PEOPLE-CENTERED DEVELOPMENT

PEOPLE-CENTERED DEVELOPMENT

Contributions toward Theory and Planning Frameworks

Edited by David C. Korten and Rudi Klauss

KUMARIAN PRESS
1984

Printed in the United States of America

Cover design by Marilyn Penrod

Library of Congress Cataloging in Publication Data

Main entry under title:

People-centered development.

(Library of management for development)
1. Economic development – Environmental aspects –
Addresses, essays, lectures. 2. Economic development –
Social aspects – Addresses, essays, lectures. I. Korten,
David C. II. Klauss, Rudi. III. Series.
HD75.6.P46 1984   338.9   84-914
ISBN 0-931816-48-3
ISBN 0-931816-31-9 (pbk.)

Preface   ix

Preface

During the 1970s bold commitments were made throughout the world to deal with three central development challenges: poverty, environmental deterioration, and the empowerment of people through increased participation in the development process. While progress has been made, it is inconsequential relative to the magnitude of the need. Within our spheres of expertise we, the editors of this volume, have been concerned with developing new capabilities in the field of development management responsive to these development priorities. We have looked at needs for new people-centered planning tools, for the reorientation of development bureaucracies using social learning technologies, and for programming strategies aimed at empowerment of people and communities. We see progress in the development and application of new concepts and tools representing an important first step. But again the progress to date remains inconsequential relative to the scope of the problem.

Continuously we confront the reality that in spite of commitment to new priorities, most development action continues to be dominated by development theories based on invalid premises and unresponsive to the three central priorities set forth above. Perhaps it is because even though those theories have been quite thoroughly discredited by a great deal of research and analysis, the development field still lacks a credible body of alternative theory that is consistent with current and emergent reality and offers useful guidance toward the accomplishment of valid human goals. As numerous authorities have observed, a useful theory proven inadequate is unlikely to be discarded until an alternative theory is available that accounts for both the facts explained by the old theory and the new facts that the old theory is unable to explain.

We have been concerned by the lack of such an alternative theory. There are of course many current intellectual contributions that are suggestive of its elements, but each deals only with a piece of a larger picture. Many, if not most, of the more valuable and provocative pieces exist outside the mainstream of development literature. We decided that one useful step might be to put together a collection of writings that we had found particularly valuable in our own thinking on the question of an alternative development theory, in a form that would encourage a broadening of the dialogue on the topic. The contributions selected do not in their present form define an alternative theory; they do suggest some of its elements. All challenge prevailing belief systems and should prove provocative to even the skeptical reader.

We have drawn contributions from many sources. They range from classic studies by well-known authors to materials drawn from lesser-known sources and writers. Given the breadth of our topic we have had to make sometimes difficult choices, not only with regard to individual selections, but also with regard to the choice of areas and issues treated—judgments to which we expect some readers will take exception.

We have made no effort to present opposing points of view on the individual issues addressed. Though many of the contributors would surely find points of disagreement among themselves, our primary interest is in helping the reader to see the ways in which these diverse contributions present a rich and surprisingly coherent perspective on fundamental issues of development policy and action.

Though some contributions have been written specifically for this volume, most have already been published. Many of the previously published pieces have been specially edited for this volume to sharpen their presentation of key issues of particular relevance to our topic in the least possible space. In each instance in which the original form of an article has been condensed or abridged, this fact is noted in an introductory footnote, and the original source is cited for readers interested in locating it. In each case the editorial changes have been reviewed and approved by the original author and, for copyrighted material, by the original publisher.

While our primary concern in preparing this volume is with those nations that have not fully shared in the benefits of economic development, this volume attempts to approach the topic of development from a relatively global perspective. The basic viewpoint is that taken by Alvin Toffler in chapter 2—that both predominantly agricultural and predominantly industrial societies face a fundamental transformation to a postindustrial form, which may be expected to resemble the current structure of agricultural societies more than that of industrial ones. The nature of the transformation will of course be substantially different for each, but to the extent that Toffler is correct, the directions of change will be toward convergence. Thus we believe that the experience of each may offer useful insights to the other and have included materials that reflect the experience and perspective of both types of societies.

Preparation of this anthology has been sponsored by the National Association of Schools of Public Affairs and Administration (NASPAA) as a contribution to the advancement of thought, teaching, and action in public administration. It is funded under Cooperative Agreement no. AID/DSAN–CA–0180 by the Office of Multisectoral Development, Bureau of Science and Technology, Agency for International Development (AID) through a project entitled "Performance Management" (no. 936–5317). One of the objectives of that project is to develop and advance knowledge in the area of people-centered program management, and the present volume is intended to help accomplish that objective. We are deeply indebted to Jerome French, Kenneth Kornher, and Jeanne North of that office and to Joe Robertson and Alfred Zuck of NASPAA for their support and encouragement in this undertaking. We hasten to add that the content of this volume is solely the responsibility of its editors and does not necessarily reflect the views of either NASPAA or AID. We also acknowledge the contributions of many colleagues from the Asian Institute of Management, the Social Development Management Network, and the Management Institutes Working Group on Social Development who have stimulated our thinking on these issues and in many instances have assisted in identifying relevant materials. Important among these have been Felipe Alfonso, Coralie Bryant, George Carner, Marcus Ingle, Gary Hansen, George Honadle, John Ickis, Frances Korten, Gabino Mendoza, Andrew Oerke, Beth Shields, Ted Thomas, and Norman Uphoff. Useful suggestions and critical comments were also received from John Cohen, John Friedmann, Bruce Johnston, Bruce Koppel, and Willis Harman. To these and other colleagues we extend our thanks.

Our special appreciation also goes to the many individuals and publishers who have given their generous permission to reproduce these materials so that they may be shared more widely, and to Jean Sonner for her support work in securing these permissions.

This anthology provides only partial coverage of relevant emerging thought and experience contributory to an alternative development theory. It is best looked upon as a partial and preliminary report on work in progress by a large and loosely defined community of scholars and practitioners. We invite readers' comments and suggestions about overlooked or forthcoming material that might be considered for future editions, should this volume prove to address a continuing need.

David C. Korten
Jakarta, Indonesia

Rudi Klauss
Washington, D.C., U.S.A.

Part One

Introduction

The industrial era was a period of unparalleled technical and economic accomplishment for human society. So substantial was its success in bringing affluence to the broad majority of the populations of Western industrial nations that it inspired a global vision of a world that might be—a world without poverty. The unquestionable success of the Marshall Plan in speeding the reconstruction of Europe following World War II provided encouragement that such a goal might be attainable. The vision rapidly captured the imagination of millions of people in nations at all stages of economic development. The presumed secret to its attainment, as articulated in the development theories of the day, was to compound rates of growth in economic output through massive investments in industrialization. The theory predicted that countries that faithfully pursued its policy prescriptions would gradually expand their modern economic sectors until their entire populations became included and thus gained access to the benefits of modern consumer society. The development strategies derived from these theories called for concentration of attention and resources on achieving the maximum possible increase in production. Management tools were developed to assist in making resource allocation decisions consistent with this priority.

While their underlying purpose was to benefit people, such strategies and methodologies were primarily production-centered. They presumed that single-minded emphasis on production would automatically translate into increased benefits for people. Thus the performance indicators and decision criteria of this period were attuned to outcomes for production rather than for people. There were, of course, calls for investments in developing human resources, but these were routinely justified on the grounds that they would yield higher payoffs in production than alternative investments—not because they would benefit people directly. Such direct benefits were looked upon somewhat disparagingly as *consumption* expenditures—a diversion of resources from investment in growth.

---

*The brief review of modern development thought that follows is based on Paul Streeten, "From Growth to Basic Needs," *Finance and Development* 16 (September 1979).

1

More than a theory was involved in shaping the prevailing production-centered definition of development purposes and of the policy prescriptions for their attainment. The vision was grounded in a deeply held and widely shared belief system backed by a rapidly growing body of social technique – a production-centered development paradigm.

The dependency theorists who came into prominence in the late 1960s were not the only ones to point out the limitations of neoclassical growth theories. Substantial criticism also emerged within the ranks of mainstream economists. Both recognized that the trickle-down effect predicted by the theory often failed to occur; indeed, a reverse "trickle-up" effect was not uncommon. The reexamination that began in the late 1960s led in the 1970s to bold commitments throughout the world to address more directly three central development challenges: elimination of poverty, preservation of the productive capacity of the environment, and empowerment of people through increased participation in the development process. These commitments were accompanied by reexamination of prevailing theory and prescriptions.*

The realization that imported labor-saving technologies were resulting in substantial increases in the productivity of the urban industrial labor force without creating jobs at rates commensurate with growth in the number of job-seekers led to a shift in emphasis from pure growth strategies to employment generation strategies. But employment generation strategies in turn proved to be based on a false assumption – namely, that the poor of developing countries were poor because they had no employment. In fact, their problem was seldom economic idleness. On the contrary, it was the endurance of long hours of difficult and largely unproductive activities from which they obtained no more than a marginal subsistence livelihood: to be unemployed was to starve. So they became adept at creating their own "employment" as petty merchants, blacksmiths, grain thrashers, and water carriers. They sold a few lottery tickets, offered themselves in prostitution, cleaned windshields at stoplights, scavenged at garbage dumps, or found any other activity that provided an opportunity to survive. With this realization, many analysts shifted their attention from the problem of increasing the quantity of available work to the problem of improving its quality.

People-centered perspectives gradually began to gain legitimacy. A major study published jointly in 1974 by the World Bank and the Sussex Institute of Development Studies called attention to possibilities for a "growth with equity" strategy directed at expanding the productive use of resources in small-scale agricultural and informal urban sectors in which the majority of the poor obtained their livelihoods. It recommended a rural strategy focused on increasing the access of the small farmer and the self-employed to land, water, credit markets, and other facilities that would allow them to increase their productivity. Its urban strategy emphasized opportunities for increasing the productivity of the self-employed and the small producer through improved access to inputs and removal of policies that discriminated against them. Still another theme was promoted by the "basic needs" school, which argued that the true measure of development progress is the extent to which the most basic needs of people are being met and that these needs should be addressed directly and immediately, by subsidy programs if necessary. A Physical Quality of Life Index was developed as an alternative to the Gross National Product as a measure of development accomplishment.

Important as they were in advancing thought and in introducing needed reforms in development priorities and actions, neither the growth with equity nor the basic needs school offered more than a partial alternative to the dominant development model. And in spite of adjustments in both priorities and prescriptions toward more people-centered perspectives, progress in addressing the three central development challenges still has remained distressingly inadequate.

The past decade has been a sobering period for development progress. Yet it also has seen remarkable advances in technology, as well as in awareness of the boundless nature of human potential and of opportunities for living in productive harmony with the natural environment. These advances lay the groundwork for establishing a people-centered alternative to the production-centered development paradigm and open up vast new possibilities for the creation of a truly human global society.

This volume brings together a number of important contributions to the growing dialogue on establishing such an alternative, organized around six major topics.

Contributors to section 2 place the current human situation in a long-term evolutionary perspective. The basic argument they develop is that both industrial and agricultural societies are in the midst of an important transition involving major changes in values, social structures, and modes of production—a social transformation toward postindustrial societal forms in which the most appropriate course for agricultural nations is largely to bypass the industrial stage. The industrial era has created most of the conditions establishing the imperatives for such a transformation. It has also created the possibility of achieving a global society in which all people would have the opportunity to realize their potentials. Both the imperatives and the possibility are examined in this section.

One imperative is that human society come to terms with the reality of life on a small planet. The implications of this reality are examined in section 3. Contributors to this section outline the basis of an alternative economics, explore the reorientation in basic values required to live in harmony with natural processes, and examine alternative organizational forms appropriate to the management of the natural resource base.

Section 4 looks at resource competition and the dynamics of poverty — the elimination of the latter being a continuing and primary challenge of the transformation. Rather than repeat the familiar litany of statistics on world poverty, these contributors examine the underlying dynamics that create and sustain these conditions. They argue that poverty is a systemic problem and suggest that it can be eliminated only through systemic changes.

Section 5 moves beyond defining problems to examining the issues underlying the choice of social techniques appropriate to people-centered purposes. The focus is on social learning theory and its application in making learning more rapid and effective in both individuals and institutions.

Contributors to section 6 argue that people-centered development also requires the application of alternative analytical frameworks and criterion functions. Just as the methodologies of the production-centered paradigm focused attention on the production system and its health, those of people-centered development must concentrate on people and their well-being. These contributors emphasize the importance of territoriality and self-reliance as guiding principles, giving preference to the use of local resources under local control to meet local needs.

The empowerment of people to control their own lives and resources, to create their livelihoods from those resources, and to direct and pursue their development as human beings is both a purpose of people-centered development and a means to its attainment. Questions of governance thus become critical. The complex issues they involve are examined by contributors to section 7. They suggest that many contemporary human institutions, from representative democracy to the large bureaucracies of business, government, and labor, tend to disempower people, removing from them control over all but a small portion of their lives. Once this happens, accountability becomes an increasingly serious problem, creating demands for control structures that are at once expensive to maintain and unresponsive even to those they are supposed to serve. A variety of alternatives are examined.

Section 8 pulls together various strands of the above arguments into a statement of some of the essential elements of a people-centered development paradigm.

Part Two

Social Transformation:
A Human Agenda

The progress of the industrial era was guided by a powerful paradigm, a product largely of Western thought and experience, that shaped the dominant direction of societal development, dictated the goals to which policy attention was directed, and spawned sophisticated methodologies for guiding human choices in directions consistent with its underlying premises. In this section Willis Harman summarizes the dominant characteristics of this paradigm and examines the forces that now render it obsolete. He goes on to outline the possibilities that he believes the current transitional period presents to human society.

While Harman writes primarily from the perspective of the United States, Alvin Toffler addresses the transformation from a Third World perspective, suggesting the opportunities that it may open to those nations that have not yet entered the industrial era.

Robert Neil examines the earlier transformations of human society, from hunting to settled agriculture, to intensified irrigated agriculture, and finally to industrialization. While for a portion of the population these transformations have represented advancement, he suggests that they have imposed on unprivileged classes ever more severe demands for additional hours of work and increased physical exertion as a condition for survival. The result is that they exist as members of the species homo sapiens with little opportunity to realize their potential humanity. Neil asks whether the next transformation will simply repeat the cycle at a still higher level of technology and suggests conditions that might allow for breaking out of the historical pattern.

Darwin viewed evolution as a competitive struggle for food, sex, and survival, in which the fit triumphed and the unfit perished. George Lock Land puts forth an alternative and more humanistic interpretation of evolution that makes an important contribution to articulating appropriate goals for people-centered development in evolutionary terms.

Finally, John Platt neatly summarizes the remarkable technological advances of the past forty years that open new opportunities to shape the present transformation in ways consistent with human outcomes.

1

Key Choices

WILLIS W. HARMAN

Few informed people now doubt that technically advanced societies like the United States are undergoing a major historical transformation to some sort of transindustrial age. This will be characterized by diminishing dominance of industrial production as a social function, by increasing prominence of service and information-related activities, and by increasing concern with value questions related to quality of life. The differences among opinions lie in how rapid and extreme this change in values, perceptions, and institutions will be. I forecast that the shift is likely to be rapid, extreme, and hazardous.

This forecast is in distinct contrast to the view that the available alternative futures comprise modest deviations from a "long-term multifold trend,"[1] with slow changes in social institutions and cultural values. It is not yet possible to discern which view is closer to correct. Both views are held by groups of reasonable men and women.

RAPID, DRASTIC CHANGES AHEAD

I propose to examine the arguments suggesting that forces toward an abrupt and drastic modification of the long-term multifold trend may lead to revolutionary social change by the 1990s. Further, this revolutionary change will be of such a nature as to reduce the discrepancy between what is seemingly good business policy and what would be good social policy.

I speak of revolutionary change very soberly. History gives us little reason to take comfort in the prospect of fundamental and rapid social change—little reason to think we can escape without the accompanying threat of economic decline and disruption of social processes considerably

---

Excerpt with minor revisions of a presentation to the White House Conference on the Industrial World Ahead, Washington, D. C., February 7–9, 1972, titled "Key Choices of the Next Two Decades," published in *A Look at Business in 1990* (U.S. Government Printing Office, Washington, D. C., 1972) and a keynote address to the 1982 AHP Annual Meeting in Washington, D. C. titled "AHP and Global Issues" published in *Association for Humanistic Psychology Newsletter*, October 1982, pp. 13–15.

greater than anything we have experienced or care to imagine. If indeed a fundamental and rapid change in basic perceptions and values should occur, a chaotic period seems inevitable as the powerful momentum of the industrial era is turned in a new direction and as the different members and institutions of the society respond at different speeds.

Accurate interpretation of this disorder is crucial. The form—and success—of the nation's policies will depend a great deal on whether the disruption is seen as accompanying a change toward a more workable system or is perceived as essentially destructive. Or, alternatively, whether it is seen as a rather bothersome episode, as a result of which things will be neither particularly better nor worse, just different.

INDICATORS OF REVOLUTIONARY CHANGE

Several clues indicate that the industrialized world may be experiencing the beginning of a sociocultural revolution as profound and pervasive in its effects on all segments of the society as the Industrial Revolution, the Reformation, or the Fall of Rome. I am not speaking of a "Greening of America," nor of the achieving of any of the popularly promoted utopias. The shape of the future will no more be patterned after the hippie movement of the 1960s than the industrial age could have been inferred from the "new-age" values of the Anabaptists.

The transformation that we call the Protestant Reformation affected all aspects of society, from the nascent science to the new capitalist commercial structure. Similarly, in the present case, we should expect impacts on the economic system, on science, on government, and on community and work life. As we look back at the Reformation, the most fundamental change appears to be in those tacitly agreed on, largely unquestioned premises that form the nucleus of any culture. Only a half dozen or so times in the history of Western civilization did this basic paradigm undergo revolutionary change. The Reformation was the most recent of these. It was characterized by a shift from the other-worldly, inner-directed, teleological paradigm of the Middle Ages to the this-worldly, outer-directed, relatively nonteleological paradigm of the industrial age.

The characteristics of the industrial-age paradigm can be summarized as follows:

> Development and application of scientific method; wedding of scientific and technological advance
>
> Industrialization through organization and division of labor; machine replacement of human labor
>
> Acquisitive materialism; work ethic; economic-man image; belief in unlimited material progress and in technological and economic growth
>
> Man seeking control over nature; positivistic theory of knowledge;

manipulative rationality as dominant theme

Individual responsibility for own destiny; freedom and equality as fundamental rights; nihilistic value perspective; individual determination of the "good"; society as aggregate of individuals pursuing own interests

In speaking of transformation we are talking about an event that is historically improbable. Since it has not yet occurred, we can make only an informed guess at the main characteristics of the substitute paradigm. If the interpretation turns out to be correct, the consequences for economic and political decision-making are profound; hence, we can ill afford not to take the possibility seriously.

The Reformation period lasted about a century. Earlier major transformations, such as the agricultural revolution, were far more dispersed in both space and time. How can such a profound shift as we are contemplating take place in the space of a decade or two? One reason is the general speedup of change. Another, of course, is the impact of modern communication media. Still another reason may lie, as we shall see, in the acceptability of the paradigm that may be replacing the beliefs and values of the industrial age.

This view of impending revolutionary change is plausible for three major reasons: (1) the complex of societal problems confronting the developed world appears to require changes in cultural values for their satisfactory resolution; (2) a replacement for the industrial-state paradigm, embodying the requisite kinds of value shifts, appears to be rising spontaneously; (3) various "lead indicators" that have preceded other cultural-change periods in history have been prominent during the past decade or so.

New values required. It is almost a truism that most of our severe societal problems are essentially the consequence of our technological and industrial successes. For example, success in reducing infant mortality has contributed to excessive population growth. Technology-created affluence poses resource-depletion and environmental problems. New materials (e.g., plastics, detergents, aluminum) have interfered with natural recycling processes. Machine replacement of manual and routine labor has exacerbated unemployment problems. Development of nuclear, biological, and chemical weapons has brought the potentiality of worldwide decimation. And so on.

The nature of these problems is such that many analysts have seriously questioned whether those basic values and premises that have shaped and supported our present technological and industrial capabilities are now suited to the humane application or even the rational control of those Faustian powers. As long as this remains a question, values that appear more suitable will be able to mobilize social power. We will return to this point later.

Emerging paradigm. Several signs visible in the United States and in other industrialized nations point to the possible emergence of a new dominant paradigm:

> Surveys and polls indicate significant value shifts among certain elite groups, such as students and corporate executives. Increased emphasis is placed on humanistic and spiritual values, quality of life, community, person-centered society, and so forth. Emphasis on materialistic values, status goals, and unqualified economic growth is diminished.[2]
>
> Numerous cultural indicators (e.g., books read, voluntary associations, song lyrics, themes of plays and motion pictures, content of magazine articles, "New Age" groups and activities) show greatly increased interest in and tolerance for the transcendental, religious, esoteric, occult, suprarational, mystical, and spiritual.
>
> New scientific interest in exploring human consciousness – subjective states, altered consciousness, unconscious processes – partly as a consequence of the availability of new research tools (e.g., biofeedback techniques) that relate inner experience to physiological correlates (e.g., galvanic skin response, body electric fields, EEG components, muscle tensions), is resulting in a new legitimation of studies of meditative states, mystical experiences, psychic phenomena, and religious experiences.

From these indicators, particularly the last, we can infer something about the direction in which values, and the dominant vision of man-in-the-universe, are likely to shift. Wherever the nature of man/woman has been probed deeply, the paramount fact emerging is the duality of his/her experience. He/she is found to be both physical and spiritual, both sides being real, and neither describable in terms of the other. At various times and places the spiritual or the material has been temporarily dominant. It is a fundamental characteristic of the emergent paradigm that it places in complementary relationship such troublesome opposites as spirit/body, science/religion, or determinism/free will, in much the same way as modern physics reconciles the previously opposing wave and particle theories of light.

The emergent paradigm appears to have characteristics something like the following:

> Complementarity of physical and spiritual experience; recognition of all "explanation" as only metaphor; use of different noncontradicting "levels of explanation" for physical, biological, mental, and spiritual reality
>
> Teleological sense of life and evolution having purpose and direction; ultimate reality perceived as unitary, with transcendent order
>
> Basis for value postulates discoverable in own inner experience as a

hierarchy of "levels of consciousness"; potentiality of supraconscious as well as subconscious influence

Goals of life—aware participation in individual growth and the evolutionary process; individual fulfillment through community; integration of work, play, learning, and growth

Goals of society—to foster development of individuals' transcendent and emergent potentialities. Economic growth, technological development, design of work roles and environments, authority structures, and social institutions all to be used in the service of this primary goal

"New naturalism, holism, and immanentism" (V. Ferkiss); "rediscovery of the supernatural" (P. L. Berger); "the politics of consciousness" (T. Roszak)

Thus the challenging paradigm assumes some sort of transcendent spiritual order, discoverable in human experience, and against which human value choices are assessed. Ultimately reality is unitary. There is a teleological sense of life and evolution having direction or purpose. Other levels of consciousness than the usual are explorable, with different appropriate forms of explanation for what is found there. Hence scientific explanation at the level of sensory experience in no way contradicts religious, philosophical, or poetic interpretations of suprasensory experience; rather, it complements them.

The new paradigm extends, rather than contradicts, the modern scientific world view, much as relativity theory extended Newtonian mechanics. Moreover, it is in its essence not new at all, having formed a central stream of thought in the humanities, in Western political tradition, and in "transcendentalist" movements in United States history.[3] Part of the growing acceptability of the "New Age" world view undoubtedly has been due to this drawing on what is already well established in the culture, together with the bridging of the "two cultures" of science and the humanities.

Lead indicators of revolutionary change. From studies of historical occurrences of revolutionary cultural and political change come the following list of typical occurrences in the period leading up to that change:[4]

Decreased sense of community
Increased sense of alienation and purposelessness
Increased occurrence of violent crime
Increased frequency of personal disorders and mental illness
Increased frequency and severity of social disruptions
Increased use of police to control behavior
Increased public acceptance of hedonistic behavior
Increase in amount of noninstitutionalized religious activities

To anyone who follows the newspapers, the list alone makes the point.

A Fundamental Problem

All the above is not to say that such a revolutionary change and paradigm shift will inevitably occur. Rather, the three assertions listed argue that among the alternative "future histories" to be considered, this possibility needs to be included. Whether or not the social forces for such a transition are gathering sufficient strength to bring it about remains to be seen. The probability is not negligible at any rate.

Consider the first of these three propositions—that the nature of society's problems necessitates significant value change for satisfactory resolution. At the risk of seeming to oversimplify, I will make this assertion much more explicit.

Industrial societies in general, and the United States in particular, are faced with one fundamental problem that is so pervasive and so pernicious that the related societal problems (e.g., poverty, unemployment, inflation, environmental deterioration, crime, alienation) will defeat all attempts at solution until that fundamental problem is satisfactorily resolved. Such resolution hinges on value change.

The problem to which I refer has puzzled Adam Smith and most economists since his time. It is the following. Individuals, corporations, and government agencies in the course of their activities make microdecisions (e.g., to buy a certain product, to employ a man for a particular task, to enact a minimum-wage law) that interact to constitute a set of macrodecisions of the overall society (e.g., a 5 percent growth rate, failing cities, polluted air and water). The problem is that *perfectly reasonable microdecisions currently are adding up to largely unsatisfactory macrodecisions.*

Some specifics will illustrate:

The tragedy of the commons. Microdecisions regarding utilization of resources (e.g., land, air, water, fuels, minerals) that are reasonable from the viewpoints of corporate management and stockholders, developers, and local governments, result in macrodecisions of resource depletion, environmental degradation, urban crowding, that are unsatisfactory to society at large.

Insufficient work opportunity. People need opportunities to contribute meaningfully to society and to be affirmed in return (commonly with wages). Individual decisions to create and accept jobs fail to result in a satisfactory full employment policy, and thus lead to the incongruity that work opportunity becomes considered a scarce commodity that needs to be rationed.

Unintended technological impact. Even with "technology assessment" we don't know how to preserve market microdecision-making regarding technological innovation and yet achieve satisfactory macrochoices with regard to technological disemployment, quality of the environment, infringements of human rights, interference with natural recycling processes, and resource depletion.

Inflation. Decisions to pass on productivity increases from technological innovation to workers in the form of increased wages, rather than apply them to reducing prices to consumers – plus demands for similar increases for service-sector workers whose productivity is not appreciably increasing – have contributed to persistent inflation.

State of the economy. Decisions of hundreds of United States-based corporations to transfer manufacturing operations to low labor-cost countries, while economically sound as individual decisions, collectively constitute a serious temporary threat to United States economy and industrial capability.

Alienation. There is presently a widespread perception that individual, corporate, and government decisions have been guided by such principles as economic growth as a self-justifying end, "the business of business is business," the affluent society, the underdeveloped world as supplier of raw materials for that affluent society, and the "technological imperative" that any technology that *can* be developed and applied *should* be – and that these notions are leading the world toward an intolerable future. Further, individuals feel themselves forced by "the system" to act in ways that they perceive as neither what they want to do, nor what would be to the general social good. The result is a serious alienation from society and its institutions.

This fundamental problem is *not* simply a matter of trade-offs – as a recent cartoon quip had it, "There's a price tag on everything. You want a high standard of living, you settle for a low quality of life." Rather, it is a flaw in the decision-making system that encourages individuals to choose on the basis of their own short-term, imprudent self-interest instead of their long-term, enlightened self-interest.

Classical economic theory attempted to explain how the market mechanism could operate to constitute, from individual self-interest microdecisions, macrodecisions that would operate for the general good. As time went on, the invisible hand clearly needed a little help in the form of governmental rule-making and umpiring, from antitrust laws to Keynesian manipulations of the money supply and interest rate. Yet the basic dilemma of unsatisfactory macrodecisions worsens, as illustrated above.

Why is the system in such trouble now, when it worked satisfactorily before? Some of the contributing factors are:

Interconnectedness, so that laissez-faire approaches are less workable

Reduction of geographical and entrepreneurial frontier opportunities

Approaching limits of natural recycling capabilities

Sharpened dichotomy between "employed" and "unemployed" (e.g., virtual elimination of the small farmer, partially or sporadically employed)

More adequate supplying of deficiency needs (improved diet, material advance) plus more education, resulting in higher expectations and keener perception of the gap between actualities and potentialities

Transition from a basic condition of labor scarcity to one of job scarcity

Approaching limits of some resources (e.g., natural gas, domestic petroleum, fresh water)

"Faustian powers" of technology and industrialization that have reached the point where they can have a major impact on the physical, technological, sociopolitical, and psychological environment

Expanded political power of labor which, forcing industrial wages to follow increasing productivity, constitutes an inflationary force

Weakening of the force of "American civil religion," partly through the eroding effect of positivistic science, and hence, weakening of the will to self-regulation in the interest of the whole

A CRUCIAL CHOICE

If this is the diagnosis, what then is the prescription?

The way in which the United States handles this fundamental dilemma is a critical aspect of the future. By and large, two significantly different approaches have their advocates.

One of these is a continuation of the collectivist trend that characterized the period since 1932 (but may have been reversed in 1980). If this path is taken, as the kinds of problems mentioned above grow more severe, they will be turned over to an expanding public sector to handle. Individual decisions will increasingly be regulated by government, through coercive controls and manipulative incentives. On this path of deprivatization it would be difficult to avoid the problems of bureaucratic giantism and increasingly coercive centralized control. Nevertheless, there are still many today who see no other real option.

The other approach involves a permanent reversal of the collectivist trend from the "New Deal" through the tattered remains of the "Great Society," and a revitalized role for the private sector. In this case, however, the nation will not return to some previous "Golden Age"; it will move forward to something not easily defined at this point, something we have never known.

The "entrepreneurial capitalism" of the nineteenth century entailed a view of economic man in a freemarket society, a state of scarcity, and minimal governmental intervention. Over the past few decades it has been replaced by "managerial capitalism," treating the person as "consumer" in an affluent industrial nation, with government regulating growth, employment, and wage-price stability. The real alternative to collectivism might be termed "humanistic capitalism." Essentially it is a strongly private-enterprise system in which humane and social and ecological values predominate over short-term economic considerations, and in which there is a strong nonprofit and voluntary sector counterbalancing the profit-making sector.

Again it is necessary to oversimplify to make the point easily. If the basic problem centers around unsatisfactory macrodecisions arising from self-interest-directed microdecisions, then the obvious thing to do is to turn the situation upside down. That is, to select appropriate macrodecisions – which is to say, national and planetary goals – that are in accord with the best available knowledge regarding human fulfillment, then to see what patterns of microdecisions would be necessary to achieve those goals.

But there is a catch. The means used to obtain those necessary individual actions have to be compatible with the ends. The United States affirms the goal to "guard the rights of the individual. . . enhance the dignity of the citizen, promote the maximum development of his [her] capabilities, stimulate their responsible exercise, and widen the range and effectiveness of opportunities for individual choice. . . to build a nation and help build a world in which every human being shall be free to dedicate and develop his [her] capacities to the fullest" (from the 1960 report of President Eisenhower's Commission on National Goals).

If we take these noble sentiments seriously, then the necessary patterns of microdecisions cannot be obtained through coercion, as tends to be the case in a planned economy. Nor can they come through manipulative behavior-shaping as has been proposed by some technocratically inclined social scientists. The only means compatible with goals such as those declared above is through learning together the nature of suitable national and global goals and the kinds of microdecisions necessary for reaching them.

In sum, the more unsatisfactory the macrodecisions (and they are getting to be pretty unsatisfactory), the stronger the corrective required. There are two routes – stronger government or major cultural transformation.

The route of transformation requires that each of us search out and remove the basic contradictions in our own belief systems, because those are contributing to the insanity of the nuclear arms race, the world economy plundering the planet on which it subsists, and all the rest.

THREE OBSOLETE CONCEPTS

A good place to begin such self-examination is with three concepts which we in modern industrial society have taken so much for granted that many persons are likely to think their abolishment a preposterous notion.

The first is the concept of war as a legitimate (an inevitable) means for settling international disputes. One may be tempted to consider this desirable but totally impracticable; the bequeathing of a nuclear "balance of terror" to all future generations regrettable but inescapable. But just imagine what might happen if (imitating the Greek comedy Lysistrata) all the women of the world were to simply say "No! War is a macho game that can't be tolerated anymore because the men's toys have become much too dangerous." It requires only a change of mind to delegitimate the authority of the nation-state to employ weapons of mass destruction. This delegitimating does not imply a centralized world government, anymore than does a supranational agency to regulate the seas, or the delivery of mail. Nor does it imply perfect people, nonaggressive, cooperative and caring. It only implies the intention to behave that way as much as possible.

But the nuclear genie is out of the bottle; the number of countries with access to nuclear weapons ineluctably rises. If world tensions are too great, if the sense of being unfairly treated is too strong, the death-dealing forces of the H-bombs could still be unleashed.

The second obsolete concept that needs replacing is the concept of development toward a mass-consumption/full-employment society. There appears no way in the present international order that many of the presently nonindustrialized countries can ever achieve an economic position remotely comparable with that of the highly industrialized countries. For one thing, the planet could not support that much mass-consumption society. Making a fair bid to replace this concept of development is an emerging concept of alternative development—human development surpassing economic development in importance; development based on native cultural roots rather than substitution of an alien western culture.

Underlying the prevailing concept of global development is a third concept so fundamental that its obsolescence is a particularly difficult proposition to accept. This is the concept of the centrality of economic institutions, and the paramountcy of economic rationality. That economic institutions dominate our society is so obvious as to hardly require comment. That this is totally reasonable—that all human activities should be increasingly carried out in the framework of the mainstream economy, that full employment in the mainstream economy is the most desirable state, that to achieve this state requires ever-increasing consumption of goods and services, that economic "bottom-line" rationality and discounting the future provides the tough-minded logic by which to make sound social decisions—that all of this is right-headed and inescapable is generally uncritically accepted. Yet it has led to and contributed to the great global problems of our day. Armament sales and diverse hedonistic pursuits are "good for the economy"; pollution control is a "growth industry". At the same time we can no longer afford (we tell one another) good schools for all; we can no longer afford to protect citizens in the streets; we can no longer afford beautification with well-kept parks and municipal gardens; young couples can no longer afford to own homes of their own.

Through the years more and more of our activities have been assimilated into the mainstream economy. We are taken care of by the food services industry, the tourism industry, the financial services industry; by the health services industry and later by the nursing homes industry; still later by the funeral homes industry; and those left behind are given "bereavement counselors" so that even in our grieving we contribute to the GNP.

Short-term "bottom-line" logic leads to decisions that are economically sound and socially disastrous. Economic discounting of the future at, say, fifteen percent a year, means that the welfare of future generations doesn't enter into present decision making.

There is an increasing awareness of the social cost of allowing economic institutions to play such a commanding role in society. In a host of experiments with informal economies, alternative economies, crafts movements, self-reliant intentional communities, etc., the consciousness of needing a new way is manifested.

Modern industrial society is exceptionally confused about values. It knows how to approach almost any "How to?"question: How to put a man on the moon? How to handle vast quantities of data in a second, or a millisecond? How to split the atom and combine the genes? But it is most unsure when faced with the question, "What for?" When you can accomplish almost any technical task imaginable, if willing to commit resources, then what is worth doing? For example, would humanity really be well served if the other cultures of the world were to continue to be progressively overwhelmed by the seductiveness and power of materialistic modern society, until the planet eventually supported one western industrial monoculture. The alternative is an ecology of diverse cultures, complementing and enriching one another, supported by a global order significantly different from the presently dominant world economy.

What would such changes imply for private enterprise as a dominant institution of our society? Here too a basic transformation is implied, commensurate with the re-examination of economic values outlined above. Rational business decisions too often turn out to have resulted in irrational squandering of natural resources, fouling of the environment, technological disemployment, debasing of persons, and—in some dimensions at least—lowered quality of life.

Those who see an inherent and insuperable discrepancy between good business policy and good social policy often assume the need for more and bigger governmental structures—looking to the government wherever private enterprise, working through the market mechanism, fails to satisfy social needs. Is there another way? Are there new, vital roles the private and voluntary sectors can play? Can the system be adjusted through a new definition of private enterprise based on new values—a humanistic capitalism— in which good business policy becomes congruent with good social policy? I believe this to be not only a real possibility, but also an emerging reality. What might be its characteristics?

SOME CHARACTERISTICS OF THE NEW PRIVATE ENTERPRISE

The transindustrial society would foster free enterprise and entrepreneurial initiative—not, however, dominated by economic goals and economic rationality to anything like the present extent. Nonprofit corporations, informal economies, and voluntary associations would play a very significant part. There would be a great deal of decentralization and formation of small organizations. The "third sector" of nonprofit and voluntary organizations would create many of the participative roles in learning activities, community planning, cable television programming, beautification, environmental enrichment, and so on, since these are not easily structured in the profit-making sector and there is good reason to avoid adding them to the bureaucracies of the public sector.

Large privately owned and managed corporations would continue to be, we may assume, the dominant economic institutions. Corporate goals would broaden to include, besides the present economic and institutional goals, authentic social responsibility and the personal fulfillment of those who participate in corporate activity. These would be included not as a gesture to improve corporate image or as a moralistically undertaken responsibility, but as operative goals on a par with profit-making and institutional security. Not production, but human productiveness, would be the goal.

Under past manpower concepts jobs were structured for efficient production, and persons were shaped, through incentive structuring, to fit the jobs. Among the consequences of these policies have been "unemployable" welfare recipients, overtrained aerospace engineers, underutilized employees, and alienated production and office workers. Those past policies, in retrospect, appear analogous to approaching the problem of air pollution by breeding smog-resistant humans. Under a new business ethos jobs would be structured to fit people. Production processes would be designed to instill pride in craftsmanship. Employees would work for pay, but also because they believe in and identify with the operative goals of their employing corporation.

Government would probably remain the organizer and regulator of large complex systems (e.g., for transportation, communication, energy supply, financial operations, and some aspects of health care, food production, and education, although these may be significantly decentralized)—systems composed of relatively autonomous self-organizing and self-monitoring subsystems, coordinated mainly by shared values and goals. Government would tend to reduce its role in the direct provision of goods and services (e.g., education, health insurance, property protection, welfare services) and instead would adjust incentives to encourage supply of these from the private sector.

In short, if this transformation should occur, private-sector institutions would assume a significantly expanded range of responsibilities (much of which would be implemented in a nonprofit mode). Large institutions that retain narrow self-serving goals, be they corporations or labor unions, would find their legitimacy questioned.

Does this sound like idealism? I mean it to be intensely practical. Let me mention three reasons why I think this new private enterprise is completely feasible, assuming that recent trends in shifting cultural values continue.

First, the public can exert tremendous power by engaging in political buying, stock purchasing, and job seeking, favoring those corporations of whose operative values it approves. Thus the balance could easily shift so that corporations that displayed serious social responsibility would have the competitive advantage, rather than the reverse. Changes in tax laws, antitrust provisions, corporate chartering laws, and so forth, might be introduced to encourage broader corporate responsibilities.

Second, requirements for effective functioning of large complex systems naturally support such values as personal honesty, openness (to ensure accurate information flow), responsibility (hence self-actualization), and cooperative trust. (The values required in the team that puts a man on the moon and gets him back are a far cry from those that suffice for operation of a used-car lot.) Thus as the production and service tasks of the society become more complex, humane values become not only moral but also functional imperatives. No doubt it would have been nice all along if we had had more of the traditional values of integrity, humility, and caring. Now, as human systems and their interactions with the earth's life-support processes have become ever more complex, this value emphasis may become a necessity if the system is to work at all.

Third, as institutions not directly accountable to the public, such as industrial conglomerates, multinational corporations, and international labor unions, become larger and more powerful relative to representative governments, their operative goals have to become more congruent with those of the overall society—else the goals of the society will become distorted toward those of the dominant institutions. Thus, political pressure will urge corporate goals toward personal fulfillment of participants, public good, and social responsibility. If multinational corporations are to be among the dominant social institutions in transindustrial society, they (to paraphrase the Declaration of Independence) will have to "derive their just powers from the consent of" all those whom their actions affect.

Thus we have postulated a future in which it is possible to see a resolution of the dilemma that the result of microdecisions is so typically an unsatisfactory macrodecision. It depends on a shift in cultural values to support the continuous examination, at the individual and local level, of microdecisions from the standpoint of how likely they are to lead to good macrodecisons. Putting the same point in different words, contemporary political, military, economic, ecological, and social crises are reflections of an underlying moral and spiritual crisis of civilization, and their resolution depends on the resolution of that deeper crisis. The underlying dilemma is that somehow humanistic and transcendental values have come to be a luxury superimposed on economic values, rather than being the measure of the appropriateness of economic values. The result is that, rather than reinforcing the best we know, economic institutions seem to be at odds with society's highest values. Until this situation is corrected, further alienation, economic decline, and social disruption will be unavoidable.

The societal transformation postulated in these remarks is either upon us or it is not — it is not our choice to make. However, we can choose either to understand and move with the tides of history, whatever they may be — or to attempt to resist them. That is a fateful choice.

2

Third Wave Development:
Gandhi with Satellites

ALVIN TOFFLER

A new civilization is emerging in our lives, which brings with it new family styles; changed ways of working, loving, and living; a new economy; new political conflicts; and beyond all this an altered consciousness as well.

The dawn of this new civilization is the single most explosive fact of our lifetimes.

It is the central event – the key to understanding the years immediately ahead. It is an event as profound as that First Wave of change unleashed ten thousand years ago by the invention of agriculture, or the earthshaking Second Wave of change touched off by the industrial revolution. We are the children of the next transformation, the Third Wave.

Much in this emerging civilization contradicts the old traditional industrial civilization. It is, at one and the same time, highly technological and anti-industrial.

The Third Wave brings with it a genuinely new way of life based on diversified, renewable energy sources; on methods of production that make most factory assembly lines obsolete; on new, non-nuclear families; on a novel institution that might be called the "electronic cottage"; and on radically changed schools and corporations of the future. The emergent civilization writes a new code of behavior for us and carries us beyond standardization, synchronization, and centralization, beyond the concentration of energy, money, and power.

This new civilization, as it challenges the old, will topple bureaucracies, reduce the role of the nation-state, and give rise to semiautonomous economies in a postimperialist world. It requires governments that are simpler, more effective, yet more democratic than any we know today. It is a civilization with its own distinctive world outlook, its own ways of dealing with time, space, logic, and causality.

Excerpted from Alvin Toffler, *The Third Wave* (New York: William Morrow, and London: Collins, 1980), chapters 1 and 23.

Above all, as we shall see, Third Wave civilization begins to heal the historic breach between producer and consumer, giving rise to the "prosumer" economics of tomorrow. For this reason, among many, it could – with some intelligent help from us – turn out to be the first truly humane civilization in recorded history.

We will look back on today as the twilight of Second Wave civilization, and be saddened by what we see. For as it came to a close, industrial civilization left behind a world in which one quarter of the species lived in relative affluence, three quarters in relative poverty – and 800,000,000 in what the World Bank terms "absolute" poverty. Fully 700,000,000 people were underfed and 550,000,000 illiterate. An estimated 1,200,000,000 human beings remained without access to public health facilities or even safe, drinkable water, as the industrial age ended.

It left behind a world in which some 20 to 30 industrialized nations depended on the hidden subsidies of cheap energy and cheap raw materials for much of their economic success. It left a global infrastructure – the International Monetary Fund, GATT, the World Bank, and COMECON – which regulated trade and finance for the benefit of the Second Wave powers. It left many of the poor countries with one-crop economies twisted to serve the needs of the rich.

The rapid emergence of the Third Wave not only foreshadows the end of the Second Wave imperium, it also explodes all our conventional ideas about ending poverty on the planet.

The Second Wave Strategy

Ever since the late 1940s a single dominant strategy has governed most efforts to reduce the gap between the world's rich and poor. I call this the Second Wave strategy.

This approach starts with the premise that Second Wave societies are the apex of evolutionary progress and that, to solve their problems, all societies must replay the industrial revolution essentially as it happened in the West, the Soviet Union, or Japan. Progress consists of moving millions of people out of agriculture into mass production. It requires urbanization, standardization, and all the rest of the Second Wave package. Development, in brief, involves the faithful imitation of an already successful model.

Scores of governments in country after country have, in fact, tried to carry out this game plan. A few, like South Korea or Taiwan, where special conditions prevail, appear to be succeeding in establishing a Second Wave society. But most such efforts have met with disaster.

These failures in one impoverished country after another have been blamed on a mind-bending multiplicity of reasons. Neo-colonialism. Bad planning. Corruption. Backward religions. Tribalism. Transnational corporations. The CIA. Going too slowly. Going too fast. Yet, whatever the reasons, the grim fact remains that industrialization according to the Second Wave model has flopped far more frequently than it has succeeded.

Is classical industrialization the only path to progress? And does it make any sense to imitate the industrial model at a time when industrial civilization itself is caught in its terminal agonies?

The Broken Success Model

So long as the Second Wave nations remained "successful"—stable, rich, and getting richer—it was easy to look upon them as a model for the rest of the world. By the late 1960s, however, the general crisis of industrialism had exploded.

Strikes, blackouts, breakdowns, crime, and psychological distress spread throughout the Second Wave world. Magazines did cover pieces on "why nothing works any more." Energy and family systems shook. Value systems and urban structures crumbled. Pollution, corruption, inflation, alienation, loneliness, racism, bureaucratism, divorce, mindless consumerism, all came under savage attack. Economists warned of the possibility of a total collapse of the financial system.

A global environmental movement, meanwhile, warned that pollution, energy, and resource limits might soon make it impossible for even the existing Second Wave nations to continue normal operations. Beyond this, it was pointed out, even if the Second Wave strategy did, miraculously, work in the poor nations, it would turn the entire planet into a single giant factory and wreak ecological havoc.

Gloom descended on the richest nations as the general crisis of industrialism deepened. And suddenly millions around the world asked themselves not merely if the Second Wave strategy could work but why anyone would want to emulate a civilization that was itself in the throes of such violent disintegration.

The First Wave Strategy

Faced by the failures of the Second Wave strategy, rocked by angry demands by the poor countries for a total overhaul of the global economy, and deeply worried about their own future—the rich nations in the 1970s began to hammer out a new strategy for the poor.

Almost overnight many governments and "development agencies," including the World Bank, the Agency for International Development, and the Overseas Development Council, switched to what can only be called a First Wave strategy.

This formula is almost a carbon copy reverse of the Second Wave strategy: Instead of squeezing the peasants and forcing them into the over-burdened cities, it calls for a new emphasis on rural development. Instead of concentrating on cash crops for export, it urges food self-sufficiency.

Instead of striving blindly for higher GNP in the hopes that benefits will trickle down to the poor, it calls for resources to be channeled directly into "basic human needs."

Instead of pushing for labor-saving technologies, the new approach stresses labor-intensive production with low capital, energy, and skill requirements. Instead of building giant steel mills or large-scale urban factories, it favors decentralized, small-scale facilities designed for the village.

Turning Second Wave arguments upside down, the advocates of the First Wave strategy were able to show that many industrial technologies were a disaster when transferred to a poor country. Machines broke down and went unrepaired. They needed high-cost, often imported raw materials. Trained labor was in short supply. Hence, the new argument ran, what was needed were "appropriate technologies." Sometimes called "intermediate," "soft," or "alternative," these would lie, as it were, "between the sickle and the combine harvester."

Centers for the development of such technologies soon sprang up all over the United States and Europe – the Intermediate Technology Development Group founded in 1965 in Britain serving as an early model. But the developing countries, too, created such centers and began pouring out low-scale technological innovations.

The Mochudi Farmers Brigade in Botswana, for example, has developed an ox- or donkey-drawn device that can be used for plowing, planting, and spreading fertilizer in single or double row cultivation. The Department of Agriculture in Gambia has adopted a Senegalese tool-frame which can be used with a single moldboard plow, a groundnut lifter, a seeder, and a ridger. In Ghana work is going forward on a pedal-driven rice thresher, a screw press for spent brewer's grain, and an all-wood squeezer to extract water from banana fiber.

The First Wave strategy has been applied on a much broader basis as well. Thus in 1978 the new government of India, still reeling from oil and fertilizer price hikes and from disappointment with the Second Wave strategies followed by Nehru and Indira Gandhi, actually banned further expansion of its mechanized textile industry and urged increased production of fabrics on handlooms instead of power looms. The intent was not merely to increase employment but to retard urbanization by favoring rural cottage industry.

There is much about this new formula that admittedly makes excellent sense. It confronts the need to slow down the massive migration to the cities. It aims to make the villages – where the bulk of the world's poor dwell – more livable. It is sensitive to ecological factors. It stresses the use of cheap local resources rather than expensive imports. It challenges conventional, all-too-narrow definitions of "efficiency." It suggests a less technocratic approach to development, taking local custom and culture into account. It emphasizes improving the conditions of the poor rather than passing capital through the hands of the rich in the hopes that some will trickle down.

Yet after all due credit is given, the First Wave formula remains just that – a strategy for ameliorating the worst of First Wave conditions without ever transforming them. It is a Band-Aid, not a cure, and it is perceived in exactly these terms by many governments around the world.

Indonesian President Suharto expressed a widely held view when he charged that such a strategy "may be the new form of imperialism. If the West contributes only to small-scale grassroots projects, our plight may be alleviated somewhat but we will never grow."

The sudden love affair with labor-intensivity is also subject to the charge that it is self-serving for the rich. The longer the poor countries remain under First Wave conditions, the fewer competitive goods they are likely to shove onto an overloaded world market. The longer they stay down on the farm, so to speak, the less oil, gas, and other scarce resources they will siphon off, and the weaker and less troublesome they will remain politically.

There is also, built deep into the First Wave strategy, a paternalistic assumption that while other factors of production need to be economized, the time and energy of the laborer needn't be – that unrelieved backbreaking toil in the fields or rice paddies is fine – so long as it is done by somebody else.

Samir Amin, director of the Institute of African Economic Development and Planning, sums up many of these views, saying that labor-intensive techniques have suddenly been rendered attractive, "thanks to a medley of hippie ideology, return to the myth of the golden age and the noble savage, and criticism of the reality of the capitalist world."

Worse yet, the First Wave formula dangerously de-emphasizes the role of advanced science and technology. Many of the technologies now being promoted as "appropriate" are even more primitive than those available to the American farmer of 1776 – closer by far to the sickle than to the harvester. When American and European farmers began to employ more "appropriate technology" 150 years ago, when they shifted from wooden to steel harrow teeth or to the iron plow, they did not turn their back on the world's accumulated knowledge of engineering and metallurgy – they seized it.

In some places, and at certain times, the First Wave strategy can improve life for large numbers of people. Yet there is painfully little evidence to show that any sizable country can ever produce enough, using pre-mechanized First Wave methods, to invest in change. Indeed, a mass of evidence suggests the exact opposite.

By dint of heroic effort, Mao's China – which invented and tried out basic elements of the First Wave formula – almost, but not quite, managed to prevent famine. This was a towering achievement. But by the late sixties, the Maoist emphasis on rural development and backyard industry had gone as far as it could go. China had reached a dead end.

For the First Wave formula, by itself, is ultimately a recipe for stagnation and is no more applicable to the entire range of poor countries than the Second Wave strategy.

In a world of exploding diversity we shall have to invent scores of innovative strategies and stop looking for models either in the industrial present – or in the preindustrial past. It is time we began to look at the emergent future.

The Third Wave Question

More than once we have seen naive attempts to "develop" a basically First Wave country by imposing on it highly incongruous Second Wave forms – mass production, mass media, factory-style education. Westminster-style parliamentary government, and the nation-state, to name a few – without recognizing that for these to operate successfully, traditional family and marriage customs, religion, and role structures would all have to be crushed, the entire culture ripped up by its roots.

By astonishing contrast, Third Wave civilization turns out to have many features – decentralized production, appropriate scale, renewable energy, de-urbanization, work in the home, high levels of prosumption, to name just a few – that actually resemble those found in First Wave societies. We are seeing something that looks remarkably like a dialectical return.

This is why so many of today's most startling innovations arrive with a comet's tail of trace memories. It is this eerie sense of *déjà vu* which accounts for the fascination with the rural past that we find in the most rapidly emergent Third Wave societies. What is so striking today is that First and Third Wave civilizations seem likely to have more in common with each other than with Second Wave civilization. They are, in short, congruous.

Will this strange congruity make it possible for many of today's First Wave countries to take on some of the features of Third Wave civilization – without swallowing the whole pill, without totally surrendering their culture or first passing through the "stage" of Second Wave development? Will it, in fact, be easier for some countries to introduce Third Wave structures than to industrialize in the classical manner?

Tomorrow's "development" strategies will come not from Washington or Moscow or Paris or Geneva but from Africa, Asia, and Latin America. They will be indigenous, matched to actual local needs. They will not overemphasize economics at the expense of ecology, culture, religion, or family structure and the psychological dimensions of existence. They will not imitate any outside model. First Wave, Second Wave, or, for that matter, Third.

Sun, Shrimp, and Chips

The surprising congruence between many of the structural features of First Wave and Third Wave civilizations suggests that it may be possible in the decades ahead to combine elements of past and future into a new and better present.

Take, for example, the issue of energy.

With all the talk about an energy crisis in the countries transitioning into Third Wave civilization, it is often forgotten that First Wave societies are facing an energy crisis of their own. Starting from an extremely low base, what kind of energy systems should they create?

Certainly they need big centralized fossil-fuel-based power plants of the Second Wave type. But in many of these societies, as the Indian scientist Amulya Kumar N. Reddy has shown, the most urgent need is for decentralized energy in the countryside rather than vast, centralized supplies for the cities.

The family of a landless Indian peasant now spends about six hours a day merely finding the firewood it needs for cooking and heating. Another four to six hours are spent bringing water from a well, and a similar amount to graze cattle, goats, or sheep.

Reddy has studied rural energy needs and concluded that the requirements of a village can easily be met by a tiny, cheap bio-gas plant that uses human and animal waste from the village itself. He has gone on to demonstrate that many thousands of such units would be far more useful, ecologically sound, and economical than a few giant, centralized generating plants.

Precisely this reasoning lies behind bio-gas research and installation programs in countries from Bangladesh to Fiji. India already has 12,000 plants in operation and has targeted for 100,000 units. China plans to have 200,000 family-size bio-gas plants at work in Szechuan. Korea has 29,450 and hopes to reach a total of 55,000 by 1985.

Just outside New Delhi, the prominent futurist writer and businessman, Jagdish Kapur, has turned ten arid, miserably unproductive acres into a world-renowned model "solar farm" with a bio-gas plant. The farm now produces enough grains, fruits, and vegetables to feed his family and employees as well as tons of food to sell at a profit to the marketplace. The Indian Institute of Technology, meanwhile, has designed a ten-kilowatt solar plant for village use to provide electricity for lighting homes, operating water pumps, and powering community television or radio sets.

The energy crisis which is part of the breakdown of Second Wave civilization is generating many new ideas for both centralized and decentralized, large-scale and small-scale energy production in the poorer regions of the planet. And there is a clear parallel between some of the problems facing First Wave and emergent Third Wave societies. Neither can rely on energy systems designed for the Second Wave era.

What about agriculture? Once again, the Third Wave leads us in unconventional directions. At the Environmental Research Lab in Tucson, Arizona, shrimp are being grown in long troughs in greenhouses, right alongside cucumbers and lettuce—with the shrimp waste recycled to fertilize the vegetables. In Vermont experimenters are raising catfish, trout, and vegetables in a similar manner. The water in the fish tank collects solar heat and releases it at night to keep temperatures up. Again, the fish waste is used to fertilize the vegetables.

A forecast of 20-year trends in world food supply prepared by the Center for Futures Research (CFR) at the University of Southern California regards as "virtually certain" new grain varieties which produce higher yields per acre on non-irrigated land—with gains as high as 25 to 50 percent. It suggests that "trickle-drip" irrigation systems, with decentralized wind-powered wells and water distributed by draft animals, could substantially increase yields while cutting year-to-year fluctuations in the harvest.

Furthermore, it tells of forage grass that, because it needs only minimal water, could double the livestock carrying capacity of arid regions; of a potential 30 percent jump in nongrain yields in tropical soils as a result of a better understanding of nutrient combinations; of breakthroughs in pest control that will cut crop losses drastically; of new low-cost water pumping methods; of the control of the tsetse fly, which would open up vast new regions to livestock farming; and many other advances.

Other possibilities pointed out by the McHales in their excellent study *Basic Human Needs* include everything from ocean farming to the use of insects and other organisms for productive work, the processing of cellulose wastes into meat via microorganisms, and the conversion of plants like euphorbia into sulphur-free fuel. "Green medicine"—the manufacture of pharmaceuticals from previously unknown or under-utilized plant life— also holds high potential for many First Wave countries.

On a longer time-scale, one can imagine much of agriculture devoted to "energy farms"—the cultivation of crops for energy production. Ultimately we may see the convergence of weather modification, computers, satellite monitoring, and genetics to revolutionize the world's food supply.

Advances in other fields also cast doubt on traditional development thinking. With wholly new composite materials many times stronger, stiffer, and lighter than aluminum, with transparent materials that are as strong as steel, with reinforced plastic mortar to replace galvanized water pipes, how long before the demand for steel peaks and production capacity is excessive? Perhaps, instead of seeking loans or foreign investment to build steel capability, the poorer countries ought to be preparing now for the "materials age"?

The Third Wave brings more immediate possibilities as well. Ward

Morehouse of the Research Policy Program, University of Lund, Sweden, argues that the poor nations should be looking beyond First Wave small-scale industry or Second Wave centralized, large-scale industry, and should focus instead on one of the key industries of the emerging Third Wave: microelectronics.

"Over emphasis on labor-intensive technology with low productivity could become a trap for poor countries," Morehouse writes. Pointing out that productivity is rising spectacularly in the computer chip industry, he argues that "it is certainly an advantage to capital-poor developing countries to get greater output per unit of capital invested."

More important, however, is the compatibility between Third Wave technology and existing social arrangements. Thus, Morehouse says, the great product diversity in microelectronics means that "developing countries can take a basic technology and adapt it more easily to suit their own social requirements or raw materials. Microelectronic technology lends itself to decentralization of production."

The Third Wave throws the need for transportation and communication into a new perspective as well. At the time of the industrial revolution, roads were a prerequisite for social, political, and economic development. Today an electronic communications system is necessary. It was once thought that communications were the outgrowth of economic development. Now, says John Magee, president of Arthur D. Little, the research firm, this "is an outmoded thesis...telecommunications is more of a precondition than a consequence."

Today's plummeting cost of communications suggests the substitution of communications for many transport functions. It may be far cheaper, more energy-conserving, and more appropriate in the long run to lay in an advanced communications network than a ramified structure of costly roads and streets. Clearly, road transport is needed. But to the degree that production is decentralized, rather than centralized, transport costs can be minimized without isolating villages from one another, from the urban areas, or from the world at large.

Not long ago, Indonesian President Suharto pressed the tip of a traditional sword against an electronic push button and thereby inaugurated a satellite communications system aimed at linking the parts of the Indonesian archipelago together—much as the railroads with their golden spike linked the two coasts of America a century ago. In so doing, he symbolized the new options that the Third Wave presents to countries seeking transformation.

Developments like these in energy, agriculture, technology, and communications suggest something even deeper—whole new societies based on the fusion of past and future, of First Wave and Third Wave.

One can begin to picture a transformation strategy based on the development of both low-stream, village-oriented, capital-cheap, rural industries and certain carefully selected, high-stream technologies, with an economy zoned to protect or promote both.

An increasing number of long-range thinkers, social analysts, scholars, and scientists believe that just such a transformation is now under way, carrying us toward a radical new synthesis: Gandhi, in short, with satellites.

The Original Prosumers

Implied in this approach is another synthesis at an even deeper level. This involves the entire economic relationship of people to the market — irrespective of whether that market is capitalist or socialist in form. It forces us to question how much of any individual's total time and labor should be devoted to production and how much to prosumption — i.e., how much to working for pay in the marketplace as against working for self.

Most First Wave populations have already been drawn into the money system. They have been "marketized." But while the wretched money income earned by the world's poorest people may be vital to their survival, production for exchange provides only part of their income; prosumption provides the rest.

The Third Wave encourages us to look at this situation, too, in a fresh way. In country after country millions are jobless. But is full employment in these societies a realistic goal? What combination of policies can possibly, within our lifetime, provide full-time jobs for all these surging millions? Is the very notion of "unemployment" itself a Second Wave concept, as hinted at by the Swedish economist Gunnar Myrdal?

The problem, writes Paul Streeten of the World Bank, is "not 'unemployment,' which is a Western concept that presupposes modern sector wage employment, labor markets, labor exchanges and social security payments. . . . The problem [is] rather, unremunerative, unproductive work of the poor, particularly of the rural poor." The remarkable rise of the prosumer in the affluent nations today, a striking phenomenon of the Third Wave, leads us to question the deepest assumptions and goals of most Second Wave economists.

Perhaps it is a mistake to emulate the industrial revolution in the West, which saw the transfer of most economic activity out of Sector A (the prosumer sector) and into Sector B (the market sector).

Perhaps what is needed for most people is part-time employment for wages (possibly with some transfer payments) plus imaginative new policies aimed at making their prosumption more "productive." Indeed, linking these two economic activities more intelligently to one another may be the missing key to survival for millions.

Practically speaking, this might mean providing "capital tools for prosumption" — just as the rich countries now do. In the affluent countries we see a fascinating synergy springing up between the two sectors, with the marketplace providing powerful capital tools for use by the prosumer: everything from washing machines to handdrills to battery testers. Misery in the poor countries is often so extreme that to speak of washing machines or power tools seems, at first glance, wildly out of place. Yet is there no analogue here for societies moving beyond First Wave civilization?

The French architect-planner Yona Friedman reminds us that the world's poor do not necessarily want jobs—they want "food and a roof." The job is only a means to this end. But one can often grow one's own food and build one's own roof, or at least contribute to that process. Thus in a paper for UNESCO, Friedman has argued that governments should encourage what I have called prosumption by relaxing certain land laws and building codes. These make it hard (often, indeed, impossible) for squatters to build or improve their own housing. What Friedman and others are beginning to say is that anything that helps the individual prosume more effectively may be just as important as production measured in conventional GNP terms.

Second Wave propaganda today unfortunately conveys to even the world's most remote and poorest people the idea that the things they make themselves are inherently inferior to the worst mass-produced junk. Rather than teaching people to despise their own efforts, to value Second Wave products and downgrade what they themselves create, governments should be offering prizes for the best or most imaginative self-built homes and goods, the most "productive" prosumption. The knowledge that even the world's richest people are increasingly prosuming may help change attitudes among the very poorest. For the Third Wave casts into a dramatic new light the entire relationship of market to nonmarket activities in all the societies of the future.

The Third Wave also raises non-economic and non-technological concerns to primary importance. It makes us look at education, for example, with fresh eyes. Education, everyone agrees, is central to development. But what kind of education?

When the colonial powers introduced formal education into Africa, India, and other parts of the First Wave world, they transplanted either factory-style schools or set up miniature, tenth-rate imitations of their own elite schools. Today Second Wave education models are being questioned everywhere. The Third Wave challenges the Second Wave notion that education necessarily takes place in a classroom. Today we need to combine learning with work, political struggle, community service, and even play. All our conventional assumptions about education need to be re-examined in both the rich countries and the poor.

Finally, the Third Wave encourages us to look behind conventional Second Wave assumptions with respect to motivation as well. Better nutrition is likely to raise the entire level of intelligence and functional competence among millions of children—at the same time that it increases drive and motivation.

And so, not merely in the fields of energy or technology, agriculture or economics, but in the very brain and behavior of the individual, the Third Wave brings the potential for revolutionary change.

The Starting Line

The emerging Third Wave civilization does not provide a ready-made model for emulation. Third Wave civilization is itself not yet fully formed. But for the poor as well as the rich it opens novel, perhaps liberating, possibilities. For it calls attention not to the weaknesses, poverty, and misery of the First Wave world, but to some of its inherent strengths. The very features of this ancient civilization that seem so backward from the standpoint of the Second Wave appear as potentially advantageous when measured against the template of the advancing Third Wave.

The congruity of these two civilizations must, in the years ahead, transform the way we think about the relations between rich and poor on the planet. Samir Amin, the economist, speaks of the "absolute necessity" of breaking out of the "false dilemma: modern techniques copied from the West of today, or old techniques corresponding to conditions in the West a century ago." This is precisely what the Third Wave makes possible.

The poor as well as the rich are crouched at the starting line of a new and startlingly different race into the future.

3

What Makes History Happen?

ROBERT E. NEIL

The human species had already spread all over the globe long before it began having anything that could properly be called a history. Early men had an anthropology, but not a history.[1] For most of its existence the species homo sapiens was just as history-less as any other animal species. We do speak of the prehistory of man but not of the mouse. The human species is unique in this respect: at some point we started having a history, and we are the only species on this planet that has one. Now it should be noted that this aspect of human uniqueness is much more recent than the more obvious one, high intelligence. Prehistoric men were just as intelligent as their descendants, but they were history-less just the same. Further, where intelligence is something that was provided to us by biological evolution, history is something that we have acquired for ourselves.

These reflections raise another question: what is history? In ordinary parlance, the word "history" is used simply as a rough synonym for "the past." But, as we have seen, most of the past is not history. What is it, then, that sets off historied humans from prehistoric ones? I would say that people begin having a history when their society produces specific events of on-going chronological significance. The cave-painting hunters of prehistoric France doubtless had their ups and downs from day to day and year to year, but they did not experience sequences of specific events of on-going chronological significance like the calling of the Estates-General, the storming of the Bastille, and the decapitation of Louis VXI. Thus "history" may be defined as follows: it is an accumulation of casually related events that render the present substantially different from the past and that will render the present substantially different from the future. The reason that early men did not have a history is that they were wild animals. Perhaps that statement may sound a trifle provocative, but all that I mean by it is that early humans lived by hunting and gathering their food just as all the other wild animals did and still do. Now the daily hunting and collecting of food is an eventless

Excerpted from Robert E. Neil, "What Makes History Happen?," *Oberlin Alumni Magazine*, Autumn 1981, pp. 26–31.

existence. Things happen, of course—a baby is born or a reindeer gets away—but this has no chronological significance. These are happenings rather than events, and happenings do not generate linear change.

Humans living in an eventless state of nature must be viewed in ecological rather than historical terms. But the converse is not true: when humans make the breakthrough to history, they do not escape from ecology. Hence it is essential to note some facts about human ecology that antedated history and that now coexist with it.[2]

The life of any animal, including homo sapiens, depends on two ecological factors: its niche and its breeding strategy. Borrowed from architecture, the term "niche" means the resources available to an animal for survival and the techniques, whether instinctive or learned, that it uses to exploit these resources. "Breeding strategy" is an ecologist's term for reproductive patterns, or, as one of them puts it bluntly, how animals turn resources into babies. Some, like fish, use what Prof. Paul Colinvaux of Ohio State calls the small-egg gambit. Others, including all mammals, have hit on the large-young gambit. But it is the niche and not the varying breeding strategies that determines the maximum size of an animal population. My back yard provides only so much niche-space for gray squirrels, and once they have filled it, then no amount of strenuous breeding will increase their numbers. It will only increase the casualties.

Most animals suffer lots of casualties because reproductivity exceeds resources. Or, to use the terminology that I have just introduced, breeding strategy is out of balance with niche-space. This is wasteful, but a surplus of babies is the insurance policy that evolution has taken out on survival. If my gray squirrels did not fill their niche, they then would be squeezed out by some other species with overlapping tastes. On the other hand, nature will cull the surplus that the breeding strategy of any species produces and so tailor population to niche. The runts in the squirrel litter will die, and the thousands of supernumerary eggs that the female salmon lays will be eaten by other fish and birds—thereby becoming part of somebody else's niche.

Homo sapiens is not exempt from these principles. Niche will ultimately determine the maximum size of our population whatever our breeding strategy. Given that females are fertile for about a quarter of a century and that humans enjoy the unique pleasures of year-round sex, it is obvious that our breeding strategy, unless controlled somehow, would produce an unsupportable surplus. But humans, unlike squirrels or salmon, are intelligent enough to know this, and so they have done their own culling instead of waiting for nature to do the job. Population control is not a new idea. Humans have been practicing it since the dimmest prehistoric times.

How was this done? There are three effective ways to limit reproductivity—not counting celibacy, which seems to lack general appeal. One can prevent conception, interrupt pregnancy, or destroy surplus babies. But contraceptive methods, e.g. prolonged lactation, remained primitive until the vulcanization of rubber in the 1840s, while techniques of abortion were both dangerous and barbaric before the development of modern surgery, also in the 19th century. Hence prior to the Industrial Revolution infanticide played an important role in human history, though this fact is not widely publicized in high school textbooks. As late as the 18th century, for instance, the foundling hospitals in France amounted to state-run facilities for infanticide.[3] With characteristic efficiency Napoleon then had revolving boxes built into the walls of these "hotels for found infants," so that babies could be abandoned to their fate anonymously; and these Napoleonic baby boxes were still in use in the 1830s.[4]

The point is that we have always had the means of limiting our population. Surgical and pharmaceutical advances in the last century have given us less traumatic methods, but we have always had effective ones. Therefore, in theory humans were always capable of optimizing their numbers, that is, adjusting breeding strategy to niche in order to ensure a good living standard for all. An optimized population would provide each individual with what ecologists call a broad niche-space. However, so far our species has only done this once, and that, ironically, was at the very beginning of our past before we had acquired a history. Since then human societies have often stabilized their numbers—contrary to the stereotype of constant population growth—but we have never done so until niche-space had already become so narrow and so compressed that most people could not be supported as true human beings. And, as a further irony, it was this phenomenon of niche-compression, this failure to optimize population, that started history and that has kept it going.

Let us go back to prehistoric times and see how this happened. The most successful human population managers to date were the hunters of the last Ice Age. That may sound strange because the very word "Ice Age" conjures up visions of people huddled and shivering for millenia and chasing giant animals from glacier to glacier. But most people did not live on the ice. They lived on the broad grasslands south of the ice where the low rainfall of the period created perfect conditions for large grazing animals and so for their human predators. Contrary to another stereotype, hunting was an easy profession. Studies of modern hunters living under much less favorable conditions have shown that they can get along very nicely by devoting only three hours a day to their profession. Further, a hunter's niche was broad, both literally and qualitatively. He had to have plenty of space to practice his profession, and he made a very good living at it. At least this is a reasonable inference to draw from archaeological studies that show that these hunters were bigger and had more teeth left at death than most later humans.[5]

But professional skill was only one secret of this good life. The other was strict control of the population. Most humans, I suspect, want as many children as they think that they can afford. Hence there is a strong temptation to increase production in order to accommodate more people. The results are disastrous, but for most technologies it takes some time for this to become apparent. Not so for hunters. A hunter is not a producer; he takes what nature provides, and there is no way that he can induce nature to produce more. Hence any attempt to intensify a hunting culture will have immediate disastrous consequences. Too many animals killed this year will mean too few to eat next year.

Now that is not obvious to most predators, and so nature has to cull their numbers to maintain the ecological balance. But it is obvious to intelligent human predators. Their response was to gear their own reproductivity to that of the animals on which they depended. Undoubtedly they did this by taboos restricting sexual activity, by prolonged suckling to reduce the number of pregnancies, and by infanticide, just as later hunters about whom we have direct information have done. Prof. Colinvaux has written a book with the intriguing title *Why Big Fierce Animals Are Rare.*[6] The answer for most of them is that, because they require a broad niche-space, nature culls them very severely. But man, as a big fierce predator, *decided* to be rare. Human numbers did increase, of course, as hunters spread to unoccupied hunting grounds. In a given habitat, however, population had to be optimized: it was a broad niche-space or else.

This Garden of Eden chapter in the human past came to an end when the climate warmed. Water, previously trapped in the ice caps, now descended as rain, and with increased rainfall forests moved into the former prairies and savannahs. This, in turn, greatly reduced the traditional human food supply, grazing animals. What followed was an ecological disaster for both those animals and men. Because the human life-span was longer than that of most game animals, the food supply fell faster than human population could. Even if the hunters realized what was happening, and even if they restricted reproduction more severely, the fact remained that they had a tribe of an existing size to be supported right now, not next year. And they had to do this on the resources of a shrinking niche. There were only two choices: reduce the tribe by killing some of its adult members or kill proportionally more animals. Please note that this did not mean increasing the actual killrate. Just killing the traditional number meant killing proportionally more. Since tradition is very strong in tribal societies, it is unlikely that the hunters perceived that they were making a choice and falling into a trap. It was just business as usual. But following traditional hunting patterns on a shrinking resource base inevitably created a vicious circle. Dozens of species of choice game animals were hunted into extinction – all of the so-called "pleistocene megafauna" in the New World, for instance. Thereupon hunters had to turn to less meaty species, with the same destructive result. The eventual outcome of this vicious circle of carnage was that though some humans remained hunters—in much-narrowed niches—for most the only solution was a change of professions. We had to become professional farmers, a possibility that we had known in general was there but that we had always resisted.

That statement runs counter to the notion that the Agricultural Revolution was a breakthrough. Books on human development speak of the "invention of agriculture" as though it were an improvement. Actually, it was a fall-back position for out-of-work hunters. Now in cost/benefit analysis farming is more efficient than hunting as far as land is concerned, but not work. Why would hunters who could support their families on only three hours of work per day want to change over to grubbing in the soil? Modern research has shown that American Indian hunters fully understood the principles of plant propagation and profited from them as long as it did not involve the drudgery of planting and weeding. It would be ridiculous to think that ancient hunters were any less perceptive. We turned to farming out of necessity, not invention, still less choice. We accepted harder work because it was the price of survival, not because it made possible a better life.

Life was not better, for example, in terms of nutrition. In essence, the Agricultural Revolution amounted to a descent on the food chain. We stopped being carnivores and instead became herbivores. Now to a modern-day conservationist this may seem to be a good thing. After all, it is more efficient to eat plants ourselves than to eat other animals after *they* have eaten the plants; this eliminates an unnecessary link in the food chain. And zealous vegetarians will insist that since all twenty amino acids are found in plants, we can have a perfectly nutritious diet without eating animal protein. Very true, but the fact remains that when it comes to supporting human life, as opposed to life in general, a carnivorous diet is much more efficient. To get all the amino acids, we must eat lots of bulky and starchy plants. Meat contains them in a highly concentrated form. Thus, though individuals in affluent societies may turn themselves into herbivores by choice, when we look at the human past and see whole societies or entire classes turning to vegetarianism, it is a sure sign of straitened circumstances: meat has become too dear. Mass conversion to vegetarianism does not reflect preference, moral rectitude, or higher spirituality; it reflects scarcity. Meat is more efficient to eat but less efficient to produce, so it has to be abandoned. For this reason, diet has long been one of the elementary forms of class status. In medieval Europe, for instance, nobles were carnivores; peasants, herbivores.[7]

But if agriculture in many ways represented a comedown rather than a breakthrough for homo sapiens, this does not detract from the significance of what had happened. For the first time in the story of animal life, a species had created a new niche for itself with new resources and new learned techniques for exploiting them. We had created a new human job or profession; we had emerged as a species capable of creating entirely new niches in response to changed ecological circumstances. No other animal can do this. To be sure, domesticated animals can adapt to living in a new niche created for them by us as part of the larger human niche. But in the wild each animal has only one profession. Kodiak bears do a very professional job of being Kodiak bears, but then they have no career alternatives. They do not suddenly start planting asparagus. But now their hairless primate cousin was doing just that.

And doing pretty well at it too—at least at first. Simple village agriculture is not terribly arduous except at certain peak times of year. Otherwise there is a good deal of leisure time. True, there are plenty of chores to be done, but there is no need to regiment just how and when. It isn't vital that the roof be rethatched today instead of tomorrow. Further, once sheep and goats had been domesticated, meat could still be part of the diet. Indeed, a captive animal population was a more reliable source of food in some ways than a wild one, especially when it could be supported on stubble and slop inedible by humans. So it is probably a mistake to allow the term "subsistence agriculture" to suggest that the early villagers were engaged in a constant struggle for mere survival.

If they were, then how can one explain the remarkable increase in their numbers? According to one recent estimate, the population of the Middle East rose by a factor of 40 between 8000 and 4000 B.C.—from only about 100,000 to over 3 million. The explanation of this is that people began having more children because they thought that they could afford them. In the short run larger families can actually be an advantage in village agriculture. If the land will support more people, and if there is no pressing need to limit population, then there will be a very strong temptation to let it grow, especially because, as we have seen, the principal method of limiting it, infanticide, was so drastic.

Well, population did grow, not just in the Near East but also in other regions where agriculture had been developed: and at first the results may have seemed beneficial—more little hands to help with the weeding, for instance. But once the pattern of large families had been established— another tradition with its own inertia—it generated an ecological cycle analogous to what had happened to the hunters, though in this case the motive force was rising human rather than falling animal numbers.

In order to understand this, let us leave our villagers for a moment and look at a universal human problem. To support a larger population at the existing living standard, it is necessary to intensify production. That means using more resources and energy. But that, in turn, causes depletion, falling productivity, and so falling living standards. Here, for once, that overused word "counterproductive" is precisely on target. One starts off trying to support more people at the present living standard and ends up by lowering their living standard. What does one do then?

There are several possibilities. Option #1: a society might decide to stabilize production, reduce population, and thus recoup the former living standard. That is what a completely rational society might do in theory, but I doubt that many actual societies are sufficiently hard-boiled to do it in practice. Option #2: one could cut one's losses by stabilizing production and population and just accepting the new, lowered living standard. But that alternative, as a deliberate policy, runs contrary to human nature—people want to get ahead or, as a minimum, hold their own. Option #3: a society could intensify production still further in an effort to recapture or even raise the living standard of the growing population. But this would only produce another downward spiral of resource depletion, falling productivity, and hence still lower living standards. And if this pattern were repeated often enough, eventually the point would be reached at which it would no longer be possible to intensify production any further with the available technology. Population would then have to be stabilized either by man or by nature, and there would be no choice about accepting the resultant rock bottom living standard. Thus, the unintended result of following option #3 would be the same as option #2, but at the lowest possible level. If I may coin an antonym, this would be a pessimized instead of an optimized population.

There is, of course, a fourth possibility, through which a society can escape from this trap. It can invent an entirely new, much more productive technology. And this will be hailed as salvation by those who do not realize that the game is merely starting all over.[8]

By the middle of the third millenium B.C. the descendants of the neolithic villagers whom we left a moment ago had learned all of this the hard way, and in so doing they had started history. As their population grew, they intensified production by planting more crops, domesticating new animals, opening up virgin land, and emigrating to start new villages. When none of these things alleviated demographic pressure, the villagers responded by inventing an improved technology. They learned how to domesticate animals for traction, which enabled them to switch from manual horticulture to true field agriculture based on plowing. For a time this changed technology probably enabled them to produce a surplus; the archaeological remains of facilities for grain storage suggest that. But the new stage of intensification eventually produced its predictable result—depletion of environment. Deforestation and soil erosion became problems, and broad tracts of once arable land underwent "desertification," to use a 1981 word for an old, old problem. Furthermore, since some of the meatiest animals were now a vital source of energy, they could no longer be used for food. Just the opposite, the ones that could not subsist on stubble had to be fed out of the grain surplus previously reserved for humans. Thus intensification of production produced a double decline in nutrition coupled with the much harder work of plowing. The ecological niche-space for the individual had been compressed—physically as well as economically because of the greater population density.

Once again a new technology was called in to break the vicious circle of rising populations and falling living standards—irrigation agriculture. And as before, the familiar pattern of intensification, depletion, diminishing returns, and so forth ensued. But this time the end result was utter disaster for most of the bloated population. They found themselves in what Prof. Harris calls the "hydraulic trap." They had been reduced to robots—mere BTUs of work—on giant irrigation projects, where they received a minimum diet of exclusively vegetable calories in return for their ceaseless toil. In effect, two-legged beings had joined four-legged ones as part of the captive animal population. Niche-space had been compressed to the point of mere survival.

As a result, population growth stopped at last, owing mainly to increased child mortality from natural causes and to a higher level of infanticide. Recent studies show that population then remained stable in Mesopotamia, Egypt, northern India, and China for centuries—in the case of China, for almost two millenia. Option #3 had indeed led to option #2 at the basement level.

Nevertheless, this descending spiral, this process of *de*volution, had produced progress, at least for a minority. The hydraulic trap for the many was the big opening for the few. Large-scale irrigation agriculture required artisans, tradesmen, and merchants, for one thing. But, above all, it required what Harris calls "extremely despotic agromanagerial bureaucracies" to harness the resources of entire river valleys. In other words, an irrigation economy required a multi-niche society instead of a single-niche community.

Let me explain that Delphic statement. Animals have a single niche: there is only one way to be a gray squirrel or a Kodiak bear. Early men were in roughly the same situation. Though arrows and spears may differ from one tribe to another, there is basically only one way to be a hunter-gatherer. The same goes for subsistence farming. Certainly no one would argue that there are several different ways to be a subsistence farmer in the same little village. There are sex and age differences, but everybody has the same niche. That is the reason why history did not begin with agriculture. Though the invention by an animal of a new niche for itself was unprecedented, nevertheless as long as everyone in the community lived in the same new niche, events did not yet replace mere happenings. Indeed, sedentary village life would seem even more eventless than a free-wheeling hunting career.

An irrigation-based existence was therefore entirely different from any previous mode of life. Not only had a multitude of new niches been invented, but these various niches coexisted with each other in the same population. Previously, humans, living in their niche, had coexisted with various animal species, each living in its niche. But now human inhabitants of the same locality lived in different niches. That is what I mean by saying that a multi-niche society had replaced a single-niche community.

It was this development, in my view, that started history. Interactions among individuals living in the same niche do not produce events of on-going chronological significance. A sequence of happenings in a village or tribe does not constitute a narrative to rivet the attention of a historian, though it may well illustrate some general behavior pattern of interest to an anthropologist. But the decision of an Egyptian pharaoh to construct a pyramid or of a Babylonian king to impose a law code generates a chain of subsequent events that does have narrative thrust because it is sui generis. Likewise, the gradual corruption of an imperial bureaucracy milking the peasants and how this produced revolt and the overthrow of a dynasty is a story of specific importance. Thus, to answer two of our original questions, history begins with the appearance of the first multi-niche societies, and what causes history to begin is the interaction for the first time between entirely different niches in the same population. Such interaction produces change rather than just variations on the same theme. It produces futures instead of mere repetitions of the present.

But let us carry our analysis a step further. What is it that sets these different niches off from each other? One difference is clearly functional: a peasant tilling the land is producing food, while a potter at his wheel is producing jars. There is a food-making niche and a jar-making niche. But this functional difference based on the division of labor is nowhere near as important as the difference in the width of niches. In a multi-niche society a few people have broad, comfortable niches, while the rest, whether peasants or potters, have narrow, compressed ones. This difference reflects the fact that most societies, until recently, produced such small surpluses that they could only afford a few broad niches. In other words, long after civilization had come into being, it remained a luxury for a privileged few: there could only be a few human-being chiefs; the rest had to be homo-sapiens Indians. Egalitarian doctrines have no relevance whatever to such societies, because an equal sharing of the small surplus would simply have meant slightly improved homo-sapiens status for everyone and human-being status for no one. And that provides us with one answer to the third of our original questions: what makes history continue to happen? It is a struggle over the limited surplus in a multi-niche society. Or, to put it another way, it is a struggle over the relative width of the niches, and over who is going to occupy them.

Now that may sound like nothing more than a restatement in an exotic vocabulary of the familiar Marxist doctrine of class struggle. But I said that this provides only one answer, not the answer, to the question of why history continues to happen.

Historically speaking, class struggle is the exception rather than the rule. Most multi-niche societies to date have developed coexisting castes as an alternative to conflicting classes. In a caste society niche-space is allocated on a hereditary basis. One is born into a given niche, and it has fixed parameters, though other niches have different ones. This is what the English found in India, and they professed to be horrified by it. Yet in medieval England the serf and the noblemen were exactly the equivalents of the untouchable and the high-caste Indians of the nineteenth century. A caste society rations niche-space by hereditary categories, and this minimizes social tensions of a destabilizing kind, because inequities are perceived as part of the natural order of things rather than as the result of exploitation by individuals. Indeed, one could make a case for the proposition that the more levels of inequity that there are in a caste society, the stabler it will be.

This, then, takes us to the other factor that makes history continue to happen. In a caste society the surplus is concentrated in a high-caste elite, and what they do with it—whether to raise armies or write books— generates events of ongoing chronological significance. I might add at this point that written history—that is, history based upon records rather than just relics—reflects this dual situation. On the one hand, it tells what the privileged niche did with the other niches, and, on the other hand, it tells what the privileged niche did with itself and its surplus. It should also be noted that writing did not come out of the blue to make recorded history possible. Just the opposite, it was an invention that became necessary once there was a history to be recorded. Why should anyone invent writing to record the eventless existence of hunters and subsistence farmers? The beginning of history brought the beginning of writing, not the other way around.

So far our analysis applies to any given society with its limited surplus. But human societies do not exist in isolation. Hence it is not surprising that the competition for niche-space within societies should be paralleled by competition for niche-space between societies. From an ecological standpoint, trade, war, colonization and imperialism are nothing but an intersociety struggle over niche-space, just as class conflict is a struggle over intrasociety niche-space. Consider, for example, the colonial movement, the "push to the East" in medieval Europe. What was it, after all, if not simply the seizure of the niche-space of less well organized peoples east of the Elbe River by their more advanced and demographically pressed western neighbors? And what was the so-called "rise of the West" in the modern period but the grabbing by Europeans of the niche-space of peoples who were still mainly in the village or tribal stage?

But the "rise of the West" also illustrates how something analogous to a caste system within a single society can be projected onto relations between multiple societies. Just as privileged elites faced and still face the unprivileged masses in particular civilizations, so the developed countries now face the underdeveloped ones. The old distinction between the aristocracy and the common folk within individual countries is now exactly paralleled by the distinction between have and have-not countries. We have developed a global set of caste distinctions—as such labels as "third" and "fourth world" clearly show. Whole countries of high-caste elites face whole countries of serfs and untouchables.

In any event, whether one concentrates on class or caste divisions, from the moment that history began with the appearance of multi-niche societies until just recently the Leitmotiv of significant chronological changes was always the struggle over a limited surplus. Or perhaps a better term would be "scarce surplus," because nobody was deliberately limiting it. To paraphrase Abbott and Costello, the question was always "who's got the surplus?" Which was another way of asking "who's got the civilization?"

But if this is what made history happen in the past, what of the present and the future? Have the rules been changed by so-called "modernization"?

In one way they have, at least temporarily. The Industrial Revolution of the last two centuries has enabled some societies to have broad niches, in comparison to earlier times, for nearly everybody. Instead of being scarce, the surplus became so enormous that nearly all the homo sapiens in these societies could be promoted to human beings. There were still chiefs and Indians, of course, but they all shared civilization as a consumption commodity. This experience has given rise to a pair of convictions about the future: first, that this situation has now become the norm where it exists, and second, that it should and will become the norm where it does not yet exist.

I believe that these are delusions. What we have really seen in the last two centuries is not the dawn of a fundamentally different era, as the term "modernization" suggests, but rather the onset of yet another cycle in the old pattern that has so often given our species a new technology, intensification of production, depletion of resources, diminishing returns, and falling living standards. When I first started saying this twenty years ago, I was met by nearly universal incredulity and so had to fight for my case. Today, alas, that is hardly necessary: the signs of niche-compression are all around us. For example, the Nobel laureate economist Wassily Leontief has calculated that even if we did not intensify production any further but stabilized it, we would nevertheless consume in what is left of this century three or four times the mineral resources that were heretofore consumed since history began.[9] That would be bad enough, but does anyone seriously think that we are going to stabilize output? All that one hears these days, so it seems, is the cry for increased productivity—that is, for still further intensification. And if further intensification is our "solution," then the history of previous cycles offers guidance to what to expect: mounting social unrest as niches narrow, increasing government repression as a response to it, the appearance of a de facto caste society to allocate niches and ration the shrinking surplus, and aggressive attempts by desperate strong states to acquire additional niche-space from weaker peoples. That by no means exhausts the catalogue, but it provides adequate food for thought, because this is what has actually happened under analogous circumstances in the past.

However, there is one way in which the present cycle may turn out to be entirely different from the previous ones. Any intensification of production requires larger inputs of energy. That was true when animals were harnessed and when people were regimented into working harder. In other words, intensification in the earlier cycles meant greater inputs of muscle power. That kind of intensification was therefore self-limiting: once the maximum amount of muscle work had been extracted from people and their animals, intensification had to stop. But that did not endanger the very survival of the technology, since muscle power is a renewable source of energy. Hence, when intensification reached the self-limiting point, the result was merely stagnation. But that, in turn, meant that intensification in a muscle-based technology was self-limiting in another respect: once the supply of muscle power could not be increased any further, it was likewise impossible to increase consumption of natural resources.

This time around things may be very different. For one, the supply of energy may *contract* instead of just no longer expanding. An industrial technology, unlike previous ones, depends on inanimate sources of energy. Everyone knows that currently this means fossil fuels and that fossil fuels are not renewable. The conclusion to be drawn is obvious, which is why we hear so much talk about "inexhaustible alternative sources" such as solar and tidal power and nuclear fusion.

In my opinion, people who talk in these terms have not thought through the full implications of their panaceas. Suppose, for example, that these alternatives do come on line before the fossils give out. Is this our salvation? Far from it: an inexhaustible energy source would simply mean an inexhaustible capacity to consume other resources, most of which are no more renewable than oil.

An idea like that is rather uncommon—even heretical—so let me recapitulate. The worst that can happen in a muscle-based technology is mere energy stagnation. Our industrial technology, on the contrary, is running a real danger of energy contraction. But the solution to that problem—further energy expansion—would merely pose a problem that old-fashioned muscle technologies never faced, namely, fatal depletion of non-energy resources. Either energy contraction or energy expansion would spell disaster—the one sooner, the other later—yet only the former is getting much attention, whereas the latter is actually being heralded as a solution instead of a problem.

Now that is indeed a heretical idea—the belief that new energy sources would probably do more harm than good in the long run. However, I for one firmly believe that this is the case. Let me illustrate the point by looking at what are euphemistically called the "LDCs"—the lesser developed countries.

Many good, kindhearted people think that they know what they want for the world's future—development, modernization, and hence prosperity for all humankind. Again, I wonder if these people have really thought through what they believe that they want. Development and modernization in today's high-caste countries have already produced a horrendous rundown of resources and pollution of the biosphere. But this is nothing compared to the impact that worldwide modernization would have. We have been told for years that it is wicked and intolerable that an American consumes as much as "x" Indians or "x + 1" Sri Lankans, but suppose that tomorrow Indians and Sri Lankans began consuming as much as Americans. An innocent moralist might say that that would only be equitable, but where would it leave the human race?

Well, where *would* it leave the human race? At present there are more than four billion homo sapiens on this planet, only a minority of whom can be supported as human beings. By the year 2000 A.D. the number of homo sapiens will have risen to at least six billion. And a century from now, according to the recent report of Willy Brandt's international committee, we will have to contend with between eight and fifteen billion homo sapiens. At present we are adding one million to the world population every five days.

From this I reluctantly conclude the following: the ratio of human beings to homo sapiens is bound to go down with each passing year. I also conclude that the ultimate ecological disaster, as Charles Krauthammer wrote in a recent issue of *The New Republic*, would probably be the very development of the Third World which most liberal Americans fervently advocate.[10] The planet simply couldn't take it.

Let us be clear: no amount of left- or right-wing sloganry will change the demographic facts of life. These can be summarized in our ecological terminology as follows. The breeding strategy of the species homo sapiens has produced more people than there is niche-space for human beings, despite our industrial technology. As a consequence, most homo sapiens are still in 1981 what they have always been—just BTUs for work—while civilization remains a minority luxury.

But the industrial cycle of intensification and depletion holds out a dismal possibility not previously seen. It may not just self-limit and stagnate. Instead, it may self-destruct and implode. If so, then history will have had not only a start but also a stop.

4

Directionality in Evolution

GEORGE T. LOCK LAND

For over a hundred and fifty years science has successfully evaded a major confrontation with the single question that lies at the very heart of all ideas about Man and Nature—namely, the issue of *directionality* in evolution. We have often assumed such direction on the part of Nature, referring to the observable process of development of "novelty, diversity, and higher levels of organization," but with no mechanism to explain how it could occur. In essence, if natural selection operates on a *random* or chance basis, if Darwinian concepts of repetition hold, why would Nature progress beyond novelty and diversity to higher levels? Why indeed should Man appear?

That there is a direction to evolution is clearly true; evidence surrounds us on every hand. That there is some force that makes evolution a cumulative process has been referred to time and time again by the world's greatest scientists, even if it could only be explained as a sort of "vital force" forever to remain an inexplicable mystery. Darwin himself, in later life, admitted that he had to accept some idea of inherited characteristics for, even to him, chance selection was insufficient to explain the behavior of evolution.[1] Jung observed, in 1968, that "the unexpected parallelisms of ideas in psychology and physics suggest...a possible ultimate one-ness of both fields of reality that physics and psychology study, i.e., a psychophysical one-ness of all life phenomena." Waddington too has characterized evolutionary theory as something that "in fact merely amounts to the statement that the individuals which leave the most offspring are those which leave the most offspring. It is a tautology."[2] We have been left with another circular explanation, chasing our own evolutionary tail.

Although modern biochemistry, cybernetics, and general systems have shown that blind chance combined with natural selection could keep evolution going in the direction to which the evidence points, they have only found more critical and sophisticated means once more to express the lack

Excerpted from George T. Lock Land, *Grow or Die: The Unifying Principle of Transformation* (New York: Random House, 1973), chapter 10.

of any acceptable evolutionary theory. The celebrated biologist and general systems theorist Ludwig von Bertalanffy wrote perhaps the most damning epitaph for present evolutionary theories:

> I think the fact that a theory so vague, so insufficiently verifiable and so far from the criteria otherwise applied in "hard" science, has become a dogma, can only be explained on sociological grounds. Society and science have been so steeped in the ideas of mechanism, utilitarianism and the economic concept of free competition, that instead of God, Selection was enthroned as ultimate reality. On the other hand, it seems symptomatic that the present discontent with the state of the world is also felt in evolution theory. I believe this is the explanation why leading evolutionists like J. Huxley and Dobzhansky (1967) discover sympathy with the somewhat muddy mysticism of Teilhard de Chardin. If differential reproduction and selective advantage are the only directive factors of evolution, it is hard to see why evolution has ever progressed beyond the rabbit, the herring, or even the bacterium which are unsurpassed in their reproductive capacities.[3]

While many have openly despaired of a solution to the riddle, the fact is that the very sciences that have nurtured that feeling are the ones to provide us with the new tools to resolve the dilemma. But to proceed we shall have to reformulate a few of the basic ideas in these disciplines. We shall review for a moment the facts of change and the observable effects using our perspective of three billion years of history.

Growth of Information Organization

- The basic drive of all organisms is to grow: to reproduce and to multiply.
- Growth is accomplished by accumulating capabilities to use energy and to direct its use.
- Use of energy for growth depends on the building up of information in living organisms and the success of this information in guiding the transformation of environmental materials into bodily constituents and special products to aid growth.
- Over time, the method of organically accumulating information has changed through the evolution of information holding and transmission techniques:

  Atomic bonding
  Molecular bonding
  Carbon-based heteropolymeric molecules
  Cell growth (enlargement)

    Cell reproduction (fission mitosis)
    Intercellular information exchange (conjugation and transduction)
    Cell recombination (fusion meiosis)
    Cell colonies
    Multicellular organisms

- Each evolutionary and natural selection step increased the organization of information and the capability of living forms to use energy to reproduce, and to decrease the biological waste of energy through loss of progeny. Less and less energy was required per unit of time to accomplish the same result.
- As complex, integral multicellular organisms evolved, other information-acquisition, storage, and transmission systems emerged to deal with more information – perception systems, nerve and brain systems, and communication systems.
- With improvements in external information handling systems, once more organisms increased their capacity to use energy to reproduce and to transform the environment into more of themselves.

    Multicellular organisms formed colonies
    Intraspecies symbiotic cooperation evolved

- Concomitant with the evolution and selection of species, the capacity to add information increased through learning by experience and imitative and social learning.
- With the advent of a sophisticated stereoscopic, color-perceiving system[4] and nonreproducing mammalian neurons, the possibility for acquisition and long-term storage of information increased.
- In order to transmit acquired information to progeny through imitative and verbal means, hominoid societies evolved longer infant learning periods and improved their communication techniques.
- To increase substantially the heritability of externally acquired information required the invention of improved information-holding and transmission techniques. With the development of symbolism this goal became possible.
- By the use of culturally spread information, additions of substantially larger amounts of new information to a much broader group became practical.
- As Man continually added to this externalized pool of information the infantile period was once more expanded so that a child entering adulthood could acquire the ectogenetic pool of information.
- Parallel with the development of symbolic information systems humans evolved higher levels of multiorganism communication, information exchange, and cooperative effects through:

    Families and tribes

> Villages and cities
> City-states and nations
> International organizations

- Technology and information growth followed the same pattern as a form of ectobiological extension and continually increased the use of energy to form life, life-supporting products, and higher levels of information exchange.

Thus, in psychological and cultural development extending the work of his biologic precursors, Man developed diversity, novelty, and higher levels of organization as a function of the evolving information system. The pressure of information growth continually reconstructs the "genetic" system with nature an unrelenting master of invention in developing better and better methods of carrying information forward.

Adaptation

In Darwinian terms, although it is inescapably true that environmental conditions do modify the form and behavior of organisms, the question is whether this phenomenon can truly be characterized by referring to it as an adaptation *to* the environment. A perfect "adaptation" to anything would be like the symbiotic relationship of phoresis, where associated organisms are not affected by each other (such as the bacteria carried in the hairs of a fly's leg).[5]However, the *ratio of adaptation* between an organisms are not affected by each other (such as the bacteria carried in the hairs of a fly's leg).[5] However, the *ratio of adaptation* between an organism and its environment is clearly one that demonstrates a far greater

The harmony of a quiescent environment is disturbed greatly when a living being absorbs it, dismembers it, rearranges it, and transforms it into its own living form. The environment changes substantially more than the organism. As with biological systems, this active *adapting of* and *transformation of* the environment is actually the most prominent characteristic of both biological and psychological systems.[6]

Darwin's famous finches would never have evolved from their protozoan precursors if "adaptation to" or "equilibrium" had been their goal. Obviously, organisms respond to their environment. They do "adapt." But, like a magician's misdirection, this fact has led many investigators away from seeing the underlying changes on the other side of life's basic transaction: the perpetual enhancement of the capacity of living organisms to *change the environment* into themselves, their progeny, and the special products that served their life and growth. Those Galapagos finches, like all living things, dismantled and totally reorganized parts of their environment as they grew. In its simplest terms, they ate their environment and made it into more finches! By looking closely and at the same time broadening our perspective we can see that evolution and growth are far more an adaptation of the environment than solely the reverse. This modification of the environment provides the basic clue to the resolution of the paradox of evolution. It provides the machinery by which evolution can *accumulate.*

Energy and Life

By enlarging our perspective of information beyond the idea of germ cell genetics, we can begin to comprehend a large body of phenomena. Just as Newton was able to correct Galileo by extending observations from weight on this planet to the moon and planets and as Einstein broadened this view even more, our role here is to seek to coordinate a larger number of facts and phenomena drawn from remoter areas. To do this at levels so far un-expressed here would involve volumes, but we can attempt to grasp a basic-ally new perspective of evolution and behavior by a brief reconsideration of life, energy, and matter.

What is it that causes information to accumulate at higher levels of organization? The bridge to understanding encompasses a single basic prin-ciple related to the idea of "information." Information is something that "determines the probabilities of an event." Examined closely, this introduces the idea that *information is a form of energy,* for energy causes events or "work." It causes atoms to bond and molecules to form; it provides our food and our thoughts. In each case, however, energy must be in very particular and specific forms or "frequencies" to do its work. It must be expressed in a form that can be "understood" at every level. In this light, energy is information (in both kinetic and potential forms).

Growth is a phenomenon that depends on the linking of information, that is, the finding of congruent meaning in its joining. As growth occurs, new phenomena come into being as expressions of higher levels of organiza-tion. A photon of light is emitted from the sun and, through photosynthesis, becomes plant life, converting carbon dioxide into oxygen and into the vegetative informational nutrition that sustains animal life. As this level of organized information is absorbed in the animal world, it reaches new heights of organization, joining in larger and larger molecules, becoming cells and the energy to drive them. It can ultimately become the material by which we move, speak, and think. If information is in an inappropriate form—as a chemical, for example—it can become toxic and cause life to cease. Yet it constantly finds the right forms to support life and to support its own transformation to becoming parts of larger organizations.

At the psychological level of growth, the use of information is recapit-ulated. We learn by communicating with one another using the same mechanics as are used in physical informational processes, through what is called "electromagnetic radiation." Just as an atom "knows" what informa-tion it can accept for growth and does this at the level of the photon, the unit of "light energy," so we accept data or not, depending on its frequencies of energy. Vision, for example, is able to absorb particular photons, or spectra, of light. The configuration of the "light energy" gives us information. Just as the light falling on the page is absorbed by dark letters and reflected by the lighter page, the energy enables us to get "data" from these words. Through one form of information energy or another, through all of our senses, we are able to grow.

We are increasingly better able to understand, as another case in point, that information is power or "capital." Far beyond the effect of money or land or machines, the organization or organism that successfully grows is able to do so as a function of the information it possesses. Monolithic organizations have been decimated by much smaller groups who have a new idea. The force of an "idea whose time has come" is irresistible.

It is all very well to call energy "information," but the meaning of this information carries us far beyond the boundaries of "living organisms." It plummets us to the microcosmic universe of atoms and electromagnetic radiation. It impels a postulate to help understand or, at least, explain what is really happening: *Along with the process of entropy there is another process occurring in parallel, that of "syntropy"*; information (as energy) constantly produces new combinations, producing diversity and higher levels of organization.

While matter is being disorganized by the forces of entropic breakdown, it is at the same time being organized by syntropy. Entropy runs "downhill" as organized matter continually decays, and syntropy runs "uphill" as matter is continually being put together in more cohesive ways. Syntropy acts very differently from the accepted transactions in the physical universe, just as idea exchange contravenes the basic concepts of economics. The sum is becoming greater than the parts.

As a matter of fact, the function of entropy is *complementary* to that of syntropy. Because no organization of information can reach an absolute state, entropy aids our reorganization by helping break down old materials. It is the catabolic function of the physical universe just as syntropy is anabolic. Life cannot exist without death, for life would have nothing to resynthesize into higher organizations if it were in static equilibrium. As the great biologist Haldane put it, "Normal death must apparently be regarded from the biological standpoint as a means by which room is made for further more definite development of life."[7] Death contributes to life in a specific causal chain. Decay is the handmaiden of creation.

As an illustration of the radical difference between the entropy of some manifestations of energy and the syntropy of information, consider the Second Law of Thermodynamics as it applies to two bodies of unequal temperatures that are brought together. In time, heat energy will distribute itself evenly between the two bodies, and in contact with a wider environment as well, will continually equalize and redistribute their heat. The order of heat runs "downhill," from organization to chaos. Yet, if we consider *information as a function of energy,* we see the reverse phenomenon. The two bodies, rather than diffusing their data, can actually *increase their order and organization.* Two atoms, molecules, cells, or humans can exchange and share information, and will, in time, through evolution, continually organize it to higher levels.

Yet the foundation of physics assumes the verity of the law of Entropy: that the universe is progressing into disorder. Time and time again experiments have demonstrated the facts of the Second Law of Thermodynamics. And the facts are true—as far as they go. Unfortunately a great deal of scientific thinking is based on investigation of what we can only characterize as *closed systems,* systems isolated from their normal environment. A researcher will do his best to isolate his experiment so that it will not be affected by outside influences or "perturbations." In doing so he in fact creates an *isolated system,* one which has *no* choice but to behave in an entropic manner as it is removed from interactive growth with the larger system. Even in our age of sophisticated science this artificial methodology continues—violating the advice given by Max Planck over four decades ago when he said, "The assumption that the orderly course of a process can be represented by an analysis of it into temporal and spacial processes must be dropped. The conception of wholeness must therefore be introduced in physics as in biology."

The results of such experiments provide a distorted picture of reality— from the behavior of atoms to that of men. What we really learn from such data is the type of behavior to expect from a *deprived* sub-system.[8] Animals, men, and molecules when subjected to "test-tube" isolation naturally fall back on lower forms of growth.

Attempts to provide more holistic environments for experiments invariably lead to unexpected results, that is, unexpected in the light of entropic laws. A case in point is the now classical "origin of life" experiment. Less than a decade ago a young graduate student, Stanley Miller, at the University of Chicago tested the possibility of organic compounds arising "spontaneously" in the simplified environment of the primeval earth. Creating a considerably more realistic—holistic—laboratory copy of this environment, methane, ammonia, hydrogen, and water, he subjected it to another common environmental agent, an electric spark much like lightning. The result was the formation of several amino acids and formaldehyde— complex building blocks of life. Following these astonishing results laboratory upon laboratory has duplicated this experiment with the same results. Melvin Calvin's work and other investigations have shown that such simple environments when subject to *any* form of natural energy input, heat, ultraviolet rays, etc., will form not only simple amino acids but complex compounds including adenine, quanine, uracil, and various sugars.[9] We can see that "chance" alone cannot explain such consistent results. There is an inevitability to such phenomena.

From the standpoint of classical ideas of entropy, the laws of universal decay have been likened to such things as the behavior of masses of different billiard balls. All matter, we have been told, would behave like an orderly arrangement of billiard balls which, in the presence of an outside force, will become progressively disarranged until no order exists. This seems reasonable; billiard balls do not rearrange themselves into orderly patterns. Yet in the Miller experiment above, what we are really seeing is an initial situation of mass disorder in which order occurs spontaneously. Imagine a billiard table with a thousand numbered balls in random disarray, which upon being struck by an outside force—a player shooting a high-energy ball into their midst—would suddenly arrange themselves into orderly rows and columns by their numbers! This is exactly like what Miller and many others experienced with atoms and molecules in their laboratories. Nature, instead of further disordering things, was *ordering* them.

We can see why such results were unexpected. When we are asked to think of billiard balls we are not invited to include the *players*. If we were to observed a billiard room instead, we would expect to see people disarranging and rearranging the balls—a very different phenomenon. It is a more holistic environment. One could have objected at this point by saying that humans are involved in the billiard room and are thus using their *intelligence* to provide order from disorder; however, since this is what we can now see is happening in all natural processes, we can only assume that even the most simple things contain intelligence. It is an intelligence dedicated to providing ever higher levels of organized, mutualized inter-relationships; they are syntropic rather than entropic.

The human syntropic machine is indeed something special, particularly if we look at the accumulation of energy potentials. One way to do this is to measure the energy reserve of animals versus Man. It was shown, shortly after the turn of the century, by the physiologist Rubner[10] that while mammals are characterized by energy reserves which average 16,000 kilocalories, Man's average energy exceeds 700,000 kilocalories! This and other of his studies demonstrated that high levels of activity actually *increase* the working potential of organisms. Once more, the facts are in sharp disagreement with classical laws. Intensive work is supposed to contribute to the wear and destruction of a system. Yet we can see that work, in truth, enhances the capabilities of an organism to do *more* work. As has been pointed out in recent research by Arshavsky, this "stands the test from the point of view of so important and basic a criterion as the life-span." Energy begets energy.[11]

In engineering practices there is also a tendency to see things in isolation. An engineer would say, "The harder you work this machine, the more wear will occur—it will run downhill." Yet, we must recognize that a machine, any machine, does not exist in isolation, it is an indivisible part of a system. What must be considered is *why* we have the machine. If it is to manufacture something, its working is dependent on the demand for the product and the economic potential of the manufacturing company. If the company is in order, the more the machine works, the more earnings it achieves, the more need there is to improve it (as competition emerges in a successful market), and finally it replaces itself by having translated its work into another form. Considered within the *system*, it contributes to subsequent reordering at higher levels. It is a part not apart and is mechanically syntropic. A badly designed machine would not perform the same syntropic function and, being "unfit," would be extincted in short order. Even an inanimate bit of matter such as this is still subject to the basic laws of nature—grow or die.

By removing the artificial constraints of "solitary confinement" in the laboratory and taking an interrelational, growth, or "systems" perspective of the "laws of Nature," we are left with the irrefutable facts of a physical and mental universe that violate some of the most ancient and basic principles of science. It is from this point of view that transformation theory postulates the "*directed* ontogenetic change" of evolution.

Sameness or Differentness

The idea of evolution toward organized systems can lead to concepts that predict an ultimate humdrum sameness. Both to Man and Nation this is an intolerable idea. The continuing interaction between living organisms and their relationship with the broad environment involve, as well, organizational changes that are characterized by an upward swing of both integration *and* differentiation. We allow larger amounts of distinct information to be expressed and then synchronously mesh these multitudes of differentness into high-order interdependent interactions. As anything becomes more organized it can actually tolerate more distinctiveness. A molecule is more complex, yet it is simpler to describe than its component atoms. In human terms the "liberation" of races, women, youth, music, clothes, and so forth, has created the possibilities, and the fact, of creating more complementary and mutually enriching relationships. For instance, the European Anglo-Saxon once practiced genocide, physically and culturally, with the American Indian. The level of growth of the early American colonies did not permit the absorption of these differences. Today, we see the reverse; efforts are being made to rediscover the heritage of these cultures and to absorb them. We accept more differentness from each other and at the same time grow more closely together.

Although attempts are made to explain these many ordering phenomena as "progress" or "humanization" or in other equally vague terms, it is possible to see them in the light of irreversible and basic laws of the known universe. Our recent efforts to stop non-decay in the ecological movement, to encourage "biodegradable" materials, illustrate our need to maintain the dynamics of universal growth. We do not now and probably never will realize a balanced or equilibrium state, for this would be a denial of the most fundamental laws of being. Those who maintain that we must stop or slow our "growth" simply do not understand that there are various forms of growth and that growth cannot be arrested. What they unknowingly espouse is a surpassing of older and lower growth forms and the movement of our species to a higher level of organization and growth, that is, to mutuality.

The freedom to form new alternative combinations and mutualisms increases at every new level of evolution from the atomic level to the molecular level to the organic. Each step makes it possible to form more new and different juxtapositions; as a consequence, we naturally find more compounds than there are elements, more words than there are letters, and so forth. At the human social-psychological level, the possibilities of new combinations are, for all practical purposes, infinite. In such an evolving "deterministic" universe, as more organized mutualized growth occurs, the *less* individually deterministic it becomes. The freedom to grow is only mediated by the need to grow *with* the system of life. As long as an idea or behavior can be made to contribute in some way, any way, it survives, just as does an atom or molecule as part of a compound.

5

The Greatest Evolutionary Jump in History

JOHN PLATT

I have a somewhat unusual view of the human situation today. I think we are passing through an evolutionary leap of unprecedented magnitude. This can be seen in the accompanying table, A Classification of Major Evolutionary Jumps, which compares our great technological developments since World War II with the largest evolutionary jumps of similar kinds in previous epochs. Many of our jumps in the last 40 years, as shown in the right-hand column, would appear to be comparable to the biggest jumps in the whole 4-billion-year history of life on earth, if judged by their probable long-run consequences, say for the next thousand years or million years or billion years.

So today nuclear missiles are the most overwhelming weapons ever known. Our new contraceptives are having global effects, but are now overshadowed by recombinant-DNA technology which might be able to create millions of new species. In the long run, solar-electric power may be as important as photosynthesis, which has been our main energy source for 2 billion years. Television is watched for hours every day by half the human race, and is changing the family, the school, commerce, politics, and the development of our brains. This electronic revolution may be a more dramatic extension of our nervous system and vision than the first development of image-forming eyes, 600 million years ago. Electronic data-processing has changed all the operations of science, business, and government, and will knit together every future society. And the possibility of working and living in space is a step whose beginnings today are hardly more than the coming ashore of the lungfish. The simultaneous convergence of all these development fitting together into a great evolutionary jump, in this short period, is absolutely staggering.

In the world of nature, our activities are also producing a unique evo-

From Frank Feather, ed., *Through the 80's: Thinking Globally, Acting Locally* (Washington, D.C.: World Future Society, 1980).

A Classification of Major Evolutionary Jumps

Eras	Early life	Multi-cellular	Early human	Post-glacial	Modern	Present Transformation
Time (years before present)	4000 M–	1000 M–	3 M–	10,000–	600–	40–
Functional areas						
Genetic mixing and control	SEX-CROSSING	Migration		DOMESTICATION AND BREEDING	DISEASE-CONTROL, CONTRACEPTION	MOLECULAR BIOLOGY, RE-COMBINANT DNA
Energy conversion	PHOTOSYNTHESIS	PLANT-EATING	FIRE	AGRICULTURE (wind, hydro)	COAL-STEAM, ELECTRICITY	NUCLEAR FISSION, (FUSION), SOLAR ELECTRIC, (SPACE POWER)
Encapsulation and habitats	CELLS ocean niches	Shell, skin, bark LAND	Clothes all climates	CITIES all continents	West "frontier"	SPACE CAPSULES, (SETTLEMENTS) Arctic, ocean
Methods of travel	Drift	Fins, feet, wings	Boats	Horses, WHEELS, SHIPS	RAILROAD, AUTO, AIRPLANE	Jet, ROCKET
Tools and weapons	Chemical	Teeth, claws	TOOLS, WEAPONS	METAL	MACHINES, GUNS, EXPLOSIVES	AUTOMATION, ROCKETS, NUCLEAR WEAPONS
Detection and signaling	Chemical	HEARING, VISION, echo-location	SPEECH	WRITING	PRINTING telephone, radio	ELECTROMAGNETIC SPECTRUM – RADAR, Laser. TELEVISION
Problem-solving and storage	DNA CHAINS	NERVOUS SYSTEM AND BRAINS	Oral memory, prediction	MATH, SCIENCE, LOGIC	SCIENCE-TECHNOLOGY	ELECTRONIC DATA-PROCESSING FEED-BACK CONTROL
Mechanisms of change	Accident and SELECTION	Foresight, REINFORCEMENT	THOUGHT	INVENTION	RESEARCH AND DEVELOPMENT	SYSTEMS-ANALYSIS AND DESIGN PROJECTS (Manhattan, Apollo)

lutionary epoch, with new radioactive wastes, with the peaking and exhaustion of fossil fuels, with possible global changes of climate in the next few decades, and the probable extinction of hundreds of thousands of species because of the destruction of their habitats—an event that has had no parallel since the last great extinction 65 million years ago.

For the human race and for life on earth, this all adds up to a "system-break," as Boulding has called it. These order-of-magnitude accelerations in recent epochs and recent decades are like the accelerating changes in the moments just before the fracture of a metal—or the birth of a baby. On a graph, if the time-periods of the table are spread out on a linear scale, the unique evolutionary peak in the last 40 years is like a knife-edge on a knife-edge.

With this simultaneous eruption of great new forces and powers, it is not clear that we can modify or even foresee the future very successfully, even for a 10- to 20-year period. As with the birth of a baby, or the coming ashore of the land animals, there is a combination of inevitability and surprise. As late as 1937, Lord Rutherford, the discoverer of the nucleus of the atom, said that the idea of getting out atomic energy was "moonshine"— when it was only 5 years away; and in the 1960s, hardly a single biologist anticipated the recombinant-DNA developments of 1973. But it is obviously urgent and essential to try to see how much is really inevitable or really surprising and how much is still subject to some human social design and control.

It is especially important, at this moment of global birth, not to waste our energies in resisting or in lamenting or in copying the past. The baby's history in the womb is of very little use to it in its new situation. What the new baby must suddenly do is to learn how to breathe and cry and swallow, and we must likewise find out quickly and successfully how to manage our great new powers in the world ahead, if we are to survive. The difference is that the baby, as the descendant of millions of successful babies, has all the needed information already encoded in its genes. But the human race, in this first attempt to build a global society, with totally new tools, has no such fail-safe mechanism or inherited knowledge of how to do it. It becomes crucial to have adequate look-out and design systems, with forecasting and computer systems-modeling and future courses and organizations. We will have to use all our commitment and all our skills at anticipatory problem-solving, so as to do it right the first time, or the whole human experiment may come to an end, in any of a dozen ways.

The social design and construction problem is central. As with the Federalists two hundred years ago, with their first social-feedback ideas or "checks and balances," we must think harder than we have ever thought before about how to design and create the components of a self-stabilizing world society. We must generate anticipatory global institutions with adequate powers, and yet find ways of preserving democratic methods of mutual problem-solving and collective self-management in a multicultural world, if our new baby planet is not to tear itself apart.

Evidently we need some major advances in the general principles of anticipatory cybernetic democratic design. Such principles in fact might even be derivable from some of the powerful new developments in social science in the last 40 years, such as systems theory, decision theory, game theory, reinforcement theory, global modeling, the theory of justice, or other social inventions. We might find more subtle and effective democratic feedback concepts and mechanisms that would make it much easier to correct the defects in existing institutions or to devise new self-correcting institutions of novel kinds.

The world of the year 2000 will be far more different from the world of 1980 than the world of 1800 was from 1780, or the world of 1930 was from 1910. And the future beyond that will be almost unimaginably different from the twentieth century.

Part Three

Coming to Terms with Life
on a Small Planet

Taking a long-term view of human well-being, people-centered development places high priority on achieving a harmonious and productive relationship between people and their natural environment – one that enhances natural productivity and creates new potentials for human development. The basic issues involved in the distinction between exploitative and harmonious partnerships are nowhere more sharply articulated than in the now-classic essay by Kenneth Boulding. Boulding differentiates between "cowboy" and "spaceship" economics – contrasting ways of conceptualizing human production-consumption systems. The former encourages free exploitation of the environment – mining it for its nonrenewable resources and using it as a limitless waste dump. Indeed it honors such behavior as productive citizenship contributing to economic health. The latter views this behavior as nothing short of criminal. While the real world is never so simple as our intellectual abstractions, the essay highlights in a dramatic way how tools of measurement and analysis serve to define the problem and to produce prescriptions supportive of a particular belief system.

Elizabeth Dodson Gray goes a step beyond Boulding in a poetic exploration of the potential for a mutually enhancing partnership between humanity and its natural environment – a form of growth through mutuality consistent with Land's evolutionary vision (chapter 4).

As resource competition increases, the classic problem of managing open-access resources becomes more acute, as demonstrated by Garret Hardin. Hardin examines the problem and various approaches to its resolution. All involve a restriction of access – what some would view as a restriction of freedom. Hardin argues that definitions of freedom are necessarily situational and change with changing circumstances.

Connor Bailey follows with a modern case study of the problem articulated by Hardin, that of an open-access fishing ground in the Philippines. Bailey examines various approaches to limiting access and concludes that the most viable would involve the fishing communities that depend on the fishing grounds in setting and enforcing their own rules, in the best interests of their members. While they are easier to advocate than to accomplish, the basic principles of community resource management articulated by Bailey are rapidly gaining acceptance as a promising approach to the complex issues of land and water management in Third World countries.

6

The Economics of the
Coming Spaceship Earth

KENNETH E. BOULDING

We are now in the middle of a long process of transition in the nature of the image which man has of himself and his environment. Primitive men, and to a large extent also men of the early civilizations, imagined themselves to be living on a virtually illimitable plane. There was almost always somewhere beyond the known limits of human habitation, and over a very large part of the time that man has been on earth, there has been something like a frontier. That is, there was always some place else to go when things got too difficult, either by reason of the deterioration of the natural environment or a deterioration of the social structure in places where people happened to live. The image of the frontier is probably one of the oldest images of mankind, and it is not surprising that we find it hard to get rid of.

Gradually, however, man has been accustoming himself to the notion of the spherical earth and a closed sphere of human activity. A few unusual spirits among the ancient Greeks perceived that the earth was a sphere. It was only with the circumnavigations and the geographical explorations of the fifteenth and sixteenth centuries, however, that the fact that the earth was a sphere became at all widely known and accepted. Even in the nineteenth century, the commonest map was Mercator's projection, which visualizes the earth as an illimitable cylinder, essentially a plane wrapped around the globe, and it was not until the Second World War and the development of the air age that the global nature of the planet really entered the popular imagination. Even now we are very far from having made the moral, political, and psychological adjustments which are implied in this transition from the illimitable plane to the closed sphere.

Economists in particular, for the most part, have failed to come to grips with the ultimate consequences of the transition from the open to the closed

From Henry Jarrett, ed., *Environmental Quality in a Growing Economy* (Baltimore: The Johns Hopkins University Press, 1968), pp. 3–14. Published for Resources for the Future, Inc. Copyright © 1966 by The Johns Hopkins University Press.

earth. One hesitates to use the terms "open" and "closed" in this connection, as they have been used with so many different shades of meaning. Nevertheless, it is hard to find equivalents. The open system, indeed, has some similarities to the open system of von Bertalanffy,[1] in that it implies that some kind of a structure is maintained in the midst of a throughput from inputs to outputs. In a closed system, the outputs of all parts of the system are linked to the inputs of other parts. There are no inputs from outside and no outputs to the outside; indeed, there is no outside at all. Closed systems, in fact, are very rare in human experience, in fact almost by definition unknowable, for if there are genuinely closed systems around us, we have no way of getting information into them or out of them; and hence if they are really closed, we would be quite unaware of their existence. We can only find out about a closed system if we participate in it. Some isolated primitive societies may have approximated to this, but even these had to take inputs from the environment and give outputs to it. All living organisms, including man himself, are open systems. They have to receive inputs in the shape of air, food, water, and give off outputs in the form of effluvia and excrement. Deprivation of input of air, even for a few minutes, is fatal. Deprivation of the ability to obtain any input or to dispose of any output is fatal in a relatively short time. All human societies have likewise been open systems. They receive inputs from the earth, the atmosphere, and the waters, and they give outputs into these reservoirs; they also produce inputs internally in the shape of babies and outputs in the shape of corpses. Given a capacity to draw upon inputs and to get rid of outputs, an open system of this kind can persist indefinitely.

There are some systems—such as the biological phenotype, for instance the human body—which cannot maintain themselves indefinitely by inputs and outputs because of the phenomenon of aging. This process is very little understood. It occurs, evidently, because there are some outputs which cannot be replaced by any known input. There is not the same necessity for aging in organizations and in societies, although an analogous phenomenon may take place. The structure and composition of an organization or society, however, can be maintained by inputs of fresh personnel from birth and education as the existing personnel ages and eventually dies. Here we have an interesting example of a system which seems to maintain itself by the self-generation of inputs, and in this sense is moving towards closure. The input of people (that is, babies) is also an output of people (that is, parents).

Systems may be open or closed in respect to a number of classes of inputs and outputs. Three important classes are matter, energy, and information. The present world economy is open in regard to all three. We can think of the world economy or "econosphere" as a subset of the "world set," which is the set of all objects of possible discourse in the world. We then think of the state of the econosphere at any one moment as being the total capital stock, that is, the set of all objects, people, organizations, and so on, which are interesting from the point of view of the system of exchange. This total stock of capital is clearly an open system in the sense that it has inputs and outputs, inputs being production which adds to the capital stock, outputs being consumption which subtracts from it. From a material point of view, we see objects passing from the noneconomic into the economic set in the process of production, and we similarly see products passing out of the economic set as their value becomes zero. Thus we see the econosphere as a material process involving the discovery and mining of fossil fuels, ores, etc., and at the other end a process by which the effluents of the system are passed out into noneconomic reservoirs—for instance, the atmosphere and the oceans—which are not appropriated and do not enter into the exchange system.

From the point of view of the energy system, the econosphere involves inputs of available energy in the form, say, of water power, fossil fuels, or sunlight, which are necessary in order to create the material throughput and to move matter from the noneconomic set into the economic set or even out of it again; and energy itself is given off by the system in a less available form, mostly in the form of heat. These inputs of available energy must come either from the sun (the energy supplied by other stars being assumed to be negligible) or it may come from the earth itself, either through its internal heat or through its energy of rotation or other motions, which generate, for instance, the energy of the tides. Agriculture, a few solar machines, and water power use the current available energy income. In advanced societies this is supplemented very extensively by the use of fossil fuels, which represent as it were a capital stock of stored-up sunshine. Because of this capital stock of energy, we have been able to maintain an energy input into the system, particularly over the last two centuries, much larger than we would have been able to do with existing techniques if we had had to rely on the current input of available energy from the sun or the earth itself. Thus supplementary input, however, is by its very nature exhaustible.

The inputs and outputs of information are more subtle and harder to trace, but also represent an open system, related to, but not wholly dependent on, the transformations of matter and energy. By far the larger amount of information and knowledge is self-generated by the human society, though a certain amount of information comes into the sociosphere in the form of light from the universe outside. The information that comes from the universe has certainly affected man's image of himself and of his environment, as we can easily visualize if we suppose that we lived on a planet with a total cloud-cover that kept out all information from the exterior universe. It is only in very recent times, of course, that the information coming in from the universe has been captured and coded into the form of a complex image of what the universe is like outside the earth; but even in primitive times, man's perception of the heavenly bodies has always profoundly affected his image of earth and of himself. It is the information generated within the planet, however, and particularly that generated by man himself, which forms by far the larger part of the information system. We can think of the stock of knowledge, or as Teilhard de Chardin called it, the "noosphere," and consider this as an open system, losing knowledge through aging and death and gaining it through birth and education and the ordinary experience of life.

From the human point of view, knowledge or information is by far the most important of the three systems. Matter only acquires significance and only enters the sociosphere or the econosphere insofar as it becomes an object of human knowledge. We can think of capital, indeed, as frozen knowledge or knowledge imposed on the material world in the form of improbable arrangements. A machine, for instance, originated in the mind of man, and both its construction and its use involve information processes imposed on the material world by man himself. The cumulation of knowledge, that is, the excess of its production over its consumption, is the key to human development of all kinds, especially to economic development. We can see this pre-eminence of knowledge very clearly in the experiences of countries where the material capital has been destroyed by a war, as in Japan and Germany. The knowledge of the people was not destroyed, and it did not take long, therefore, certainly not more than ten years, for most of the material capital to be reestablished again. In a country such as Indonesia, however, where the knowledge did not exist, the material capital did not come into being either. By "knowledge" here I mean, of course, the whole cognitive structure, which includes valuations and motivations as well as images of the factual world.

The concept of entropy, used in a somewhat loose sense, can be applied to all three of these open systems. In the case of material systems, we can distinguish between entropic processes, which take concentrated materials and diffuse them through the oceans or over the earth's surface or into the atmosphere, and anti-entropic processes, which take diffuse materials and concentrate them. Material entropy can be taken as a measure of the uniformity of the distribution of elements and, more uncertainly, compounds and other structures on the earth's surface. There is, fortunately, no law of increasing material entropy, as there is in the corresponding case of energy, as it is quite possible to concentrate diffused materials if energy inputs are allowed. Thus the processes for fixation of nitrogen from the air, processes for the extraction of magnesium or other elements from the sea, and processes for the desalinization of sea water are anti-entropic in the material sense, though the reduction of material entropy has to be paid for by inputs of energy and also inputs of information, or at least a stock of information in the system. In regard to matter, therefore, a closed system is conceivable, that is, a system in which there is neither increase nor decrease in material entropy. In such a system all outputs from consumption would constantly be recycled to become inputs for production, as for instance, nitrogen in the nitrogen cycle of the natural ecosystem.

In regard to the energy system there is, unfortunately, no escape from the grim Second Law of Thermodynamics; and if there were no energy inputs into the earth, any evolutionary or developmental process would be impossible. The large energy inputs which we have obtained from fossil fuels are strictly temporary. Even the most optimistic predictions would expect the easily available supply of fossil fuels to be exhausted in a mere matter of centuries at present rates of use. If the rest of the world were to rise to American standards of power consumption, and still more if world population continues to increase, the exhaustion of fossil fuels would be even more rapid. The development of nuclear energy has improved this picture, but has not fundamentally altered it, at least in present technologies, for fissionable material is still relatively scarce. If we should achieve the economic use of energy through fusion, of course, a much larger source of energy materials would be available, which would expand the time horizons of supplementary energy input into an open social system by perhaps tens to hundreds of thousands of years. Failing this, however, the time is not very far distant, historically speaking, when man will once more have to retreat to his current energy input from the sun, even though this could be used much more effectively than in the past with increased knowledge. Up to now, certainly, we have not got very far with the technology of using current solar energy, but the possibility of substantial improvements in the future is certainly high. It may be, indeed, that the biological revolution which is just beginning will produce a solution to this problem, as we develop artificial organisms which are capable of much more efficient transformation of solar energy into easily available forms than any that we now have. As Richard Meier has suggested, we may run our machines in the future with methane-producing algae.[2]

The question of whether there is anything corresponding to entropy in the information system is a puzzling one, though of great interest. There are certainly many examples of social systems and cultures which have lost knowledge, especially in transition from one generation to the next, and in which the culture has therefore degenerated. One only has to look at the folk culture of Appalachian migrants to American cities to see a culture which started out as a fairly rich European folk culture in Elizabethan times and which seems to have lost both skills, adaptability, folk tales, songs, and almost everything that goes up to make richness and complexity in a culture, in the course of about ten generations. The American Indians on reservations provide another example of such degradation of the informaion and knowledge system. On the other hand, over a great part of human history, the growth of knowledge in the earth as a whole seems to have been almost continuous, even though there have been times of relatively slow growth and times of rapid growth. As it is knowledge of certain kinds that produces the growth of knowledge in general, we have here a very subtle and complicated system, and it is hard to put one's finger on the particular elements in a culture which make knowledge grow more or less rapidly, or even which make it decline. One of the great puzzles in this connection, for instance, is why the take-off into science, which represents an "acceleration," or an increase in the rate of growth of knowledge in European society in the sixteenth century, did not take place in China, which at that time (about 1600) was unquestionably ahead of Europe, and one would think even more ready for the breakthrough. This is perhaps the most crucial question in the theory of social development, yet we must confess that it is very little understood. Perhaps the most significant factor in this connection is the existence of "slack" in the culture, which permits a divergence from established patterns and activity which is not merely devoted to reproducing the existing society but is devoted to changing it. China was perhaps too well-organized and had too little slack in its society to produce the kind of acceleration which we find in the somewhat poorer and less well-organized but more diverse societies of Europe.

The closed earth of the future requires economic principles which are somewhat different from those of the open earth of the past. For the sake of picturesqueness, I am tempted to call the open economy the "cowboy economy," the cowboy being symbolic of the illimitable plains and also associated with reckless, exploitative, romantic, and violent behavior, which is characteristic of open societies. The closed economy of the future might similarly be called the "spaceman" economy, in which the earth has become a single spaceship, without unlimited reservoirs of anything, either for extraction or for pollution, and in which, therefore, man must find his place in a cyclical ecological system which is capable of continuous reproduction of material form even though it cannot escape having inputs of energy. The difference between the two types of economy becomes most apparent in the attitude towards consumption. In the cowboy economy, consumption is regarded as a good thing and production likewise; and the success of the economy is measured by the amount of the throughput from the "factors of production," a part of which, at any rate, is extracted from the reservoirs of raw materials and noneconomic objects, and another part of which is output into the reservoirs of pollution. If there are infinite reservoirs from which material can be obtained and into which effluvia can be deposited, then the throughput is at least a plausible measure of the success of the economy. The gross national product is a rough measure of this total throughput. It should be possible, however, to distinguish that part of the

GNP which is derived from exhaustible and that which is derived from reproducible resources, as well as that part of consumption which represents effluvia and that which represents input into the productive system again. Nobody, as far as I know, has ever attempted to break down the GNP in this way, although it would be an interesting and extremely important exercise, which is unfortunately beyond the scope of this paper.

By contrast, in the spaceman economy, throughput is by no means a desideratum, and is indeed to be regarded as something to be minimized rather than maximized. The essential measure of the success of the economy is not production and consumption at all, but the nature, extent, quality, and complexity of the total capital stock, including in this the state of the human bodies and minds included in the system. In the spaceman economy, what we are primarily concerned with is stock maintenance, and any technological change which results in the maintenance of a given total stock with a lessened throughput (that is, less production and consumption) is clearly a gain. This idea that both production and consumption are bad things rather than good things is very strange to economists, who have been obsessed with the income-flow concepts to the exclusion, almost, of capital-stock concepts.

There are actually some very tricky and unsolved problems involved in the questions as to whether human welfare or well-being is to be regarded as a stock or a flow. Something of both these elements seems actually to be involved in it, and as far as I know there have been practically no studies directed towards identifying these two dimensions of human satisfaction. Is it, for instance, eating that is a good thing, or is it being well fed? Does economic welfare involve having nice clothes, fine houses, good equipment, and so on, or is it to be measured by the depreciation and the wearing out of these things? I am inclined myself to regard the stock concept as most fundamental, that is, to think of being well fed as more important than eating, and to think even of so-called services as essentially involving the restoration of a depleting psychic capital. Thus I have argued that we go to a concert in order to restore a psychic condition which might be called "just having gone to a concert," which, once established, tends to depreciate. When it depreciates beyond a certain point, we go to another concert in order to restore it. If it depreciates rapidly, we go to a lot of concerts; if it depreciates slowly, we go to few. On this view, similarly, we eat primarily to restore bodily homeostasis, that is, to maintain a condition of being well fed, and so on. On this view, there is nothing desirable in consumption at all. The less consumption we can maintain a given state with, the better off we are. If we had clothes that did not wear out, houses that did not depreciate, and even if we could maintain our bodily condition without eating, we would clearly be much better off.

It is this last consideration, perhaps, which makes one pause. Would we, for instance, really want an operation that would enable us to restore all our bodily tissues by intravenous feeding while we slept? Is there not, that is to say, a certain virtue in throughput itself, in activity itself, in production and consumption itself, in raising food and in eating it? It would certainly be rash to exclude this possibility. Further interesting problems are raised by the demand for variety. We certainly do not want a constant state to be maintained; we want fluctuations in the state. Otherwise there would be no demand for variety in food, for variety in scene, as in travel, for variety in social contact, and so on. The demand for variety can, of course, be costly, and sometimes it seems to be too costly to be tolerated or at least legitimated, as in the case of marital partners, where the maintenance of a homeostatic state in the family is usually regarded as much more desirable than the variety and excessive throughput of the libertine. There are problems here which the economics profession has neglected with astonishing singlemindedness. My own attempts to call attention to some of them, for instance, in two articles,[3] as far as I can judge, produced no response whatever; and economists continue to think and act as if production, consumption, throughput, and the GNP were the sufficient and adequate measure of economic success.

It may be said, of course, why worry about all this when the spaceman economy is still a good way off (at least beyond the lifetimes of any now living), so let us eat, drink, spend, extract and pollute, and be as merry as we can, and let posterity worry about the spaceship earth. It is always a little hard to find a convincing answer to the man who says, "What has posterity ever done for me?" and the conservationist has always had to fall back on rather vague ethical principles postulating identity of the individual with some human community or society which extends not only back into the past but forward into the future. Unless the individual identifies with some community of this kind, conservation is obviously "irrational." Why should we not maximize the welfare of this generation at the cost of posterity? "*Après nous, le déluge*" has been the motto of not insignificant numbers of human societies. The only answer to this, as far as I can see, is to point out that the welfare of the individual depends on the extent to which he can identify himself with others, and that the most satisfactory individual identity is that which identifies not only with a community in space but also with a community extending over time from the past into the future. If this kind of identity is recognized as desirable, then posterity has a voice, even if it does not have a vote; and in a sense, if its voice can influence votes, it has votes too. This whole problem is linked up with the much larger one of the determinants of the morale, legitimacy, and "nerve" of a society, and there is a great deal of historical evidence to suggest that a society which loses its identity with posterity and which loses its positive image of the future loses also its capacity to deal with present problems, and soon falls apart.[4]

Even if we concede that posterity is relevant to our present problems, we still face the question of time-discounting and the closely related question of uncertainty-discounting. It is a well-known phenomenon that individuals discount the future, even in their own lives. The very existence of a positive rate of interest may be taken as at least strong supporting evidence of this hypothesis. If we discount our own future, it is certainly not unreasonable to discount posterity's future even more, even if we do give posterity a vote. If we discount this at 5 per cent per annum, posterity's vote or dollar halves every fourteen years as we look into the future, and after even a mere hundred years it is pretty small—only about 1½ cents on the dollar. If we add another 5 per cent for uncertainty, even the vote of our grandchildren reduces almost to insignificance. We can argue, of course, that the ethical thing to do is not to discount the future at all, that time-discounting is mainly the result of myopia and perspective, and hence is an illusion which the moral man should not tolerate. It is a very popular illusion, however, and one that must certainly be taken into consideration in the formulation of policies. It explains, perhaps, why conservationist policies almost have to be sold under some other excuse which seems more urgent, and why, indeed, necessities which are visualized as urgent, such as defense, always seem to hold priority over those which involve the future.

All these considerations add some credence to the point of view which says that we should not worry about the spaceman economy at all, and that we should just go on increasing the GNP and indeed the gross world product, or GWP, in the expectation that the problems of the future can be left to the future, that when scarcities arise, whether this is of raw materials or of pollutable reservoirs, the needs of the then present will determine the solutions of the then present, and there is no use giving ourselves ulcers by worrying about problems that we really do not have to solve. There is even high ethical authority for this point of view in the New Testament, which advocates that we should take no thought for tomorrow and let the dead bury their dead. There has always been something rather refreshing in the view that we should live like the birds, and perhaps posterity is for the birds in more senses than one; so perhaps we should all call it a day and go out and pollute something cheerfully. As an old taker of thought for the morrow, however, I cannot quite accept this solution; and I would argue, furthermore, that tomorrow is not only very close, but in many respects it is already here. The shadow of the future spaceship, indeed, is already falling over our spendthrift merriment. Oddly enough, it seems to be in pollution rather than in exhaustion that the problem is first becoming salient. Los Angeles has run out of air, Lake

Erie has become a cesspool, the oceans are getting full of lead and DDT, and the atmosphere may become man's major problem in another generation, at the rate at which we are filling it up with gunk. It is, of course, true that at least on a microscale, things have been worse at times in the past. The cities of today, with all their foul air and polluted waterways, are probably not as bad as the filthy cities of the pretechnical age. Nevertheless, that fouling of the nest which has been typical of man's activity in the past on a local scale now seems to be extending to the whole world society; and one certainly cannot view with equanimity the present rate of pollution of any of the natural reservoirs, whether the atmosphere, the lakes, or even the oceans.

I would argue strongly also that our obsession with production and consumption to the exclusion of the "state" aspects of human welfare distorts the process of technological change in a most undesirable way. We are all familiar, of course, with the wastes involved in planned obsolescence, in competitive advertising, and in poor quality of consumer goods. These problems may not be so important as the "view with alarm" school indicates, and indeed the evidence at many points is conflicting. New materials especially seem to edge towards the side of improved durability, such as, for instance, neolite soles for footwear, nylon socks, wash and wear shirts, and so on. The case of household equipment and automobiles is a little less clear. Housing and building construction generally almost certainly has declined in durability since the Middle Ages, but this decline also reflects a change in tastes towards flexibility and fashion and a need for novelty, so that it is not easy to assess. What is clear is that no serious attempt has been made to assess the impact over the whole of economic life of changes in durability, that is, in the ratio of capital in the widest possible sense to income. I suspect that we have underestimated, even in our spendthrift society, the gains from increased durability, and that this might very well be one of the places where the price system needs correction through government-sponsored research and development. The problems which the spaceship earth is going to present, therefore, are not all in the future by any means, and a strong case can be made for paying much more attention to them in the present than we now do.

It may be complained that the considerations I have been putting forth relate only to the very long run, and they do not much concern our immediate problems. There may be some justice in this criticism, and my main excuse is that other writers have dealt adequately with the more immediate problems of deterioration in the quality of the environment. It is true, for instance, that many of the immediate problems of pollution of the atmosphere or of bodies of water arise because of the failure of the price system, and many of them could be solved by corrective taxation. If people had to pay the losses due to the nuisances which they create, a good deal more resources would go into the prevention of nuisances. These arguments involving external economies and diseconomies are familiar to economists, and there is no need to recapitulate them. The law of torts is quite inadequate to provide for the correction of the price system which is required, simply because where damages are widespread and their incidence on any particular person is small, the ordinary remedies of the civil law are quite inadequate and inappropriate. There needs, therefore, to be special legislation to cover these cases, and though such legislation seems hard to get in practice, mainly because of the widespread and small personal incidence of the injuries, the technical problems involved are not insuperable. If we were to adopt in principle a law for tax penalties for social damages, with an apparatus for making assessments under it, a very large proportion of current pollution and deterioration of the environment would be prevented. There are tricky problems of equity involved, particularly where old established nuisances create a kind of "right by purchase" to perpetuate themselves, but these are problems again which a few rather arbitrary decisions can bring to some kind of solution.

The problems which I have been raising in this paper are of larger scale and perhaps much harder to solve than the most practical and immediate problems of the above paragraph. Our success in dealing with the larger problems, however, is not unrelated to the development of skill in the solution of the more immediate and perhaps less difficult problems. One can hope, therefore, that as a succession of mounting crises, especially in pollution, arouse public opinion and mobilize support for the solution of the immediate problems, a learning process will be set in motion which will eventually lead to an appreciation of and perhaps solutions for the larger ones. My neglect of the immediate problems, therefore, is in no way intended to deny their importance for unless we at least make a beginning on a process for solving the immediate problems we will not have much chance of solving the larger ones. On the other hand, it may also be true that a long-run vision, as it were, of the deep crisis which faces mankind may predispose people to taking more interest in the immediate problems and to devote more effort for their solution. This may sound like a rather modest optimism, but perhaps a modest optimism is better than no optimism at all.

7

Moving with the Natural Grain of Life

ELIZABETH DODSON GRAY

Now I must begin again. I must begin with a new woman, with the one who goes to the Nursing Home.

It is evening and I have the lonesome feeling that I am far from home, but I do not know where home is.

Here there is no support. There is nothing I can do but survive. The time is at the turning. Evening is turning into night. The arc of the sky is filled with great bands of sunset. Birds are flying high. It is a lonely time for me. I feel lost and far away from home. But where is home? I have never found it.

So after the supper had been cleared away, I stepped out into the night. My night. It was black night and the stars were my stars, I was alone with them. It was so still, the only sound was the tide coming, coming in, coming in. It was a pulse. It was there, it never stopped. It said be still and know that I am here. The timing of the pulse was the timing of my pulse. So I am the child of the tide.[1]

From Elizabeth Dodson Gray, *Green Paradise Lost* (Wellesley, Mass.: Roundtable Press, 1979), pp. 118–26. Copyright © 1979 by Elizabeth Dodson Gray. Reprinted by permission of Roundtable Press. In addition, permission to reprint material quoted in this chapter from the following sources has been obtained: Ian L. McHarg, *Design with Nature* (Garden City, N.Y.: Doubleday and Co., Doubleday Natural History Press, 1971), p. 11. Barry Commoner, *The Closing Circle: Nature, Man and Technology* (copyright © 1979 by Alfred A. Knopf, Inc.; reprinted by permission); Howard T. Odum, *Environment, Power and Society* (copyright © 1979 by John Wiley and Sons, Inc.; reprinted with permission); Erik Eckholm and Lester R. Brown, *Spreading Deserts: The Hand of Man* (Washington, D.C.: Worldwatch Institute, 1977); Jean Hersey, *The Shape of a Year* (copyright © 1967 by Jean Hersey; reprinted by permission of McIntosh and Otis, Inc.); May Sarton, *Plant Dreaming Deep* (copyright © 1968 by May Sarton; used by permission of W. W. Norton and Company, Inc.); and Beatrice Willard, et al., "The Ethics of Biospheral Viability," in Nicholas Polunin, ed., *Growth without Ecodisasters* (reprinted by permission of Macmillan, London and Basingstoke).

LIVING LIGHTLY ON THE EARTH

A child of the tide will be sensitive to the pulse of natural cycles and to the flow or lay of the land. We have few examples of this in our present way of operating. But what this would mean for our living with the sea and dunes and sandbars and shallow bay of the New Jersey Shore is described by the landscape architect Ian McHarg in *Design with Nature*.

> . . . The sand dune is a very recent formation [geologically]. It will change its configuration in response to autumn hurricanes and winter storms and will sometimes be breached. . . The New Jersey Shore. . . is continuously involved in a contest with the sea; its shape is dynamic.[2]

McHarg points out that the relative stability of the dunes and the string of coastal islands they form is dependent for that stability upon vegetation — reeds, sea grasses, certain shrubs and trees — which anchor the sand against the actions of waves and wind. He then goes on to analyze from an ecologist's viewpoint what each of the several rows of dunes formed by the action of waves and wind provides for the shoreline's stability, what their tolerances and vulnerabilities are, and precisely how humans must design their human activities to fit within such natural tolerances — or upset that stability of the dunes.

> We now have the broad outlines of an ecological analysis and a planning prescription based upon this understanding. A spinal road could constitute a barrier dune and be located in the back-dune area. It could contain all utilities, water, sewer, telephone and electricity and would be the guardian defense against back-flooding. At the widest points of the backdune, settlement could be located in communities. Development would be excluded from the vulnerable, narrow sections of the sandbar. The bayshore [facing the mainland] would, in principle, be left inviolate. The beach [facing the ocean] would be available for the most intensive recreational use, but without building. Approaches to it would be by bridges [inland from the ocean beach] across the dunes, which would be prohibited to use. Limited development would be permitted in the trough, determined by groundwater withdrawals and the effect upon vegetation.[3]

McHarg points to Holland, which in order to reclaim land below sea level does adapt its human settlements to the shapes and needs of its shoreline.

> The dune grass, hero of Holland, is an astonishingly hardy plant, thriving in the most inhospitable of environments. Alas, it is

incapable of surmounting the final crucial test of man. In the Netherlands, the vulnerability of dune grasses to trampling is so well understood, that dunes are denied to public access; only licensed naturalists are permitted to walk on them. . . . If you would have dunes protect you, and the dunes are stabilized by grasses, and these cannot tolerate man, then survival and the public interest is well served by protecting the grasses. But in New Jersey they are totally unprotected. Indeed nowhere along our entire eastern seaboard are they even recognized as valuable.[4]

In everything—from farming to building human settlements—human activity must conform itself, McHarg says, to the "lay of the land" and its natural cycles and processes. *For ultimately human productivity can only be sustained over time by a partnership with natural productivity.*

The farmer is the prototype. He prospers only insofar as he understands the land and by his management maintains its bounty. So too with the man who builds. If he is perceptive to the processes of nature, to materials and to forms, his creations will be appropriate to the place; they will satisfy the needs of social process and shelter, be expressive and endure. As indeed they have, in the hill towns of Italy, the island architecture of Greece, the medieval communities of France and the Low Countries and, not least, the villages of England and New England.[5]

When the child of the tide can claim the natural processes as part of herself/himself, we will be sensitive out of kinship and caring, not out of "responsibility" and "duty." We will be like sailors and those who design their boats and their sails, attentive to how the wind blows, how the waves move, and how the tides run, in order to know how best to sail *with* the boat, *with* the sails, and *with* the elements.

As a Hand Slips into a Glove

"Ecological reconnaissance" has been suggested as a practical way to make sure human developments fit appropriately within natural systems. Dr. Beatrice Willard, who made the suggestion, has had extensive experience as a field ecologist, in addition to serving in the Executive Office of the President on the prestigious three-member Council on Environmental Quality. She writes:

I spent a day of ecological reconnaissance of the alpine tundra with the design engineer, locating for him within the route of a proposed high-tension line both the transient, unstable life-systems and the permanent, mature ones. By doing this the engineer was able to locate transmission-line towers so as to avoid the mature stands — some of which are several thousand years old, judging from the depth of soil accumulated. Without this knowledge, the engineer would have eradicated thousands of years of tundra development with a few hours work, for he had proposed a tower for the center of one of these old stands.

So it is with all development. . . . With prior ecological investigation, design and development can be planned so as to maintain game migration routes, fisheries, winter grazing grounds, grass beds, striped bass spawning areas, zones of seismic activity, mature old stands of vegetation, marshes, woods, prairies, and other habitats for rare plants and animals. . . . [All this] can be done best and cheapest when a comprehensive plan is developed in the earliest stages. It is much more difficult, for example, to accomplish habitat rebuilding or restoration of a species' population after construction on the project has begun. But it may be relatively simple to work around a segment of habitat which should be saved. . . . *Actions can harmonize with ecosystems, as a skilled hand slips adroitly, gently, smoothly into a glove, with little or no disruption of either the hand or the glove.*[6]

In the past, however, we have been too preoccupied with our anthropocentric pretensions to bother even to observe the way the natural systems worked. Although a few specialists may have studied these things, we have arranged our major and minor human systems across the grain of the way nature works. Our use of water to flush away human wastes is a classic example. Even a casual look at organic matter decaying to enrich the soil would have shown us that organic wastes should be returned to the earth to decay and enrich it. Yet we are now stuck with stupid arrangements and massive capital investments in flushing our toilets into sewers, rivers and oceans — and still further great investments in vast sewage treatment facilities to clean water which shouldn't have been dirtied in the first place. Meanwhile, back on the farm and in our gardens the soil is stripped of nutrients which never come back as wastes, and we restore the soil with chemical fertilizers made from precious (and also depleting) natural gas. This availability of artificial fertilizers has led farmers to using more than the crops can absorb; the cash crops never lack for fertilizer and grow like crazy, but the excess is washed — you guessed it — into rivers and lakes by rains, threatening our waters with a new hazard, "eutrophication" or so many nutrients that water grasses (like the cash crops) grow like crazy and clog our waterways, ponds and lakes.[7]

It is all very senseless and unperceptive of the natural grain of life. It tells us a great deal about the arrogant rationality of the human animal, that we created such arbitrary human systems without any attempt to fit them into the vast natural systems—*of which we are a part, even though we thought we were above.* The truth is that whether it is a sewerage system or an industrial production line, men have created arbitary and linear systems in vast conceptual disregard of the fact that the world is based upon circular flows and functions in vast systems of recycling. The straight lines and singlemindednesss of linear systems do not fit into such circles; they disrupt them.

NATURE MAGNIFIES WELL-DESIGNED SYSTEMS

Our task as architects of the future is to redesign and restructure our linear human systems until they are congruent with natural systems, until they do recycle. Beyond this we might even be clever enough, as Howard T. Odum suggests, to design human systems so well that we help natural systems work for us, thus magnifying our efforts.[8]

Let me illustrate this. I was in church one Sunday morning when the sun poured through a stained glass window in such a way that the whole window shimmered and danced with colors which had come alive in the power of the sun. The other stained glass windows in the church were dark and almost black. I suddenly realized that the stained glass windows were designed so that without the natural power of the sun they were nothing. But when the sun came through at just the right angle and time of day and year, the sun joined with that colored glass to do what no colored glass could do on its own. We must do this too. We must be humble enough and kindred enough with natural systems of which we are a part to design our human systems so responsively, so sensitively, that we do *with* nature what we cannot do alone—shine, shimmer and dance in a healthy symbiosis of those who together enjoy the goodness of creation.

John Todd and the New Alchemy Institute in Woods Hole, Massachusetts, have developed a number of such ways natural and human systems can work together. The waste of one part becomes food for another, and it all takes place in a naturally powered, symbiotically integrated and cascading and multiplying way.[9] John Todd describes how he first learned to do this:

> It occurred to me that here I'd been in university since 1957, thirteen or fourteen years in academia—and many of these students had been in almost as long as I had—and we simply weren't trained in sensitive stewardship. We didn't know anything. Science hadn't trained us to be able to answer the most fundamental questions: How do you make that piece of earth sing, and how do you make it support those that live there? Degrees in agriculture, disease ethology, ecology . . . nothing!

So I decided we had to figure a way. I decided each student is going to study one component of this place. You're gonna do rocks, you're gonna do earthworms, you're gonna do grasses, you're gonna do herbs, you're gonna do snails, you're gonna do wind, you're gonna do sun, you're gonna do ferns...fourteen components. And there's two things you're gonna do before you pass this course: one is to find out what's here and in what abundance, and the second is you're gonna teach somebody else what you've learned.

Several months later...people were camping out, living in trees, stuff like that...and they grumbled like hell! Studying earthworms was not their idea of graduate school. But then they started to teach one another, and all of a sudden, like the scales falling from our eyes, a piece of land came alive. One of the students found a plant that only grows where there's water! So we dug down and found water! And it happened in a place where we could build a series of little dams like steps down the valley, and with the sun there, all of a sudden we had a driving wheel for the whole system. Another student found miner's lettuces, which meant we had a sort of balanced soil association, and the guy with the worms was able to collaborate. All of a sudden we had gardens, and the wind guy figured out a source of energy. And all of a sudden we were talking for the first time like we knew what we were talking about, even though we had just barely got the doors open! And here was this piece of land which was no longer an inhospitable enemy. Everywhere we were finding allies. Without knowing what was there, we never would have gotten the door open far enough to see what was inside. It was very heavy for me.

There has never been any doubt for me since that time that the way to go is to be whole. Know the sun, know the plants, know the soil, know the people, know the shelter...have them all interlaced, begin from there.[10]

The person who interviewed John Todd sums up the New Alchemy experience:

The essential requisite for the success of New Alchemy—and everyone here seems to sense it—is not money (though of course money is needed, or they will go under). It is this sense of a balanced interdependence with each other and with nature and an understanding of the delicacy of that balance. It is what John Todd calls the concept of interconnected webs. What New Alchemy provides is more than just hardware, more than just a solar-heated, wind-powered greenhouse/aquaculture complex that is inexpensive to construct, operates almost anywhere, and produces no-cost food—in itself a unique and important gift to the world—but a tangible way to use the environment constructively instead of destructively, a way to live in harmony with our own ecosystem, a way to use the sun and the wind and the elements to produce nourishing food. And *that* is alchemy.[11]

Fitting human life within natural cycles is not only for future new human settlements but it appears also to be the way to wiggle past critical environmental problems created by past patterns of human settlement or by natural fluctuations in climate and precipitation. Erik Eckholm and Lester Brown write in *Spreading Deserts: The Hand of Man* how—

In the desert, as elsewhere, planners have much to learn from the plants, animals, and cultures that have withstood centuries of extraordinarily adverse environmental conditions. If the ecological balance historically maintained by most nomadic groups was rather wretched, predicated as it was on high human death rates, these people used the life-defying desert remarkably resourcefully. In popular mythology, nomads are often pictured as aimless wanderers. But in fact, nomadic movements nearly always harmonize with the seasonal rhythm of climate and plant life. They are geared to permit animals to find adequate forage throughout the year and to permit the regrowth of grazing lands.

A return to an earlier historical age is no more desirable than likely. . . . Rudimentary modern medicine has trickled into the arid zones well ahead of advanced agricultural technology, helping push down death rates. Moreover, national boundaries now divide natural ecological zones artificially and restrict the traditional movements of nomadic groups, while the spread of sedentary agriculture further limits migrations. . . . Although many traditional nomadic practices are no longer viable, adopting some modernized version of the nomadic way of life may be the only way that those in the arid desert fringes can safely exploit these areas' protein-producing potential. Regional management schemes, in which clan leaders regulate grazing and migratory movements according to natural conditions and the advice of range specialists, represent one possibility.[12]

WHEN THE EARTH IS MYTHED AS FEMALE

As I write this, I am not at all sure male culture can muster the sensitivities necessary to do this fitting in. Let me tell you a curious story. Recently my husband and I were in Iceland for an international conference on the future of the global environment. A highlight of the bus tour of the capital city of Reykjavik was a visit to the studio of their eminent local sculptor Asmundur Sveinsson. He has another statue "Music of the Sea," which is a woman's body, sitting down, wide open and exposed in the pelvis, with one leg back and one forward. She is leaning back, her head flung back, with one arm forward and out, and the other arm back. But she is laced with ropes that cut into her knees and breasts and are strung like a musical instrument to each of her hands. I as a woman winced in pain as I looked at that statue; I could feel the vagina exposed and the breasts hurting where the ropes laced through them.

When Matthias Johannessen was writing a book about Sveinsson, he asked the sculptor about this statue. "But it's a female figure," the sculptor replied, "I made her breasts like a boat. And her feet grow out of the wave which again turns into a thigh. It's all waves. And the hand is holding the strings. The music of the sea."[13] You can see here, quite unself-conscious in Asmundur Sveinsson, the deep equation of the woman and nature, the symbolization of this in the body of the woman, and the total lack of sensitivity to what is *done to* the body of the woman. So long as men consciously or unconsciously symbolized natural processes as female—and "female" means to them controlled and subordinated—then our fitting into nature will be delayed and distorted by the male need to control and subordinate.

Fascinated with the sculptor's lack of sensitivity to what was being done to the body of the woman in "Music of the Sea," I began using a postcard photograph of the statue as a litmus test or Rorschach test with some of our most perceptive male friends and colleagues. I made a startling discovery. Men do not identify with the body of that woman! Men do not sense her vaginal vulnerability in the pose of that statue, and (even more curious!) they do not feel the pain of those ropes laced into her breasts and knees.

I found this surprising. And chilling for the future of the earth. Eugene Bianchi's words come to mind about what happens between a woman and a man when he rapes her: "As a subhuman, her terror and pain call forth no empathy."[14] This is for me the predicament of the earth today. The male culture which is raping her does not identify (perhaps cannot identify) with the body of the earth which he myths as feminine. And because he cannot identify with it, he cannot seem to feel the mute pain.

ENTERING INTO RESPONSIVE DIALOGUE

Women are trained by their usual life-experience to be adept at non-verbal communication. The circumstances of their mothering force them to spend years responding to the needs of children, who even after they can speak often cannot identify what it is they need. As Tolstoy wrote somewhere, "The need is cry enough!" Have men ever such training in their life experiences? Can they understand the mute cry which has no words when nonetheless it speaks?

Jean Hersey in *The Shape of a Year* gives us in passing a number of examples of listening to non-verbal communications. She writes about the humans' need for water as well as that of plants during a drought:

> It's all very well as a gardener to relate closely to nature and nature's ways, but it also has a slight drawback. When rain is needed I feel sort of parched, too. Of course, on the other hand, when rain does come, we gardeners have a tremendous sense of joy and relief, and can almost feel the earth absorbing water and roots replenishing themselves.

> What the little wren has to tell when he perches on top of a garden post in the bright sunlight is beyond words. In some way he communicates his mood of joy and ecstasy and we quicken in response to fresh green everywhere, to a warming sun, and to merely being alive at the moment and listening to a small wren.

> When you speed along in the car what do you know of the melody of a brook? Wind in meadow grass? The humming of bees in the clover? The subtle differences of bird songs, the crackle of some-one's brush fire? As you walk each of your five senses seems to sharpen. There are the smells of the countryside which you never notice behind car windows, the fragrance of wild honeysuckle and the drifting scent of pear blossoms over someone's hedge.

> You learn a lot about people when you take them walking in the woods. . . . Sometimes we start out speaking of everyday affairs, and after a few minutes the pauses in the conversation grow longer. The wood itself begins to speak and we fall silent. The sounds of a stream, of the wind in the tree-tops, the whir of a startled woodcock flying off, all seem more important than what we might say.[15]

To those who can so listen, so feel, so respond, living becomes a responsive dialogue. The child of the tide flows *with* the current of life just as the wind, flowing through my wind chime, produces the beauty of sound. May Sarton writes of this same responsive dialogue with the current of life in her existence as a person and poet:

> I am more aware now than I was during his life of how much Quig's friendship, his very existence even apart from our rela-tionship, did to help me forge out the position of these last years

about my work. It is good for a professional to be reminded that his professionalism is only a husk, that the real person must remain an amateur, a *lover* of the work. Whatever we do well is done spontaneously for its own sake, in just the way Quig suddenly decided that he had to get up to the schoolhouse room and paint, or, equally spontaneously, had to make muffins! I am, I think, more of a poet that I was before I knew him, if to be a poet means *allowing life to flow through one rather than forcing it to a mold the will has shaped*; if it means learning to let the day shape the work, not the work, the day, and so live toward essence as naturally as a bird or a flower.[16] (Emphasis added.)

8

The Tragedy of the Common

GARRETT HARDIN

At the end of a thoughtful article on the future of nuclear war, Wiesner and York[1] concluded that: "Both sides in the arms race are...confronted by the dilemma of steadily increasing military power and steadily decreasing national security. *It is our considered professional judgment that this dilemma has no technical solution.* If the great powers continue to look for solutions in the area of science and technology only, the result will be to worsen the situation."

I would like to focus your attention not on the subject of the article (national security in a nuclear world) but on the kind of conclusion they reached, namely that there is no technical solution to the problem. An implicit and almost universal assumption of discussions published in professional and semipopular scientific journals is that the problem under discussion has a technical solution. A technical solution may be defined as one that requires a change only in the techniques of the natural sciences, demanding little or nothing in the way of change in human values or ideas of morality.

In our day (though not in earlier times) technical solutions are always welcome. Because of previous failures in prophecy, it takes courage to assert that a desired technical solution is not possible. Wiesner and York exhibited this courage; publishing in a science journal, they insisted that the solution to the problem was not to be found in the natural sciences. They cautiously qualified their statement with the phrase, "It is our considered professional judgment...." Whether they were right or not is not the concern of the present article. Rather, the concern here is with the important concept of a class of human problems which can be called "no technical solution problems," and, more specifically, with the identification and discussion of one of these.

It is easy to show that the class is not a null class. Recall the game of tick-tack-toe. Consider the problem, "How can I win the game of tick-

From *Science* 162 (13 December 1968): 1243–48. Copyright © 1968 by the American Association for the Advancement of Science.

tack-toe?" It is well known that I cannot, if I assume (in keeping with the conventions of game theory) that my opponent understands the game perfectly. Put another way, there is no "technical solution" to the problem. I can win only by giving a radical meaning to the word "win." I can hit my opponent over the head; or I can drug him; or I can falsify the records. Every way in which I "win" involves, in some sense, an abandonment of the game, as we intuitively understand it. (I can also, of course, openly abandon the game—refuse to play it. This is what most adults do.)

The class of "No technical solution problems" has members. My thesis is that the "population problem," as conventionally conceived, is a member of this class. How it is conventionally conceived needs some comment. It is fair to say that most people who anguish over the population problem are trying to find a way to avoid the evils of overpopulation without relinquishing any of the privileges they now enjoy. They think that farming the seas or developing new strains of wheat will solve the problem—technologically. I try to show here that the solution they seek cannot be found. The population problem cannot be solved in a technical way, any more than can the problem of winning the game of tick-tack-toe.

What Shall We Maximize?

Population, as Malthus said, naturally tends to grow "geometrically," or, as we would now say, exponentially. In a finite world this means that the per capita share of the world's goods must steadily decrease. Is ours a finite world?

A fair defense can be put forward for the view that the world is infinite, or that we do not know that it is not. But, in terms of the practical problems that we must face in the next few generations with the foreseeable technology, it is clear that we will greatly increase human misery if we do not, during the immediate future, assume that the world available to the terrestrial human population is finite. "Space" is no escape.[2]

A finite world can support only a finite population; therefore, population growth must eventually equal zero. (The case of perpetual wide fluctuations above and below zero is a trivial variant that need not be discussed.) When this condition is met, what will be the situation of mankind? Specifically, can Bentham's goal of "the greatest good for the greatest number" be realized?

No—for two reasons, each sufficient by itself. The first is a theoretical one. It is not mathematically possible to maximize for two (or more) variables at the same time. This was clearly stated by von Neumann and Morgenstern,[3] but the principle is implicit in the theory of partial differential equations, dating back at least to D'Alembert (1717-1783).

The second reason springs directly from biological facts. To live, an organism must have a source of energy (for example, food). This energy is utilized for two purposes: mere maintenance and work. For man, maintenance of life requires about 1600 kilocalories a day ("maintenance calories"). Anything that he does over and above merely staying alive will be defined as work, and is supported by "work calories" which he takes in. Work calories are used not only for what we call work in common speech; they are also required for all forms of enjoyment, from swimming and automobile racing to playing music and writing poetry. If our goal is to maximize population it is obvious what we must do. We must make the work calories per person approach as close to zero as possible. No gourmet meals, no vacations, no sports, no music, no literature, no art. . . . I think that everyone will grant, without argument or proof, that maximizing population does not maximize goods. Bentham's goal is impossible.

In reaching this conclusion I have made the usual assumption that it is the acquisition of energy that is the problem. The appearance of atomic energy has led some to question this assumption. However, given an infinite source of energy, population growth still produces an inescapable problem. The problem of the acquisition of energy is replaced by the problem of its dissipation, as J. H. Fremlin has so wittily shown.[4] The arithmetic signs in the analysis are, as it were, reversed; but Bentham's goal is still unobtainable.

The optimum population is, then, less than the maximum. The difficulty of defining the optimum is enormous; so far as I know, no one has seriously tackled this problem. Reaching an acceptable and stable solution will surely require more than one generation of hard analytical work—and much persuasion.

We want the maximum good per person; but what is good? To one person it is wilderness, to another it is ski lodges for thousands. To one it is estuaries to nourish ducks for hunters to shoot; to another it is factory land. Comparing one good with another is, we usually say, impossible because goods are incommensurable. Incommensurables cannot be compared.

Theoretically this may be true; but in real life incommensurables *are* commensurable. Only a criterion of judgment and a system of weighting are needed. In nature the criterion is survival. Is it better for a species to be small and hideable, or large and powerful? Natural selection commensurates the incommensurables. The compromise achieved depends on a natural weighting of the values of the variables.

Man must imitate this process. There is no doubt that in fact he already does, but unconsciously. It is when the hidden decisions are made explicit that the arguments begin. The problem for the years ahead is to work out an acceptable theory of weighting. Synergistic effects, nonlinear variation, and difficulties in discounting the future make the intellectual problem difficult, but not (in principle) insoluble.

Has any cultural group solved this practical problem at the present time, even on an intuitive level? One simple fact proves that none has: there is no prosperous population in the world today that has, and has had for some time, a growth rate of zero. Any people that has intuitively identified its optimum point will soon reach it, after which its growth rate becomes and remains zero.

Of course, a positive growth rate might be taken as evidence that a population is below its optimum. However, by any reasonable standards, the most rapidly growing populations on earth today are (in general) the most miserable. This association (which need not be invariable) casts doubt on the optimistic assumption that the positive growth rate of a population is evidence that it has yet to reach its optimum.

We can make little progress in working toward optimum population size until we explicitly exorcize the spirit of Adam Smith in the field of practical demography. In economic affairs, *The Wealth of Nations* (1776) popularized the "invisible hand," the idea that an individual who "intends only his own gain," is, as it were, led by an invisible hand to promote...the public interest."[5] Adam Smith did not assert that this was invariably true, and perhaps neither did any of his followers. But he contributed to a dominant tendency of thought that has ever since interfered with positive action based on rational analysis, namely, the tendency to assume that decisions reached individually will, in fact, be the best decisions for an entire society. If this assumption is correct it justifies the continuance of our present policy of laissez-faire in reproduction. If it is correct we can assume that men will control their individual fecundity so as to produce the optimum population. If the assumption is not correct, we need to reexamine our individual freedoms to see which ones are defensible.

The Tragedy of Freedom in a Commons

The rebuttal to the invisible hand in population control is to be found in a scenario first sketched in a little-known pamphlet[6] in 1833 by a mathematical amateur named William Forster Lloyd (1794–1852). We may well call it "the tragedy of the commons," using the word "tragedy" as the philosopher Whitehead used it.[7] "The essence of dramatic tragedy is not unhappiness. It resides in the solemnity of the remorseless working of things." He then goes on to say, "This inevitableness of destiny can only be illustrated in terms of human life by incidents which in fact involve unhappiness. For it is only by them that the futility of escape can be made evident in the drama."

The tragedy of the commons develops in this way. Picture a pasture open to all. It is to be expected that each herdsman will try to keep as many cattle as possible on the commons. Such an arrangement may work reasonably satisfactorily for centuries because tribal wars, poaching, and disease keep the numbers of both man and beast well below the carrying capacity of the land. Finally, however, comes the day of reckoning, that is, the day when the long-desired goal of social stability becomes a reality. At this point, the inherent logic of the commons remorselessly generates tragedy.

As a rational being, each herdsman seeks to maximize his gain. Explicitly or implicitly, more or less consciously, he asks, "What is the utility to *me* of adding one more animal to my herd?" This utility has one negative and one positive component.

1. The positive component is a function of the increment of one animal. Since the herdsman receives all the proceeds from the sale of the additional animal, the positive utility is nearly $+1$.

2. The negative component is a function of the additional overgrazing created by one more animal. Since, however, the effects of overgrazing are shared by all the herdsmen, the negative utility for any particular decision-making herdsman is only a fraction of -1.

Adding together the component partial utilities, the rational herdsman concludes that the only sensible course for him to pursue is to add another animal to his herd. And another; and another. . . . But this is the conclusion reached by each and every rational herdsman sharing a commons. Therein is the tragedy. Each man is locked into a system that compels him to increase his herd without limit — in a world that is limited. Ruin is the destination toward which all men rush, each pursuing his own best interest in a society that believes in the freedom of the commons. Freedom in a commons brings ruin to all.

Some would say that this is a platitude. Would that it were! In a sense, it was learned thousands of years ago, but natural selection favors the forces of psychological denial.[8] The individual benefits as an individual from his ability to deny the truth even though society as a whole, of which he is a part, suffers. Education can counteract the natural tendency to do the wrong thing, but the inexorable succession of generations requires that the basis for the knowledge be constantly refreshed.

A simple incident that occurred a few years ago in Leominster, Massachusetts, shows how perishable the knowledge is. During the Christmas shopping season the parking meters downtown were covered with plastic bags that bore tags reading: "Do not open until after Christmas. Free parking courtesy of the mayor and city council." In other words, facing the prospect of an increased demand for already scarce space, the city fathers reinstituted the system of the commons. (Cynically, we suspect that they gained more votes than they lost by this retrogressive act.)

In an approximate way, the logic of the commons has been understood for a long time, perhaps since the discovery of agriculture or the invention of private property in real estate. But it is understood mostly only in special cases which are not sufficiently generalized. Even at this late date, cattlemen leasing national land on the western ranges demonstrate no more than an ambivalent understanding, in constantly pressuring federal authorities to increase the head count to the point where overgrazing produces erosion and weed dominance. Likewise, the oceans of the world continue to suffer from the survival of the philosophy of the commons. Maritime nations still respond automatically to the shibboleth of the "freedom of the seas." Professing to believe in the "inexhaustible resources of the oceans," they bring species after species of fish and whales closer to extinction.[9]

The National Parks present another instance of the working out of the tragedy of the commons. At present, they are open to all, without limit. The parks themselves are limited in extent—there is only one Yosemite Valley—whereas population seems to grow without limit. The values that visitors seek in the parks are steadily eroded. Plainly, we must soon cease to treat the parks as commons or they will be of no value to anyone.

What shall we do? We have several options. We might sell them off as private property. We might keep them as public property, but allocate the right to enter them. The allocation might be on the basis of wealth, by the use of an auction system. It might be on the basis of merit, as defined by some agreed-upon standards. It might be by lottery. Or it might be on a first-come, first-served basis, administered to long queues. These, I think, are all the reasonable possibilities. They are all objectionable. But we must choose—or acquiesce in the destruction of the commons that we call our National Parks.

Pollution

In a reverse way, the tragedy of the commons reappears in problems of pollution. Here it is not a question of taking something out of the commons, but of putting something in—sewage, or chemical, radioactive, and heat wastes into water; noxious and dangerous fumes into the air and distracting and unpleasant advertising signs into the line of sight. The calculations of utility are much the same as before. The rational man finds that his share of the cost of the wastes he discharges into the commons is less than the cost of purifying his wastes before releasing them. Since this is true for everyone, we are locked into a system of "fouling our own nest," so long as we behave only as independent, rational, free-enterprisers.

The tragedy of the commons as a food basket is averted by private property, or something formally like it. But the air and waters surrounding us cannot readily be fenced, and so the tragedy of the commons as cesspool must be prevented by different means, by coercive laws or taxing devices that make it cheaper for the polluter to treat his pollutants than to discharge them untreated. We have not progressed as far with the solution of this problem as we have with the first. Indeed, our particular concept of private property, which deters us from exhausting the positive resources of the earth, favors pollution. The owner of a factory on the bank of a stream – whose property extends to the middle of the stream – often has difficulty seeing why it is not his natural right to muddy the waters flowing past his door. The law, always behind the times, requires elaborate stitching and fitting to adapt it to this newly perceived aspect of the commons.

The pollution problem is a consequence of population. It did not much matter how a lonely American frontiersman disposed of his waste. "Flowing water purifies itself every ten miles," my grandfather used to say, and the myth was near enough to the truth when he was a boy, as there were not too many people. But as population became denser, the natural chemical and biological recycling processes became overloaded, calling for a redefinition of property rights.

How to Legislate Temperance?

Analysis of the pollution problem as a function of population density uncovers a not generally recognized principle of morality, namely: *the morality of an act is a function of the state of the system at the time it is performed.*[10] Using the commons as a cesspool does not harm the general public under frontier conditions, because there is no public; the same behavior in a metropolis is unbearable. A hundred and fifty years ago a plainsman could kill an American bison, cut out only the tongue for his dinner, and discard the rest of the animal. He was not in any important sense being wasteful. Today, with only a few thousand bison left, we would be appalled at such behavior.

In passing, it is worth noting that the morality of an act cannot be determined from a photograph. One does not know whether a man killing an elephant or setting fire to the grassland is harming others until one knows the total system in which his act appears. "One picture is worth a thousand words," said an ancient Chinese; but it may take 10,000 words to validate it. It is as tempting to ecologists as it is to reformers in general to try to persuade others by way of the photographic shortcut. But the essence of an argument cannot be photographed: it must be presented rationally – in words.

That morality is system-sensitive escaped the attention of most codifiers of ethics in the past. "Thou shalt not . . ." is the form of traditional ethical directives which make no allowance for particular circumstances. The laws of our society follow the pattern of ancient ethics, and therefore are poorly suited to governing a complex, crowded, changeable world. Our epicyclic solution is to augment statutory law with administrative law. Since it is practically impossible to spell out all the conditions under which it is safe to burn trash in the back yard or to run an automobile without smog-control, by law we delegate the details to bureaus. The result is administrative law, which is rightly feared for an ancient reason – *Quis custodiet ipsos custodes?* –

"Who shall watch the watchers themselves?" John Adams said that we must have "a government of laws and not men." Bureau administrators, trying to evaluate the morality of acts in the total system, are singularly liable to corruption, producing a government by men, not laws.

Prohibition is easy to legislate (though not necessarily to enforce); but how do we legislate temperance? Experience indicates that it can be accomplished best through the mediation of administrative law. We limit possibilities unnecessarily if we suppose that the sentiment of *Quis custodiet* denies us the use of administrative law. We should rather retain the phrase as a perpetual reminder of fearful dangers we cannot avoid. The great challenge facing us now is to invent the corrective feedbacks that are needed to keep custodians honest. We must find ways to legitimate the needed authority of both the custodians and the corrective feedbacks.

Freedom to Breed is Intolerable

The tragedy of the commons is involved in population problems in another way. In a world governed solely by the principle of "dog eat dog"—if indeed there ever was such a world—how many children a family had would not be a matter of public concern. Parents who bred too exuberantly would leave fewer descendants, not more, because they would be unable to care adequately for their children. David Lack and others have found that such a negative feedback demonstrably controls the fecundity of birds.[11] But men are not birds, and have not acted like them for millenniums, at least.

If each human family were dependent only on its own resources; *if* the children of improvident parents starved to death; *if*, thus, overbreeding brought its own "punishment" to the germ line—*then* there would be no public interest in controlling the breeding of families. But our society is deeply committed to the welfare state,[12] and hence is confronted with another aspect of the tragedy of the commons.

In a welfare state, how shall we deal with the family, the religion, the race, or the class (or indeed any distinguishable and cohesive group) that adopts overbreeding as a policy to secure its own aggrandizement? To couple the concept of freedom to breed with the belief that everyone born has an equal right to the commons is to lock the world into a tragic course of action.

Unfortunately this is just the course of action that is being pursued by the United Nations. In late 1967, some thirty nations agreed to the following:[14]

> The Universal Declaration of Human Rights describes the family as the natural and fundamental unit of society. It follows that any choice and decision with regard to the size of the family must irrevocably rest with the family itself, and cannot be made by someone else.

It is painful to have to deny categorically the validity of this right; denying it, one feels as uncomfortable as a resident of Salem, Massachusetts, who denied the reality of witches in the seventeenth century. At the present time, in liberal quarters, something like a taboo acts to inhibit criticism of the United Nations. There is a feeling that the United Nations is "our last and best hope," that we shouldn't find fault with it; we shouldn't play into the hands of the archconservatives. However, let us not forget what Robert Louis Stevenson said: "The truth that is suppressed by friends is the readiest weapon of the enemy." If we love the truth we must openly deny the validity of the Universal Declaration of Human Rights, even though it is promoted by the United Nations. We should also join with Kingsley Davis[15] in attempting to get Planned Parenthood-World Population to see the error of its ways in embracing the same tragic ideal.

Conscience Is Self-Eliminating

It is a mistake to think that we can control the breeding of mankind in the long run by an appeal to conscience. Charles Galton Darwin made this point when he spoke on the centennial of the publication of his grandfather's great book. The argument is straightforward and Darwinian.

People vary. Confronted with appeals to limit breeding, some people will undoubtedly respond to the plea more than others. Those who have more children will produce a larger fraction of the next generation than those with more susceptible consciences. The difference will be accentuated, generation by generation.

In C. G. Darwin's words: "It may well be that it would take hundreds of generations for the progenitive instinct to develop in this way, but if it should do so, nature would have taken her revenge, and the variety *Homo contracipiens* would become extinct and would be replaced by the variety *Homo progenitivus*."[16]

The argument assumes that conscience or the desire for children (no matter which) is hereditary – but hereditary only in the most general formal sense. The result will be the same whether the attitude is transmitted through germ cells, or exosomatically, to use A. J. Lotka's term. (If one denies the latter possibility as well as the former, then what's the point of education?) The argument has here been stated in the context of the population problem, but it applies equally well to any instance in which society appeals to an individual exploiting a commons to restrain himself for the general good – by means of his conscience. To make such an appeal is to set up a selective system that works toward the elimination of conscience from the race.

Pathogenic Effects of Conscience

The long-term disadvantage of an appeal to conscience should be enough to condemn it; but it has serious short-term disadvantages as well. If we ask a man who is exploiting a commons to desist "in the name of conscience," what are we saying to him? What does he hear? — not only at the moment but also in the wee small hours of the night when, half asleep, he remembers not merely the words we used but also the nonverbal communication cues we gave him unawares? Sooner or later, consciously or subconsciously, he senses that he has received two communications, and that they are contradictory: (1, the intended communication) "If you don't do as we ask, we will openly condemn you for not acting like a responsible citizen"; (2, the unintended communication) "If you *do* behave as we ask, we will secretly condemn you for a simpleton who can be shamed into standing aside while the rest of us exploit the commons.

Everyman then is caught in what Bateson has called a "double bind." Bateson and his co-workers have made a plausible case for viewing the double bind as an important causative factor in the genesis of schizophrenia.[17] The double bind may not always be so damaging, but it always endangers the mental health of anyone to whom it is applied. "A bad conscience," said Nietzsche, "is a kind of illness."

To conjure up a conscience in others is tempting to anyone who wishes to extend his control beyond the legal limits. Leaders at the highest level succumb to this temptation. Has any President during the past generation failed to call on labor unions to moderate voluntarily their demands for higher wages, or to steel companies to honor voluntary guidelines on prices? I can recall none. The rhetoric used on such occasions is designed to produce feelings of guilt in noncooperators.

For centuries it was assumed without proof that guilt was a valuable, perhaps even an indispensable, ingredient of the civilized life. Now, in this post-Freudian world, we doubt it.

Paul Goodman speaks from the modern point of view when he says, "No good has ever come from feeling guilty, neither intelligence, policy, nor compassion. The guilty do not pay attention to the object but only to themselves, and not even to their own interests, which might make sense, but to their anxieties."[18]

One does not have to be a professional psychiatrist to see the consequences of anxiety. We in the Western world are just emerging from a dreadful two-centuries-long Dark Ages of Eros that was sustained partly by prohibition laws, but perhaps more effectively by the anxiety-generating mechanisms of education. Alex Comfort has told the story well in *The Anxiety Makers*;[19] it is not a pretty one.

Since proof is difficult, we may even concede that the results of anxiety may sometimes, from certain points of view, be desirable. The larger question we should ask is whether, as a matter of policy, we should ever encourage the use of a technique the tendency (if not the intention) of which is psychologically pathogenic. We hear much talk these days of responsible parenthood; the coupled words are incorporated into the titles of some organizations devoted to birth control. Some people have proposed massive propaganda campaigns to instill responsibility into the nation's (or the world's) breeders. But what is the meaning of the word responsibility in this context? Is it not merely a synonym for the word conscience? When we use the word responsibility in the absence of substantial sanctions are we not trying to browbeat a free man in a commons into acting against his own interest? Responsibility is a verbal counterfeit for a substantial *quid pro quo*. It is an attempt to get something for nothing.

If the word responsibility is to be used at all, I suggest that it be in the sense Charles Frankel uses it.[20] "Responsibility," says this philosopher, "is the product of definite social arrangements." Notice that Frankel calls for social arrangements – not propaganda.

Mutual Coercion Mutually Agreed Upon

The social arrangements that produce responsibility are arrangements that create coercion, of some sort. Consider bank robbing. The man who takes money from a bank acts as if the bank were a commons. How do we prevent such action? Certainly not by trying to control his behavior solely by a verbal appeal to his sense of responsibility. Rather than rely on propaganda we follow Frankel's lead and insist that a bank is not a commons; we seek the definite social arrangements that will keep it from becoming a commons. That we thereby infringe on the freedom of would-be robbers we neither deny nor regret.

The morality of bank robbing is particularly easy to understand because we accept complete prohibition of this activity. We are willing to say "Thou shalt not rob banks," without providing for exceptions. But temperance also can be created by coercion. Taxing is a good coercive device. To keep downtown shoppers temperate in their use of parking space we introduce parking meters for short periods, and traffic fines for longer ones. We need not actually forbid a citizen to park as long as he wants to; we need merely make it increasingly expensive for him to do so. Not prohibition, but carefully biased options are what we offer him. A Madison Avenue man might call this persuasion; I prefer the greater candor of the word coercion.

Coercion is a dirty word to most liberals now, but it need not forever be so. As for the four-letter words, its dirtiness can be cleansed away by exposure to the light, by saying it over and over without apology or embarrassment. To many, the word coercion implies arbitrary decisions of distant and irresponsible bureaucrats; but this is not a necessary part of its meaning. The only kind of coercion I recommend is mutual coercion, mutually agreed upon by the majority of the people affected.

To say that we mutually agree to coercion is not to say that we are required to enjoy it, or even to pretend we enjoy it. Who enjoys taxes?

We all grumble about them. But we accept compulsory taxes because we recognize that voluntary taxes would favor the conscienceless. We institute and (grumblingly) support taxes and other coercive devices to escape the horror of the commons.

An alternative to the commons need not be perfectly just to be preferable. With real estate and other material goods, the alternative we have chosen is the institution of private property coupled with legal inheritance. Is this system perfectly just? As a genetically trained biologist, I deny that it is. It seems to me that, if there are to be differences in individual inheritance, legal possession should be perfectly correlated with biological inheritance—that those who are biologically more fit to be the custodians of property and power should legally inherit more. But genetic recombination continually makes a mockery of the doctrine of "like father, like son" implicit in our laws of legal inheritance. An idiot can inherit millions, and a trust fund can keep his estate intact. We must admit that our legal system of private property plus inheritance is unjust—but we put up with it because we are not convinced, at the moment, that anyone has invented a better system. The alternative of the commons is too horrifying to contemplate. Injustice is preferable to total ruin.

It is one of the peculiarities of the warfare between reform and the status quo that it is thoughtlessly governed by a double standard. Whenever a reform measure is proposed it is often defeated when its opponents triumphantly discover a flaw in it. As Kingsley Davis has pointed out,[21] worshippers of the status quo sometimes imply that no reform is possible without unanimous agreement, an implication contrary to historical fact. As nearly as I can make out, automatic rejection of proposed reforms is based on one of two unconscious assumptions: (1) that the status quo is perfect; or (2) that the choice we face is between reform and no action; if the proposed reform is imperfect, we presumably should take no action at all, while we wait for a perfect proposal.

But we can never do nothing. That which we have done for thousands of years is also action. It also produces evils. Once we are aware that the status quo is action, we can then compare its discoverable advantages and disadvantages with the predicted advantages and disadvantages of the proposed reform, discounting as best we can for our lack of experience. On the basis of such a comparison, we can make a rational decision which will not involve the unworkable assumption that only perfect systems are tolerable.

Recognition of Necessity

Perhaps the simplest summary of this analysis of man's population problems is this: the commons, if justifiable at all, is justifiable only under conditions of low-population density. As the human population has increased, the commons has had to be abandoned in one aspect after another.

First we abandoned the commons in food gathering, enclosing farm land and restricting pastures and hunting and fishing areas. These restrictions are still not complete throughout the world.

Somewhat later we saw that the commons as a place for waste disposal would also have to be abandoned. Restrictions on the disposal of domestic sewage are widely accepted in the Western world; we are still struggling to close the commons to pollution by automobiles, factories, insecticide sprayers, fertilizing operations, and atomic energy installations.

In a still more embryonic state is our recognition of the evils of the commons in matters of pleasure. There is almost no restriction on the propagation of sound waves in the public medium. The shopping public is assaulted with mindless music, without its consent. Our government is paying out billions of dollars to create supersonic transport which will disturb 50,000 people for every one person who is whisked from coast to coast three hours faster. Advertisers muddy the airwaves of radio and television and pollute the view of travelers. We are a long way from outlawing the commons in matters of pleasure. Is this because our Puritan inheritance makes us view pleasure as something of a sin, and pain (that is, the pollution of advertising) as the sign of virtue?

Every new enclosure of the commons involves the infringement of somebody's personal liberty. Infringements made in the distant past are accepted because no contemporary complains of a loss. It is the newly proposed infringements that we vigorously oppose; cries of "rights" and "freedom" fill the air. But what does "freedom" mean? When men mutually agreed to pass laws against robbing, mankind became more free, not less so. Individuals locked into the logic of the commons are free only to bring on universal ruin; once they see the necessity of mutual coercion, they become free to pursue other goals. I believe it was Hegel who said, "Freedom is the recognition of necessity."

The most important aspect of necessity that we must now recognize, is the necessity of abandoning the commons in breeding. No technical solution can rescue us from the misery of overpopulation. Freedom to breed will bring ruin to all. At the moment, to avoid hard decisions many of us are tempted to propagandize for conscience and responsible parenthood. The temptation must be resisted, because an appeal to independently acting consciences selects for the disappearance of all conscience in the long run, and an increase in anxiety in the short.

The only way we can preserve and nurture other and more precious freedoms is by relinquishing the freedom to breed, and that very soon. "Freedom is the recognition of necessity"—and it is the role of education to reveal to all the necessity of abandoning the freedom to breed. Only so, can we put an end to this aspect of the tragedy of the commons.

9

Managing an Open-Access Resource: The Case of Coastal Fisheries

CONNER BAILEY

Most of the coastal fisheries of Southeast Asia are approaching or have exceeded maximally sustainable yields, because of tremendous increases in fishing effort over the last two decades. Ever increasing numbers of small-scale fishermen and the introduction of highly effective gear types such as the trawl have combined to pose a serious threat to these valuable but vulnerable resources. There is growing recognition of the need to establish effective management schemes to assure the long-term sustainability of high yields from coastal fisheries.[1] Effective action requires coming to terms with the problem of allocating the resources among competing groups of fishermen and finding viable means of enforcing that allocation.

The Sea as an Open-Access Resource

Unlike most agriculture and forestry lands which involve specific property rights, the sea generally is regarded as common property or an open-access resource. Essentially anyone is eligible to become a fisherman and exploit the resource as he can. In Southeast Asia it is common for landless agricultural laborers[2] and unemployed urban workers[3] to take up fishing as an occupation of last resort. Sons born to fishermen seldom have opportunities to move out of fishing and so remain with their father's trade. Consequently, growing numbers of persons come to depend for their livelihoods on this limited resource. Access to a fishery may be open, but success in exploiting it depends to a large extent on the availability of capital to

International Center for Living Aquatic Resources Management (ICLARM) contribution no. 135. Abstracted from Conner Bailey, "Access to and Management of Coastal Marine Resources: The Fishing Communities of San Miguel Bay, Philippines" (Paper prepared for the Canadian Council for Southeast Asian Studies/Institute of Southeast Asian Studies (Singapore) joint seminar, "Village-Level Modernization: Livelihoods, Resources, Cultural Continuity," Singapore, 21–24 June 1982; and Conner Bailey, "Natural Resource Management: A Basis for Organization of Small-Scale Fishermen," *Rural Development Participation Review* (Ithaca, N.Y.: Rural Development Committee, Cornell University, Winter 1982), pp. 19–22.

invest in efficient gear. *Open* access is not the same as *equal* access. The problem is particularly severe in shallow coastal fishing grounds where the vast majority of Southeast Asia's fishermen—mostly small-scale operators—are concentrated. Rapid growth of trawler fleets which directly compete with small-scale fishermen has increased the pressure and introduced a serious problem of distribution of benefits from the fisheries.

Policy Options

In regions such as Southeast Asia, social and economic goals often conflict in the management of coastal fisheries. Where governments focus on economic goals, policies are likely to be dictated by the desire to insure adequate supplies of fish at prices affordable by local consumers, to increase foreign exchange earnings from the export of fisheries products such as shrimp, and to increase economic efficiency (profitability) in the fishery sector. Such policy criteria tend to favor the larger, more capital-intensive fishing units such as trawlers, which are highly productive in terms of size of catch, highly effective in capturing shrimp, and yield higher rates of profit than fishing units operated by small-scale fishermen.[4]

In contrast, social goals in fisheries management would emphasize the creation of employment opportunities and an equitable return for the largest number of those needing employment. These criteria favor policy support for small-scale production units which employ substantially more people per unit of investment, result in a wider and more equitable distribution of income, and spread ownership of capital over a substantial number of households.

Where the fisheries resource is already fully exploited, the operation of trawlers in shallow coastal waters not only results in diminished production by small-scale fishermen, but may also reduce quality and total value of the catch. Small-scale fishermen as a whole use selective fishing gear such as gill nets or hooks and lines which tend to exploit relatively large specimens of their target species. In contrast, trawlers are nonselective, capturing anything in the paths of their nets, including immature forms of commercially valuable species. Indeed, the major portion of a trawler's catch usually consists of such "trash fish" which are sold for fish-meal processing. Especially when operating in shallow coastal waters which serve as nursery grounds, trawlers exert a damaging influence on a vulnerable resource.

The Case of San Miguel Bay

In 1979 a two-year interdisciplinary research project was launched to study the fisheries of San Miguel Bay, Philippines,[5] where large numbers of small-scale fishermen were operating in competition with a growing fleet of trawlers. San Miguel Bay is located in the Bicol Region of southern Luzon Island. The bay's shoreline is roughly horseshoe-shaped and has a surface area of approximately 840 square kilometers. Forty percent of the bay is less than four fathoms (7.3 m) and 80 percent less than seven fathoms (12.8 m) in depth.[6] Catch per unit of effort data indicate that the bay is one of the most productive fishing grounds in the Philippines, but that production has leveled off in recent years. The bay's fisheries resources are maximally exploited in terms of catch in weight.[7]

SOCIO-ECONOMIC CONDITION

There are approximately 3,500 fishing households in the forty-four coastal communities surrounding San Miguel Bay. The total population of these households is 24,000 persons, of whom 5,600 regularly operate as fishermen in the bay.[8] Few of these households own or have access to agricultural land and economic alternatives to fishing are distinctly limited.

Nearly three-quarters of the bay's small-scale fishermen reported in a survey that their catch has declined over the past two years.[9] At the same time investment costs (wood, synthetic netting, engines) and operational costs (especially fuel) have increased considerably, while fish prices at the beach have increased only slightly. A large plurality of the fishermen surveyed expressed willingness to change both occupation and place of residence if they could thereby increase their income. Despite net outmigration between 1939 and 1980, the population of these coastal communities has grown at the rate of 2 percent per year and has more than doubled during this period.[10] Given the limited alternatives to fishing in this area, it is likely that the number of fishermen operating in the bay has increased at a similar rate.

THE BAY'S SMALL-SCALE FISHERIES

Small-scale fishermen operate relatively simple and inexpensive boats and gear. The most common type of boat is the *banca*, a light outriggered craft with a hollowed log keel and marine plywood sides, sometimes powered by a 16 HP gasoline engine. No significant concentration of ownership of boats and gear exists among the bay's small-scale fishermen; 58 percent of our fishermen respondents classified themselves as owner-operators.[11]

Few trawlers operated in the bay prior to 1970. During the early 1970s the "Norway" style of otter trawl used by large commercial trawlers was adopted for use in shallower waters and quickly proved its profitability, resulting in a rapid increase in numbers of small and medium trawlers and in the level of total fishing effort exerted on the bay's fishery.

Trawlers constitute a distinct category of fishing unit despite the fact that most trawlers operating on the bay displace less than three tons. As such they are legally defined as small-scale fishing units and fall under the jurisdiction of local municipal governments. Small trawlers may operate *legally* in all waters over four fathoms (7.3 m) in depth. Trawlers displacing over three tons ("medium trawlers") are legally classified as "commercial" fishing units, whose operations are controlled by the national government through the Bureau of Fisheries and Aquatic Resources (BFAR). Medium trawlers are legally restricted to waters deeper than seven fathoms (12.8 m).[12] This distinction is important, as only 20 percent of the bay is *legally* available to medium trawlers while 60 percent is exploitable by small trawlers. (There are also a number of "large" trawlers displacing between 60 and 120 metric tons, but these operate primarily outside the bay.)

While investment requirements in 1982 for small-scale gear range from 100 pesos for a push net to 13,000 pesos for a motorized gill net, small and medium trawlers cost 55,000 pesos and 70,000 pesos, respectively. Twenty-five percent of the bay's trawler fleet is owned by one person. Eight persons own another 34 percent of the fleet. The 75 small and 20 medium trawlers operating in San Miguel Bay employ a total of 500 fishermen and account for 47 percent of the total volume of catch landed.[14] The remaining 53 percent of the catch is distributed among over 5,000 small-scale fishermen.

POLICY IMPLICATIONS

It is obvious that the trawlers of San Miguel Bay represent a significant concentration of fishing power controlled by relatively few individuals who employ a small fraction of the total fisheries workforce. Moreover, owners of trawlers earn most of the pure profits (total returns less fixed, variable, and opportunity costs) from the bay, though owners of medium trawlers have incurred substantial losses, primarily due to higher fuel costs for operating larger engines.[15] The more numerous small trawlers, however, are highly profitable.[16]

Fish and shrimp yields from the bay are extraordinarily high, though there is no evidence to show that total catches have declined due to the high level of effort applied to the fishery.[17] It is, however, unlikely that increased production from the bay is possible through increased fishing effort.

The critical issues are distributional. Pauly states that reduction of trawling effort would have a direct positive impact on the catch landed by small-scale fishermen, thus presumably having a positive distributional result, as virtually all of the major species landed by trawlers are exploitable by small-scale fishermen using existing gear. Conversely, there appears to be little likelihood of increasing the catch of the small-scale fishermen unless effective restrictions are placed on the numbers of trawlers and/or their zones of operation. Such action might reduce economic "efficiency" measured by conventional profitability criteria, but it could be expected to improve substantially the livelihoods of the 90 percent of the fishermen who now account for only 53 percent of the catch. Moreover, since the fine mesh nets used by trawlers land large volumes of undersized commercially valuable fish species while the small-scale fishermen use more selective gear, such a policy might increase the economic value of the total catch by shifting production toward larger fish directly consumed by humans.

Efforts to reduce trawling effort would run directly contrary to current public policies which seek to improve the lot of the small-scale fishermen by providing them with access to credit with which to purchase larger boats and more sophisticated gear. In 1981 most of the governmentally subsidized loans provided to fishermen in the San Miguel Bay area were for construction of new small trawlers. These loans are supposed to be given only to small-scale fishermen, but in actuality the new trawlers will be controlled by existing trawler operators, who act as guarantors for otherwise unsecured loans issued through local rural banks.[18] In situations such as San Miguel Bay, where the resource is already heavily exploited, this type of loan program will further increase the aggregate fishing power of a few individuals and further skew access to the resource. Under these circumstances such well-intentioned credit programs contribute to the problem, not to its solution.

The basic solutions to the lack of control over fishing effort are political and organizational. A significant improvement in the lot of the small-scale fishermen might be achieved simply by enforcing the existing ban on all trawling in the 40 percent of the bay which is less than four fathoms deep. If the six municipal mayors whose jurisdictions include the shoreline of San Miguel Bay together were to decree an end to trawling within the seven-fathom mark (as they are empowered to do under a presidential decree), the area reserved for small-scale fishermen would be extended to 80 percent of the bay.

A major contributor to the present lack of enforcement is the existence of cross-cutting administrative jurisdictions which in turn dilute responsibility and encourage corruption. Municipal governments, the Bureau of Fisheries and Aquatic Resources, the Coast Guard, and the police are all expected to play a part in enforcement of fisheries regulations. When responsibility is so divided and unclear, enforcement suffers. In the San Miguel Bay area, trawlers are frequently observed operating in areas of less than four fathoms depth and do so with impunity because of the absence of effective enforcement. The incentive to trawl the shallower water is mainly the shrimp resource, which is most abundant in the shallows.

Community Management of the Fisheries Resource

Any solution must recognize the inherent physical difficulties in enforcing fishing restrictions where economic incentives invite violation, as they do in San Miguel Bay. For the government to patrol all fishing grounds where illegal fishing is suspected would require a heavy investment in boats, fuel, and personnel. Approaching the problem primarily in terms of the expenditure of public funds to enforce a centrally mandated regulation is not likely to prove a viable option. It is too expensive and the opportunities for circumvention of a centrally administered system are too great.

The most promising solution is one built on the motivation and resources of the small-scale fishermen themselves. If properly organized, the small-scale fishermen could themselves take part in monitoring and reporting illegal fishing. In the course of their daily activities, these fishermen witness what happens at sea. They know who is responsible for illegal fishing, but individually lack the confidence and political influence necessary to turn their complaints into effective administrative or judicial action. They know by experience that individual complaints and even petitions will have no lasting effect. For example, in 1977 a number of fishermen from San Miguel Bay petitioned the president of the Philippines in regard to illegal fishing by trawlers. In response, funds were released for the construction of a boat for use by the police. For the past several years this boat has been beached, the engine removed for repairs. On its side can still be read the boat's name: *The Enforcer.*

With the support of an organization of their peers, small-scale fishermen could be integrated into legitimate local political processes and be able to lobby effectively for their interests. Because under existing law municipalities are charged with the regulation of near-shore marine resources (one of the few cases in the Philippines where control over important natural resources is decentralized), local organizations of small-scale fishermen can exert effective political pressure. Only by acting in concert can effective pressure be exerted on political leaders and enforcement agencies. The mobilization of this political effort in response to a clear threat to their livelihoods offers the best hope of eliciting organizational solidarity among people who are more often noted for their individualism.

The record of previous attempts to establish organizations among small-scale fishermen is strewn with failures. If such efforts are to be successful they must address real needs and result in real improvements in the well-being of the community. Too often in the past, efforts inspired by well-intentioned planners and administrators were based on misperceptions of the problem, such as the presumption noted earlier that the primary need is for captial to buy larger boats and more sophisticated equipment. Another common mistake is to assume that the condition of the small-scale fishermen is a consequence of being locked into a disadvantageous position vis-à-vis middlemen and that marketing cooperatives can break this dependency. To be sure, there are unscrupulous middlemen, but the vast majority earn a modest living while providing essential services which a formal (much less an official or government-managed) organization is unlikely to provide.

In extreme cases, such efforts to displace local buyers may exacerbate existing cleavages within communities while exchanging one set of dependency relationships for another. Marketing efficiency rarely is enhanced by replacing private entrepreneurs with salaried personnel, especially from the civil service.

The focus of organizing efforts in fishing communities should be directed to the central problem, the collective management of the commons according to rules established by the local community, to the equitable benefit of all the community's members.

Part Four

Resource Competition and the Dynamics of Poverty

As cynics commonly note, the poor have always been with us. Unfortunately the development efforts of the past several decades have done little to change this basic reality. If the situation is to be changed, it is essential to understand why so many well-intentioned development efforts in the past have been beneficial to only a few, while some have even deepened the poverty of the many. Contributors to this section deal with the problem from a variety of perspectives. But the basic patterns of resource competition and of exploitation, intentional or otherwise, by those who control even the meager resources of those who do not, are remarkably consistent. On the positive side, these contributions also reveal and document the creative abilities of the poor, which allow the more fortunate of them to survive in spite of the systemic biases that commonly frustrate their efforts to improve their lot and sometimes even their efforts to survive. Full utilization of these abilities offers the primary hope for improving on the development efforts of the past. The key is to reduce the constraints which the poor face in putting those abilities to work. Such action must be based on in-depth understanding of their dynamics.

Jeffrey Nugent and Pan Yotopoulos open this section with an analysis of why the equilibrating mechanisms which orthodox development economics argues will result in broad distribution of the benefits of increased production do not work as predicted. Their analysis makes a substantial contribution toward explaining why the policies advocated by orthodox theory have commonly produced outcomes contrary to those intended. Their study also sets forth an economic argument for application of the principle of local self-reliance in the formulation of economic policies.

In chapter 12, Izzedin Imam takes us from the abstractions of economic theory to the practical realities of the poorest of the poor in the rural villages of Bangladesh and what it means to live at the very margin of survival. Here is the story of poverty in its most degrading and dehumanizing form, as told by those who experience it.

The dynamics of seasonality, highlighted in Imam's study, are elaborated by Robert Chambers, Richard Hurst, David Bradley, and Richard Feachem. A pervasive feature of rural poverty, seasonality creates severe pressures on the very poor, commonly pushing the weakest into a downward spiral of increasing dependency and despair. The authors forcefully demonstrate the implications of seasonality for any development effort directed to the rural poor.

George Carner's study of Philippine poverty takes the household as the basic analytical unit and the household survival strategy as its organizing conceptual framework. His study provides important insights into why in many instances the situation of Third World poor is steadily deteriorating, in spite of — even because of — well-intentioned development efforts intended to alleviate the conditions of their poverty.

That the pervasive reality of resource competition is not limited to the rural poor is graphically illustrated by Simon Fass, in a study of water supply services in Port-au-Prince, Haiti. His study documents the consequences of this competition and its disproportionally negative impact on the very poor.

The dynamics of concentration and marginalization also have a geographical dimension, as brought out by Michael Lipton. He demonstrates the pervasive nature of urban bias and the dynamics which sustain it to the disadvantage of rural areas and rural peoples.

The final essay in this section, by Osvaldo Sunkel, views the problem of marginalization and concentration from the perspective of a dependency theorist, providing a summary of the central arguments of that school. His analysis of the dynamics of the international system is provocative and not easily dismissed, even though his implicit ideological assumption that the problems noted are unique to capitalist economic systems is easily challenged.

10

Orthodox Development Economics versus the Dynamics of Concentration and Marginalization

JEFFREY B. NUGENT AND PAN A. YOTOPOULOS

Income growth, unemployment, and inequality are probably the three most typical characteristics of the recent experience of developing countries (LDCs).[1] While poor performance on employment and income distribution is hardly unique as a historical phenomenon, in the particular context of contemporary LDCs it may have been largely unanticipated. In the view of mainstream orthodox development economics, it is the take-off which is difficult. After development has been initiated, and once it has been 'put on the turnpike', its trickling down and its spread will be almost automatic. The real surprise of the recent experience, then, is that unemployment and inequality have been increasing at a time that LDCs have been growing at historically unprecedented rates. While the engine of growth has been running strong, the accessories of growth either have failed to function or have been systematically offset by disequilibrating forces, leaving development to trickle up, rather than down.

Admittedly, the recent literature in development economics has begun to own up to these failures by pointing to exogenous factors such as inappropriate government policies, market imperfections, and information costs. Such an approach in our opinion is timid and falls short of the mark. It is the purpose of this paper to suggest as an alternative explanation that the processes which generate the backwash effects of development are endogenous to the system. In this sense phenomena such as unemployment and inequality become the logical, although not exclusive, consequences of excessive reliance on the market mechanism at the early stages of development. Should our analysis be correct, the appropriateness of the market

---

Excerpted from "What Has Orthodox Development Economics Learned from Recent Experience?," *World Development* 7 (1979): 541–54. Copyright © Pergamon Press Ltd. Reprinted with permission.

as an important foundation of orthodox economics for the context of LDCs must be called into question.

We begin with a description of the various equilibrating mechanisms inherent in the orthodox approach to development economics and contrast this approach with an alternative disequilibrium view of development. We then present an anatomy of failure of the equilibrating mechanisms that operate through migration, technological change, capital formation, international trade, monetization and other forms of institutional change, and we describe their disequilibrating characteristics. In the final section we pull the arguments together and go on to explain why some conventional policies, instead of spreading development, may actually increase its backwash effects.

The Orthodox and the Disequilibrium Paradigms Contrasted

Three interrelated ideas, which are part and parcel of the body of theory known as neoclassical economics, have had profound influence in shaping the orthodox economics of development.[2] These ideas have provided the theoretical building blocks for the study of development economics and have outlined the kind of policies appropriate for achieving economic development.

The first idea is that development is a gradual, continuous and cumulative process, which can effectively rely on marginal adjustments. Equilibrium positions are thought to be stable and the price mechanism serves as the beacon for summoning the required adjustments and thus becomes, in itself, an important device for promoting economic development. The corollary of this view is that static, partial equilibrium techniques are sufficient for analysing economic development.

Second, is the idea that growth is harmonious and that order is created out of conflict and selfish drives through the operation of automatic, equilibrating mechanisms—the neoclassical counterpart to the Invisible Hand of classical theory. These mechanisms guarantee that development generally benefits all major income groups. In the ruling paradigm of a harmonious world, rich and poor, capitalist and labourer, all work together for increased output to mutual advantage.

Third, is the optimism concerning the future possibilities for continued development and its spread among groups and across nations. Exchange is capable of leading to a Pareto-optimum position which benefits everybody, at least in the sense that the gainers have the potential to compensate the losers. The neoclassical theory of international trade is an even more definite statement of the proposition that free exchange will spread the benefits of development across the world through specialization and the division of labour.

The ruling paradigm of the economics of development rests on the classical-neoclassical view of a world in which change is gradual, marginalist, non-disruptive, equilibrating, and largely painless. Incentives are the bedrock of economic growth. Once initiated, growth becomes automatic and all-pervasive, spreading among nations and trickling down among classes so that everybody benefits from the process. This view is analogous to the communicating vessels of elementary hydraulics: the pressure in the vessel with higher initial endowments leads to raising the water level in the other vessels. The mechanism that trips off change and restores equilibrium is the pressure created by non-identical endowments. Its impulse is transmitted through the pipeline that connects the vessels. Analogously, development is initiated by incentives arising from inequality and is promoted by the market mechanisms that connect the rich and the poor. According to this paradigm, therefore, what is required for development is to create the proper incentives, to perfect the market mechanisms, and thereby to initiate the changes that lead to self-propelled take-offs. The incurably optimistic payoff is the general spread of development and the homogenization of the rich and poor to the extent they become indistinguishable – at least up to exogenous factors like the quantity of talents they possess or their tastes for risk-taking.

While the neoclassical paradigm views development as a cumulative process ruled by equilibrating mechanisms and centripetal tendencies, the disequilibrium paradigm suggests that economic development, at least in its early stages, acts like the suction principle in inducing biformity. It nourishes the towering heights of *polarity* at one extreme at the same time it creates *marginalization* at the other extreme. Just as cream rises to the top, development trickles up for a while to benefit those who are well-endowed; and as sediment becomes mired at the bottom, the victims of development are crowded into the periphery.

In the discussion that follows we present some examples of such development-generated, inequality-increasing systematic biases that help illustrate the paradigm of development disequilibrium, and contrast it with the orthodox paradigm.

Unemployment and Migration Within A Disequilibrium System

As Keynes suggested, in a monetary economy the unemployed cannot signal their desire for goods until they are hired and receive the money wages they spend. As a result, in a period of recession the signal sent to producing firms is not that of shortage of supply but rather is one of slack sales and accumulating inventories, which the producing firms attempt to correct by laying off workers, thus leading to further production cutbacks and pushing the economy ever further into recession. Orthodox Keynesian economists called this a failure in effective demand which they showed could be offset by an exogenous monetary or fiscal stimulus.[3] The "New Keynesians" now go one step further in emphasizing that a monetary market economy has an inherent tendency to move away from the Walrasian centre of gravity into states of chronic disequilibrium. For example, given some amount of unemployment, inflation and financial instability may combine to push the economy even further away from full employment.[4]

In the employment models that have been used in the economics of development, such considerations have been notably absent. Be they of classical[5] or neoclassical[6] origins, such models have been long on controversy over whether or not and why workers are paid their marginal product and short on the implications for unemployment. The presumption in this analysis is that unemployment and agricultural underemployment, if they exist at all, contain in themselves the potential for achieving development at virtually zero cost. If they exist, they live on borrowed time, soon to disappear along with the ugly-headed demon called dualism through rural-urban migration.

In a world of homogeneous labour and complete information, employment at a marginal product lower than the opportunity cost of labour – the urban wage rate – is irrational. Except for transaction costs, thanks to the power of the "Invisible Foot," such models imply that labour can be transferred costlessly to the urban sector and can begin immediately earning wage rates higher than those in rural areas. Since labour is assumed to be homogenous in quality, the migrants are the surplus, marginal or unemployed workers of the agricultural sector. As such the process of migration is equilibrating in the sense that it raises the marginal productivity of labour for those remaining in agriculture, while lowering that for those in the recipient (urban) sector. Under competitive product and capital markets, the capitalist's rent is entirely saved and invested. Capital formation is not subject to economies of scale, and labour-displacing technology has not yet been admitted as a problem. As a result, even starting from humble beginnings, industrial capital absorbs more labour and plants the seed for future investment and further labour absorption. Eventually, surplus labour disappears along with the wage differential and hence dualism itself. In the process the inequality in the distribution of labour income (though perhaps not overall income) will be reduced and indeed eliminated.[7] Economic development in this model is the gradual, harmonious and optimistic process of the orthodox neoclassical paradigm.

The role assigned to migration and the Invisible Foot in restoring equilibrium in the long run is, however, not congruent with the combination of three phenomena which have been consistently observed in recent historical experience. First, there are generally extremely high rates of migration from the agricultural to the non-agricultural sector. Second, these massive migration flows persist unabated despite the fact that unemployment rates in urban areas have tended to increase. Third, despite the high unemployment rates in urban areas, the wage differentials between agriculture and non-agriculture are maintained, if not increased, and sectoral dualism becomes even more accentuated.

In contrast to the traditional mode, the development disequilibrium approach considers migration the epitome of the polarization-marginalization process. The quality of the migrants becomes the crux of this issue. Unlike the stampede of the Invisible Feet of faceless and homogeneous workers posited by the neoclassical model, the alternative interpretation considers migration a highly selective process. Namely, it is thought that the migrants are largely the younger, better educated, more ambitious, healthier, more self-confident, adjustable, risk-taking, infra-marginal workers. As such, they need not linger unemployed in the cities, waiting for industrial expansion to create more marginal jobs for them to occupy. Instead, in the analysis of Thurow and Lucas,[8] they can enter employment immediately and even move to the head of the queues for the better-paying jobs, prompting employers to raise the skill requirements of higher and middle level jobs. The result of this upgrading of the skill requirements of such jobs is the eventual displacement of the marginal urban workers who are forced to join the ranks of the unemployables, the *Lumpenproletariat* of the cities.[9] By their employment alone the migrants contribute to polarization in the urban sector and to the marginalization of previously employed workers. By their departure from the rural sector they transfer out of agriculture a valuable portion of its human capital investment and further contribute to its marginalization.

Technological Change, Capital Accumulation and Biformity

Technological change, especially the variety imported by LDCs from DCs, has been increasingly characterized by the following features: (1) the increasing importance of economies of scale, (2) the increasing degree to which capital is used relative to labour at given factor prices, and (3) the decreasing flexibility in production processes, especially the increased difficulty of substituting plentiful factors of production (labour) for scarce ones (capital).[10] The primary importance attached to scale in the choice of technology,[11] coupled with the often limited size of the domestic market, forces the LDCs that have no easy access to large foreign markets to operate domestic production in small, high cost modern units, or in large but underutilized ones. In the latter case the importation of modern technology preempts the markets of the indigenous firms that operate with intermediate scale and technology, allowing only the crafts sector to survive on account of an increasing gap in wage rates vis-à-vis the modern firms.[12]

The importation of technological change often results in narrowing the so-called technological shelf. Instead of being smooth and continuous as assumed in neoclassical production theory, the technological shelf is getting more scalloped and eventually it reduces to two alternative techniques: the modern technique utilized by the cream of the world's firms, and the traditional technique practised by the increasingly marginal crafts sector. Sutcliffe[13] has demonstrated that, even as early as the 1950s, the variation in factor proportions actually practised in DCs and LDCs alike in manufacturing (exclusive of crafts) was remarkably low in most industries and especially in those industries that might be thought attractive to LDCs, such as food processing, beverages, metal products, basic metals, furniture and fixtures, paper, printing and publishing, non-metallic minerals, miscellaneous manufacturing and all kinds of machinery. The range has undoubtedly continued to shrink in recent years. Moreover, the operation of the market has biased the direction of technological change toward market-oriented commercial ventures and has increased technological dualism, making it ever more difficult for LDCs to succeed in indigenous technological change and industrialization. When the technological gap was smaller and the technological shelf more continuous, as for example in mid-19th century France, the start-up costs of adapting modern technology apparently represented no more than 6–8 months of wages of the average worker. Now, with a greater technological gap and a more discontinuous shelf of choices, the start-up costs for the transfer of modern technology have been estimated to average some 30yr of wages of the average worker.[14]

The experience of comparative latecomers to the ranks of DCs, like Japan and Russia, may indeed be instructive in this regard. By the latter third of the 19th century the technological gap had already become quite large, and it is significant that these countries succeeded in closing the gap while only gradually emerging from the protective cloak of isolation. Historical studies of both countries have shown that indigenously developed capital goods industries played an important role in their technological and economic development. In contrast, and at the same time, indigenous attempts at industrialization and technological development were being snuffed out in many LDCs via enforced colonial dependence in the guise of free trade.[15]

In contemporary LDCs, and in contrast to these historical success stories, technological change operating with the benefit of trade and exchange mechanisms has succeeded primarily in inducing further polarization and marginalization. The increasing capital and decreasing labour requirements of modern technology have merely accentuated the scarcity of capital and abundance of labour in the traditional sector. While the cream of the firms at the top end of the scale has succeeded in absorbing modern technology and in attracting scarce capital, the marginalized producers are increasingly crowded out.

The characteristics of technological change carry over also to the process of capital accumulation and make capital mobility operate so as to increase biformity instead of spreading development.

As the indivisibilities of capital become more important, the dependability of the traditional rate-of-return signalling mechanism declines. Potential investors require not only more capital to start with, but also more know-how and more information about the plans of actual or potential competitors, about future technology, etc., because such factors are of critical importance in determining the present value of their investments. These requirements are, however, selectively available only to the firms that are especially successful, large and experienced, and which are already important in their industry or within the international economy. Such firms are also in a better position to mobilize capital from domestic and foreign financial institutions (or parent firms abroad), to obtain know-how and to reduce risk and uncertainties by their own actions, such as by centralization, government protection and regulation, or by diversifying product lines and their portfolio of assets.

International Trade in Development Disequilibrium

International trade and exchange is probably considered the most effective weapon in the orthodox arsenal of equilibrating development-spreading mechanisms.

The formal foundation for linking trade and development was provided by early Ricardian analysis demonstrating that countries, poor or rich, would have a comparative advantage in at least one commodity and that the benefits from trading it would be divided among trading partners. Even under its original assumptions (labour is the only factor of production and all resources are fully utilized and mobile domestically and perfectly immobile at the international level), there is nothing to guarantee that trade would take place within the terms-of-trade bands that are beneficial to all. In the more realistic Heckscher-Ohlin world of many factors and commodities and of technology identical between countries but different among sectors, the spread of development takes place in the process of factor-price equalization.[16] This occurs as countries export commodities intensive in the factor they are well-endowed with and import commodities intensive in their scarce factor of production, achieving therefore equalization of factor prices through trade even though international factor mobility may be limited.[17] However, the typical LDC, well-endowed in unskilled labour but poorly endowed in capital, would be able to export only those commodities in which its technical efficiency parameter is identical to that of DCs.[18] As our discussion of technological change has suggested, it is no mean feat to eliminate the inter-country technological gap in any given industry, let alone over a range of commodities sufficiently large and important to generate enough trade to eliminate the large factor price differentials between countries. Furthermore, adopting the DC technology implies also the adoption of the DC factor proportions and thus defeats the possibility of absorbing the large amounts of plentiful labour that would be required for equalizing factor prices between countries.

Instead, two other alternatives are more likely under the conditions of international trade that confront contemporary LDCs. As trade-disequilibrium theorists have suggested,[19] in a capitalistic world of unequal initial factor endowments, the capital of the well-endowed country may buy out the comparatively advantaged industry in the poorly endowed country. The increase in efficiency in that case coincides with foreign control and under those circumstances trade will not necessarily benefit the less developed partner and development is confined to the foreign enclave.[20]

The other alternative is that some internationally traded factors of production come in a package controlled by international firms with global operations (MNCs). The investment package available to LDCs also includes technology, enterprise, management and marketing, besides the traditional component of savings. The transfer of savings and technology can result in improvement in the balance of payments and can induce the spreading and equilibrating effects of international trade. The control of the inelastic factors of enterprise, management and marketing, on the other hand, may secure for the MNCs and their affiliates important monopoly rents on a global scale which, in the context of oligopolistic and oligopsonistic output markets cannot be competed away and passed on to consumers. It is this advantage from participation in international marketing, and their ability to maximize profits on a global, rather than national, scale, that make MNCs and their local affiliates competitive rather than complementary with local factors of production, thereby impeding the growth of local concerns, and eventually making them wither.[21]

Money, Finance and Institutional Changes

It is common for neoclassical analysis to treat the financial mechanism in a most truncated fashion. The fundamental proposition of the quantity theory of money is that money is neutral, in the sense that relative prices, output and incomes do not depend on the quantity of money. At the micro level this implies that prices are exogenously given and independent of the individual's initial endowments of wealth and power. The validity of the classical dichotomy was, of course, successfully challenged on both theoretical and empirical grounds,[22] but seemingly to no avail as far as the orthodox paradigm of economic development is concerned. We suggest two additional reasons why orthodoxy is wrong, especially in the LDC context.

First, the prices that count are seldom known, generally only expected. As a result, in LDC economies typified by production processes with relatively long gestation lags, decisions based on money prices will be correct only if expectations are correct, i.e., if all prices are correctly foreseen. Unanticipated price changes imply sub-optimal decisions on the part of individual decision-makers. If errors in price expectations were only random, their effect on decision would be of little consequence for long-run development. The problem is, however, that such errors are typically not random; they are inherently systematic and have the effect of biasing decisions and the distribution of real income in the direction of greater inequality. The larger and more regular participants in the market are at a distinct advantage in anticipating prices as compared to the smaller and less frequent participants. This is just one form of market activity of the producer or consumer and the 'on-the-job-training' that he receives through such participation.

Moreover, even aside from errors in expectations, actual prices and costs are systematically distorted in favour of the wealthy. On the production side, and irrespective of whether there exist *physical* economies of scale, the small producer is likely to be hampered by *financial* diseconomies because of small scale. We may take agriculture as an example. The small farmer suffers from being able to purchase only small quantities of inputs and to sell only small quantities of output at a time. Indeed, the cost of collecting milk when each farmer has but one cow is prohibitive as is that of distributing fertilizers, seed and other modern inputs to the small farmer.[23] With little security to offer for loans and thereby unable to obtain credit on reasonable terms, the small farmer is undercapitalized in storage capacity and has to sell his produce at harvest time when prices are low. These are conventional costs of market operation that are reflected in market prices and which must be borne by the small farmer.[24]

Similar financial disadvantages of small size exist also on the consumption side, where the market institutions become biased against the marginal and the poorer of the market participants. It appears that economic development is accompanied by a standardization of tastes making possible the expansion of the market to the benefit of consumers. This is true, however, only for the consumers who have already achieved a minimum level of initial endowments. The effect on the poor, on the other hand, can well be detrimental because the way of life they must pursue in order to subsist is made more expensive by the way of life of the rich. Mass merchandizing, for example, conveys its benefits disproportionately on those who can afford to use it – the consumers who have an automobile for transportation to the shopping centres, the ones who have refrigerators and storage space, and who can afford to buy in quantity. For the marginal individuals whose alternative sources of supply are crowded out, the hidden costs of transport, finance, pilferage and spoilage may far exceed the benefits of the lower prices that mass merchandizing provides.

When prices are either incorrectly foreseen or systematically biased in one direction or another, effective demands instead of notional demands are relevant. The systematic distortion of market prices against the poor and in favour of the rich – or in favour of those who have power and exercise control, as a Marxist would have added – can only be ignored if the poor refuse to participate in the market. To a certain extent this happens since the poor are the real experts in being poor and have devised means and institutions (e.g., the "paracommercial" market of the informal sector) to bypass the market. To the extent the poor are co-opted or forced into the market, the disequilibrium and inequality-increasing effects of the market bias cannot be ignored. Co-opting may take place when individuals, anticipating only intended expenditure, are misled into believing that the observed price and quality are those applicable also to their own case, irrespective of their scale of transactions. Participation in the market may be forced when individuals find themselves locked into indebtedness or long-term contracts, or when the reinforcement mechanism of development-associated taste-changes has foreclosed non-market alternatives by making the production and consumption shelf more discontinuous.

The important point is that no matter how individuals first get into the market, it is most likely difficult to pull out of it. The institution of the market sucks people into it and on a sustained basis imposes biases favourable to the experienced and the rich and unfavourable to the inexperienced and the poor. Even though a production and consumption system may be neutral to scale, the market exchange system built on it is seldom scale-neutral. Most often it is systematically biased to incorporate the threat of economic cannibalism – in which the strong consume the weak.

Moreover, the fact that the market is ruled by money acts to the disadvantage of rural people and more generally the poor in additional ways. The money used by the rural and urban poor is, of course, the same money used by the urban rich. But its relative availability is controlled by urban elites, naturally with their own interests primarily in mind. What is optimal monetary policy for the urban rich, who have numerous alternative assets for storing wealth and whose capital and services may be financed by the inflation tax arising from expansionary policy, is by no means necessarily optimal also for the rural poor, who with relatively few forms of assets other than money are forced to pay the inflation tax on their monetary holdings. The existence of market dualism, in fact, virtually guarantees the distinct sub-optimality as far as the rural and the poor are concerned of the uniform currency area of the nation-state. For example, while counter-cyclical monetary policy can be advisable for urban producers with short gestation lags and relatively long-term labour contracts as in developed countries, such policies can be entirely inappropriate for rural activities dominated by long gestation lags in production and short-term labour contracts.

Another feature of markets based on money (to which Keynes alerted us but which has been lost in the orthodox literature of development economics) is their instability. One aspect of instability is, of course, that of dynamic equilibrium positions. As Harrod and Nikaido have alerted us,[25] as soon as a market economy drops off the knife edge of its equilibrium growth patch, it inevitably moves further and further away from equilibrium, no matter how flexible the relative factor prices are. At a more micro level, participation in the market is like a roller coaster ride which the small and poor are particularly ill-equipped to handle. For large producers adequately cushioned against unexpected adversities, income instability is a bonus wherein one has the incentive to save and invest.[26] Without the benefits of such cushions, in good times the poor are unable to think ahead to savings and investment, and in bad times they are forced to cut consumption levels temporarily below subsistence levels (with predictable adverse effects on future health and productivity).

Orthodox development theory advocates freeing the individual from the incentive-inhibiting shackles of the extended family.[27] We suggest, on the contrary, that the market-induced break-up of the extended family and of the traditional organization of economic activities around it, amounts in fact to the disintegration of an institution which otherwise can play a unique role in bring about efficiency and development with a minimum of inequality. The extended family is an institution that provides for complementarity, specialization, conservation and credit without dependence on money, and thus obviates the biases and distortions to which the market gives rise. At the same time, its intimacy facilitates technical or X-efficiency by instilling a maximum of cooperation, and by minimizing the amount of energy and time that needs to be spent on monitoring individual inputs and outputs. The fact that the extended family spans generations insures that it induces an appropriate degree of conservation and environmental protection, and it increases investment and therefore dynamic efficiency. The extended family is the epitome of a successful team, with team productivity (or utility) being something considerably greater than the sum of individual marginal productivities (or utilities). Modern sector teams can eventually be put together, but the time that typically transpires between the break-up of the extended family and the creation of effective, cohesive modern-sector teams is simply too long. In the meantime, individual members of the family are left disoriented, divorced, alientated—easy prey to the forces of marginalization and inequality mentioned above.

We do not mean to imply that everything about the break-up of traditional institutions and the shoring up of the market is bad and that everything that preserves the status quo is good. Indeed, the creation of effective markets is an important part of the development process. However, since the force of suction and the processes of creaming, on the one hand, and marginalization, on the other, are also inherent in the market's development, we suggest that it is important not to lose sight of the advantages of traditional institutions in maintaining order and balance amid the otherwise increasing disorder of the universe.

Policy Implications of the Alternative Paradigms

The point which this paper has tried to convey is that the process of development in market-oriented LDCs is not necessarily dominated by automatic, equilibrating, and development-spreading effects, as the traditional orthodox paradigm implies. Although they are sometimes subtle and elusive, in our opinion the disequilibrating, biformity-creating processes of marginalization and polarity can be important and thereby can help explain a basic characteristic of recent development experience, of growth with ever greater inequality. We do not, however, wish to imply that the various mechanisms and effects we have ascribed to the disequilibrium paradigm bear exclusive responsibility for growth with inequality. Nor do we wish to deny the role that inappropriate policies, market imperfections, and other exogenous factors have played in this experience.

We would suggest, however, three things. First, in view of the pervasiveness and multiplicity of market imperfections in individual LDCs, we deem it appropriate to call attention to a corollary of the second-best principle which states that removal of one or more of these imperfections may not improve welfare as long as other such imperfections and distortions remain. Only an unrealistically successful frontal attack on all distortions and market imperfections simultaneously can raise welfare and remove the sources of the disequilibrating impulses and systematic biases we have referred to above. Second, if such imperfections could be removed, the costs of doing so is often prohibitive. Third, in view of the generality of this experience across countries of widely differing policy mixes and even socioeconomic systems, we suggest that disequilibrating mechanisms, such as those we have underscored, may constitute a more fundamental explanation of the recent experience and therefore deserve more detailed empirical investigation than alternative explanations.

Should our view of the important role of disequilibrating mechanisms in the development process be correct, what policy implications would follow and how would these differ from those derived from the orthodox approach to development economics? Let us emphasize that the difference in policy implications between the two paradigms lies not in the presence or absence of intervention per se, but rather in the scope and nature of such intervention. In general, while the orthodox paradigm condones intervention as an attempt to correct for market imperfections in order to allow market forces to operate more freely, the disequilibrium paradigm advocates intervention in order to offset the systematic biases attributable to the operation of the market in the early stages of development.

A few examples of contrasting policy recommendations may help to clarify the differences. In keeping with our emphasis on capital market imperfections, let us begin with policies aiming at offsetting such imperfections. The orthodox advice is to bolster the ability of financial institutions to deliver financial services to small, traditional, but hard-to-reach potential clients. Recommendations for subsidized credit schemes, and the creation of more banks in rural areas may also be part of the orthodox line. From the disequilibrium perspective we would suggest that the costs of reaching such peripheral individuals are likely to be very great, and that even when such investments are made, it is again likely to be the large and experienced participants in the market-cum-credit-and-money game who gain the most.

Another imperfection we have dwelled upon concerns information. With fluctuations in prices of inputs and outputs and very imperfect information about their future trajectories, orthodox policy recommendations often include information systems, price supports, stabilization schemes or credit-cum-insurance programmes. However, since they benefit market participants in proportion to their initial participation in the market, such schemes favour early and larger participants in the market game at the expense of small latecomers.

What are the alternatives to orthodox policies? In our opinion, several complementary policy actions may be undertaken. First, the viability of subsistence (non-market) activities, and of the beneficial aspects of traditional institutions, such as the extended family, needs to be assured. This can be done, among other ways, by bringing to the non-commercial sectors social security systems, and modes of self-reliance and by removing artificial incentives for their participation in the market. Second, activities can be undertaken to strengthen the availability, effectiveness and competitiveness of "seed loans" repayable in kind and other forms of non-monetary credit to provide alternative paths to accumulation, technological change and technical and allocative efficiency than through market dependence. Third, crop and other types of insurance schemes should be modified so as to protect the traditional sector against the risks of bad weather, bad advice, etc., with respect to family labour inputs instead of for out-of-pocket costs of market labour only or more typically of capital and other purchased inputs. Fourth, and perhaps only as a last resort, the market links between the traditional and modern sectors should be deliberately sabotaged, at least until such time as the small, marginal individuals and firms are in a better position to participate more effectively and on more equal terms in the market game.

Lest this sound like total folly, let us suggest that the broken market links can be replaced by internal links, thereby creating the halfway house of *para*commercial activities within which comparative advantage, specialization of labour and labour-intensive, small scale, intermediate technologies can flourish, yet without the inequality-exaggerating bias, dynamic instability and price illusion of the market. Products, information and services can be exchanged within the paracommercial sector through a system of local fairs. At higher levels of aggregation exchange between communities and countries at similar levels of development can be encouraged as in the formation of customs unions among LDCs at similar levels of development.

This damming up of the economy must be viewed only as a holding action for providing the necessary time and resources to tackle the most immediate problems of poverty and destitution. It is inspired by the principle that, when threatened, societies (not unlike the amoeba) fragment into small groups in order to survive. Small size, with no important life-lines to the rest of the world, can better serve in absorbing the shocks of social derailments. As development takes hold, however, and employment increases in the spectrum between the paracommercial and the commercial sector – in the traditional agricultural and industrial sectors, in the public sector, and finally in the modern agricultural and industrial sector – the lifelines among the various sectors can be restored. Factor movements, such as the exodus from the paracommercial small farms into commercial activities, can then again be encouraged. The purpose of damming up the economy is to develop the local turf, instead of prematurely transferring the benefits of development to the advanced sectors. The paracommercial sector can be seen as a hothouse that nurtures the new seedlings until they are ready to be transferred into the shark-tank competition of commercial activities – and to survive.

11

Peasant Perceptions: Famine

IZZEDIN I. IMAM

Famine is never far from the consciousness of the vast majority of the population of Bangladesh—especially that half of the rural population that has no resource other than the labor it can sell. Every few years, famine comes sweeping across the landscape, leaving a trail of destruction and dislocation in its wake. In the interim, precarious survival strategies are mapped out, meager resources are garnered, and dependency relationships are created to form a community web providing some security in meeting basic needs. Then famine strikes again, carving its way through all the savings and potentialities that have been painstakingly created.

Government and nongovernment agencies are, of course, aware of the plight of the poor and are seeking solutions. Besides relief and aid programs various ways are constantly sought to increase the ability of the population to withstand the years of poor crops with minimum harm. Yet very little attention has been given to finding out how those people who bear the full brunt of the attack—the landless and near-landless peasantry—respond to and seek to protect themselves from the ravages of famine. Even less attempt has been made to obtain their reactions to the relief activities to which they are subjected.

The Bangladesh Rural Advancement Committee (BRAC) recently conducted a research study intended to fill in some of these gaps. The information was collected during four group discussion sessions involving some fifteen landless village leaders held over a period of two days at BRAC's Training and Resource Center in Savar. Most participants were from the northern areas of Bangladesh particularly prone to famine, such as Rowmari in Rangour District, Sherpur in Melanda District, and Jhinaigati in Jamalpur District. An agenda, in the form of a checklist prepared in advance by the researchers, outlined key issues and questions to ensure that all the areas of interest would be covered during the four sessions without limiting the scope of discussion. The discussions were kept informal and open-ended

Excerpted form Izzedin I. Imam, *Peasant Perceptions: Famine* (Dacca, Bangladesh: Bangladesh Rural Advancement Committee, July 1979).

to allow the landless to speak for themselves. The researchers facilitated the discussion and recorded the points made. This report is based on the notes from these discussions. Because there are other authoritative accounts available of the physical damage which results from malnutrition and starvation, our report concentrates on how socioeconomic structures and networks of relationships are maintained, intensified, or dismantled during times of famine.

Conditions and Causes

Initial comments of the participants reflected a resignation to famine as a simple consequence of natural events such as a delay in the arrival of the rains or excessive floods, a fate preordained for them and beyond their control. It would be easy to come away after a brief, superficial hearing thinking that the landless of Bangladesh can comprehend famine only as blind misfortune, unchangeable and beyond human interference.

However, as one gently probes for more incisive answers and establishes a more open dialogue, one comes to be impressed by their thorough and sophisticated understanding of one of the most important determinants of the *consequences* of famine – one that commonly escapes the notice of conscientious researchers. This is the important human element that determines the severity of suffering experienced. It is on this dimension of the problem that the participants can shed unique light as they begin to reveal how the structure of relationships in the village community prevents the hardships of famine from being borne equitably by all its members. These relationships allow those who occupy positions of influence and wealth further to widen the gap between themselves and those in a dependent situation. For example, the participants reported that once a natural calamity triggers expectation of a food shortage, the large landowners begin to divert food supplies into storage and wait for the prices to rise – thus turning adversity into their opportunity.

But the landless have no such option. Furthermore, the drop in production also reduces the demand for their labor – the only resource they possess. Wage rates fall and the wage laborers find themselves at the mercy of those who can offer work or who have cash to offer in return for their few possessions.

The worst reports were related by participants from Rowmawi, Rangpur, and the various subdivisions of Jamalpur. Their daily wage rates as of the time of our study, July 1979, were reported to be between Tk. 1.00 and Tk. 2.00 plus provision of one or two meals.[1] Some employers also provided the laborer a small quantity of uncooked rice to take home in the evening. For example, one participant reported that he was served *panta* (cooked rice soaked in water) for breakfast, wheat *khichuri* (a mixture of wheat and pulses cooked together) for lunch, and was given a half seer of *kaun* to take home at the end of the day. He explained that had he been served an evening meal by the employer he probably would have consumed more than half a seer.² In addition to the meals and food he was paid a wage of Tk. 1.00 with which to feed his family. The price of rice in his area was Tk. 6.00 per seer that month.

In such a situation, often the only recourse is to start selling off the only possessions the household may have. Generally, the landless pawn their goods to money lenders, a term generally applied to anyone with surplus assets, such as the landowners. The hope is always that one day the loan will be repaid and the object recovered. But this virtually never happens. The interest charged on the loan is usually so crippling that the debtor has next to no chance of being able to repay the principal in the time allotted and the object passes into the possession of the money lender.

The sum lent is usually one-half to one-third the actual value of the object pawned and interest may run as high as 300 percent per year. Even so the borrower is usually made to feel obligated and from then on is expected to assume a subservient position vis-a-vis the lender. One participant from Rowmari told of an elder cousin who had pawned a set of earrings to his richer relative. Eventually he repaid the total sum of Tk. 350.00 due. Still, as a person under obligation, he felt that to ask his cousin to return the earrings would violate the social norms governing such a relationship. Moreover, he lived in dread of the day he might have to ask his relative for another loan and did not want to jeopardize his future chances.

Pawning usually begins with those items which are expendable, such as ornaments or jewelry. Eventually as the desperate need for cash to buy food increases, every household item, including utensils, may be pawned or sold at any available price.

Landlords were reported to keep an eye open for opportunities to increase their holdings and eagerly to seize any opportunity to push those with a very small amount of land to sell it at deflated prices. Famines offer such opportunity, since the marginal landholders are often as desperate in their need for cash as are the totally landless. Moreover, they are reluctant to show any resistance to those on whom they depend for employment. The larger landowners thus find themselves in a position to name any price they wish and if the crisis is sufficiently deep may acquire lands at prices less than half their normal value. As with household items, the land is usually mortgaged rather than sold outright. But rarely does it come back to its original owner. The exact terms differ with the individual case. In one transaction occurring in early 1979 reported by participants from Burichong, Comilla, a man had to mortgage a small piece of land valued at Tk. 500 for only Tk. 150. He had soon spent this amount on food and returned to the landlord to borrow more. He was told he would get another installment only if he gave up all rights to the land. Later when he was again in need of money he had to take up employment for this same landlord at a daily wage of Tk. 3.00, in an area where the daily wage in normal times had been Tk. 10.00. The landlord reportedly claimed that times being difficult, he could not afford to pay a higher wage. He was, however, known to be stockpiling paddy in anticipation of a rise in price.

People may attempt to supplement their incomes by a variety of means, such as selling fruit trees or bamboo plants or collecting firewood to sell. In Rowmari, those who have the skills earn some income by weaving. As a last resort the household head may leave his family and set off to an uncertain destination in hope of finding employment. Cases were reported of people migrating from Jessore to India, where they might receive a daily wage of Tk. 5.00. Some from Comilla migrate to Sylhet in hope of becoming fishermen. Some of those who migrate return periodically to give any earnings to their families. But anxieties over whether those who migrate will return grow with time, as commonly they do not. The wives left behind may take up employment doing chores in the richer households, living off the leftovers of the rich family's meals. One woman in Rowmari who could no longer stand the cries of her hungry children hung herself—leaving them behind with no one to care for them. A case was reported from Melanda, Jamalpur, of a woman who was said to have sold her four children and turned to begging.

Participants repeatedly talked of losing a sense of direction and any idea of where to turn next. Said one participant from Sherpur, Jamalpur, "The boat was floating. Now it has sunk. We see an unending sea all around." In desperation some turn to crime. A cobbler in Melanda, Jamalpur, unable to find any more hides in the market, began systematically poisoning the cows in his area with the help of two collaborators.

This feeling of utter helplessness was reiterated again and again, as was the hostility toward those who aggravated already harsh conditions by stockpiling paddy, colluding to acquire land at low prices, and exploiting the labor of the landless at the lowest possible wages.

Effects on Social Relations

As desperation deepens, the very fabric of the community begins to come apart. Some of the most important institutions in the society, such as marriage, the joint family, and sibling solidarity, come to be seen as burdens; and the network of cooperation that in normal times ensures sharing and security becomes increasingly unreliable.

Marriage, in normal times, is perceived as an opportunity to extend one's network of relations. However, we were told the story of a landed man in Rowmari whose two daughters both married grooms who came in to live with their father-in-law and to rely on his support. Rather than extending his network, the two grooms became an enormous burden on him and he did not know what to do with them.

In another case, we could observe the last remnants of village efforts to rescue an unfortunate neighbor. A man from Melanda, Jamalpur, was driven to such desperation after four days without eating that he decided to sell his child. The community intervened and supported them through contributions until things improved. But things did not improve and the father slipped back into a state of hopelessness. By this time conditions had become so unstable that the participant who related the story did not expect the community would be willing to expend its resources to prevent the dissolution of the family.

One participant from Melanda expressed great unwillingness to accept his sister into the household that he shares with his brother, a sentiment that would have been virtually unthinkable in normal times.

The relationship of the son-in-law to his wife's father was traditionally marked with a great deal of deference, cordiality, and mutual respect. A son-in-law who charged his father-in-law with being unable to provide sufficient comforts would have been subject to strong sanctions. Yet we were told of an incident in Melanda where a son-in-law began to complain bitterly and threaten divorce because his father-in-law could not afford to entertain him in comfort or to provide sarees for his daughter.

Quarrels over ownership of property become acute, even among siblings. One participant's sister sold a fruit tree that belonged to him after they had quarreled. The man in question, being too weak to prevent the new owner from claiming the fruit, neatly side-stepped the issue by selling the tree to a third man. The two rival owners are now fighting with each other to gain possession of the tree.

Looking forward, the participants all predicted increasing hardship. They foresaw food supplies becoming even smaller. Migrations were expected to continue, with more families being abandoned and community cooperation continuing to decline. Anxiety would continue over the health of children and their survival would become increasingly unlikely. Deaths and suicides would continue to multiply as social bonds loosened and obligations between kin were increasingly ignored. The very links that bind society together were seen to be endangered.

Reactions to Relief Programs

An important concern of our inquiry into famine was to determine how famine relief efforts are perceived by those who are most affected. Famine relief and Food For Work (FFW) programs are always conceived and designed in the central offices of the agencies concerned, isolated from the views of those who will receive the assistance. Do the famine victims feel that these programs make much difference to their plight? We raised this question and found some of the answers fairly startling.

The very first reaction was one of complete dissatisfaction with the relief and FFW programs. Although we were a little apprehensive about what sort of significance we could attach to any answers that were being given to BRAC, a potential relief-giving agency, we were genuinely impressed by the persuasiveness of some of their arguments. There was a general consensus that FFW was always preferable to relief. The initial consideration seemed to be an ethical one: it is ethically more acceptable to be given some relief in exchange for work rather than to be given relief as charity. There seemed to be a sense of pride attached to the view that they did not like simply to be given what they needed, and there was a corresponding sense of there being something demeaning about accepting relief without any return.

Underlying this, however, seemed to be an even deeper reluctance of participants to find themselves under any obligation. FFW allowed them to *claim* their food. Having put in labor, they feel that they have a right to what they get and do not have to feel that they are waiting at the mercy of others.

Gradually the significance of this concern became clear. Relief operations always seem to arrive through the intermediary of the local elite. From this realization it is a very small step to the conclusion that relief operations are themselves a subtle instrument of exploitation. In fact, all the participants' statements on relief operations revealed a strong belief that large amounts are being corruptly siphoned by influential local people, such as the chairmen and members of the Union Councils.

A participant from Sherpur claimed that FFW wheat was used by the landlords to feed laborers whom they hired for their own work. Another claimed that in Melanda, out of Tk. 1,500–worth of wheat, a large amount was sold and the rest was used to pay laborers at a lower rate than was intended by the original contributor. In another instance, when the chairman was called in to investigate a charge that the laborers were being underpaid, he was reportedly bribed to ignore the charge. Other allegations against the local organizers include padding the list of people needing relief so that the organizers can get more relief goods than really needed from the central distributing authority and then skim off the excess for themselves. The landless feel powerless in front of the local leaders on whom they depend in very many ways. One participant from Dhamrai, Dacca, said, "We have no power to talk in front of the rich, like the Chairman. We are afraid of them. We are always looked down upon and scolded. So we never know what they are writing and doing."

One of the chief complaints of the landless is the complete lack of opportunity for them to participate at any stage in the oganization of relief programs. They have no way of knowing if, and to what extent, they are being cheated. They often suggested that the relief should be handed over directly to the poorest levels of the community, which would take charge of their own distribution. In his way the "whole thing would be done in the open, and no one would be able to cheat. The poor would never think to cheat other poor people – only the rich do that." They also believe that this is the only way that they would be able to ascertain whether enough food was being allocated to their community. (Opinions varied as to how much of the actual allocations was being misappropriated – ranging from one-eighth to one-half of the total allocation.)

There was also mistrust as to the purity of the foods that were being distributed – they claimed that the flour they were given was often adulterated with sawdust or chaff. For this reason they preferred to receive wheat rather than flour because it could not be adulterated.

As the participants reflected on their shared experiences, they developed an increasingly well-reasoned analysis of their situation, arriving at a number of shared conclusions. First, they concluded that if help were to be forthcoming they did not want welfare handouts. They wanted inputs to self-help income-generating activities that would allow them to buy their own food. Specific mention was made of loans, technical assistance, training, and logistical support. Second, they concluded that unity was the key to breaking the deadlock in which they were caught. Only through collective action, they asserted repeatedly, could they make their influence felt and be able to take control of their situation. They indicated that this emphasis on collective action should extend into economic and income-generating activities. The basis of this preference was quite pragmatic, as only through working together could they achieve economies of scale based on division of labor.

The participants in this study demand more information, and more consultation. They hope eventually to break out of the vicious cycle of poverty by somehow setting themselves up in a trade or profession where they could earn sufficient incomes through their own efforts. They want aid in a form that will provide them an opportunity to break their dependence on the goodwill of people whose interests are basically opposed to their own.

We should point out in closing that the objective of this study was not to verify the truth or objectivity of the participants' comments. There can be little doubt that it we had interviewed the landlords rather than the landless a totally different picture of the situation would have been presented. The study does only what its was intended to do – to present a picture of the views and opinions held by those people who suffer with full force the ravages of famine.

12

The Seasons of Poverty

ROBERT CHAMBERS, RICHARD LONGHURST,
DAVID BRADLEY, AND RICHARD FEACHEM

This paper examines seasonal factors which are adverse for rural people, especially in tropical countries. Its main hypotheses can be presented by a scenario.[1] While this is a generalized scenario drawn as a composite from many settings, it illustrates relationships between variables that many settings seem to share. In particular, there is a widespread tendency for adverse factors to operate concurrently during the wet seasons and for these to hit the poor segments of the population harder than the more well-to-do. Typically the scenario develops as follows.

Toward the end of the dry season, water becomes scarce. There is a rise in the labor and energy required to fetch water and to water livestock, and also to gather food and to clear and manure fields. The poorer people begin to suffer more than others. They have less food because they have been able to grow less, because they have fewer livestock, because they may lose a higher proportion of their food reserves in storage, and because they have less money. They may eat less in order to save food for the crucial time of cultivation. Work is scarce and wages are low at this time of year. Some migrate in search of work and food.

The rains bring the start of crisis and of the "hungry season" or "lean period." For cultivators, future food supplies and cash income depend upon timely agricultural operations during an often brief period for land preparation. Poorer farmers are often constrained by lack of inputs—whether seeds, fertilizers, water or draft power. They may have to obtain these from richer farmers or merchants with whom they are forced into dependent and exploitative relationships, and they may obtain them late or not at all. For those with land, heavy and urgent energy demands have to be met.

Excerpted from Robert Chambers, Richard Longhurst, David Bradley, and Richard Feacham, "Seasonal Dimensions to Rural Poverty: Analysis and Practical Implications" (Discussion paper 142, presented at the Institute of Development Studies at the University of Sussex, Brighton, England, February 1979).

If draft animals are used, they are weak from lack of grazing during the dry season. For both small farmers and laborers, heavy manual labor for land preparation (often by men), for transplanting (often by women), and for weeding (often by women) comes at this time when food is short. Laborers benefit from being able to get work, but many are in negative energy balance and lose weight. At the same time, food prices are high and transport problems in the rains make it difficult for either central authorities or the open market to relieve local shortages. Anticipating hard work, mothers give their children only a diminished and less regular food supply with their milk. Food preparation becomes more hurried and the diet less varied and nutritious. Less time is spent on cooking, housecleaning, water collection, fuel gathering and childcare, and more of the women's time is spent on agricultural operations.

Diseases vary in their seasonality, but some of the more serious and debilitating peak during or just after the rains. These usually include malaria and sometimes diarrheal diseases, especially where the wet season is also the hot season. Guinea worm also peaks at this time, as do infections of the skin. The development of protein-energy malnutrition contributes to low immune response. Coinciding with a peak labor demand, when failure to cultivate, transplant, weed, or harvest may critically affect future income and food supplies, infections increase the risks and vulnerability of rural people. This is when the poorer people must work in order to earn enough to tide them over until the next agricultural season. This is also a bad time for mothers and children. Births peak, but body weights of mothers and of babies at birth are both low, and neonatal mortality also peaks. The calorific value of the milk supply of lactating mothers is low. Pregnant and lactating women are weakened by disease and work. Those in the poorer, smaller families are especially vulnerable because of the need to work when work is available.

This is a time of year when many dependent and exploitative relationships begin or are reinforced and deepened. It is when the poorer people are driven to sell or mortgage land, livestock, jewelry, their future crop, or their future labor; they beg from patrons; they become indebted to money lenders. The poor are subordinated to the less poor, the weak to the strong, the women to the men, the children to the adult, the aged to the young.

At harvest time wages are high, but the work is also hard—both the harvesting proper and the post-harvest processing. Furthermore, morbidity is still marked and weakness lingers from the food shortages and sicknesses of the lean season. Weight loss is now at its greatest. Mortality, especially among older adults, peaks in response to the high energy demands and the weakened physical condition. Food prices are low, which may be good for some of the landless, but generally is bad for tenants, sharecroppers, and small cultivators who have to sell their harvest to raise cash to repay loans taken earlier at high interest rates, and for the ceremonies that are soon to follow.

After harvest, things improve for a time. Food is available, and food intake recovers in both quantity and quality. Body weights rise. Morbidity and mortality decline. There are ceremonies, celebrations, marriages. There is a peak in rates of conception. And then gradually the cycle begins all over again.

In appraising this scenario, several factors combine to prevent nonrural dwellers from realizing how severe the adverse conditions in the wet season may be for the poorer rural people. Rural poverty tends to be underperceived anyway, especially as it affects women and children. But in addition, the wet season is neglected because of problems of travel and tarmac bias; because agricultural activities in the wet season are more likely to be observed than what goes on in villages and inside dwellings where the sick and the undernourished are more likely to be found; and because of difficulties in wet season research. The incidence of diseases in the wet season is also liable to be underestimated, since a low proportion of those affected may attend clinics and hospitals (where records are kept), because of difficulties in travel, seasonal shortages of money, weakness, and the priority of agricultural work.

Practical Implications

Seasonal analysis has practical implications. The most central, affecting most or all rural development programs and initiatives, is the importance of seasonality for the choice, design, and timing of activities. Contrary to much past practice, rural planning should have seasonal analysis of poverty as one of its central concerns, and priorities should be related to what happens at the worst times of the year.

The benefits from this approach may be high where the poorer rural people are able to sustain an adequate livelihood for part, or even most, of the year, but are unable to support themselves during a lean period. If a government objective is the provision of basic needs and adequate livelihoods to all citizens, then a focus on the lean period may often have higher returns in terms of livelihoods created—helping many people over the threshold—than attempts to create fewer entirely new livelihoods around the year. An alternative to this approach is to raise food and income floors during favorable times and improve savings and storage in order to enable the poorer rural people to tide over the lean period. Some sector-specific suggestions follow.

Health

Plan public health action to give priority to diseases which coincide with critical periods of the year. While there is much local variation, these may include malaria, the diarrheas, guinea worm, and skin infections, all of which tend to peak during the rains and the time of food shortages and high agricultural activity.

Ensure adequate health services during critical periods through (1) issuing drugs to rural clinics to fit the seasonality of morbidity and of agricultural work; (2) regulating staff leave so that rural staff are at their posts during the critical times of the year and on leave at the least critical; and (3) improving the mobility of staff at certain times of the year.

Concentrate health services in areas where poorer people are numerous and seasonal morbidity coincides with and limits agricultural activities.

Plan health education to fit the pattern of the seasons.

THE FAMILY

Identify the strategies used by poor people to mitigate seasonal stresses. Avoid programs or actions that weaken those strategies and seek measures to support and strengthen them.

Devise tools and techniques to relieve the drudgery and energy drain during periods of intense crisis for those who are most adversely affected (poorer households, and women in particular), concentrating especially on those domestic activities which are unpaid and where therefore paid labor will not be displaced.

Organize communal childcare at times of high demand for women's labor.

Provide food supplies for vulnerable groups (e.g., pregnant and lactating women) and their families at times of food shortage and stress.

Arrange annual leave and school holidays to enable families to muster their full strengths for the most testing times in agriculture.

AGRICULTURE AND FOOD

Improve short- and long-term weather forecasts and communicate the results.

Take steps to even out agricultural labor demands and food and income flows through (1) developing irrigation and improving water management; and (2) using farming systems analysis and agricultural research to make appropriate improvements in intercropping, serial cropping, minimum tillage, and breeding for drought-avoidance and drought resistance.

Improve food storage, both through crops that store in the soil, such as cassava-manioc, and through methods applicable to other crops, especially in small quantities under village conditions.

Maintain adequate national and regional buffer food stocks.

Where appropriate, decentralize government food stores to have food available in areas prone to seasonal shortages.

Implement purchase and pricing policies that (1) provide a floor price for food crops at which the government will intervene as a buyer; and (2) prevent prices from rising above a ceiling by releasing food stocks on the market.

Operate monitoring systems (e.g., with reporting of local food prices) to give early warning of local food shortages.

Government Planning and Administration

Use off-season public works selectively and carefully, to provide work and income flows consistent with seasonal demands.

Examine the timing of the financial year and mitigate adverse effects (for example, does it end just before the rains, making it difficult to stock rural clinics with drugs and to supply agricultural inputs in time?).

Exploit slack seasons for the mobilization, education, and organization of deprived groups, such as landless laborers.

Examine the seasonal peaks and troughs in demand on the time of government field staff, and adjust programs accordingly.

The seasonal mode of analysis should not divert attention from more basic issues. Many of the adverse effects of seasonality, as they are linked with rural poverty, would often be more sharply reduced by reforms which counter urban bias and redistribute land and water assets. Before such reforms, seasonally oriented programs might enable the poorer rural people to gain more adequate, secure, and continuous flows of food and income and more stable health, and these might help to establish the physical, psychological, and social preconditions for political organization and pressure to achieve those reforms. If, after the reforms, the poorer families had direct control of adequate means of production and received adequate returns for their labor, they might then be less vulnerable to adverse seasonal effects. Seasonally oriented programs would still be needed, but the need would be less acute.

13

Survival, Interdependence, and Competition Among the Philippine Rural Poor

GEORGE CARNER

By any measure, at least 45 percent of all households in the Philippines are poor. That is 3.5 million families. While these households share in common some problems and owe their poverty to the same underlying causes, households differ significantly in how they cope and the degree to which they are afflicted by poverty. Farmers are invariably identified as poor, yet marginal rice and corn farmers on 3 hectares of upland pursue a very different survival strategy with different outcomes than efficient paddy farmers on 1.5 hectares of fully irrigated land. Location clearly contributes to poverty differentials. Farmers in Cagayan Valley are more vulnerable to typhoons and have less access to technology, inputs, and markets than farmers in Nueva Ecija. Poverty has a seasonal dimension. Upland farmers may grow only one crop a year, with very little farm income accruing in the off-season, which may last six months. Compare this to certain farmers who are so busy raising two and even three crops a year on irrigated land, they must hire on laborers to meet the workload. As one group pursues its strategy for economic survival it may affect another group's success in attaining a minimum livelihood. The double crop farmers' demand for labor opens jobs for upland farmers in their off-season. On the other hand, certain forest squatters who clear fragile lands for agriculture may help precipitate soil erosion, floods, and siltation, which undermine productivity among farmers farther down the watershed and even among fishermen, whose catch may ultimately decline. Survival strategies revolve around access to resources and jobs. In the scramble, these poor groups are in competition not only with the wealthy and powerful but with each

Copyright © 1982 by The Regents of the University of California. Reprinted from *Asian Survey* 22, no. 4 (April 1982): 369–84, by premission of The Regents. This paper draws on the extensive research carried out by the USAID mission to the Philippines over a two-year period under the direction of the author and reported in its *Country Development Strategy Statements* for FY 1982 and FY 1983. The views expressed are those of the author.

133

other as well. In the sugar fields of Negros, the seasonally migrant *sacada* workers compete with the permanent *dumaan* workers.

Such diversity suggests that efforts to devise appropriate rural development programs must begin by identifying who these various groups are and what kinds of survival strategies they adopt, keeping in mind their interdependence and recognizing that they may be in direct competition.

Who Are the Poor?

It is no easy task to come up with a precise answer to this question. The normal methodological problems and measurement difficulties are further complicated by the fact that poor households engage in a variety of activities. What is a principal occupation for one group may be a sideline for another. Nevertheless, it is possible to begin to categorize households in a rough yet meaningful manner with reference to their resource base, how they manage it, and the income they derive. Analyzed in this fashion, three broad groups emerge as the most disadvantaged among the poor: landless agricultural workers, upland farmers, and sustenance fishermen.

These groups encompass nearly two-thirds of all poor households found in rural areas of the Philippines. Rural poor are also found among lowland rice farmers, especially in rainfed areas, but the degree of poverty does not appear to be as acute or its incidence as prevalent.

Survival Strategies

The overriding goal of the very low income household is to produce or earn enough to eat. In a real sense malnutrition is a basic indicator of how successful a household's survival strategy is. Access to land for subsistence production partially insulates the household from rising food costs, providing an important form of food security.

If food needs are not being adequately met there are a number of ways households cope. One is for household members to diversify their employment activities. Even the most demeaning jobs are taken, despite low pay. Provision of food makes a job especially attractive. Women may take up basket making, sewing, weaving, and other types of crafts that can be produced at home and in the off-season.

If these activities are still insufficient, they will turn to the village support system. A wealthier relative may provide credit or a little land to grow vegetables. Feasts and holidays offer occasions to supplement the diet. Those who provide food and festivities to their barrio mates increase their own social currency. The village system of kinship ties and reciprocal arrangements provides security. This security, along with strong emotional ties to the community, underscores why income levels alone are not the major determinants of occupation or place of residence. Even in the face of declining income and opportunity, the very poorest persist with the knowledge that one's friends and family will share whatever relative excess they may possess. The value of family and community makes up for some of the shortfalls. This may hamper economic progress, but it helps the poor survive.

Another coping mechanism is simply to do more with less. Basically this means cutting down on food consumption and other essentials.

Ultimately, if the possibilities for surviving in the village decline to the breaking point, the household faces the stark choice of leaving. The decision is probably not abrupt. In practice, a son or a daughter is sent to the city or a husband begins seasonal migration to other areas. In this way the household is able to diversify its income sources beyond the village, while avoiding a break and the accompanying risk of total failure. Remittances from household members who have migrated often permit a family to reestablish a minimum livelihood within the village. On the other hand, if a migrant is successful in establishing a firm footing in the new area, the entire family may join him.

Within this general pattern each of the three groups we have identified pursues a variety of strategies, depending on their specific resources and constraint patterns. Even so, within each group wide diversity is apparent, but again subgroups of households with similar decision calculus and tactics are discernible.

Landless Agricultural Workers

The landless agricultural rural worker can be defined "as one who works in agriculture but possesses neither ownership nor recognized rights to farm the land and who earns 50% or more of his total income from wages or payment in kind."[1] Essentially this definition encompasses farm laborers on rice and corn lands and hired workers on sugar and coconut lands. While statistics on this type of worker vary, it is estimated that *at least* 1,150,000 or 7.5 percent of the total Philippine labor force and 14.3 percent of the total number of persons employed in agriculture fall into this group,[2] accounting for some 500,000 to 700,000 households. At least half of these households work on rice farms, while about one-third work in sugar fields, and the remaining sixth work on coconut lands and other crops.

Household income varies widely between farm laborers and plantation workers. Among farm laborers, those receiving a share of the crop tend to be better off than the wage earners. Among plantation workers, coconut laborers do better than sugar laborers and permanent laborers receive more income than casual workers.[3] Productivity and cropping intensity are also important variables in the landless laborer's earnings. Irrigated paddy production provides much more rice income to the worker receiving a fixed share of each crop. At the other extreme, as sugar lands are taken out of production in response to plummeting international prices, sugar workers are locked out of jobs. Most landless workers derive up to one-fourth of their total income from secondary sources.[4] Duck raising and piggery are the most prevalent supplementary income activities, followed by handicraft manufacturing, vending, fishing, and carpentry. Opportunities for supplementary income appear greater for farm laborers and, to a lesser extent, for coconut workers than for sugar plantation laborers. Thus total household income for landless agricultural workers may be estimated at between 2000 and 3000 pesos for the vast majority. This represents around half the income required for a minimally adequate diet for a family of six.

The landless are not completely without assets. Their possessions are mostly limited to a temporary house, usually on a rent-free plot. Few own their house lot. They may have some livestock, a few farm implements, and perhaps a radio.[5] Ownership of a carabao is an important asset as it increases significantly a laborer's wage rate or crop share. Finally given heavy competition for available employment, the worker's health becomes a tangible asset (or liability).

Survey after survey suggests a high rate of dissaving permitted by regular indebtedness to relatives, friends, employers, and local money lenders. The heterogeneity and powerlessness of landless subgroups precludes their organizing into effective economic groups. Only plantation workers show any inclination to join organizations such as unions. But these tend to be controlled by plantation owners.[6]

The social makeup of the landless further confirms their disadvantaged condition. The majority of household heads, though younger than farmers, still have only between four and six grades of schooling, and a significant number have no schooling. The chances for their children's going beyond the sixth grade are limited by the household's need for the child's earnings and its inability to shoulder the costs of further schooling. Nutrition levels are very low, especially among sugar plantation workers, where three meals a day are not always possible, rice and fish are not eaten daily, and meat is not seen but once or twice a month.[7] Access to basic health and family planning services is infrequent.

Landlessness in the Philippines is a function of population growth, land fragmentation, the spread of large commercial plantations, eviction of tenants by landowners opposed to land reform, and the fixing of land tenure in rice and corn areas.[8] The growing number of landless are in effect precluded from acquiring land and largely depend on family, communal, or plantation ties for employment that is poorly paid and, for the majority, seasonal. Two examples will serve to illustrate this dependence and the deterioration in their terms of employment as competiton increases: the *Sagod* system of labor in lowland rice areas and the *Pakiao* system in the sugarcane plantation of Negros Oriental.

The Sagod system, also known as Gama, is a labor arrangement that has emerged since 1973 whereby landless workers (and small farmers) contract to do weeding for free in exchange for exclusive rights to harvest the weeded portion in return for a share of the harvest. This guarantees the laborer a rice income. High-yielding rice technology has nearly doubled the man-days required in rice cultivation. Weeding has become a major operation, for which small and larger farmers alike hire in. This system provides more stable employment and security for more laborers within the village, to the exclusion of outside competitors. The major drawback is that the laborers must work harder than before and without pay. This represents a decline in real wages and deprives the laborer of income at weeding time, often forcing him to go into debt to carry his family through to harvest. It also has the effect of freezing out landless laborers from outside the village.[9] This is indicative of the trend of small farmers, often former tenants, becoming owner-operators under land reform and then leaving most of the tilling to the growing numbers of landless.[10] At the same time, the owner-operators are beginning to adopt labor-saving techniques that further reduce returns to labor. Now that weeding is not a cost to the farmer, he is able to plant by broadcasting rather than transplanting—for which he formerly had to pay outside laborers. Likewise, the farmer is introducing mechanical threshing at harvest time and deducting the cost of the operator from the laborer's share. At the same time laborers are threshing less but harvesting more plots. This tends to accentuate competition for available work.

The Pakiao system is found in many areas and crops, and governs 80 percent of the work on sugarcane haciendas in Negros. It involves paying a flat rate per hectare for a given operation (e.g., plowing, weeding). The most difficult work is assigned a higher rate, but since it requires more laborers or longer time to complete, it may in fact provide no more pay and sometimes even less pay than a flat daily rate.

The system is a legal way of undercutting the minimum-wage law, to the detriment of the sugar workers.[11] The widespread practice of hiring laborers on a temporary basis is another way of paying lower wages and keeping workers in line. The workers' ignorance and lack of organization and the absence of alternative employment opportunities leave them little recourse for opposing this system.

The seasonality of most employment open to the landless helps explain the patterns of rural-to-rural migration as members of landless households move between rice, sugar, and fishing in search of supplemental work. Competition is heavy, especially in the more productive areas, where upland farmers, fishermen, and even lowland farmers make their labor available for a share of the rice harvest or supplemental cash.

Upland Farmers

Upland farmers are mostly subsistence farmers of marginal land on rolling hills and steep mountain slopes. At least three main categories of farmers are found in upland areas: indigenous kaingineros, marginal kaingineros, and upland rice/corn farmers.[12] The first two engage in shifting and the third in settled agriculture. The indigenous kainginero is generally an illiterate, non-Christian farmer who subsists on various crops suitable for annually shifting cultivation, produced on remote, illegally occupied tropical rain forest land.[13] Marginal kaingineros are mostly literate, Christian farmers who have migrated from the lowlands. They derive about 70 percent of their income from annual and perennial crops produced by slash-and-burn/weed-and-burn operations on marginal accessible forest, bush, and grasslands, generally recognized as agricultural rather than forest reserves. Upland rice/corn farmers rely on plowed, rolling-slope land generally to produce corn in the dry season and rice in the wet season. By one estimate there are a total of 500,000 kainginero households.[14] Marginal kaingineros make up over half the total and are growing at a faster rate than indigenous kaingineros, owing to migration by lowlanders in search of land, as access routes to the uplands expand.[15] Little data is available on the total number of upland rice/corn farming households, but we can estimate them at around one million households.[16]

Estimated household incomes for kaingineros fall in the 2,000–3,000 peso range.[17] Most of their income is in the form of root crops (e.g., camote and cassava) and some upland rice which is consumed largely within the household.[18] A few fruit trees, two pigs, and/or a few chickens provide additional subsistence income. Marginal kaingineros tend to have a somewhat higher cash income, to the extent that they have greater access to markets for cash crops. Average annual income for upland rice/corn farmers was estimated at approximately 3,500 pesos in 1974 with lower incomes for tenants and subsistence white corn farmers as compared to mixed rice and cash corn farmers. This represents about three-fourths the income needed to meet minimum food requirements. Corn farmers generally use traditional varieties of white corn, especially, as high-yielding varieties are available mostly for yellow corn and require higher inputs levels. Yields for traditional varieties average only 0.4 metric tons per hectare, largely due to the prevalence of downy mildew and low soil fertility. Low farmgate prices, market isolation, and limited knowledge hamper adoption of higher-yielding technology.[19] Many rice and corn farmers also engage in mixed cropping of coconuts, bananas, fruit trees, and vegetables. For additional cash income, upland rice and corn farmers, along with the less isolated marginal kaingineros, look to secondary sources. Income from off-farm agricultural as well as nonagricultural employment ranges as high as 70 percent of total income for some households, attesting to the inadequacy of the marginal lands to provide enough production for subsistence needs. These income sources include rattan gathering, firewood and handsawn timber, gum copal, abaca (hemp) stripping, piecework on lowland farms and copra making.[20] Housewives and other household members contribute about 25 percent to total household income from off-farm sources. Indigenous kaingineros, on the other hand, earn no more than 10 percent from off-farm sources, which is a reflection more of limited opportunities than of less need.

Women play an important role in upland production. They plant the roots and vegetables and manage the poultry and pig raising while caring for the children. They often market these products. Women also contribute substantially to the planting and harvesting of rice and corn. They know the best species of wood for cooking, though the men help in the collecting. As in most Filipino households, the woman administers the purse and shares in the making of household purchasing decisions.

Most kaingineros exercise squatter's rights on the land they cultivate and are essentially transient.

Population pressure and more intensive land use (and abuse) is upsetting the delicate ecobalance in the uplands and is further limiting the farmers' already low returns. Given an adequate fallow cycle after the first three crops, soil fertility and land productivity may remain relatively stable. As the kaingin plot is replanted sooner, because of competing pressure on the land, soil quality rapidly declines. Marginal kaingineros are often the most destructive of land fertility because of their inherited, inappropriate lowland farming practices and the more permanent nature of their crops.[21] The plow-method practices used by rice/corn farmers on rolling hills worsen leaching and soil erosion, contributing to low soil fertility. The declining fertility and productivity of the uplands helps explain the seasonal migration of upland farmers to the lowlands in search of supplementary income.

In general, education, health and nutrition services are limited. A lack of teachers and schools coupled with the irregular demands of slash-and-burn agriculture in the case of kaingineros and off-farm employment in the case of upland rice/corn farmers will continue to limit educational opportunities for their children and thus upward social mobility.

One may expect a growing degree of competition among the three groups of uplanders as their resource base degenerates. This has already happened in Mindanao.

The potential for competition seems greater between kaingineros and entities concerned with maintaining forests as perennially renewable sources of economic, environmental, and social benefits. Kaingineros desire unrestricted access to land for slash-and-burn farming. This places them in direct conflict with (1) government agencies attempting to maintain an environmental balance between forested lands, pasture lands, and lands cleared for agriculture, and (2) loggers who practice sound forest-management methods, including selective logging, sustained yield cutting cycles, reforestation and protection of logged-over/regenerating forest lands.

Illegal loggers or legally established but irresponsible loggers, whose tenure in the forest is transitory, are generally not in conflict with marginal kaingineros. These loggers treat forests as immediate but temporary sources of income. Once they have removed all marketable-sized logs of commercially acceptable species they abandon the area and pose no threat to the kainginero. The marginal kaingineros enter to cut and burn the remaining immature, unmarketable-sized trees and brush, which would over time mature and reestablish dense vegetative cover on the upland.[22]

But indigenous kaingineros from cultural minority tribal groups often perceive forest areas as their own personal ancestral lands and may not recognize government authority to alienate, control, or regulate the exploitation of timber, minerals, water and other resources – particularly the land itself. Though slash-and-burn farming is declared illegal by government, tribal groups consider it essential to sustain life. Log production supplies building materials, taxes, and foreign exchange – and so is licensed by government. Minority groups resent established loggers cutting trees on the ancestral lands. Violence is all too often the result, as indigenous kaingineros attempt to assert supremacy and uphold their ancestral rights over the logger's attempts to exercise their government-granted rights to exploit timber. The usual result is further displacement of the minorities to more and more remote areas.

Sustenance Fishermen

Sustenance fishermen are small-scale, traditional fishermen who fish both inland waters and marine coastal waters within three miles of the coastline. There are approximately 600,000[23] sustenance or "municipal" fishermen located in 10,000 coastal fishing villages throughout the country.[24]

Despite the relative importance of the industry, average annual income for sustenance fishing households amounted to about 3,900 pesos in 1975[25] for an average family of 6.3 members, including income from sources other than fishing. More than one-third of these households supplemented their incomes by working in agricultural and service jobs. Often sustenance fishing is taken up as an occupation of last resort by landless families unable to find other forms of employment.

Low income levels are a function of low productivity, which on a national basis averages 1.33 metric tons per fisherman annually, and the low prices they received (1.50–2.50 pesos per kilogram).[26] Incomes within fishing communities vary according to asset ownership, particularly ownership of a vessel. While 74 percent own some fishing gear (including hand-held instruments, barriers and traps, set lines, and nets), the majority of fishermen (60 percent) do not own boats. Instead they rent small boats, crew for small boat owners, hire as laborers on larger crafts, raft-fish with hooks and lines, or net fish on shorelines. Forty-seven percent of the bancas are motorized, which significantly increases the catch. After expenses are deducted, the remaining income is divided, with the banca owner usually receiving at least half of the share. Fishermen often end up indebted to middlemen and banca owners.[27]

Another contributing factor to the sustenance fisherman's low standard of living has been the rapid rise in energy cost relative to fish prices, resulting in overall decline in their real income from 1972 to 1979. This trend is likely to continue.[28] They also suffer from practices destructive of the resource base, such as overfishing, dynamite fishing, use of fine mesh nets, competition with fishermen using more advanced methods, destruction of coral beds and mangroves, and pollution. Marketing problems include diminishing availability of fish landings, spoilage, lack of transport to market, price uncertainty, lack of pricing information, and price controls by middlemen.

The fundamental problem of the coastal fishermen is their underlying dependence on a common-property, open-access resource (with finite limits of natural production) and on a product which is highly perishable once caught, and insufficient opportunities for alternative sources of food and income. The Philippine National Environmental Protection Council (NEPC) considers that the coastal waters are already fully exploited. Consequently there is little prospect for improving the incomes of fishermen from increased fish production. Indeed further increases in capital investment may only heighten the problem.

Cycles Undermining Survival

The preceding discussion points up the resourcefulness of poor households in managing very limited productive assets and exploiting available opportunities for securing and stabilizing family income streams. That they should not have more success is not surprising, given three mutually reinforcing vicious cycles that undermine their individual survival strategies. Indeed, the surprise is that they survive at all.

The first cycle is that of population pressure. While for the individual poor household children represent wealth and security, in the aggregate, rapid population growth presses in upon the natural resource base. In 1900 there were 7 million Filipinos. Today the population approaches 47 million. By 2000 there will be between 70 and 75 million Filipinos, even if a replacement fertility rate is achieved by then. Yet the physical resources will not have increased. In fact, the trend is toward degradation and depletion, in part owing to accelerated use by large numbers of people. Population pressures limit the poor's access to land, lead to increasing competition for available jobs, and overburden available social services – compounding health and nutrition problems.

The second cycle is the serious and rapid environmental decline threatening the future of the Philippines.[29] Deterioration of the resource base results in corresponding decreases in the productivity on which the survival strategies of most poor households depend. Ironically, the poor in their desperate efforts to survive add to the degradation.

This relationship is most evident in the rapid loss of forest cover over large areas of the country. Slash-and-burn farming[30] and excessive logging and pasturing have depleted vegetative cover, leading to heavy runoff of tropical rains, which has in turn resulted in serious erosion of the soil. The upland farmer's productivity suffers first. When soil fertility deteriorates to the point that it will not sustain a food crop, he must move on to other upland areas if available, or join the ranks of the landless agricultural workers or urban squatters. Most of the 5 million hectares (one-sixth of the total land mass of the Philippines) classified as denuded and degraded areas are abandoned farm or forest lands that have reverted to unproductive *imperata* grasslands.[31]

Forest destruction is beginning to affect the supply of cooking fuel. Some 70 percent of all households in the country are dependent on wood to cook the food they consume.[32] As the sources of wood diminish and population increases, the cost of firewood is bound to rise. With rising prices forest exploitation will accelerate further.

Forests are nature's main reservoir for water storage. As more forest lands are denuded, streams, rivers, and lakes supply proportionately less water during the dry season. Man-made reservoirs fill up with silt and irrigation water supplies are reduced. Lowland farmers are forced to decrease the amount of land they can plant in the dry season, which results in lower yields, less employment, and smaller incomes.

Forest destruction is also responsible for the silt that ultimately enters the coastal ecosystems, destroying coral reefs that feed many species of fish and other marine life. Meanwhile, mangrove ecosystems are being cleared for housing, fishponds, and industrial sites. Both processes disrupt the food chains that supply marine life and the spawning grounds of important commercial species of marine life. The sustenance fishermen operating in shallow coastal waters are directly affected. Siltation of coral reefs, destruction of mangrove ecosystems, and illegal fishing methods such as dynamiting reduce fish populations and fish catches.

The third cycle is the most perverse, and that is the growth cycle itself. In the Philippines, as in most developing *and* industrialized countries, the pressing needs of industrialization and export promotion engender accelerated exploitation of natural resources. The irony is that in generating national economic benefits, the very resources required for sustained growth are depleted. But the special tragedy in countries such as the Philippines is that the pattern of growth in many respects undercuts the poor's efforts to survive. For example, commercial logging to sustain expanded timber exports competes with upland agriculture and contributes to the rapid forest denudation, with its adverse effects on upland soil fertility, lowland irrigation systems, and coastal fishing grounds. Sugar, coconut, banana, and coffee export expansion favors plantation agriculture and ties up substantial land assets in the hands of the few, to the detriment of the landless agricultural workers. Efforts to develop agricultural alternatives (such as alcogas) to imported energy tend to promote further plantation expansion. Commercial fisheries have been encouraged to adopt the latest technology to contribute to export balances. In the process the coastal waters have been overexploited and sustenance fishermen have seen their livelihoods threatened. While the poorer households are the major producers of these primary products, the returns accrue disproportionately to marketing and banking concerns. The profits are not even reinvested in the expansion of rural employment and productivity. Instead they go to finance Manila-based capital-intensive industry, in which few jobs are created.

Meanwhile, the poor are becoming increasingly dependent on the sale of their labor services as a source of income. The current labor force is growing at an annual rate of about 3.5 percent, with an estimated 500,000 new entrants added yearly to an already substantially underemployed labor force, especially in the rural sector.[33] Current labor absorption patterns fail to provide anywhere near adequate employment opportunities for all those seeking jobs. The greed of the growth machine all too often trades off long-term equitable development for quick economic returns. Income distribution remains skewed and benefits trickle up to the wealthy more rapidly than they trickle down to the poor.

Conclusion

Unless these cycles can be broken, increasing numbers of poor people will be displaced, abandoning their current strategies, ultimately making their way to the large cities. Action is required on two fronts simultaneously. First, initiation or strengthening of policies to encourage slower population growth, sound management of the environment, and balanced, equitable development. Second, specific attention to the needs of the various landless, upland, and fishermen groups, with a view to helping them improve upon their survival strategies and remove the obstacles in the way to a more successful standard of living. There are few if any universal answers to the problems of the rural poor. It all depends on the locally specific conditions of each defined group. The challenge is to tailor programs to each group, using impact rather than administrative expediency as the guiding principle for interventions.

14

The Political Economics
of Drinking Water

SIMON M. FASS

An in-depth examination of one small segment of the public service sector in Haiti, specifically water distribution management in Port-au-Prince, highlights the severe consequences which deficient administration can bring to bear upon a relatively large number of people. Failure to provide equality of access through administrative means has resulted in a severe form of water resource competition within an urban setting in which the poor are the ultimate losers. Little has been done to overcome these deficiencies, in part because of the political influence of those in a position to profit from the existing situation.

The Municipal Distribution System, 1976

In early 1976 an average of 740 liters of water per second (l/s) entered the water distribution system of Port-au-Prince. For its total population of 640,000 at the time, this amounted to an average of 100 liters per person each day (lcd).[1] Six hundred and forty l/s were drawn from rivers and sources on Morne l'Hospital, a mountain rising to 1,000 meters to the south of the city, 40 l/s from river sources to the west, and 60 l/s from wells in the Cul de Sac plain to the north. Because deforestation and erosion had reduced the water absorption capacity of major watersheds on the mountainside, the municipal water authority, CAMEP, had come to rely more heavily on pumping from wells in the plain. This water was on the margin of potability because of salt water infiltration caused by excessive pumping in periods of drought.

The major pipes of the distribution system covered most of the urban area and fed about 30,000 legal and clandestine private connections, 36

A more extensive treatment of issues raised in this chapter and the role of international technical assistance in such problem areas is provided in Simon M. Fass, "Water and Politics: The Process of Meeting a Basic Need in Haiti," *Development and Change* 13 (London: Saga Publications, 1982): 347–64.

"official" standpipes in various states of disrepair, and 100 fire hydrants. In transport between source and consumer, about 50 percent of water input leaked out of the system. For the most part the loss was due to breaks and leaks in pipes, but much of it occurred because connections to reservoirs in homes and establishments were not equipped with automatic shut-off valves, or sometimes any valves at all. When such reservoirs, including swimming pools, were full, the overflow spilled into the streets. Since there were no metering devices or enforced penalties for not having valves, and the water tariff was on a flat-rate basis, subscribers had little incentive to invest in appropriate valves.[2] The United Nations estimated that control mechanisms at private connections could have reduced losses to a more reasonable range of 30 to 35 percent.[3]

Individuals installed reservoirs because of irregular distribution and pressure of water flows. Heavy demand fluctuations, variations in rainfall, limited public storage capacity, and high distribution losses caused the irregularities. Subscribers had to be prepared for periods of several days, sometimes weeks, between deliveries through the pipes.[4]

The 30,000 legal and clandestine private connections in 1976 provided direct service to only about 150,000 residents (i.e., 5 consumers per household). The number of people using rainfall catchment methods, private wells, or tanker truck deliveries was less than 1 percent of the total urban population. The remaining 490,000 residents were in theory serviced by the 36 officially designated standpipes that were supposed to exist at the time. In reality only 27 standpipes functioned. The others had long since been destroyed. The total outflow from the operating standpipes on any given day did not exceed 1.4 million liters. Thus under the best of circumstances their total supply could not provide more than 2.8 liters per person each day for 490,000 residents presumably dependent on them. To put this in perspective, a single flush of a modern toilet facility requires 19 litres. In practice, water wastage at the standpipes normally ranged from 30 percent to 50 percent of total outflow. Many were located at great distances from residential areas. Half functioned for five hours or less each day and at unpredictable intervals. Variations in pressure and number of spigots at each standpipe could generate outflows as low as 200 liters an hour in some cases, and correspondingly lengthy queues. In fact, no more than about 55,000 final consumers actually obtained water directly from the standpipes each day.[5]

The extreme scarcity caused by the municipal distribution system led the city's population to adapt in a number of ways. There were a number, something on the order of 40,000, who relied on leaks and breaks in pipes. It was common to knock a hole in a pipe, if necessary digging into the street to find one, plugging it with a wooden spike when not in use, and attaching a short rubber hose from the hole to a bucket when drawing water from it. Such users were in effect constructing their own standpipes. However, since most of the readily available pipes connected subscribers with trunk lines, and since subscribers were generally families with means, penalties for this practice could sometimes be quite severe. This method of obtaining water was not widespread.

A more common practice, providing water to some 95,000 residents, was sharing among neighbors. In a number of areas, high, middle, and low income homes are located side by side. In such neighborhoods, the proportion of families with connections tend to be relatively high, and so the number of individuals requesting water from a particular subscriber on any given day, usually in the form of a request to a household servant, is low, typically less than 10 or 12. Since the number of demands was low enough not to cause too much inconvenience, and since good neighborly relations are highly valued by most people, higher income families did and do accede to the demands whenever their own reservoir supplies seemed more than adequate. An additional benefit to subscribers was that the incentive to break pipes is reduced.

The majority of nonsubscribers, however, some 300,000 low income residents who lived in downtown areas with relatively few private connections, were obliged to buy water from fixed and mobile vendors. The shortage of water outlets had in effect given rise to a rather substantial private market for a publicly-provided service.

The Private Water Market, 1976

The private water market in 1976 contained three principal sets of vendors.[6] The first set were tanker truck operators who drew water from fire hydrants and transported it to industrial and commercial establishments, and to about 1,200 higher income homes located in areas without piped service or with very irregular service. Charges for truck supply varied between U.S. $3.00 and U.S. $6.00 per m³, depending on availability and delivery distance. Average consumption by these 6,000 regular residential consumers was 100 lcd, or a total of about 600 m³ per day. The gross revenues of truckers, who paid nothing for water, either in the form of user charges or in the form of license fees, amounted from these consumers alone to an average of $2,700.00 per day, $980,000 per year, and an annual return of $39,000 per truck.[7]

Even high income families considered the $68.00 monthly expenditure for water excessive, and the municipal water authority, CAMEP, was under constant pressure from the families to extend pipes into new areas, or to fix pipes and increase flows in areas where the system had broken down. At the time a connection involved a one-time fee of $25.00, and flat-rate user charges of about $0.12 per m³ generally cost households between $20.00 and $25.00 a year.

There were substantial profits to be made, and many truck operators engaged in a number of competitive activities to limit supply. These sometimes included the use of influence to restrict entry by additional truckers (e.g., by making it bureaucratically difficult for potential competitors to obtain import licenses for vehicles, or to clear vehicles from customs), and the use of sabotage. More often truckers were known to break pipes in order to create demand for transported water over the extended periods required to locate the breaks and repair them. CAMEP's system maintenance operations were invariably compromised.

The second set of vendors, representing the key source of supply for the private water market, consisted of some 2,000 households which had connections to the system and sold water in lower income areas to neighboring consumers and/or to mobile sellers who would transport it further afield. Consumer families, or small groups of families could sometimes arrange subscriptions with such suppliers and pay monthly fees of anywhere from $1.00 to $5.00 for unlimited quantities. This practice, however, was rare and typically limited to transactions between property-owners and nearby tenants. The common method was to sell water by the bucketful (about 18 liters per bucket).

The minimum price, in effect during the rainy season if water was flowing in the pipes, was two cents a bucket, or about $1.10 per m^3. In the dry season the typical price would be ten cents, equivalent to $5.60 per m^3. During drought periods, as happened in 1975 and 1977, unit prices could readily reach anywhere from $10.00 to $20.00 per m^3 for several months at a stretch. At these times consumers had to pay 100 to 150 times the typical unit price charged to their urban counterparts in the United States.

Gross revenues to the 2,000 sellers amounted to $1.87 million a year, with individual returns ranging anywhere from $500 to $2,000 annually.[8] The outlay necessary to generate such income streams, required about $100.00 for a concrete reservoir and, if legal, the $25.00 connection charge and $20.00 annual water fee noted earlier.

Although entry into this market was somewhat limited, there being only a relatively small proportion of the population with the resources and influence necessary to obtain connections and build reservoirs, competition between vendors was intense, as were efforts to manipulate prices. It was not uncommon for CAMEP crews, or sometimes individual "contractors," to be paid for installing clandestine connections or for cutting off the legal or illegal connections of others. Valve operators could be persuaded by such means to open water flows to one area under their jurisdiction and to close it to another, thus creating scarcities which could drive prices up and shift demand from one group of vendors to another. When water was exceptionally scarce, even public standpipes did not escape the competitive effects.

They would be subject to deliberate destruction or, more frequently, come under the control of certain locally powerful men who would levy fees for access to them.

When the municipal system functioned properly in the rainy season, water was abundant. Reservoirs of most connected families were full and standpipes provided longer hours of service at high pressure. Consumption demands were easily supplied and most residential consumers would purchase directly from connected vendors. In the dry season, or when the system did not operate as it was supposed to, it would become quite difficult to continue the practice. Competition among buyers for limited supplies would transform queues into street fights, and adolescents who would otherwise fetch water would be prevented by parents from doing so. Simultaneously, the long wait and/or the greater distances across which individuals had to transport water limited the number of adults who could dedicate the time necessary to obtain it during daylight hours. There was a much higher return on the use of time in most other activities, particularly those linked to income-generation. Sellers, on their part, would also limit the number of individuals who were permitted access to their reservoirs, in order to manage financial transactions better.

The third set of vendors were mobile vendors who bought water from connected households and transported it to consumers. A hardened group of women who put up with a great deal of physical abuse from each other at water sources and a great deal of verbal abuse from antipathetic customers, they numbered 14,000 at the peak, or about 4.5 percent of the urban labor force.

The margin charged by the vendors in ordinary circumstances was one cent per bucket, or two if the transport distance was long. These were margins on top of whatever the vendors themselves paid to connected families, and thus could represent unit price differences to consumers anywhere from 35 percent to 100 percent greater than at the sources. Under extreme scarcity these vendors might obtain margins of two to four cents a bucket, earning as much as $0.40 to $0.80 per day. For 1976, the aggregate net earnings of mobile vendors came to $930,000, or approximately $5.50 a month for each vendor.[9]

Total expenditures by consumers in the private water market thus amounted to about $3.8 million a year, a quarter being paid largely by a very small group of high income residents and the balance by some 300,000 low income families. The former would pay an average unit price of $4.50 per m^3, the latter an average of $2.30 per m^3, and the families connected to the municipal system, if they paid anything, an average of between $0.80 and $0.12 per m^3, excluding the disbursements necessary for "expediting payments" to crews and contractors. By contrast, CAMEP's total annual revenue from the sale of water was $650,000 during the same period.

The price structure resulting from the various operations of the water market yielded a highly skewed distribution of consumption. Residents with private connections, almost exclusively composed of higher income families, were able to consume an average of 156 lcd. The 180,000 residents who could by one means or another get water free of charge obtained between 15 and 32 lcd, depending on the type of source. The 300,000 inhabitants who purchased water in the private market restricted usage to an average of 11 lcd, meaning of course that a large number of them limited consumption to less than that figure. Thus, at the extremes, 23 percent of the population received 75 percent of total consumption; and another 47 percent of residents, 11 percent.

Impacts on the Population

At a unit market price of $0.0023 per liter (i.e., $2.30/m³) on the average, a typical family of five individuals would have had to spend about $4.00 a month in order to consume 11 lcd. In 1976 about 40 percent of urban families had incomes of $20 per month or less, 30 percent obtained something between $20 and $40 per month, and 14 percent between $40 and $60 per month.[10] For each of these groups the purchase of 11 lcd would in principle have represented, respectively, 25 percent or more of income, 10 to 25 percent, and 7 to 10 percent. Given all the various daily demands placed on the use of money, many families found it impossible to spend 25 percent of what they had just for water. Surveys in various neighborhoods indicated that the maximum feasible expenditure was in the range of 13 to 15 percent in most cases.[11] At the same time, the use of water for such basic needs as drinking, cooking, laundering, and washing made it equally impossible to permit consumption to fall below a certain minimum amount, which household surveys suggested was on the order of 2 to 4 lcd.

Families responded to the squeeze in a number of ways. The poorest of them, with incomes of less than $10 per month, used purchased water only for cooking and drinking. They used surface runoff for cleaning themselves and traveled on foot or by public conveyance to rivers on the periphery of the city to wash clothes, the price of transport being less than the purchase price of enough water with which to do laundry. They might also launder and wash less often. In addition, they would expend more effort queuing and fighting their way to standpipes, locating or making breaks in pipes, or carrying water over great distances from higher income areas where they could find water at no charge.

These practices incurred enormous risks. Besides that of arrest and beating if caught making or even using a broken pipe, a major hazard was that of illness caused by contaminated water or by residence in areas with disastrous sanitary conditions, susceptibility to which was aggravated by the extra energy expended by already malnourished bodies to trudge 20 kilogram buckets of water or bundles of clothing across several kilometers each day.[12] With the risk of illness came the possibility of seriously compromising the capacity to generate income streams. Curative medical services would require such families to curtail other expenditures further, to dig into savings, or to incur heavy debts. Almost all productive economic activities were very time-extensive, and the removal of a significant proportion of household labor from market activities for an extended period, especially when such activities had already suffered from a diversion of capital toward health care, could readily wipe a family out. In the case of the poorest of the city's inhabitants, perhaps 30 to 40 percent of the total, the ability to obtain safe water was absolutely critical to personal and economic well-being, such as it was, let alone survival.

Prospects for Improvement

The government had recognized, long before 1976, that supply and distribution of drinking water was an urban service in need of constant improvement and expansion. For this reason, in 1964 it created the municipal water authority, CAMEP, as a spin-off from a national water service established in 1892. The authority's purpose was to organize and manage water service for the capital city.

But CAMEP suffered from serious administrative inadequacy. Weak personnel management thwarted whatever attempts were made to install water meters, identify clandestine connections, oblige valve operators to provide regular service, identify and repair leaks and breaks rapidly, collect water charges consistently, etc. Furthermore while the city expanded in one direction, CAMEP had a tendency to plan and invest for its movement in another direction. To a very large extent, it was an almost hopeless administrative capability which gave cause for the private water market to become as important as it did, and in turn, for the market to generate the vicious impacts described earlier, on low income families.

CAMEP officials candidly admitted to international assistance agencies throughout the late 1970s that things were not as they should be, but argued that budget limitations resulted in a salary structure which left personnel open to accepting whatever private supplements were available. In addition, employment at CAMEP, as in most public service institutions, was often acquired through political influence. The influence that provided a job could also protect it, and CAMEP management had little scope to invoke penalties against its employees. The same reason was given for CAMEP's inability to control clandestine connections or to charge fees to such connections when located, and its habit of running pipes out to single or small groups of high-income homes in an almost chaotic fashion.

If the population of Port-au-Prince should continue to grow at its historical rate of 6.1 percent a year (1971–76), there will be 1.1 million people in the city by 1985. Since no new capital works are likely to be operational by then, source flows will remain at 900 ls. As a result, average supply will drop from a level of 100 lcd in 1976 to 70 lcd in 1985. The number of subscribers, optimistically, might reach about 40,000 and provide service to some 200,000 people. Another 200,000 persons might be able to get water free of charge from subscribers or from breaks in the system, leaving a balance of some 700,000 people with recourse only to what remains of 27 standpipes which functioned in 1976 and of 10 added on the periphery of the city in 1976 (by an Interamerican Development Bank–financed improvement project)—or to the private market. The prospect would seem to be for increasing real prices on the private market and corresponding declines in consumption among this group.

This scenario could be avoided by technical means, specifically by increasing the number of standpipes in operation. The capital outlay required for, say, 100 standpipes is currently about $100,000, more or less equivalent to the annual total cost for one foreign consultant. Recurrent costs might amount to about $10,000 per year. That is really all that is required to significantly help almost three-quarters of a million people by 1985.

Yet short-term political considerations may confound any attempt to bring this about. The projected decline in per person source flows will most likely cause CAMEP to give higher priority to supplying subscribers than the standpipes. This would therefore minimize interest in building more of the latter, which, in CAMEP's view at least, mean simultaneous wastage of a physical and political resource. In addition, the increase in the number of connected vendors, involving perhaps 3,000 families by 1985, would give CAMEP serious pause to consider the consequences of investments in standpipes that would eliminate all or part of a multimillion-dollar income stream. In effect, certain of the so-called deficiencies in CAMEP's administration are useful to the persons who benefit from them. Indeed, in the political circumstances of Haiti, they are perhaps absolutely necessary.

The Interamerican Development Bank which is assisting Haiti with improvements in its water system sees the problem as an issue to be addressed gradually by building standpipes at a rate consistent with CAMEP's ability to maintain them. The government doesn't see it as an issue to be dealt with at all.

15

Urban Bias in World Development

MICHAEL LIPTON

The most important class conflict in the poor countries of the world today is not between labour and capital. Nor is it between foreign and national interests. It is between the rural classes and the urban classes. The rural sector contains most of the poverty, and most of the low-cost sources of potential advance; but the urban sector contains most of the articulateness, organisation and power. So the urban classes have been able to "win" most of the rounds of the struggle with the countryside; but in so doing they have made the development process needlessly slow and unfair. Scarce land, which might grow millets and beansprouts for hungry villagers, instead produces a trickle of costly calories from meat and milk, which few except the urban rich (who have ample protein anyway) can afford. Scarce investment, instead of going into water-pumps to grow rice, is wasted on urban motorways. Scarce human skills design and administer, not clean village wells and agricultural extension services, but world boxing championships in showpiece stadia. Resource allocations, within the city and the village as well as between them, reflect urban priorities rather than equity or efficiency. The damage has been increased by misguided ideological imports, liberal and Marxian, and by the town's success in buying off part of the rural elite, thus transferring most of the costs of the process to the rural poor.

The poor—between one-quarter and one-fifth of the people of the world—are overwhelmingly rural: landless labourers, or farmers with no more than an acre or two, who must supplement their income by wage labour. Most of these countryfolk rely, as hitherto, on agriculture lacking irrigation or fertilisers or even iron tools. Hence they are so badly fed that they cannot work efficiently, and in many cases are unable to feed their infants well enough to prevent physical stunting and perhaps even brain damage. Apart from the rote-learning of religious texts, few of them receive

Reprinted by permission of the publishers from Michael Lipton, *Why Poor People Stay Poor: Urban Bias in World Development* (Cambridge: Harvard University Press, 1977), pp. 13–21. Copyright © 1977 by Michael Lipton. First published in Great Britain by Maurice Temple Smith, London, 1979.

any schooling. One in four dies before the age of ten. The rest live the same overworked, underfed, ignorant and disease-ridden lives as thirty, or three hundred, or three thousand years ago. Often they borrow (at 40 per cent or more yearly interest) from the same moneylender families as their ancestors, and surrender half their crops to the same families of landlords. Yet the last thirty years have been the age of unprecedented, accelerating growth and development! Naturally men of goodwill are puzzled and alarmed.

How can accelerated growth and development, in an era of rapidly improving communications and of "mass politics," produce so little for poor people? It is too simple to blame the familiar scapegoats – foreign exploiters and domestic capitalists. Poor countries where they are relatively unimportant have experienced the paradox just as much as others. Nor, apparently, do the poorest families cause their own difficulties, whether by rapid population growth or by lack of drive. Poor families do tend to have more children than rich families, but principally because their higher death rates require it, if the ageing parents are to be reasonably sure that a son will grow up, to support them if need be. And it is the structure of rewards and opportunities within poor countries that extracts, as if by force, the young man of ability and energy from his chronically stagnant rural background and lures him to serve, or even to join, the booming urban elite.

The disparity between urban and rural welfare is much greater in poor countries now than it was in rich countries during their early development. This huge welfare gap is demonstrably inefficient, as well as inequitable. It persists mainly because less than 20 per cent of investment for development has gone to the agricultural sector, although over 65 per cent of the people of less-developed countries (LDCs), and over 80 per cent of the really poor who live on $1 a week each or less, depend for a living on agriculture. The proportion of skilled people who support development – doctors, bankers, engineers – going to rural areas has been lower still; and the rural-urban imbalances have in general been even greater than those between agriculture and industry. Moreover, in most LDCs, governments have taken numerous measures with the unhappy side-effect of accentuating rural-urban disparities: their own allocation of public expenditure and taxation; measures raising the price of industrial production relative to farm production, thus encouraging private rural saving to flow into industrial investment because the value of industrial output has been artificially boosted; and educational facilities encouraging bright villagers to train in cities for urban jobs.

Such processes have been extremely inefficient. For instance, the impact on output of $1 of carefully selected investment is in most countries two to three times as high in agriculture as elsewhere, yet public policy and private market power have combined to push domestic savings and foreign aid into nonagricultural uses. The process has also been inequitable. Agriculture starts with about one-third the income per head of the rest of the economy, so that the people who depend on it should in equity receive special attention not special mulcting. Finally, the misallocation between sectors has created a needless and acute conflict between efficiency and equity. In agriculture the poor farmer with little land is usually efficient in his use of both land and capital, whereas power, construction and industry often do best in big, capital-intensive units; and rural income and power, while far from equal, are less unequal than in the cities. So concentration on urban development and neglect of agriculture have pushed resources away from activities where they can help growth *and* benefit the poor, and towards activities where they do either of these, if at all, at the expense of the other.

Urban bias also increases inefficiency and inequity *within* the sectors. Poor farmers have little land and much underused family labour. Hence they tend to complement any extra developmental resources received — pumpsets, fertilisers, virgin land — with much more extra labour than do large farmers. Poor farmers thus tend to get most output from such extra resources (as well as needing the extra income most). But rich farmers (because they sell their extra output to the cities instead of eating it themselves, and because they are likely to use much of their extra income to support urban investment) are naturally favoured by urban-biased policies; it is they, not the efficient small farmers, who get the cheap loans and the fertiliser subsidies. The patterns of allocation and distribution within the cities are damaged too. Farm inputs are produced inefficiently, instead of imported, and the farmer has to pay, even if the price is nominally "subsidised." The processing of farm outputs, notably grain milling, is shifted into big urban units and the profits are no longer reinvested in agriculture. And equalisation between classes inside the cities becomes more risky, because the investment-starved farm sector might prove unable to deliver the food that a better-off urban mass would seek to buy.

Moreover, income in poor countries is usually more equally distributed within the rural sector than within the urban sector.[1] Since income creates the power to distribute extra income, therefore, a policy that concentrates on raising income in the urban sector will worsen inequalities in two ways: by transferring not only from poor to rich, but also from equal to less equal. Concentration on urban enrichment is triply inequitable: because country-folk start poorer; because such concentration allots rural resources largely to the rural rich (who sell food to the cities); and because the great inequality of power *within* the towns renders urban resources especially likely to go to the resident elites.

But am I not hammering at an open door? Certainly the persiflage of allocation has changed recently, under the impact of patently damaging deficiencies in rural output. Development plans are nowadays full of "top priority for agriculture."[2] This is reminiscent of the pseudo-egalitarian school where, at mealtimes, Class B children get priority, while Class A children get food.[3] We can see that the new agricultural priority is dubious from the abuse of the "green revolution" and of the oil crisis (despite its much greater impact on *industrial* costs) as pretexts for lack of emphasis on agriculture: "We don't need it," and "We can't afford it," respectively. And the 60 to 80 percent of people dependent on agriculture are still allocated barely 20 per cent of public resources; even these small shares are seldom achieved; and they have, if anything, tended to diminish. So long as the elite's interests, background and sympathies remain predominantly urban, the countryside may get the "priority" but the city will get the resources. The farm sector will continue to be squeezed, both by transfers of resources from it and by prices that are turned against it. Bogus justifications of urban bias will continue to earn the sincere, prestige-conferring, but misguided support of visiting "experts" from industrialised countries and international agencies. And development will be needlessly painful, inequitable and slow. It is not my wish to overstate the case for reducing urban bias. Such a reduction is not the *only* thing necessary. But a shift of resources to the rural sector, and within it to the efficient rural poor even if they do very little for urban development is often, perhaps usually, the *overriding* developmental task.[4]

Urban bias does not rest on a conspiracy, but on convergent interests. Industrialists, urban workers, even big farmers, *all* benefit if agriculture gets squeezed, provided its few resources are steered, heavily subsidised, to the big farmer, to produce cheap food and raw materials for the cities. Nobody conspires; all the powerful are satisfied; the labour-intensive small farmer stays efficient, poor and powerless, and had better shut up. Meanwhile, the economist, often in the blinkers of industrial determinism, congratulates all concerned on resolutely extracting an agricultural surplus to finance industrialisation. Conspiracy? Who needs conspiracy?

Does the need for a high share of rural resources last for ever? Does not development imply a move out of agriculture and away from villages? Since all developed countries have a very high proportion of resources outside agriculture, can it make sense for underdeveloped countries to push more resources *into* agriculture? And – a related question – as a poor country develops, does it not approach the British or U.S. style of farming, where it is workers rather than machines or land that are scarce, so that the concentration of farm resources upon big labour-saving farms begins to make more sense?

The best way to look at this question is to posit four stages in the analysis of policy in a developing country towards agriculture. Stage I is to advocate leaving farming alone, allowing it few resources, taxing it heavily if possible, and getting its outputs cheaply to finance industrial development, which has top priority.

The second stage in policy for rural development usually arises out of the failures of Stage I. In Stage II, policy-makers argue that agriculture cannot be safely neglected if it is adequately to provide workers, materials, markets and savings to industry. Hence a lot of resources need to be put into those parts of agriculture (mainly big farms, though this is seldom stated openly) that supply industry with raw materials, and industrial workers with food. That is the stage that many poor countries have reached in their official pronouncements, and some in their actual decisions. Stage II is still permeated by urban bias, because the farm sector is allocated resources not mainly to raise economic welfare, but because, and insofar as, it uses the resources to feed urban-industrial growth. Development of the rural sector is advocated, but not for the people who live and work there.

In Stage III, the argument shifts. It is realised that, so long as resources are concentrated on big farmers to provide urban inputs, those resources will neither relieve need nor—because big farmers use little labour per acre—be used very productively. So the sequence is taken one step further back. It is recognised, not only (as in Stage II) that efficient industrialisation is unlikely without major growth in rural inputs, but also (and this is the distinctive contribution of Stage III) that such growth cannot be achieved efficiently or equitably—or maybe at all—on the basis of immediately "extracting surplus." Stage III therefore involves accepting the need for a transformation of the *mass* rural sector, through major resource inputs, *prior* to substantial industrialisation.

It is at Stage III that I stop. I do not believe that poor countries should "stay agricultural" in order to develop, let alone instead of developing. The argument that neither the carrying capacity of the land, nor the market for farm products, is such as to permit the masses in poor countries to reach high levels of living without a major shift to non-farm activities seems conclusive.

The learning process, needed for modern industrialisation, is sometimes long; but it is fallacious for a nation, comprising above all a promising but overwhelmingly underdeveloped agriculture, to conclude that, in order to begin the process of learning, a general attack on numerous branches of industrial activity should be initiated. A far better strategy is to concentrate first upon high-yielding mass rural development, supported (partly for learning's sake) by such selective ancillary industry as rural development makes viable. Rapid industrialisation on a broad front, doomed to self-strangulation for want of the wage goods and savings capacity that only a developed agricultural sector can provide, is likely to discredit industrialisation itself.

16

The Dynamics of
Dependency and Marginality

OSVALDO SUNKEL

In a dependent underdeveloped economy, the dynamism of the system is basically derived from the expansion of primary export activities and import-substituting industrialization. It is important, therefore, to determine the effects of these forms of economic expansion on access by the people to the sources of a reasonable and stable income, i.e., employment opportunities, access to property, possibilities for the exercise of entrepreneurial, technical, artisanal and professional activities, and/or participation in income transfer systems.

The conventional approach, utilized normally in planning models and in employment projections, assumes that employment is a function of the availability of capital, assuming technology to be homogeneous and constant or improving at a fixed rate. In this way, the amount of capital needed to employ one person at an average level of productivity can be estimated and, therefore, also the rate of investment necessary to employ an active growing population. The problem appears then to be one of achievement of a rate of savings which will finance a level and expansion of investments sufficient to "absorb" the growing labour force; in other words, if the economy can be made to grow rapidly enough – and this is mainly a function of the rate of investment – there will be no unemployment. If internal savings are not adequate to reach such a rate of capital formation, it is assumed that a complement of foreign financing, assistance and investment may and probably will solve the problem.

This view is not only far too simple but also far too mechanical. To begin with, the crucial assumption of technological homogeneity, implicit in the model, but rarely explicitly stated, is in total contradiction to the heterogeneity which characterizes precisely those economies where margin-

Excerpted from "Transnational Capitalism and National Disintegration in Latin America," *Social and Economic Studies* 22 (1973): 132–76. Grateful acknowledgement is made to *Social and Economic Studies* for permission for this use.

157

ality prevails. If, to simplify the argument, we assume that there exist only two levels of technology – modern and primitive, the former capital-intensive and the latter labour-intensive – and that the productive capacity of the modern sector grows faster than that of the primitive sector, the rate of investment, as well as the average amount of capital per person employed will have to grow in order that a *constant* rate of employment may be maintained – at least until the weight of the sector of primitive technology becomes relatively insignificant. If the modern sector, apart from expanding relatively faster than the primitive sector, further replaces to some extent its output, technological modernization would result on the one hand, in the *creation* and on the other, in the *destruction* of employment opportunities. If demand remains constant during this process of technological substitution, an increase in investment in the modern sector would create idle capacity and unemployment, since the number of persons employed per unit of capital in the modern sector is less than in primitive activities. In this way, it is conceivable that an *increase in the rate of investment* could lead to an *increase in the rate of un- and underemployment,* and therefore, of marginality. In fact, I would suggest that this is not just an extreme hypothetical situation, but is perhaps the best working hypothesis to explain the growing problem of unemployment, underemployment and marginality in Latin America.

To justify this assertion it becomes essential, to begin with, to drop the highly restrictive and unrealistic assumption of the constancy of total demand made, for the sake of simplicity, in the foregoing argument. In fact, this assumption is not necessary; in order for the hypothesis to hold, it is sufficient if the increment in total demand induced by the increase in net investment produces an additional increment in employment that is smaller than the net employment (reduction of employment at the primitive level less creation of employment at the modern level) created by the initial new investment. This is very likely to happen if the distance between the modern and primitive levels of technology is very wide, if the proportion of employment in the primitive sector is very large, and if the employment multiplier of investments in the modern sector is very low.

These situations are quite frequent in most of our countries. It should be noted that this analysis has been conducted in terms of levels of technology and not, as is usually the case, of sectors of activity. In other words, we are thinking of a horizontal classification of the economy, separating the modern and primitive levels in all sectors of economic activity. In this way it becomes apparent that the technological innovations which are introduced at the upper margin of the modern level replace technological processes that are being abandoned at the lower margin of the primitive level. In plain words, computers, satellite communication, automated electric power plants, etc., are in effect replacing the accountant, the smith, the water mill, the coach, etc.

On the other hand, the income generated by additional investments in the modern sector mainly enlarges the incomes of middle and higher income groups, whose demand expands proportionally to a greater extent in consumer durables and modern services where highly capital-intensive technologies prevail. This fact, together with the high marginal import propensity of these groups considerably reduce the employment-creating effect of investments in the modern sector. In this way, the multiplier effects of employment creation at the modern level will probably be lower than the unemployment caused by the replacement of economic activities at the primitive level and its negative multiplier effects.

A few examples may contribute to a better understanding of our approach. The effect on the labour market of the relatively fast growth of the modern activities and the consequent disruption of the more primitive activities is quite clear: the demand for skilled human resources grows very rapidly while the demand for unskilled manpower slackens. As a consequence, a tendency towards improvement of wages of qualified personnel (except under conditions of rapid expansion of higher and technical education) and a relative stagnation or decline in the wages of unskilled labour is observable. This phenomenon has been perceived clearly in the agricultural sector and in the traditional export sector. These activities react to the decline in demand with reduction of production and employment; the decline in demand is still followed by processes of technological modernization which substantially reduce the level of employment. This gives rise to an important outflow of unskilled manpower which adds to the ranks of the urban marginal groups.

The same phenomenon can be examined from the point of view of the different types of occupation which provide access to sources of income. The expansion of the modern sector normally implies the installation of relatively large enterprises, and this will increase the number of large firms. But given the oligopolistic conditions which generally prevail, this will also limit the possibilities of expansion of medium and small-sized firms, as well as of artisanal work. Frequently, the expansion of large firms in extractive, commercial, industrial or other activities will result from the penetration of foreign subsidiaries. This may have the effect of limiting or excluding medium and small, and even large, national entrepreneurs, particularly when this process involves an acute tendency of concentration of the ownership of markets or means of production, land, water, foreign exchange, credit, technology and know-how, etc. Furthermore, inequalities in the labour market and the concentration of property will tend to accentuate the unequal distribution of income, with the consequent reinforcement of a structure of demand which contributes to the dynamization of capital-intensive activities. This process involves an acceleration of obsolescence of existing products and processes, leading to unnecessary and premature replacements of installed capacity, generally with considerable savings of manpower. In this and many other ways, impolicy, or lack of policy, contributes to a restriction of the access of the population to sources of income.

If what has been suggested in the foregoing analysis is correct, the problem of marginality looks much more serious and unmanageable than is normally assumed, both because it probably will worsen in the near future and also because such partial policies as popular participation or integration as well as such global policies as population control or indiscriminate acceleration of economic growth do not reflect the true dimensions and nature of the problem. An adequate consideration of the question of marginality requires an approach that incorporates this phenomenon as one of the inherent processes of dependent underdevelopment, where appropriate consideration is given to those questions of technology, institutions, income distribution, concentration of property, structure of consumption and production, etc., which have a more pronounced and direct influence on the accessibility of the population to the sources of income.

The Relationships between the Processes of International and National Polarization

The examination of the internal and international processes of polarization clearly suggests a further step in the analysis. If we look at countries as composed of developed and underdeveloped functions, groups and regions, and remember the basic characteristics of the international economy – the penetration of the underdeveloped economies by the economies of the developed countries through the extractive, manufacturing, commercial and financial transnational conglomerates – it becomes apparent that there must be a close correlation and connection between the extension of the developed economies into the underdeveloped countries, and the developed, modern and advanced activities, social groups and regions of these countries.

From such a perspective of the global system, apart from the distinction between developed and underdeveloped countries, components of importance can be observed:

a) a complex of activities, social groups and regions in different countries which conform to the developed part of the global system and which are closely linked transnationally through many concrete interests as well as by similar styles, ways and levels of living and cultural affinities;

b) a national complement of activities, social groups and regions partially or totally excluded from the national developed part of the global system and without any links with similar activities, groups and regions of other countries.

In this conception of the phenomena associated with the development-underdevelopment continuum which implicitly claims to incorporate the aspects of domination-dependence and marginality which form an inherent part of it, the so-called developed countries would be those where the developed structure—economic, social and spatial—prevails, while the backward and marginal activities, social groups and regions would appear as exceptional, limited and secondary situations.

Conversely, the so-called underdeveloped countries would be those in which the phenomenon of marginality affects a significant proportion of the population, activities and areas, and therefore would appear as an urgent and acute problem, not only in relative terms but also for the reason that large segments of population are affected by it at extremely low absolute levels of living. The modern activities, social groups and areas would, on the other hand, constitute more or less restricted portions of these countries.

We shall now present a graphic model combining the different elements. It is assumed, for the sake of simplicity, that our model of the international system consists of only one dominant developed country and two under-developed and dependent countries (see figure 1).

The International System

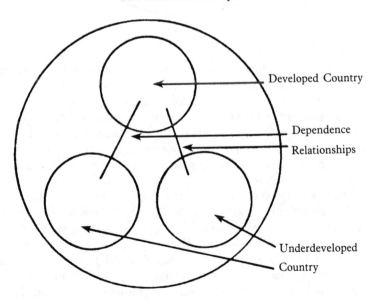

FIGURE I

It is assumed that each country within the system – both the developed and the underdeveloped ones – manifests a certain degree of heterogeneity in the levels of development, modernity, progress and incomes. Solely for the sake of convenience we shall reduce heterogeneity to its simplest expression, viz., duality. This enables us to distinguish between integrated and marginal or segregated sectors (see figure 2).

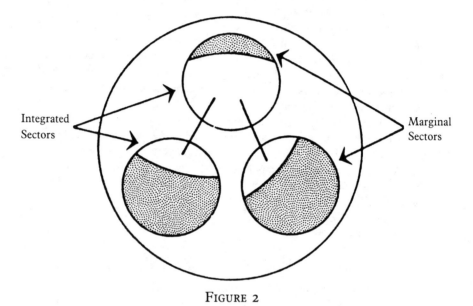

Integrated Sectors

Marginal Sectors

FIGURE 2

Finally, overlapping with the two previous figures, and in accordance with the basic categories of our analysis, we shall assume that at the heart of the international system is an international or transnational kernel or nucleus, consisting of (1) a matrix of national integrated sectors, (2) segregated individual national segments formed by the segregated or marginal sectors of each country, and (3) the relationships between (2) above and the integrated segments. The diagramatic expression corresponding to this idea is shown in figure 3.

The interpretation so far advanced suggests that the international system contains an internationalized nucleus of activities, regions and social groups of varying degrees of importance in each country. These sectors share a common culture and "way of life," which expresses itself through the same books, texts, films, television programmes, similar fashions, similar groups of organization of family and social life, similar style of decoration of homes, similar orientations to housing, building, furniture and urban design. Despite linguistic barriers, these sectors have a far greater capacity for

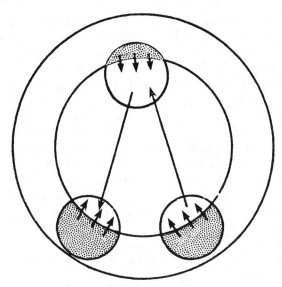

FIGURE 3

communication among themselves than is possible between integrated and marginal persons of the same country who speak the same language. An advertisement in *Time* magazine expresses this idea with the perfection to be expected from publicity aimed precisely at the international market constituted by the nucleus of internationalized population:

> *Time*'s 24 million readers are apt to have more in common with each other than with many of their own countrymen. High incomes. Good education. Responsible positions in business, government and the professions. *Time* readers constitute an international community of the affluent and influential, responsive to new ideas, new products and new ways of doing things. (*The Economist*, 16–22 May 1970, p. 81)

For this international community, inhabiting different countries — developed and underdeveloped — to have similar patterns of consumption, it must also have similar patterns of income. However, it is well known that the average levels of income *per capita* of developed nations are greater by a factor of considerable magnitude than that of underdeveloped countries. But these averages are highly questionable, particularly if the national universe which they claim to represent is highly heterogeneous, as is particularly the case in underdeveloped economies, where income distribution is very unequal. In fact, depending upon whether greater or lesser weight is attached to the modernized, integrated or internationalized segment of each underdeveloped economy, more or less significant proportions of the population in these economies will accumulate substantial shares of total income, thereby obtaining *per capita* incomes similar to those prevailing in the developed countries. In the case of Chile, for example, with an average *per capita* income of about U.S.$600, the privileged 10 per cent of the population which receives about 40 per cent of the total income has a *per capita* income of U.S.$2,400, a figure significantly higher than the average for any European economy.

We shall now consider the trends of *per capita* income of the integrated and segregated segments of population. Although empirical evidence on this matter is extremely scanty, it is generally agreed that while income distribution in the developed countries has been more or less constant or slightly improved, in the underdeveloped countries income inequalities, at least between the extremes, has probably widened. It may well be that the total income accruing to the middle and higher income sectors grows faster than the national average, since – as will subsequently be shown – it is directly or indirectly associated with the activity of the transnational conglomerates which grow at substantially faster rates than national economies – both developed and underdeveloped. In contrast, the population growth of the higher income sectors tends to be substantially below the national average both in developed and underdeveloped countries. Therefore, *per capita* incomes of these sectors must increase much faster than the national average in both types of countries. The marginal groups, on the contrary, experience population growth rates higher than national averages and income growth rates which are lower than the national averages, and therefore, *per capita* incomes would have to grow at rates lower than national averages; and this would hold again for both developed and underdeveloped economies. Therefore, according to this analysis, income distribution should deteriorate in both types of countries. However, this tendency may be overcome in the developed countries by means of income redistribution policies which may have a significant effect because of the relatively small size of the lower income groups in an economy relatively characterized by generally high average levels of income. In contrast, in the underdeveloped countries such income redistribution policies do not have similar results because the relative size of low income sections of the population is very big. This may be one of the main reasons why income redistribution policies, when applied by these countries, tend to favour well organized middle and lower middle income groups rather than the poorer sectors of the population.

This analysis sheds some new light on the subject of the "growing income-gap" between developed and underdeveloped countries, of which much is made in the academic literature of development. It rests precisely on the comparison of *per capita* average income trends in both types of nations. In terms of our approach – which does not accept national averages

on account of the heterogeneity of underdeveloped national economies—
and the transnational character of certain segments of these economies, the
growing gap between the rich and poor nations is rather a conceptual and
statistical illusion, which hides the much more significant fact of a growing
gap between rich and poor within the underdeveloped countries, in circumstances where the *per capita* incomes of the higher income groups in
these countries are similar to the absolute levels and growth rates of the
average *per capita* income of the developed countries.

The Internal Productive Structure and the National Transfer Mechanisms

The analysis of the income differentials which allow local minorities in
the underdeveloped countries to maintain international consumption patterns
leads us to the question of how these incomes originate. From a logical
point of view, only four sources of high incomes can exist in underdeveloped economies: a) high productivity activities, b) income transfers from
sectors of high productivity to social groups not linked to these activities,
c) monopolistic exploitation of goods and/or factor markets in low productivity activities, and d) income transfers from abroad.

These four sources of high incomes are obviously not mutually exclusive; on the contrary, they complement and reinforce each other. In fact,
the social groups linked more closely to the high productivity activities have
therefore the capacity to acquire a larger bargaining strength and to exercise
greater pressure over the transfer mechanisms and also the capacity to
exercise a larger degree of monopoly power in their markets of inputs and
outputs. On the other hand, the fact that a certain social group is closely
linked to a high productivity activity does not mean that it cannot in turn
be exploited by other internal or external groups.

The activities of relatively higher productivity in Latin American countries have traditionally been the primary export sectors, which have always
enjoyed comparative advantage. The manufacturing industry has also shared
this advantage by virtue of the policy of industrial protection and the internal
structure of incomes. This does not mean that the entire population linked
in some way to these activities—as workers, employees, owners, buyers,
providers, etc.—will necessarily enjoy high incomes. It merely means that
these activities permit the generation of a large total income due to the
high average productivity per person, which in turn results from a relatively
high degree of capitalization per person and the relatively favourable prices
of goods which they produce. The distribution of this income among groups
which participate in its generation will depend on institutional conditions
in respect of the nature of the property relationships of natural resources
and capital, and the degree of their concentration. It will also depend upon

the general characteristics of the labour, goods and capital markets.

In cases in which the volume of income generated is considerable and centred in very few establishments, with a small, strongly unionized, skilled labour force, the salary of workers would be substantially higher than average. In diametric opposition to this is the position of the large mass of unskilled workers—scattered throughout a large number of small establishments where traditional forms of ascription rather than a labour market prevent effective unionization—whose real income would tend to be kept at a low level, perhaps not much higher than in the more primitive rural activities.

Nevertheless, in all these cases there exist privileged groups which obtain incomes similar to those prevailing in developed countries.

Moreover, in countries where middle and working class groups have acquired some influence over the state, governments usually become important agencies of income redistribution, acquiring by means of taxation, foreign exchange policies or other mechanisms a part of the income generated in high productivity activities, and then redistributing it to middle and working class sectors in a variety of ways. Thus, sectors which are not associated in any way with the higher productivity activities are in a position to make use of the state apparatus as a transfer mechanism and thereby obtain access to higher incomes which will also allow them to adopt, at least partially, the life style and patterns of consumption of the international community.

There are yet other groups which, without in any way being associated with high productivity activities, are still able to secure high incomes, as happens, for example, when institutional conditions allow certain persons to capture a large proportion of the incomes of many other people with whom they have some kind of economic relationship as workers, buyers, sellers, etc. This happens generally where there is a high degree of concentration of ownership or control of the means of production or other sources of income, and/or oligopsonistic or oligopolistic situations in the market for goods and services. Even though these situations exist in high productivity sectors, they are more clearly observable in the more primitive and traditional activities, in rural areas, in handicraft and small industries, and many service activities: commerce, non-institutionalized financial markets, etc. These are generally economic activities which are highly labour-intensive and have a low *per capita* productivity, but where salaries can be kept low due to the abundant supply of unskilled labour, and where markets can be very imperfect due to institutional power arrangements.

Finally, small high-income groups which do not derive their incomes from any of the sources mentioned above can be found in every country. This is the case with persons who obtain their income from abroad because they are part of a foreign economic, administrative, cultural, religious, military or political structure, or of an international organization. This is normally a marginal group in most countries.

The high income groups, with internationalized consumption patterns, obtain their incomes from a very heterogeneous productive structure which is not compartmentalized but is, on the contrary, closely integrated and institutionally interrelated. Only a relatively small part of this productive structure, which differs in nature and importance from country to country, has levels of productivity sufficiently high to allow certain groups to sustain these patterns of consumption; the low productivity of the larger part of the productive structure, on the contrary, must be organized on an exploitative basis in order to provide minority groups with high incomes. Moreover, strong transfer mechanisms must be present if a wider range of groups, including those not directly or indirectly associated with high productivity activities, are to achieve the internationalized pattern of consumption. In other words, the magnitude of the high income sector is a function, in the first place, of the economic magnitude of the high productivity activities, and secondly of its political capacity to obtain a larger share of the incomes generated by that sector. Thirdly, it is a function of the capacity of the group to extract a part of the income generated in the low productivity activities through the maintenance of an institutional structure in the factor and goods markets and in the income transfer mechanisms, which will restrict the access of large sectors of the population to the sources of reasonable and stable incomes. If broad features of this analysis which need more detailed and careful scrutiny are correct, it could be inferred that the presence and expansion of the internationalized consumption sector of high incomes is not independent of the presence and expansion of a marginalized sector, nor of the capacity of the former to strongly influence the evolution of the productive structure, the nature of the productive structure, the nature of the transfer of technology, internal income transfers, and the pattern of consumption.

Part Five

Social Learning and
the Nature of Planning

Production-centered development has been supported by its own organizational models and decision-making methodologies. Generally it has favored command-system forms of organization, which respond to formal central plans based on the decision rules and methodologies of rational decision analysis. Dealing with defined problems in stable environments, such systems can be relatively efficient. But they tend to be unresponsive to local variety and to make little use of the creative energies of most of their members.

People-centered development favors the organizational models of self-organizing systems, which operate in a more organic fashion. The structures and information flows of self-organizing systems are geared to the goal-setting and problem-solving processes of their various subsystems, so that innovative and adaptive action—that is, learning—occurs continuously throughout the total system. They attempt to utilize the creative abilities of all their participants.

Social learning theory provides an important part of the theory base for people-centered development. Edgar Dunn, Jr. sets forth the basic arguments of social learning theory, which deals with the unique ability of humans and human groups to function as learning organisms, that is, to engage in behavior directed to changing or reprogramming behavior. Dunn examines how the experimental processes of social learning differ from those of the classical physical sciences and argues that the limited contributions of the social sciences to the solution of social problems can be traced to a failure to embrace this distinction.

David Korten provides a link between Dunn's epistemological concerns with social learning theory and the seeming intractability of rural poverty. He examines the limitations of development programming procedures based on the epistemological models of the classical physical sciences and demonstrates through a number of case studies how an alternative approach more consistent with the principles of social learning theory has produced results in addressing rural poverty in Asia.

The broader implications for social problem solving of the relationship between social learning and planning theory are examined by John Friedmann. Russell Ackoff takes the point a step further, noting that development itself is not a product of production, but rather of learning. This reconceptualization leads Ackoff to look at development from quite a fresh perspective and to suggest important implications for the ways in which professional planners define their roles.

17

The Nature of Social Learning

EDGAR S. DUNN, JR.

The most striking thing about evolutionary history is that the operation of phylogenesis in its generalizing mode created improvements in organism adaptability until it generated learning organisms. Thus, the behavioral reprogramming of organism behavior that is phylogenesis gradually evolved a program (genotype) that provided the organism with the power to reprogram itself—to act as a true learning system at the organism level. In the human species the learning organism reached the point where learning becomes largely socialized because the dominant aspect of the individual organism's learning environment is the presence of and the sharing with other learning organisms.

In this way there emerged a process of social evolution distinct from biological evolution and a process of social learning distinct from a purely stochastic learning process. This process takes place at two levels—the level of the individual and the level of the group.

The major elements in an individual's learning and personality formation are associated with his social environment. He learns by sharing in a range of acquired information through communication and social system participation. Individual behaviors form group clusters to exploit the behavioral amplification that specialization and exchange can afford. Thus, individual learning and behavior are shaped by the nature of the group activities in which the individual participates and through which he is molded, and which in turn, are frequently molded by him.

Social learning also takes place at the level of the group, where the result is not the transformation of individual behavior but the transformation of group behavior. Either the collective membership of the group or some leadership élite undertakes to monitor the group behavior with reference to group goals. Serious deviations constitute problems which must be resolved through technological innovation and social reorganization.

Social learning subsumes both social system learning and the socialized

Excerpted from Edgar S. Dunn, Jr., *Economic and Social Development: A Process of Social Learning* (Baltimore: The Johns Hopkins University Press, 1971), pp. 239–45. Published for Resources for the Future, Inc. Copyright © 1971 by The Johns Hopkins University Press.

learning of the individual. Its operation at the two levels is obviously inter-related. Since the orientation of this book is a social science one, we have been predominantly concerned with the way in which the process works to transform social systems. The essence of what we have learned about the operation of the process is as follows.

Social behavior is not identical with social learning. Two of the unique aspects of the human social process continue to operate in the absence of social learning. Behaviors directed to evaluating and organizing behavior are continuously employed in maintaining social processes that are homeo-static in character. There they operate to modify the mix and flow of estab-lished modes of behavior in response to established behavioral criteria associated with the monitoring of moderate environmental changes.

Since social systems frequently encounter situations, in which such predetermined forms of adaptation are inadequate, rarely can they long escape the necessity for social learning. Then they must display the third unique component of the social process—behavior directed to changing behavior. In this learning process both behavior-evaluating behavior and behavior-organizing behavior continue to operate, but they become trans-formed into aspects of behavior-changing behavior. They operate together to form a process of social learning.

This we identify as a process of evolutionary experimentation —a process that is different in important respects from the experimental process known to classical science. Social system evolution is the result of a problem solving process that is an implicit if not explicit form of hypothesis testing— but is problem solving and testing of a different order.

Classical experimental physical science takes place at two levels: analysis and system design. At the level of analysis it is concerned with understanding the operation of deterministic physical systems from the posture of an external observer. It commonly tests hypotheses about the nature of the system by observing the effect upon components of the system of changes in exogenous parameters, usually under highly controlled conditions. In this way it seeks to identify laws or universal relationships. At the level of system design, these relationships or laws are applied to the design of deterministic systems like machine systems, creating artifacts that amplify human behavior. The design of these systems is engineered from the posture of an external manipulator. To the extent that the valuation process is involved, it is concerned only with instrumental values or efficiency criteria at the design stage.

In social systems problem solving and hypothesis testing take on a differ-ent character. The basic point of departure is the fact that the social system experimenter is not exogenous to the system. He exists as an endogenous component of the system he is attempting to understand and transform. He is not dealing with the understanding and design of fully deterministic systems. He is immersed in the act of social system self-analysis and self-transformation. He is the agent of social learning—a purposive, self-actuating, but not fully deterministic process. He is not interested to the same degree in establishing universals because the social system which engages his activity is phenomenologically unique and both its structure and function are temporary in character. He is engaged, rather, in formulating and testing developmental hypotheses. The developmental hypothesis is a presupposition that, if the organization and behavior of the social system were to be modified in a certain way, the goals of the system would be more adequately realized. This developmental hypothesis is not tested repeatedly under nearly identical or controlled conditions. Rather, it is tested by the degree to which goal convergence is realized as a result of the experimental design. Problem solving—hypothesis formulation and testing—is an iterative, sequential series of adaptations of an adaptable, goal-seeking, self-activating system. It can be characterized as evolutionary experimentation.

This process calls into play the other two unique processes in its support. Because by its nature social learning involves social reorganization, behavior-organizing behavior is involved. We have seen that an organization is defined by a set of boundary conditions. These boundary conditions are a set of social system goals and the controls imposed upon component systems to assure that their behavior supports the total system goals. Developmental hypotheses arise out of the anomalies of social organization when the social system controls do not adequately serve the social system goals. They are tested through social system reorganization designed to bring the system goals and controls into consonance.

Evolutionary experimentation can be seen to exhibit both a normal and extraordinary mode. In normal problem solving the emphasis is upon the reorganization of the system controls. It involves the reorganization of subsystem boundaries under the control of the total system goals. It does not threaten the context of the system. As we have seen, this mode of problem solving is frequently inadequate. The developmental hypotheses and the associated subsystem reorganizations are not sufficient to bring about consonance of total system goals and controls. Thus, evolutionary experimentation occasionally manifests itself as a paradigm shift or a displacement in the operating context of the total system. It comes to deal, not with the reorganization of controls, but with the reformulation of total system goals as well.

This makes plain that behavior-evaluating behavior is also an essential servant of evolutionary experimentation. In the case of normal problem solving, attention is restricted to a consideration of the adequacy of instrumental goals and criteria. Subsystem goals may come under consideration because they are in conflict with the target goals of the total system. They are either placed under additional constraints by the reorganization of control subsystems or they are directly subjected to the reorganization of their own goals and controls. In this mode, however, even the revision of subsystem goals is undertaken under the control of total system goals. In the case of evolutionary experimentation that is manifest as a paradigm shift, it is the target goals of the total system that are subject to revision. This makes plain that the social scientist concerned with developmental problems cannot abstract from normative or value-laden issues. The process of evolutionary experimentation is essentially a normative process; one of its consequences is the evolution of social values.

Throughout social history the operation of this process of social learning has been hazardous and haphazard because its conduct has not been efficient and because it has been predominantly concerned with instrumental goals. In effect, the process of social learning has not understood itself sufficiently well to rationalize itself as an efficient process with a coherent purpose.

Because the process has not been understood and consciously applied, social change has frequently been dominated by an attempt to implement change by processes incompatible with the reality of social evolution. Acting on the basis of inadequate paradigms and metaphors, we have been inclined to practice a form of social engineering. It is presupposed that the change agents can act as though they are external to the process and have the knowledge and power to design a terminal state that will bring about consistent goals and controls in a deterministic fashion. Also acting on the basis of an inadequate paradigm of the social process, an attempt to freeze the social status quo—to create and maintain static social system boundaries—is frequently evident. Both of these impractical modes are clearly impossible, but the attempt to impose them upon social change has a tendency to exacerbate the traumatic and unpredictable consequences of the process.

The other part of the difficulty stems from the fact that social learning is being applied more efficiently in one of its modes than the other because it is only partly understood. The resulting disproportion has had serious social consequences. The conscious and efficient practice of physical science and the design of physical systems has been perfected to the point where normal social system problem solving is dominated by the reorganizations associated with new physical technology—the redesign of machine subsystems and their control. This has had the effect of accelerating the rate at which organizational crises occur—in particular, the rate of those that can only be resolved by paradigm shifts. This accelerated need for social reorganization is not matched by an appropriate understanding of social system learning. We do not yet see the implications of normal problem solving for the control of human subsystems (involving the consistency of individual and total system goals), nor do we see clearly how to engage purposively in the process of controlling paradigm shifts. This has led to an accelerating rate of painful, reactive, major social reorganizations. The revision of the target goals of social systems is as yet largely uncoordinated, fragmentary, and opportunistic.

One concludes that amelioration of many of the world's worst social ills, if not the long-run survival of the social process itself, must hinge upon our ability to make the practice of social learning more orderly and rational.

First, we need to devote concentrated attention in social science to understanding the process. Second, at every stage and level of our understanding we need to apply what we know to conscious, orderly practice and control of the process. This implies that developmental hypotheses should be more objectively and consciously formulated by the group. The evolutionary experiment should be frankly conceived as an experiment and deliberately provided with information feedback that monitors goal convergence and sets the stage for the next round of experimentation. The seductive appeal of utopian social engineering must be put aside. Third, we need to innovate organizational forms and procedures that efficiently integrate the goals and controls of social learning itself. Fourth, we need to acknowledge that this may require an over-arching social goal or value that serves as a final test for evolutionary experiments — that guides the formulation of developmental hypotheses and passes judgment upon paradigm shifts.

We have suggested that this over-arching goal is the development of the growth motives of the human individual. If this suggests that, as a consequence, social evolution becomes teleological in a way not matched by cosmological or biological evolution, it should be pointed out that this is not a terminal state or a transcendent teleology of the kind associated with the orthogenetic fallacy; nor is it the conventional teleology of social action formed by the pursuit of instrumental goals and social maintenance. It is a process teleology. It suggests that human beings can establish the process of human development as the goal of the process of social evolution. Both the process and the goal are understood to be open to further transformation as we advance in the practice and understanding of them.

By asserting the normative priority of human development as our social goal, we add to the internal consistency of the social learning paradigm as well as to the order of the process. It provides the interface between the social learning of the individual and social system learning. It is only through establishing such a priority that group behavior and individual behavior come to be mutually reinforcing in a nonstatic world.

If this makes the social process and social science anthropocentric in character, no apology is necessary. To deny that this is appropriate would be to deny a fundamental aspect of human nature and the evolutionary process that formed it. The psychic orientation of man and his motivation to action is by nature anthropocentric just as that of the rat is rat-ocentric. Man happens to have the potential through social learning to create a controlled process that can support him in the realization and exercise of his highest human potential — perhaps even to enlarge that potential and the meaning and joy that accompanies its exercise.

18

Rural Development Programming: The Learning Process Approach

David C. Korten

One of the clear lessons of the 1970s has been that effective participation of the rural poor in the development process is more easily mandated in programming documents than achieved in the real world of program implementation. It is not, however, a new lesson. In earlier decades, experience with cooperatives and rural development produced similarly disappointing results in the context of high expectations and good intentions. Generally the cooperatives proved to be creations of government operated under government management – which provided little market power, produced few returns to members, and consequently enjoyed little or no popular support. Similarly community development, when implemented on a large scale, ended up as little more than one more set of centrally formulated programs and targets implemented through conventional bureaucratic structures and largely unresponsive to local preferences and/or needs.

In hindsight the results seem quite predictable. Yet in spite of the monotony with which the basic lessons thus learned have been repeated and the fairly substantial progress made in understanding the nature of the problem, it remains the rule rather than the exception to see in development programming: a) reliance, even for the planning and implementation of "participative" development, on centralized bureaucratic organizations which have little capacity to respond to diverse community-defined needs or to build on community skills and values; b) inadequate investment in the difficult process of building community problem-solving capacity; c) inadequate attention to dealing with social diversity, especially highly stratified village social structures; and d) insufficient integration of the technical and social components of development action.

From *Rural Development Participation Review* 2 (Ithaca, N.Y.: Rural Development Committee, Cornell University, Winter 1981), pp. 1–8. The research on which this paper is based is documented in detail in a much longer version: "Community Organization and Rural Development: A Learning Process Approach," *Public Administration Review*, September–October, 1980 pp. 480–510.

Prominent among the barriers to effective participatory programs are pressures on development financing agencies to move too much money too quickly in time bounded, pre-planned projects in pursuit of short-term results; while the need is for a flexible, sustained, experimental, action-based, capacity-building style of development effort for which both donors and recipient bureaucracies are ill-equipped. Pressures for immediate results measured by goods and services delivered drive out attention to building the capacity of the responsible institutions to provide these goods and services in ways which are responsive to local needs *and* build the local problem-solving capacity on which sustained development depends. Programming procedures which demand detailed upfront planning coupled with rigorous adherence to fast-paced implementation schedules and pre-planned specifications all but assure that the projects will be unresponsive to subsequent popular input—or even to a growing understanding of what the real problems are on the part of the project's professional staff.

Three Asian Successes

Are there options? Apparently so, as there are a number of successful experiences that provide exceptions to the more typical outcomes. These bear examination in a search for useful lessons. Three cases selected for examination for Asia share several common characteristics: a) involvement of rural people in their own advancement; b) greater than average success, with results that are not dependent on uniquely favorable settings; and c) a scale of operation that places them substantially beyond the pilot project stage.

INDIAN NATIONAL DAIRY DEVELOPMENT BOARD

India's National Dairy Development Board (NDDB), built up from the model of the Anand Milk Producers' Union, is frequently cited as an example of the potentials of cooperative organization in the Third World. By the end of 1976 it was comprised of 4,530 village cooperatives with a combined membership of 2 million farmers. The cooperative collects milk from members at village collection points twice each day, transports and processes it, and markets the processed products in major urban centers. It is known for being efficient, free of corruption, and effective in providing major benefits to even the poorest members of the village communities it serves.

But it did not begin with the NDDB operating a national-scale program. Its roots go back to the mid-forties when a group of dairy farmers grew tired of cooperating with the government-sponsored milk market program which offered them low and fluctuating prices. Boycotting the government program, they formed their own cooperative under the leadership of a farmer-member. By 1947 eight village cooperatives with 432 members had formed a cooperative union. These were difficult times for the cooperative and in 1949 they called on the assistance of Verghese Kurien whom, it seems, destiny had brought to their village. Along with the farmers, Kurien learned how the problems of milk production and marketing within a village cooperative framework could be overcome. As they learned, other cooperatives were formed and brought within the organizational umbrella. Gradually methods were refined, and the organization that was eventually to become the NDDB grew—from the bottom up—adding new layers and branches as it grew, always under the sustained leadership of Kurien. Appropriate management systems to meet the demands of the program were worked out through experience. The values of integrity, service, and commitment to the poorest member-producers were deeply imbedded in its emerging structures. Management staff were hired fresh from school, trained through experience on the job, indoctrinated in the values of the program, and advanced rapidly as the program grew.

BANGLADESH RURAL ADVANCEMENT COMMITTEE

BRAC was formed in early 1972 under the leadership of Mr. F. H. Abed, a practicing accountant, as a modest relief effort to resettle refugees in the Sulla area of Northeast Bangladesh following the war of partition with Pakistan. Those involved soon learned that relief alone was not going to overcome the miserable conditions in which even the successfully resettled refugees were forced to live, and it was decided to reorient their efforts toward village-level development.

A multi-sectoral program was evolved which included construction of community centers, functional education, agriculture, fisheries, cooperatives, health and family planning, and vocational training for women. In each sector early failures led to program modifications. For example the teaching methods and lesson plans of the functional education program were substantially revised to make them more relevant to village life. In the health program they turned to use of paramedics, with physicians reorienting their roles to be first trainers, second planners, and only lastly curers. But close monitoring of the villages in which they were working revealed to BRAC staff that they still were not producing the results they wanted. Too few of its programs were addressing the needs of the landless. Conflicting interests of landed and landless made it nearly impossible to address the interests of each within a single village association. Each sectoral activity tended to operate independently of the others. Village activities remained overly dependent on the presence of BRAC staff. The paramedics tended to concentrate on cures rather than prevention. The literacy program was not producing useable skills.

BRAC programs had fallen into the patterns of most sectoralized government sponsored rural development efforts – with similar results. Again a major review was undertaken to assimilate the lessons learned and evolve a change in strategy. The new strategy would concentrate entirely on the poorest 50% of the village population – defined operationally as those families whose livelihoods depended in part on selling labor to third parties – and program initiatives would come largely from the beneficiaries. When entering a new village, an initial survey identified members of the target group. Informal discussions at traditional gathering places served to identify the major concerns of this group and to single out those with leadership potential. Discussion groups grew until a village assembly of the poor became formalized. Leaders received training at a special BRAC center in organizing and consciousness-raising methods.

To insure against dependence on BRAC and to discourage participation by those only interested in handouts, initial activities developed by the group had to be carried out exclusively with local resources. Only when the group had proven capable in mobilizing such resources were supplemental BRAC resources offered. Education provided literacy and numeracy skills, but was designed concurrently to raise consciousness of class exploitation and to build commitment to group action. The activities dealt with truly basic needs such as demands for a rightful share in government programs; bargaining for improved wages, share cropping and landlease terms; and schemes to gain control over productive assets. Women's activities emphasized productive employment, often involving difficult physical work under a food-for-work program. All schemes were planned and implemented under the supervision of leaders from the target group.

As the strongest possible indication that BRAC's new approach was indeed responding in an effective way to strongly felt needs, the program was being self-replicated by the villages themselves. As one village set out to organize another to protect its newly negotiated gains in wages and contract terms, the landless of other villages came from miles away asking organized villages to help them achieve the same.

At about the time that BRAC moved from a sectoral to a more people-centered approach, it also established a research unit to advance the understanding of its staff of rural poverty. Questions were addressed such as: Who controls what assets in the rural village and how? How are some families able to advance themselves while others become increasingly impoverished? What is the peasant's perception of famine and credit? Participatory research techniques such as the use of peasant panels to generate data on peasant perceptions of famine and credit proved highly effective. Researchers and field workers often exchanged roles or worked jointly to insure that research was fully integrated with operations. By January 1980, 378 BRAC staff were working with some 800 villages.

THAILAND'S COMMUNITY-BASED FAMILY PLANNING SERVICES

As an official of Thailand's development planning agency responsible for observing government programs in action from 1965 to 1971, Mechai Veravaidya reached two conclusions: 1) the government's development programs were largely failing because they were designed from the top down, involved no participation of the people, and seldom provided effective follow-up on completed projects; and 2) the few gains made were rapidly overtaken by Thailand's rapid population growth. Mechai left the planning agency in 1971 and began experimenting with the idea of bringing family planning closer to the people. He tried having a doctor offer family planning services in a local school. The people responded, but he could not get a second doctor interested. He tried using student recruiters to send potential acceptors to a clinic. The doctors liked this approach, but the people didn't. After a variety of failures he tried in 1974 a totally new approach which would not be dependent on physicians. Shopkeepers were recruited in each of five villages, given a supply of birth control pills, instructed in their use, and encouraged to sell them for a small commission. Good sales led to recruitment of seventy new distributors. Expansion continued thereafter and Mechai eventually set up a new organization specifically to service his distributors and expand the program.

As the program expanded, Mechai became preoccupied with the design and operation of strong management systems consistent with the needs of the village-level operations. Continuous testing and revision resulted in important changes in supervisory, resupply, and reporting systems. New layers of management were added as required. As top management became further and further removed from field operations he instituted a requirement that each make periodic visits to the villages with local supervisors to keep them grounded in village reality. Finding donor-mandated statistical reporting systems cumbersome and of little utility, he drastically simplified reporting requirements to gather only the most basic of performance information, directly related to program operations. Color coded graphs and monthly staff meetings were mechanisms for encouraging staff to make regular use of this data. Unimpressed with the utility of conventional impact surveys which did not relate to administrative units and produced results only after the time for action had passed, he devised his own "mini-survey" method by which his supervisors gathered data from a sample of households each month, processed the data, and put it to immediate use.

The Common Feature: A Learning Process

The performance of a development program can be characterized as a function of the fit achieved between beneficiaries, program, and assisting organization. In more specific terms a given development program is likely to perform poorly in terms of advancing the well-being of a specific group unless there is a close correspondence between: beneficiary needs and program output; program task requirements and the distinctive competence of the assisting organization; and the mechanisms for beneficiary demand expression and the decision processes of the assisting organization (see figure 1).

The various programs examined in the cases above each found a particular solution to the requirement for fit appropriate to its time and circumstance. If we look to these experiences for a program or an organizational blueprint for replication elsewhere we are only likely to be disappointed. It is to the *process* of their development that we must look for the most useful lessons. The nature and significance of this process is best understood by contrasting it with a more conventional approach to development programming, understood as the "blueprint" approach.

THE BLUEPRINT APPROACH

This approach, with its emphasis on careful pre-planning, reflects the textbook version of how development programming is supposed to work. Researchers are supposed to provide data from pilot projects and other

SCHEMATIC REPRESENTATION OF FIT REQUIREMENTS

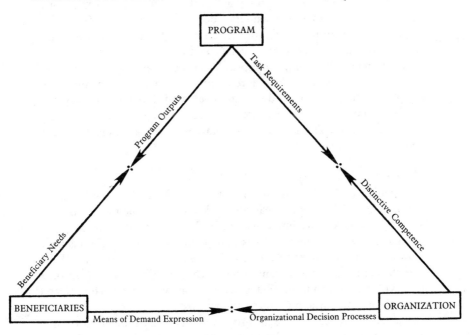

Figure 1

studies from which project designers will choose the most cost-effective designs for achieving given outcomes. Administrators of the implementing organizations are supposed to execute the project plan faithfully, much as a building contractor would follow construction blueprints, specifications, and schedules. Once implementation is complete an evaluation researcher is supposed to measure actual changes in the target population and report actual versus planned changes to the planners at the end of the project cycle so that blueprints can be revised.

Its clear-cut order, allocation of funds for precisely-stated outcomes, reliance on "hard" data and expert judgment, and the clearly-stated implementation schedules make project justification easy in budget presentations. It is a programming approach quite appropriate to certain types of development projects—most notably physical infrastructure projects—where the task and outcomes are defined, environment stable, and cost predictable. Unfortunately, however, in rural development the objectives are more often multiple, ill-defined, and subject to negotiated change; task requirements are unclear; environments are constantly changing; and costs are unpredictable. Although knowledge is severely limited, the blueprint approach calls for behaving as if it were nearly perfect. Where there is need to build institutional capacity for sustained action on unfamiliar development problems, it assumes that development actions are terminal and that hastily assembled temporary organizations will suffice. Where the need is for a close integration of knowledge-building, decision-making, and action-taking roles, it sharply differentiates the functions and even the institutional locations of the researcher, the planner and the administrator.

Awareness is becoming widespread that the blueprint approach is an inadequate response to the rural development problem, but its assumptions and procedures continue to dominate most rural development programming and to provide the core content of most training courses in development management. This is unlikely to change until viable options are understood and supported.

THE LEARNING PROCESS APPROACH

Examination of the three Asian success cases suggests that the blueprint approach never played more than an incidental role in their development. None was designed and implemented. Each emerged out of a long-term learning process in which villages and program personnel shared their knowledge and resources to create a fit between needs, actions, and the capacities of the assisting organization. Each had a leader who spent time in the villages with an idea, tried it, accepted and corrected his errors, and built a larger organization around the requirement of what he learned.

In each instance the overall process can be broken down into three stages, each with its own unique learning requirement (see figure 2). The elements of each stage can be described roughly as follows:

Figure 2 PROGRAM LEARNING CURVES

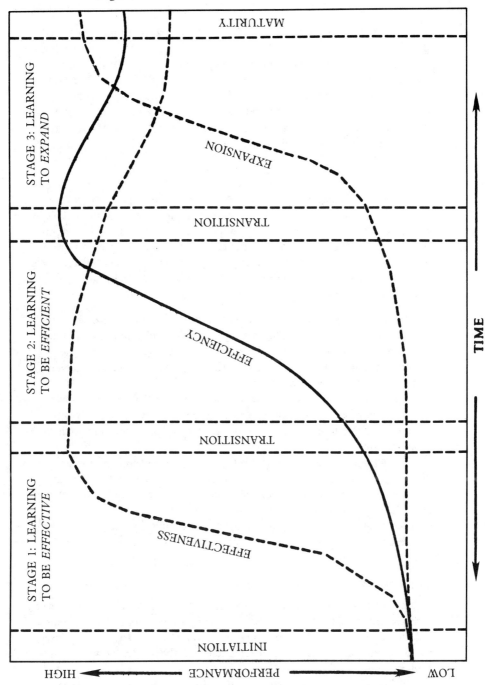

Note: There are likely to be trade-offs between effectiveness, efficiency, and expansion which will lead to some loss of effectiveness as efficiency increases, and to losses in both effectiveness and efficiency during expansion.

Stage 1: Learning to be effective. One or more teams of highly qualified personnel are sent to one or more villages which constitute their learning laboratory or pilot site. Here they develop a familiarity with the problem in question from the beneficiary's perspective and try out some promising approaches to addressing jointly identified needs. They may be supported by a variety of external resource persons with expertise in the social, managerial, and related technical sciences. Errors will be common and the resource inputs required will be high relative to results. It is assumed that rapid adaptive action will be taken as errors in initial assumptions are identified.

Stage 2: Learning to be efficient. As insights are gained into what to do, attention is redirected to learning how to do it more efficiently, eliminating activities which are relatively nonproductive and working out simplified problem-solving routines for handling critical activities within the grasp of less skilled persons. New learning laboratory sites may be selectively established to test and further refine such methods – simultaneously giving additional personnel experience in their application.

Stage 3: Learning to expand. Then attention is again redirected, this time to the phased development of a supporting organization geared to the requirements of carrying out the prescribed activities on a larger scale. It requires building into the organization the supporting skills, management systems, structures, and values.

The three stages as represented here are a simplified abstraction of what in reality may be a very disorderly and largely intuitive process. Yet the abstraction helps to explicate an alternative to the blueprint approach to programming.

A key point worth special note is that in the cases examined, there was no thought given to simply testing a program model in a pilot context and then leaving it to others to implement. To the contrary, each was distinguished by a *substantial continuity of personnel*. The people who had the experience of figuring out an original program design capable of doing the job were the same people who then built an organization around that model adapted to its requirements.

THE LEARNING ORGANIZATION

Any pre-planned intervention into a varied and constantly changing sociotechnical system inevitably will be in error by some margin; the outcome will nearly always deviate from the outcome intended. It is the response to this error that tells the true character of the organization and its leadership.

In the *self-deceiving organization* those in authority treat error as synonymous with failure and seek to place blame on some guilty party. In response, the organization's members become skilled in hiding such errors. Those in authority, thus removed from operating reality, are reassured that as a result of their "brilliant" leadership everything is going just as intended. They may impress the unwary visitors with their briefings on program accomplishments. But to more sophisticated observers the claim that a program addressed to the rural poor is working effectively exactly as originally planned is a sure indicator that mistakes are being hidden, that leadership is ineffective, and that actual program operations are probably in a state of disarray which bears little resemblance to what has been described.

In the *defeated organization* the source of error is assumed to stem from forces beyond the control of the organization's members. Thus while adverse factors may be discussed in rich detail, no action is taken. When individual members feel impotent and therefore refer all problems to their superiors for action, they render their superiors equally impotent, ultimately immobilizing the entire organization.

In the *learning organization* error is treated as an essential source of information. Since some margin of error is treated as inevitable, particularly in the early stages of the learning process, it is viewed neither as a sign of failure, nor of environment perversity. Error is discussed candidly in such organizations, but in the context of lessons learned and corrective actions being attempted. There may be no surer indicator that an organization has effective leadership.

NEW ROLE FOR SOCIAL SCIENCES

While the demand for greater sensitivity to the dynamics of social behavior in rural development programming is now notably high, the influence of the social sciences in programming decisions is notably low. Given the roles normally accepted by social scientists in relation to action programs, their limited influence is hardly surprising. In their role of summary evaluator they have mainly engaged in documenting failure long after the time for corrective action has passed. In doing social soundness assessments, they have most often been called in after the basic choices affecting project design have been made to certify that there will not be serious adverse social consequences. In testing the program concepts in pilot projects, they have been asked to certify program blueprints when in reality the results achieved will often reflect more the operational competence of the organization which has done the implementation than the specific validity of the program design. In carrying out baseline surveys there is seldom any real presumption that the data will be used as a substantive input to planning. More likely the survey was contracted only to meet a requirement set in some programming document for baseline evaluation data.

What is all too rare is for the social scientists to help an organization build its capacity to actually *use* social science knowledge and data as a normal part of its operating routine. What the case studies suggest as needed is a willingness to experiment with new research methods by researchers committed to providing action agency personnel with simple tools to facilitate their *rapid* collection and interpretation of social data directly *relevant to action* for which they are responsible. The task is to make a demystified social science available as every person's tool, turning agency personnel, and in some instances the villagers themselves, into more effective action researchers.

This most often seems to involve disciplined observation, guided interviews and informant panels rather than formal surveys; emphasizing timeliness over rigor; employing oral more than written communication; offering informed interpretation rather than extensive statistical analysis; making narrative rather than numerical presentations; and giving attention to the processes unfolding and to intermediate outcome data required for rapid adaptation, rather than dwelling on detailed assessment of "final" outcomes. Rather than provide the static profiles found in the typical socio-economic survey, it involves a quest to understand the dynamics of the socio-technical systems that govern village life, to provide a basis for operational-level predictions of the consequences of given development interventions. It means identifying target group members and behaviors in terms relevant to program action rather than simply producing aggregated statistics.

Application to an Established Bureaucracy

The framework of the learning process approach can be applied in either of two ways. One is by building an entirely new program and organization — from the bottom up — as illustrated in the three cases discussed earlier. The other is by introducing an analogue of this same process within an established organization which seeks to build a new capacity for effective village-level action. The methodologies for the latter application are presently being worked out by the Philippines' National Irrigation Administration (NIA) in an effort directed toward strengthening its capacity to work in effective support of small farmer owned and operated (communal) gravity-fed irrigation systems.

Concerned that the communal irrigation system it was assisting often fell into disrepair and disuse soon after rehabilitation construction was completed, NIA officials concluded that attention was needed to strengthen the water user associations concurrently with work on physical construction. They first selected for special attention two systems scheduled for assistance. Since the NIA had no community organizers of its own, a number of experienced organizers were hired on a temporary basis to work with NIA engineers on these systems. The idea was to integrate the social and technical aspects of the work — developing the social and technical capacity of the water user association through active involvement of its members in such activities as planning system layout, obtaining water rights and rights of way, organizing volunteer labor inputs to system construction, and exerting control over project expenditures. Known as the Laur Project, the experience established that such integration was at once important and difficult to achieve.

In one community, local power struggles emerged which led to a two-year postponement of construction plans. In the second community, a high level of cohesion greatly facilitated farmer involvement, but seldom in ways which made life easier for project staff. Delays resulted from farmer demands for scheduling and design changes. The use of volunteer labor posed unfamiliar problems of supervision worked out only through lengthy meetings. The engineers did not always welcome farmer interest in monitoring purchases and limiting the staff's personal use of vehicles operated on gasoline charged to the farmers' loan account. Particularly tense was a conflict in judgment between farmers and engineers as to whether the materials chosen for dam construction would withstand the force of local floods. Farmers said no. Engineers said yes. (The farmers won a Pyrrhic victory when the dam, finally constructed to the engineers' specifications, washed out a few months after completion.)

At this stage the pilot projects were a failure from the standpoint of any normal evaluation criteria. But it was quite evident to those involved that the weakness was not in the basic concept—it was in the as-yet-limited capacity of the NIA to make it work. And the experience provided extensive insights as to what was required to develop that capacity on both the technical and institutional sides. A major commitment to further learning was implied, involving major changes in the NIA's structure and operating procedures.

A series of new pilot projects was initiated, the designs of which were carefully worked out to incorporate the lessons of the earlier Laur experience. New personnel were brought in and thoroughly trained in these lessons. A top-level national communal irrigation committee was established to coordinate the learning process under the leadership of NIA Assistant Administrator Benjamin Bagadion, a man with total dedication to the idea of independent farmer owned and operated irrigation systems. The committee included central level NIA officials, representatives of related action agencies, and senior members of collaborating academic and research institutions—each of whom had a major day-to-day commitment to the effort. A new social science research program supported by the Ford Foundation was introduced to build within the NIA the new skills, methods, and systems it would require for its new participative approach. Social scientists from the Institute of Philippine Culture developed guidelines for rapid collection and assessment *by NIA field staff* of "institutional profiles" which contained social-institutional data critical to project selection and planning. They also observed field activities and produced monthly "process documentation" reports which provided non-evaluative narrative feedback on key process events.

Concurrently, management experts from the Asian Institute of Management assessed the fit between requirements of the new methods for assisting communals and the existing NIA management systems, advised on new management roles and procedures, assisted in planning the organizational change process, and coordinated workshops for NIA managers and engineers on the new methods. On the technical side, an agricultural engineering team from the International Rice Research Institute and the University of the Philippines at Los Banos was developing simplified methods for diagnosis and correction of common water management problems by farmers and NIA engineers, and designing water management systems suited to needs of small water user associations.

Once the new methods for assisting the communal projects seemed to be proving more successful in the second round of pilot projects or learning laboratories, a second set of 12 sites was chosen, one in each region of the country, to test their broader application and to begin building the basis for the expansion stage. As of mid-1980 the NIA was perhaps half way through the learning process on which it had embarked three and a half years earlier. It was likely to be a total of seven or eight years before the new capacity would be in place throughout the agency. Such a lengthy undertaking does not fit well with normal donor programming cycles and requires uncommon commitment, patience, and continuity of leadership. But it may be exactly the type of undertaking in which any major agency concerned with being effective in assisting the rural poor must become engaged.

Conclusion

The programming methods which gained currency in the days of large-scale capital infrastructure project construction continue to dominate development action, even though they are manifestly inappropriate to the requirements of new style programming. However, a basis can be found in current experience for the formulation of alternative and more appropriate programming frameworks and methods based on a *learning process approach* which recognizes that in working with rural people, our knowledge of what is needed and our institutional capacity to do this are both limited. There should be no call for endless research. But neither should there be continuation of blind action based on inappropriate statements of the problem and ineffectual implementing organizations. The challenge is to integrate action-taking, knowledge-creation, and institution-building into a coherent learning process, as a number of relatively more successful development programs are already doing.

19

Planning as Social Learning

JOHN FRIEDMANN

Ideas about planning have changed so much in recent years that one is tempted to speak of a genuine shift in paradigm.[1] Specifically, the change was from a "blueprint" model of planning to a social learning approach. Blueprinting means to devise a design for the future that is carried out by a central authority according to a specific program. Formal deviations from the design are permitted but must be duly noted in the plan itself which, in its remaining parts, is then adjusted to preserve its structure as an integrated whole. Essentially a form of advance decision-making, blueprinting involves a central determination of the public purpose. It must be comprehensive in its coverage and rational in the disposition of its instruments.[2]

Although it serves as the pattern for formal planning in American local government, skeptics have always questioned the model. If it survived as an ideal, it was because of the strong simplicity of its conception, and because it legitimated and confirmed state power. Planners whose background placed them in an intellectual tradition that conceived of planning as physical design writ large, sustained it. Propped up by an advanced professional degree, they were comfortable with the thought that they might be entrusted with the task of giving physical form to what they claimed to be the common will of the community. They conceived of planning, like any other activity, as being subject to the division of labor and, in this division, they meant to be the artisans of plans.[3]

Toward the end of the 1960s, this conception was badly shaken. Whatever theorists might say, historical events had cast serious doubt on the ability of the blueprint model to come successfully to grips with the major problems besetting American cities. The "best and the finest" had mired the country in the debacle of Vietnam; the cities were in crisis; faith in the liberal state had spent itself. As far as planners were concerned, these were the stirring times of "advocacy" and citizen participation.[4] The cry

---

Reprinted from *Retracking America* © 1981 by John Friedmann. Permission granted by Rodale Press, Inc., Emmaus, Pa. 18049.

was for Power to the People, and even Richard Milhouse Nixon would flash the fist salute. Senator Moynihan would later call it the "maximum feasible misunderstanding."[5]

Technocratic *hubris* had fallen out of step with the times. Instead of planning *for* people, planners now talked of planning *with* them. Though practice might not always be in line with rhetoric, the intention was clear. People were beginning to take charge of their lives within their own communities. In the 1960s, the struggle had been over poverty; in the 1970s, it was increasingly over questions of environmental quality, housing, and consumer rights. The effort was called the community movement,[6] and congenial books, such as E. F. Schumacher's *Small Is Beautiful*[7] and Ivan Illich's *Tools for Conviviality*[8] turned instant classics. As a metaphor for this movement, blueprinting was clearly inappropriate. At the same time, it was by no means certain what planning notions might replace it. And until a substitute could be found, the old beliefs and practices would linger on.

In 1973 I argued in the first edition of *Retracking America* that planning was not so much concerned with the making of plans as with "mutual learning," was less centered on documents than dialogue, and was more dependent for its results on the transactions of individual persons in specific settings than on abstract institutions. I called this planning style *transactive*, and the underlying model *social learning*.

Social learning had been foreshadowed in the work of two American philosophers who had been deeply concerned with questions of guided social change: John Dewey and Lewis Mumford. In several works,[9] Dewey had advocated a scientific, open-ended approach to planned social change. Yet though his overall vision was persuasive, he remained vague on who precisely would conduct social experiments and who would ultimately be the learners. Would it be scholars? planners? the state? particular publics? the people as a whole? Dewey refused to say. Mumford, for his part, was more specific. In his major work, *The Culture of Cities*,[10] he championed social surveys as an instrument of regional planning, but envisioned them as being carried out not by planning professionals but by the region's inhabitants themselves. For Lewis Mumford, planning was to be a form of civic action in which small groups, contributing their labor voluntarily, and assisted in their work by "experts," would learn about their habitat and then appropriately act upon this knowledge. For Mumford, planning was to be a form of human liberation; it was to be a way for the repoliticization of the Republic.

After a generation's lapse, during which these ideas failed to penetrate American consciousness, a new group of social learning theorists emerged. The first to employ the model (though he did not call it social learning) was Edgar H. Schein. His little book, *Process Consultation*,[11] had grown out of his work as a business consultant. In it he stressed the importance of a problem diagnosis that would jointly involve client and consultant in a process of mutual learning. Coming out of the same business background but with stronger theoretical grounding, Charles Hampden-Turner's *Radical Man: The Process of Psycho-Social Development*[12] argued the case for an interactive, cellular organization as the structure most conducive to corporate purpose and human development.

In the same year as *Radical Man,* the concept of social learning was explicitly introduced into the discussion about planned change by Edgar S. Dunn, a resource economist with the Ford Foundation.[13] Dunn succeeded in linking Dewey's experimentalism (with its strongly instrumental and pragmatic bias) to evolutionary theory, and posited dialogic interaction as the core of socially adaptive behavior. As virtually all other writers had done before him, Dunn stressed the importance of the small learning group (or "cell") as the setting for experimental, innovative practice.

A number of works supported and sustained the emerging paradigm.[14] In these studies, social learning was loosely used as a metaphor to suggest a cybernetic process by which organizations might adapt themselves to rapidly changing, "turbulent" environments.[15] Basic questions, such as who would learn and to what end, were not yet being asked. To do so would have required a specific context, and during the early stages of the emerging paradigm, most writers were content to indicate its nature and to praise its virtues.

In social planning, the general context is given by society. But to think productively about planning in the public domain further requires that we carefully define the object of our thinking. The problem is to devise a definition that will open up new areas of theoretical inquiry. One such definition, proposed in *Retracking America,* is the process by which scientific and technical knowledge is joined to organized action. This formulation made it possible to describe social learning as an approach to planning in which practice would be joined to theory within a single movement involving four intersecting dimensions.[16]

In this conception, social action was treated as the primary phenomenon

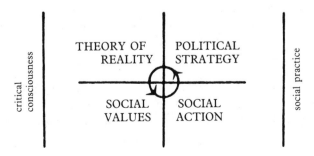

in the sense that theory responds to practice and is shaped by practice even as it serves to inform it.[17] If the currently held images of the world support success, then all is well. But if the results are negative and unexpected, as they often are, further inquiry must be conducted. Initially, this may lead only to questions about strategy, but eventually the theory itself will have to be examined. And finally, it may even become necessary to question the actor's operative values in the situation.

In this model, the characters of actor, inquirer, and planner-theorist are intermixed, and the process of "planning" comes to be embedded in the undifferentiated process of the action itself.[18] It is also fairly obvious that what is referred to here as social practice is problematical with regard to both the choice of means or strategy and outcomes; it is specifically an *innovative* practice to which the expertise of planning comes to be joined. Allocative planning, solely concerned with the distribution of finite resources among competing uses, is excluded from this model. In contrast to innovative practice, it is central in conception, comprehensive in scope, quantitative in expression, and functionally rational. Although in large organizations some sort of allocative planning is probably inevitable, the meaning of planning is far from being exhausted by allocative processes. Especially in times of social crisis, innovative practice is not only typically more prevalent, it is also considerably more important than central allocation.

If it is granted that learning processes are primarily related to innovative social practice, we may further argue that it is thereby linked to a *political struggle* in which significant innovation is asserted and must prevail against an opposition. This struggle will be especially hard in times of resource shortage (of slow or negative economic growth, for example) when attempted innovations clash with the existing powers, because they are part of a zero-sum game in which resources are reallocated to the winner.

Social learning, then, is the consequence of an innovative practice that characteristically takes the form of a political struggle to overcome the *status quo*. If we now look further at this practice-based learning, we find that it relies on a process that, by combining two kinds of knowledge – personal and theoretical or "processed" knowledge – yields an understanding greater than either could have produced by itself. Personal knowledge is the intimate knowing we have about our daily lives. Much of this knowledge is subliminal or "tacit."[19] Even though we continuously use it, we are scarcely aware of it and are generally unable to articulate it in any other form than anecdotal. Personal knowledge is nevertheless vital to human undertakings.

The process of grafting personal on processed knowledge may be called *mutual learning*, because it generally involves people with different abilities and skills who decide to work together on a common problem-solving task.

Insofar as they do this, they learn from each other and from the situation so that the cognitive maps of both are in the end transformed.

In a task-related effort, mutual learning is most effective when it is carried out through *dialogue* which involves a trusting relationship between two or more dyadic pairs.[20] Dialogue is a process of communication that flourishes in small groups. This is why virtually all social learning theorists insist on the importance of a cellular structure for organizations intent on pursuing innovative practice. The optimally sized group is surprisingly small, numbering from seven to nine members.[21] In such groups, everybody's contribution counts.

Planners appear as facilitators and mediators of group-based practices; they use their special skills in the service of the common task. In a way, then, they must not only share the abstract purposes of client groups but align themselves in ways that will abolish (or at least minimize) status differences arising from command of different kinds of knowledge. To do so means to risk oneself, countenancing the possibility of personal and/or collective failure. On the part of the planner, it means to make a serious value commitment.

For generations, social scientists have been told that scientific knowledge is "objective," and that value commitments have no place in planning, which is to be based on calculated choice alone. This belief persists despite challenges to it, most recently on epistemological grounds by Paul K. Feyerabend.[22] It persists to the point where rationality is denied to any action based on committed ways of knowing. Economists are among the more conspicuous perpetrators of this myth. If they understood that every action is a risk not only in the mathematical sense of uncertainty, but *existentially*, they would understand as well that action is impossible without a personal commitment of some sort.[23]

Markets and other institutions do not "act" of themselves; at best they can be said to behave. Every action requires an actor, and actors assume risks for which there is no economic compensation. Yet it would be strange, indeed, if risk-taking and commitment precluded "rational" thinking. On the contrary, both point to the wider rationality in which ends are no less carefully examined than the means and in which immediate ends often emerge in the course of the action itself.

The blueprint model, surviving in the form of allocative planning, is typically adapted to the requirements and predilections of bureaucratic entities, such as the state. Here, planning tends to be separated from action and at least short-range plans (such as program budgets) are claimed to have a binding character on subordinate actors who, by working through the machinery of the state "from above," attempt to give reality and substance to the plan. Innovative practice may, of course, also take place within the state's domain; more often, it will be found in civil society, asserting the will of citizens against the powers. The social learning approach is a model of politicized planning.

It is also a model of how to bring about innovative changes "from below." Decentralized, uncoordinated, and often with only minimal financial support, innovative social practice may seem peculiarly weak and ineffective. Yet it would be quite wrong to dismiss it on these grounds and to argue the alternative position that all significant social change originates with the state "from above." Cellular organization encourages the formation of *networks, social movements,* and *loose coalitions* which can be very potent forces in the struggle for structural change in basic institutional arrangements, including those of governance. In the United States, the best recent example is the feminist movement which, even as it retains a decentralized, cellular form, is able, when it is needed, to bring about concerted action (e.g., in lobbying for the Equal Rights Amendment). The environmental movement is yet another well-known instance.

States have almost always feared a genuine grassroots politics; the preferred term is participation, not empowerment. But a politicized planning requires a community that is active, that exercises some control over the conditions of its livelihood, and that can hold the state accountable. Regarded in this light, it may be a utopian project, but it is a project all the same and, as such, an object of struggle. The social learning approach to planning can make its greatest contribution here, as it works toward the transformation of the structures of political governance. The ultimate terms of this struggle would be this: that planning "from below" might accurately reflect the genuine interests of the people engaged in the social production of their lives.

20

On the Nature of Development and Planning

RUSSELL L. ACKOFF

Development, contrary to what many believe, is not a condition or a state defined by what people have. *It is a capacity defined by what they can do with whatever they have to improve their quality of life and that of others.* Therefore, development is possession of a desire for improvement and the ability to bring it about. It is more a matter of motivation and knowledge than it is of wealth.

This is not to say that wealth is irrelevant to development. It is very relevant. How much people can improve their quality of life and that of others depends not only on their motivation and knowledge, but also on what instruments and resources are available to them. For example, a man can build a better house with good tools and materials than without them. On the other hand, a "developed" man in a condition of poverty is more likely to be able to improve his quality of life and that of others, than a less developed man in a condition of wealth.

Development is a product of learning, not of production; learning how to use oneself and one's environment to better meet one's needs and those of others. Because the development process is essentially a learning process, one person cannot develop another. He cannot learn for another, but he can help another learn for himself. Therefore, *a government cannot develop a country; it can only help its country develop itself.*

Now, how can we plan for development understood in this way? The answer to this question lies in *who* does the planning because the principal benefit of planning is not derived from consuming its products, plans, but from participating in the planning process. In planning, process is the most important product. Therefore, effective development planning cannot be done for some by others. The others must do it for themselves, but they can be helped by professional planners.

Excerpted from Russell L. Ackoff, "National Development Planning Revisited." Reprinted with permission from *Operations Research* 25 issue 2 (March–April 1977): 212–18, Operations Research Society of America. No further reproduction permitted without the consent of the copyright owner.

196/SOCIAL LEARNING AND THE NATURE OF PLANNING

The proper role of the professional planner is to provide others with information, instruction, motivation, and the resources that can increase the effectiveness with which they plan for themselves.

Effective development planning must be participatory. France used such planning to bring about its remarkable recovery from World War II.[1] Paris recently used participatory planning to prepare its new development plan.[2] An urban black ghetto in Philadelphia has also been using such planning.[3] In Mexico one of my former students, Miguel Szekeley, has initiated such planning in a number of rural communities in the state of Nayarit. In the state of Puebla the Postgraduate College of the National School of Agriculture has done the same, as has a group at the Institute of Engineering of the National Autonomous University of Mexico, working with representatives of two government agencies in the state of Queretero. Even without anything like the support these rural efforts deserve, they are meeting with remarkable success.

To be sure, organizing a nation as large as Mexico to plan its own development is difficult, but, as France showed, it is not impossible.

Before trying to answer this question, I would like to point out that we have closed a significant circle. I have argued that to be developed is to be motivated for and capable of improving quality of life. I have also argued that planning one's development cannot be done effectively by others; it must be done by oneself because the development of motivation and the capability for improving quality of life—development itself—can be obtained through planning for it.

There is a major role in such planning as I have described for the operations researcher, but it is very different from the one he plays in less-than-well-developed countries today. In most of these he is practicing the conventional Anglo-American textbook version of operations research, cutting national development problems down to a size and shape that permit applications of his underdeveloped models and algorithms to them. The unit on which he focuses should not be a problem or an operation of a social system. It should be the whole system and its culture. In development planning the nature of the system being planned for, its culture, must be changed, not merely what a particular part of it does at a particular time and place.

The operations researcher working on national development planning should not assume the posture of a detached value-free objective scientist, but that of a philosopher-politician who seeks to provide others with power over themselves. He should be a proponent, take a position, and propagandize for it. Effective development planning requires whole persons, not abstractions from them. It requires professionals who can start and sustain nonviolent cultural revolutions. They in turn require a profession and a body of scientific and humanistic knowledge that enables them to do this job better than others. Operations researchers do not meet these needs now but they could develop this capability. This too, however, would require development planning. What better place is there to practice such planning than on oneself?

Part Six

Planning for Equity and Self-Reliance

The choice of analytical framework largely determines problem definition and ultimately the choice of action prescriptions. The preferred frameworks for people-centered development focus on people and their capacity to address their own needs—including their needs for growth. The contributors to this section elaborate on the basic concepts and illustrate their application.

David Korten and George Carner present a case study demonstrating application to donor agency programming of the analysis of Philippine poverty groups reported by Carner in chapter 13, above. They then elaborate on the conceptual frameworks that guide such application.

Next, John Friedmann sets forth his model of agropolitan development, which largely inverts many conventional planning prescriptions, using a territorial unit to define a people-inclusive development strategy based on the principle of self-reliance.

Finally, David Morris suggests that the potential benefits of applying the principles of local self-reliance as a guide to development action are not confined to the rural areas of Third World countries. Specifically, he illustrates how they can and have benefited many American cities.

21

Planning Frameworks for People-Centered Development

DAVID C. KORTEN AND GEORGE CARNER

The central concept of people-centered development is quite simple. It is an approach to development that looks to the creative initiative of people as the primary development resource and to their material and spiritual well-being as the end that the development process serves. A major failing of conventional development models, both socialist and capitalist, is that they become so production-centered that the needs of the production system have assumed precedence over the needs of people. Those people lucky enough to participate in the development enterprise find their lives dominated by large impersonal bureaucracies, both public and private, that exert inordinate control over their lives, including their access to sources of livelihood, and limit their opportunities for creative individual initiative. Those who do not participate, a substantial portion of humankind, live at or near the margin of subsistence, at standards intolerable in a truly human society. At the same time, the demands of that development enterprise drive human society to the destruction of its natural resource base and endanger the fragile ecosystems on which all life on earth ultimately depends.

Recognition of the dehumanizing, inequitable, and environmentally unsustainable consequences of conventional development models has stimulated a serious search for alternatives. These alternatives must surely provide substantial increases in productive output to meet the needs of a vast and growing world population, but they must do so in ways that are both consistent with the basic principles of participation and equity and sustainable.

Our own experience suggests that this search must be backed by experimentation with new planning tools that contribute to a redefinition of the development problem[1] and by efforts to achieve a reorientation in the institutions by which human societies manage productive resources—especially land and water resources—returning control to the people who depend on them for their livelihoods.[2]

Our perspective is most readily communicated by recounting a case in which we both were involved and which contributed to the development and application of new planning frameworks of the type we are suggesting may be needed. The case is from the United States Agency for International Development (USAID) Mission to the Philippines.[3]

People-Centered Planning in a Donor Mission

Donor agencies like AID have characteristically been preoccupied with transferring assistance resources in support of general economic development on a sector-by-sector and project-by-project basis.[4] While the last decade has seen a substantial emphasis on human *needs*, there has been much less attention to human *potentials* beyond requiring beneficiaries to provide volunteer labor in support of centrally initiated schemes. The experience of the USAID Mission to the Philippines illustrates how a planning approach that focuses attention on people, their potentials, and the constraints they face in their self-reliant development efforts can influence a donor's program in ways that make it more responsive to the needs of the poor, even through what is initially a purely top-down planning process.

Five years after the landmark United States foreign assistance legislation of 1973 directed the Agency for International Development (AID) to target its assistance to improve directly the lives of the poor in the Third World, AID introduced a major programming innovation. Each USAID mission was to produce a five-year rolling strategy document called a Country Development Strategy Statement (CDSS). It was a basic programming innovation intended to produce comprehensive country-specific assistance strategies based on in-depth understanding of the country in question. The guidance provided by Washington on preparing this document asked missions to address a variety of analytical questions.[5] Most significant and unconventional were the two fundamental questions, Who are the poor? What are the causes of their poverty? A serious effort by the Philippine USAID mission to address these questions as a basis for arriving at a development assistance strategy led to the creation of an analytical framework that differed significantly from the macro-socioeconomic analyses underlying more conventional development planning.

DIAGNOSING POVERTY

The framework arrived at by the mission evolved through successive iterations. The first step was to identify an income threshold that would define a poverty level. Then it was recognized that to be meaningful the analysis had to go beyond lumping the poor together as a faceless, placeless aggregate. Recognizing the household as the basic economic unit among the poor, the mission decided to use it as the unit of disaggregation. An obvious next step was to categorize households according to the main occupations of their heads. But again the standard classifications that lump together "farmers, farm laborers, fishermen, hunters, loggers and related workers" in a single category revealed little about the realities of these households that might provide a useful basis for targeting development action. In looking for a more meaningful breakdown, it became evident that one of the more significant distinguishing characteristics of rural households was the nature and size of the resource base to which they had access, and the nature of their rights of access. This led to a further disaggregation into upland farmers, paddy rice farmers, landless agricultural workers, and artisanal fishermen – the first being dependent on the uplands, the second and third on the lowlands, and the fourth on coastal waters. Then each group was divided into a number of significant subclassifications.

Initially, fairly standard socioeconomic profiles were developed for each of the groups so identified. But it soon became evident that while such profiles describe the symptoms that define poverty, they do little to reveal underlying causes. The data were again reorganized using the concept of a household survival strategy borrowed from the Cornell University studies of landless households.[6] The idea was to look at households with access to a similiar resource base in terms of how their members utilized available assets to fashion a subsistence livelihood. Generally this involved substantial diversification. For example, in a given household the husband might fish in one season and harvest coconuts in another. The wife might tend a garden and engage in small-scale trade. Other members might engage in craft activities or migrate in search of seasonal employment. Once available data were organized around the survival strategy concept, a dynamic picture emerged of the causes of the poverty that afflicted these households and of the creative efforts of individual household units to sustain their members in the midst of highly adverse circumstances. The analysis now revealed not faceless aggregate statistics, but rather real people, innovative and hardworking, a potentially productive development resource – if the major constraints they faced could be relieved (see chapter 13 in this volume for the substance of this analysis).[7]

The comparison of the survival strategies of different poverty groups provided an important but still only partial view of the causes of their poverty. To develop a more complete view, a set of macro-level analyses was overlaid on the household analysis. These analyses included examination of employment patterns in the economy at large, population dynamics, land-use patterns, urban-rural and regional disparities, and macro-economic trends and policies. They provided the contextual background for a better understanding of the limited outcomes the poverty groups achieved from their survival strategies. For one thing, this analysis helped to highlight the increasing competition for limited land and water resources as a result of population growth and economic expansion. This competition exists among poor households, between the rich and the poor, and, of particular significance for questions of development strategy, between the modern sector (where the impressive statistical gains in economic growth are to be found) and the traditional sector (on which the majority of the population depends for its livelihood).

The mission's poverty analysis provided an explicit and common definition of the poverty problem, an important first step in formulating strategy. It clearly identified the major rural groups with a high incidence of poverty, specifically, landless agricultural workers, upland farmers, and artisanal or sustenance fishermen. These represented not only the majority of the poor in the Philippines, but also groups that had been largely neglected by government and donor development efforts during the 1970s, when the emphasis in rural development had been on raising rice production, primarily that of small farmers with access to irrigated lands. The analysis revealed that the irrigated rice farmers represent less than 15 percent of the rural poor of the Philippines and are in general the least disadvantaged. Thus the production-centered approach of past agricultural policy had unwittingly bypassed the vast majority of the rural population by assuming that small farmers were a homogeneous group.

The poverty group analyses served as the basic input to a series of brainstorming sessions held within the mission and open to all staff. It was during these sessions that a consensus on the nature of the problem was reached and the initial round of strategic choices was made.

THE OUTCOME

The assistance strategy that emerged from these discussions took generating productive employment as its central focus. Yet it was also noted that the survival patterns and requirements of poor households argue for a strategy different from more conventional employment strategies, which simply rely on accelerated creation of employment in the modern sector of the economy to absorb surplus labor.

The mission's analysis noted that poor households display considerable resourcefulness, to the extent of fashioning a self-help economy structured to provide the production, marketing, credit, transportation, insurance, health care, and other facilities essential to their survival and advancement. This economy is composed of household production units, farm and non-farm, that produce goods and services consumed mainly by the poor themselves.

The analysis concluded that the mission's strategy should build on this resourcefulness and natural survival motivation by helping the government of the Philippines to expand the options and resources available to these households. Such an approach would start with efforts to increase farm production for consumption at home and within the local community before encouraging a market orientation. This analysis recognized the need for innovative mechanisms of resource control to provide more equitable access to land and water resources and incentives to small producers for intensive and sustainable resource utilization. It also accepted that poor households diversify their employment activities and increasingly rely on off-farm income sources. Small-scale local manufacturing and services were noted as important parts of this traditional economy and were earmarked for assistance.

Two important themes were thus identified as critical to the concept of people-centered planning. The first was an emphasis on supporting and building from the self-reliant efforts of the poor to address their own needs. The second was an implicit recognition that while the modern sector is the primary source of conventional economic growth, the traditional sector is the primary source of livelihood for most poor households – and that the two sectors are in competition for resources. These themes have helped to distinguish between a simple employment strategy and a people-centered employment strategy – one normally focuses on expansion of the modern economy, the other builds on the strengths of the traditional or "people's" economy.

A third theme was subsequently identified as central to relevant action on the analysis – the need for new or substantially reoriented institutional capabilities supportive of a people-centered development strategy. The result has been a number of projects designed to assist key development agencies in learning to build the capacities of poor beneficiaries for productive, self-reliant management of local resources.

Data Presentation as a Determinant of Problem Definition

We have become impressed as a result of this experience with the significance of the selection and presentation of planning data in shaping problem definition and the subsequent choice of corrective action. To illustrate, conventional economic plans are based on analysis of indicators of the health and progress of the macroeconomy (e.g., economic growth rates, foreign exchange balances, sectoral production and employment, and development of capital infrastructure). Quite naturally, needed development actions are defined in terms of policies and investments designed to spur the growth of the lagging sectors as identified by these indicators.

Where concern for social outcomes has become prominent, planners have drawn on highly aggregated social indicators that are quite useful in spotlighting deficiencies in educational levels, health care, nutritional status, and so forth. The statistics themselves define the problem in terms of deficiencies in services relative to some desired standard; the logical response is to undertake actions directed to making up these deficiencies. This translates into funding commitments to the requisite service programs, and too often leads to unsustainable burdens on public budgets and central administrative systems.

Another approach where poverty is a central concern is to disaggregate economic and social data by geographical area so as to highlight relatively depressed areas. The logical action, it would seem, is to concentrate investments in the relatively depressed areas. But while this may benefit the area, there is no assurance that it will benefit the people in those areas who are most depressed. The mission's analysis revealed that some of the major concentrations of particularly depressed households were found in provinces which economic statistics identified as relatively high performers in terms of the amount and value of total production.

The frameworks used for data collection and analysis in the case study we cite focused attention on people, their livelihood strategies, and the particular barriers to improved household-level performance they faced. The poor became visible, not as potential welfare cases, but as hardworking, creative individuals sustaining themselves under difficult circumstances. The logic of such an analysis dictates a search for measures to relieve those constraints. Defining the poverty problem in these terms is relatively uncommon in development circles, in part because the data employed are not organized or presented in formats that suggest such a definition.

Much work has been done in recent years on methods to introduce social soundness analysis into project assessment.[8] The weakness of these efforts, however, has been that they have focused on assessing project choices already made. While they may shape the details of project design, they seldom challenge its premises or contribute to a redefinition of the development problem on which its identification was originally based. We are suggesting that social and environmental analysis be used as the point of departure in defining the problem, shaping the development strategy, setting the framework for programs of action, and, finally, identifying individual projects within those programs. It is a simple and, to many people, a fairly obvious concept, but one that is quite radical from the perspective of prevailing development practice.

Production-Centered versus People-Centered Development

Advocates of conventional practice will no doubt maintain that all development is ultimately for the purpose of benefiting people. But the evidence is by now substantial that focusing on production systems is not an effective approach to realizing the productive potentials of the great mass of the population, nor to creating a production system responsive to their needs. Simply characterized, production-centered development has concentrated on:

> Industry over agriculture, yet agriculture is where the majority of the world's people obtain their livelihoods;
>
> Urban over rural areas, yet rural areas are where the majority of people live;
>
> Concentrated over broadly based ownership of productive assets, with the outcome that development investments benefit the few more than the many;
>
> Optimal use of capital over optimal use of human resources, with the consequence that capital is employed while people are not;
>
> Exploitation of natural and environmental resources to achieve short-term increments in physical wealth over management practices that sustain and increase the yields of these resources, resulting in destruction of the environment and rapid depletion of the natural resource base;
>
> Efficiency of interdependent large-scale production units based on international comparative advantage over the diversity and adaptability of small-scale units organized to achieve relative local self-reliance, resulting in economies that are energy-inefficient, lack adaptability, and are prone to serious disruption from breakdown or political manipulation in any part of the system.

Open- versus Closed-System Economics

Production-centered development has been driven by the models of conventional open-system economics that view both people and environment as exogenous variables.[9] People are treated as any marketable production resource, to be purchased when their marginal return to the firm exceeds their marginal cost and dismissed when it does not. The social and environmental costs of the firm's decisions are largely externalized or passed on to the general public, while gains are internalized or privatized. The "real" costs of natural resources to the economic system are presumed to be only the cost of extracting them. Disposal of waste is treated as costless, since it is simply dumped into the environment. The primary measure of system performance is the total throughput – the Gross National Product – on the presumption that this is a proxy for the human well-being produced by the system. It is in fact a measure of the health and performance of the production system, not of the people system.

In people-centered analysis people and environment are the primary endogenous variables, the point of departure for development planning. It draws its basic perspectives and analytical methods from the emerging science of human ecology – the study of interactions between human and ecological systems. It demands what Boulding calls "spaceship economics," the economics of a closed or bounded system in which the physical and mental well-being of the ship's inhabitants, not its rate of throughput, constitutes the measure of performance of the life-support system.

Functional versus Territorial Perspectives

John Friedmann and Clyde Weaver have drawn a parallel distinction between the functional and territorial perspectives in planning and economic organization.[10] They point to the transnational corporation as the ultimate expression of the functional perspective. Such corporations operate largely beyond the jurisdiction of the national state and without loyalty to place or people, shifting their location and adjusting their labor force as dictated by the efficiency demands of the production process in search of optimum returns to available capital.

Emphasizing the principles of the economies of scale and externalizing social and environmental costs, such organizations tend to be hierarchically structured, with power concentrated at the top and well removed from the consequences of local actions. They have a preference for homogenizing individual cultures to create mass global markets for their standardized products, preferring for reasons of efficiency to adapt the consumer to their mass-based products rather than to diversify the product in response to local preferences. Most large government bureaucracies, though largely immune to the demands of the marketplace, are also hierarchically structured around functionally defined and centrally determined purposes and expect consumer demands to conform similarly to the standardized services offered.

The territorial perspective outlined by Friedmann and Weaver contrasts quite sharply with the functional perspective. An individual is a member of a territorial unit, whether nation, province, district, or neighborhood – on the basis not of his or her temporary economic utility to that unit but of residence. The territorial jurisdiction is appropriately concerned with the well-being of all its members in perpetuity. Its guiding principle in economic decision-making is to achieve an optimum relationship between the resource base defined by its territorial boundaries and the needs of its members for sustainable improvements in well-being. A central priority in territorial management is to achieve a structuring of relationships within the territorial boundaries consistent with this outcome. The basic principle is that the community has a responsibility to ensure a floor for all its members in regard to satisfying basic needs, in return for which it has a right to expect a productive contribution consistent with the individual's abilities. Within this framework, any increment of productive contribution that a given member can make to the total production of the community is a positive gain and should be so valued, even though by reason of some incapacity the marginal value of that contribution may not equal or exceed the marginal cost of the individual's maintenance.

Organization by place tends to sustain cultural heterogeneity (what George Honadle refers to as the "cultural gene pool"), diversity, and local self-reliance. These outcomes are achieved through specialization based on small production units, leading to substantial adaptability at both local and global levels.

Friedmann and Weaver caution that the territorial perspective should not be confused with conventional regional planning—most of which reflects more a functional than a territorial perspective and suffers from most of the limitations of that perspective.

Achieving a reorientation from a predominantly function- or production-centered to a predominantly territorial or people-centered approach to development is an ambitious undertaking. We suggest that one of many requirements is the further development and application of people-centered planning frameworks along the lines suggested by our case study. Only by clearly defining development in terms of people and their continued well-being can we expect to achieve broadly based sustainable improvement in productive output responsive to the needs of all people.

22

Agropolitan Development: A Territorial Approach to Meeting Basic Needs

JOHN FRIEDMANN

Our proposed approach to meeting basic needs through application of territorial power begins with five assumptions. *First,* most of the world's population live at unacceptably low levels of material consumption. *Second,* most of the world's population are engaged in the production of use values outside the exchange economy. *Third,* every territorially integrated national community must be able to meet the basic needs of its members or eventually lose its claims to legitimacy. *Fourth,* the strengthening of territorial power that is implied in a basic needs approach to development does not exclude the necessity of judiciously using transnational power in meeting national needs. *Fifth,* the basic-needs approach is intended as a general model of development in which production and distribution are treated as facets of the same process of *equal development*. It is not meant to be an instrument for containing poverty in a context of transnational development.[1]

Basic needs refer to the sum of reciprocal claims in a territorially integrated society. In such a society, everyone is regarded as simultaneously a producer and consumer.[2] Needs are basic to the extent that their satisfaction is regarded as essential for a dignified human existence.[3] As such, they represent an entitlement: each member has a rightful claim on his community for their satisfaction. But this entitlement implies a reciprocal claim. The community can ask for useful contributions from each member of its work.[4]

Basic needs, in the sense of survival, may be further regarded as a variable subset of a more general category of *human needs*. Two additional types of need may be distinguished: social and individualized. *Social* needs are needs of the collectivity (they are regarded as essential for the collectivity's survival and well-being). Transportation, for instance, is such a need and requires

---

Excerpted from John Friedmann and Clyde Weaver, *Territory and Function: The Evolution of Regional Planning* (Berkeley and Los Angeles: University of California Press, 1979), chapter 8. Copyright © 1979 by the authors; reprinted by permission.

an allocation of resources. So are universities, even though not everyone may be able to attend one; they are not yet a survival need. Finally, *individualized* needs are those for which the collectivity assumes no specific responsibility. They remain each person's own concern, such as his/her choice of companionship, travel, or taste in food and clothes. Within certain bounds, intended to safeguard the wider interests of the collectivity, they are an expression of personal preference, and the collectivity remains silent about them.

These distinctions are derived from the historical experience with resource allocation in the Jewish kibbutz.[5] There the historical path in the evolution of human needs may be briefly described as follows. In the early days of the movement, nearly all the needs of kibbutzim members were those of survival, thus they were satisfied collectively. As the kibbutzim movement grew more prosperous, a category of *social* needs was added, expanding more rapidly than basic or survival needs, which tended to level off. Operationally speaking, social needs were those whose satisfaction was hedged in by certain rules and procedures, reflecting communal preferences. Individual members had to apply for them to the kibbutz. But as the movement became still more prosperous, *individualized* needs began to appear and to establish their own claim on the community's resources. Provision was made for them by paying each member an allowance in money for which no account needed to be rendered. In recent years, individualized needs have increased more rapidly than either social or basic needs and so has the cash economy of the kibbutz. Whether this trend should be allowed to continue unchecked has become a major issue of ideological debate.

It is clear from this account that the satisfaction of basic needs will not for very long remain the sole objective of national development. It is merely a *first target* in societies where the majority of the people fall below an absolute level of poverty. In a comprehensive sense, development may be regarded as a process of individuation. As basic needs are met, social needs appear, and as these, in turn, are satisfied, individualized needs become relatively more significant.

Basic needs must not become a fetish for planners. The object of planning is to create those conditions in the real world that will nourish human beings who are "rich in needs".[6] This requires the continued development of the productive forces and more particularly the *development of the bases of communal wealth*: land and water, good health, knowledge, and skills.

The Agropolitan Approach to a Basic Needs Strategy

In the following pages we set forth guiding principles for a territorial approach to a basic needs strategy. We shall call it the "agropolitan" approach.[7] The specific setting we have chosen is that of densely populated, agrarian societies characterized by low profiles of social development, high rates of population increase, incipient urban-based industrialization, high external dependency, and rising indices of inequality. Such societies are typically found in Asia and parts of Africa. Outside the appropriate geographical setting for agropolitan development, other forms of territorially-based planned development would be more fitting.

We propose agropolitan forms as an approach to the development of large segments of the world periphery – the new regions of economic backwardness and dependence which have always been a concern of regional planners. Additionally, our discussion is intended to break the current impasse in regional studies: a new paradigm is needed.

The reader will undoubtedly perceive some similarities between our version of agropolitan development and China's experience over the past twenty years. This is the result, not of a conscious effort to hold up the Chinese example for universal emulation, but of structural features that obtain from working within the same framework of assumptions: for instance, that the first-stage objective of development should be the satisfaction of *basic needs*; that development should be organized on a *territorial basis*; that questions of *production and distribution should be jointly solved*; and that the resource base for the development of *productive forces must be continuously expanded*.[8]

We will discuss the major elements of the agropolitan approach under four headings, including (1) the basic conditions for its realization, (2) the territorial framework, (3) the expansion of production, and (4) the role of the state.

The Basic Conditions

Three conditions are essential to successful agropolitan development: (1) selective territorial closure; (2) the communalization of land and water resources; and (3) the equalization of access to the bases for the accumulation of social power. They are difficult conditions to fulfill; yet, without them, only limited progress can be made.

Selective territorial closure refers to a policy of enlightened self-reliance at relevant levels of territorial integration: district, region, and nation. This condition flies straight in the face of the ideology of free trade and comparative advantage and the attempts of transnational enterprise to organize a functionally integrated world economy under its tutelage. Selective closure is a way to escape from the fetishism of growth efficiency; it is an expression of faith in the abilities of a people to guide the forces of their own evolution. It means to rely less on outside aid and investment, to involve the masses in development, to initiate a conscious process of social learning, to diversify production, and to pool resources. It means learning to say "we" and to assert a territorial interest.

The *communalization of land and water resources* is the second condition for agropolitan development. In poor agrarian societies, productive wealth occurs chiefly in the form of land and water. Communalizing this wealth means that the power to determine the ultimate uses and disposition of land and water rests with the appropriate territorial community. In most peasant societies, this is an ancient practice, vestiges of which may be found to this day, as in Mexico's indigenous tradition of the *ejido*.[9]

Communalization may take a variety of forms. All that is asserted here is the *priority interest of the community in the basic conditions of its sustenance*. Whereas individuals seek short-term gains, territorial communities must ensure the long-term survival and well-being of the group. Communalization legitimizes the expression of this interest.

In the context of a basic-needs strategy, communalization is essential. Only the community can guarantee the satisfaction of the basic needs of its members, and to allocate benefits accordingly it must have access to the fruits of its own labour. The full mobilization of available resources, which agropolitan development implies, is possible only where the benefits from such an effort are understood to flow in roughly equal measure to everyone in the community. Where benefits are appropriated primarily for private use, so that the gains accrue unequally, even the initial effort is not likely to be made, and the productive potential of the community will be realized only in part.

The third condition for agropolitan development is the *equalization of access to the bases for the accumulation of social power*. Social power is here conceived as a resource capable of raising the individual's sense of potency. Where access to the use of social power is unequal, the power of the few to dominate the many is enhanced. Where it is more equally distributed, the ground is prepared for entering upon freely co-operative relations.

It is freely co-operative relations that are the well-spring for an active life. They release new energies, generate new ideas in practice, and are capable of transforming what would otherwise be burdensome chores into work that is joyful.

Social power is an inexhaustible resource whose potential capacity increases with use. The long-term development of the human race must be based on this remarkable product that flows more freely the more we use of it. *But it becomes truly available only to those who help to produce it!*

There are many bases for the accumulation of social power. They include:

- productive assets in land, water, and tools
- financial resources
- relevant information
- knowledge and skills
- social and political organization

The next question is more difficult: what is intended by the phrase, "equalization of access?" In the present context, it means that within territorially integrated communities, everyone is to have an equal chance of gaining access to the use of common resources for production and adaptive use. This emphasis on a probability calculus is intended. Whereas resources of social power may be placed within the reach of everyone, not everyone may wish to use them, or to use them for the same or even similar ends. Complete equality of outcomes can only be enforced by resorting to Draconian measures. Human beings are diverse in their nature, and a mechanical egalitarianism is contrary to the very essence of what it means to be human.[10]

The Territorial Framework

Agropolitan districts are the smallest territorial units that are still capable of providing for the basic needs of their inhabitants with only marginally important resource transfers from outside.[11]

In view of the need for face-to-face encounter in the governance of agropolitan affairs—a form of governance that concerns questions of both production and distribution, and mindful of a population density criterion that would require at least 200 persons per square kilometre of cultivated land—agropolitan districts may be designed to have a total population of between 15,000 and 60,000.[12] The inclusion of a country town within the district would raise their total by an additional 5–20,000 people. Speaking in rough numbers, we suggest agropolitan districts that would range in population size from 20,000 to 100,000.

This derivation of agropolitan districts applies only to rural areas. In cities, *agropolitan neighbourhoods* may be variously defined within approximately the same overall population limits.[13] According to this procedure, many smaller towns will obviously fall within rural agropolitan districts, while medium-sized cities would constitute districts in their own right.

THE EXPANSION OF PRODUCTION

Applying the principle of territoriality to problems of economic organization means strengthening the territorial economy at all relevant levels, above all, the agropolitan district and the level immediately superior to it, or the region. And strengthening the territorial economy means to encourage self-reliance in the management of economic affairs.[14] From this, a number of correlative principles may be derived:

–development should aim at diversifying the territorial economy;
–development should aim at the maximum development of physical resources consistent with principles of conservation;
–development should encourage the expansion of regional and interregional (domestic) markets;

–development should be based as much as possible on principles of self-finance;

–development should promote social learning.

These five principles of a self-reliant territorial development will now be separately discussed.

Diversifying the territorial economy. In predominantly agrarian societies, diversification has two possible meanings: first, diversifying agricultural production (e.g. food crops where industrial crops are common and vice versa); and, second, augmenting the level of industrial production and service activities in rural areas. (In urban areas, this would take the form of facilitating the growing of agricultural crops and small livestock.)

The diversification of area economies is a way of overcoming the contradictions between city and countryside. It is also a way for making agropolitan districts and regions more capable of dealing with adversity, more ingenious in overcoming difficulties, and also – because more interdependent – more communally oriented.

Michael Goldberg has argued that the lowest units in a hierarchically structured system tend also to be the most specialized, the least adaptable, and the most readily replaceable units.[15] Although his language is borrowed from ecology, Professor Goldberg is speaking of the small enterprise or firm in a capitalist economy. This firm, indeed, is replaceable. But an agropolitan district with tens of thousands of inhabitants is not; *it must survive.* And if it is to survive, it must diversify its economy; it must become rather like one of Professor Goldberg's "higher" units where adaptability facilitates resilience to changes in environment. But in stressing resilience, Professor Goldberg fails to mention that the most adaptive human systems are also the most likely to display a high order of creativity in problem-solving. Polivalence in economic structure may thus be highly correlated with innovativeness, social learning, and development.

Diversification in rural agropolitan districts will, at a minimum, require electric energy, radio or telephone communication, regular water supply, drainage, and year-round, all-weather transport to other areas.[16]

Can it be assumed, however, that non-agricultural activities could be efficiently located in rural areas? Experience in both China and the advanced industrial and post-industrial regions in Western Europe and the United States has shown that the answer to this question is affirmative.[17] Urban-industrial concentrations are an historical phenomenon; they are not necessarily the lowest-cost locations.[18] For many industries, especially those oriented towards mass markets, generalized labour skills, and agricultural raw materials, decentralized locations may be as economical or more so. The same may be said of convenience services that are best located within walking or bicycling distance from their potential clients. These considerations suggest that the existence of economies of scale (and thus of economies of concentration) has been vastly overstated. The lowest level of a real economy may be efficiency integrated on a pedestrian or bicycle scale, that is, on the scale of a typical agropolitan district.[19]

Maximum physical development constrained by the need for conservation. The need to develop the physical quality of life is obvious and essential. But physical development is difficult to accomplish, because what needs to be done is often not valued by market economists.

The remuneration of work tasks in the process of production must be evaluated in a social rather than market perspective. Where a sufficiency of livelihood is guaranteed, and labour is not fully used, every contribution to production represents a gain, however slight, to the community. And in an economy in which survival is still the major issue, everything contributing to this objective represents a social gain.[20]

But the maximum development of physical resources does not mean, as it does under industrial capitalism, that resources may be exploited with a view to maximum immediate gain for individuals. *The territorial community has a history that translates forward into time.* Future generations are nearly as important as those living, the only difference being the uncertainty of future knowledge (technical innovations, emergents). For this reason, territorially organized communities tend to value the future more highly than communities which are integrated primarily on a basis of function. This holds as well for agropolitan communities, where resource use must be managed in perpetuity.[21]

Application of this principle raises the important question of use-value production which we discussed earlier in this chapter. In almost all agropolitan districts, there will be unused time during at least some part of the year. To the extent that work can be mobilized for the production of use values for the community, *in return for a guarantee of basic needs*, the productive base of the community can be expanded. This may be regarded as the classical form of primitive accumulation. Its major initial object in rural areas would undoubtedly be land and water management (anti-erosion controls, small flood control and irrigation projects, land reclamation schemes), the development of local energy resources, transport improvements, and the construction of various social facilities such as schools, clinics, assembly halls, and recreation areas.

Expanding regional and interregional (domestic) markets. Under the prevailing doctrine of unequal development, the only way to expand domestic markets is something like the following sequence

> foreign demand → manufactured exports → expansion of secondary and tertiary employment → increased demand for agricultural products → increased demand for domestic manufactures → increase in

domestic production and employment.[22]

In this sequence, everything follows its "natural" course. The only trouble with the sequence is that it is wrong. Domestic mass markets are created, not by foreign demand for the products of low-cost labour but by increasing the productivity of the masses through agropolitan development! The new industry should be devoted to the production of wage goods, or simple products, including tools in daily use. The variety of such goods is small and the technology of their production is straightforward. Wage goods can be manufactured in small enterprises that are dispersed among agropolitan districts. In this way, people get experience with inventing and with making things. They learn about machines and common business practices.[23]

To build up wage-goods production at home, mass production with advanced technology must be severely limited.[24] Jet planes cannot be matched with gliders in a race!

Successful home production of wage goods will eventually create a demand for machinery and simple transport equipment. This, too, can be produced at home. The new sequence will, therefore, look like this:

increased agricultural productivity + industrial diversification in de-centralized locations (principally wage-goods production) → increased occupation of labour → increased demand for wage goods → increased demand for machinery and simple transport equipment → technological and product innovations → enhanced capacity for export of domestic manufactures abroad.

Agropolitan development builds strength from within, based on its own resources, its own skills, its own discoveries and learning. It does not expect a transfusion of strength from "donor" countries abroad. It does not count on miraculous transformations, nor on results without effort. And so it begins with a development that will satisfy basic needs as, in doing so, it creates new ones.

If the countryside is endowed with basic infrastructure – for instance, if an internal communications and transport network is built up that will connect agropolitan districts and regions with each other – large cities will lose their present overwhelming advantage. The economy will then turn inward upon itself, discover its hidden energies and assets, and, in a "natural" learning progression, modernize itself from within.

Manufacturing industry will be second in a logical sequence of steps. The first is the continuous upgrading of agricultural productions, starting with overall increases in the physical volume of food and basic fibres, followed, in due course, by increases in the productivity of farm land and the productivity of workers.[25]

The development of industry will be tied into this sequence, beginning with agricultural processing and going on to the manufacture of tools and other equipment of use to peasants and workers in their daily lives. Dispersed among the villages and fields, small industries will provide a source of work and income, in a mode of production that is intimately related to the emerging agropolitan structure of society in which the contradictions of industrial capitalism – between city and countryside, production and consumption, work and leisure – are progressively resolved.

Following principles of self-finance. Self-reliance implies some form of self-financing. Yet it is said that poor people, who perforce must provide the bulk of resources, are incapable of saving. Engel's law is invoked to prove this, showing that most of poor people's income is spent on necessities, especially on food. This is true, of course, and not particularly surprising. But if they are properly motivated, even poor people – that is, the great mass of the population in agrarian societies – are capable of extraordinary efforts – witness the remarkable investments in self-built housing throughout the world,[26] or the substantial village-bound remissions of money earned by relatives in the city,[27] or the amounts saved by poor people to finance the education of their children.[28] When poor people do *not* save, it is usually for one of three reasons: because they live below the threshold of subsistence; because family obligations are more immediately pressing; or because what they have managed to put aside is forcibly taken from them – for instance, when the government bulldozes self-constructed housing in shanty towns, landlords extract exorbitant rents, moneylenders collect astronomical interest payments, or the terms of trade with the city are rigged by government against the countryside.

The first and foremost rule of self-finance is therefore this: to establish conditions that will secure for the benefit of oneself and one's family the effort saved out of present consumption. Peasants are not more altruistic than other people.[29] Yet they are capable of exceptional sacrifice if the benefits to them, including improvements in the territorial community that yield a *common benefit,* are clear and direct.

To ensure that effort given up to the community results in benefits to the masses, the basic conditions of agropolitan development must be fulfilled: selective territorial closure – to prevent the outbound transfer of resources; the communalization of wealth – to prevent the appropriation of communal benefits for private gain; and the equalization of access to the bases of social power – to prevent the accumulation of social surplus in the hands of those whose access is privileged.

A further condition for self-finance is that the employment of local resources in different tasks should be left, as much as possible, to the decisions of the appropriate institutions at district and regional levels. Not only is the central allocation of resources for local benefit a virtual impossibility, but the democratic doctrine that the people have a right to share in the decisions that involve the collective use of their own resources must be respected. In principle, local, regional, and national plans should be dovetailed into each other. But particularly at district and sub-district levels, what the people want, as opposed to what the state would like to happen, constitutes a proper subject for discussion between them and, indeed, for extensive negotiation. Agropolitan planning, along with other forms of planning, requires a substantial margin of uncertainty.[30]

Promoting social learning. Social learning occurs whenever the institutions comprising the agropolis show an enhanced capacity for dealing with the problems that confront them. It is not, strictly speaking, a descriptive term, referring to a modality of institutional performance. The social learning approach to problem-solving points instead to both structural forms of social relations and to specific practices that will promote it.[31]

The practice of group evaluation and self-criticism is an especially valuable technique. So are campaigns whose principal purpose is to encourage social learning. Such campaigns would be conducted periodically with the full panoply of group discussions, field observations, experimental trials, and interdistrict contests. Suitable topics would include improved irrigation practices, environmental sanitation, youth culture, small livestock production, group decision-making, marketing, infant care, afforestation, and water management. Follow-up work would be done by local cadres. For the idea is not to teach some set of abstract skills, but to induce new practices. And for this local village cadres are essential. They will provide the link to supporting central services and encourage those innovative practices through which effective learning will occur.

Care should also be devoted to the design of channels for the routine exchange of information among agropolitan districts themselves. Some information exchange will happen spontaneously, of course, as limited functional relations develop among districts and regions, but special measures to promote the sharing of information on relevant local experiences will make this evolutionary process more effective. Officers might be appointed for each district to develop information networks and to facilitate cross-district learning. For example, regular visits to neighbouring districts might be organized to observe livestock breeding techniques, the results of new hybrid strains, bio-conversion technology, solar energy production, improved methods of grain storage, and so forth. The inauguration of a new school, or the completion of an irrigation or small hydro-electric project might be cause for region-wide celebration, dramatizing the event and encouraging its emulation. The object of all these activities would be to improve actual practice and to teach the general principle that development is not "imported" but produced through one's own efforts.

THE ROLE OF THE STATE

Each agropolitan district is a self-governing unit whose authority over its own productive and residentiary activities, considered jointly, is restrained only by the concurrent needs of all other districts and the combined needs of the larger community of which they form a part. This limitation on autonomy is balanced by the requirement that the level of development of productive forces across all districts shall be approximately equal.

Self-reliance requires self-finance, and self-finance calls for self-government. The political autonomy of agropolitan districts is a fundamental principle and may be exercised through assemblies, with delegates sent by component functional and territorial units, representing productive and residentiary interests respectively. Planning and other technical personnel should be attached to the assemblies in order to bring all possible formal knowledge to bear on their decisions.

But even though they are autonomous, agropolitan districts are not sovereign units. They are parts of a larger territorial system — the nation — that, in turn, is linked into the all-embracing functional system of the world economy.

In social formations that are organized on the basis of agropolitan principles, the role of the state is at once protective, developmental, facilitative, regulatory, and redistributive. It is *protective* by securing territorial boundaries against outside, predatory forces and keeping the peace among the constitutive units of the state. It is *developmental* by co-ordinating national policies for both structural change and growth, and by undertaking projects of common benefit which exceed the ability of agropolitan districts. It is *facilitative* in that, through its own resources, it stands prepared to support agropolitan districts (and regions) in the realization of their own projects. It is *regulatory* by maintaining those critical balances within the system of social relationships that will permit both change and growth to occur without excessive disruption of the system as a whole. And it is *redistributive* in that it takes surplus resources from rich districts to equalize redevelopment possibilities in less favoured areas.

In agropolitan society, the central state is a strong state. Increased power at district and regional levels requires a growth of power at the centre. It follows that a system of agropolitan governance is not without its own sources of conflict. Conflicts will arise among territorial units (districts and regions), each with its special interests to defend, and there will always be differences in local and/or personal viewpoint. But agropolitan governance is not intended to sublimate conflicts into a greater harmony; *it is to provide a legitimate forum for articulating conflicts and searching for appropriate means of resolution.*

The Parallel Economy

The foregoing description of the agropolitan approach to development is an attempt to set forth the conditions of a better life for the billions of peasants and urban workers in the periphery of the world economy. It is an approach that tries to bring together questions of production and distribution in the same solution by shifting the bulk of developmental activities to where the people are, an approach which stresses a development *from within* in which human energies are released in freely co-operative relations. Starting with basic needs, it is also a development which, in parallel with the general development of productive forces, allows for the gradual emergence of individual needs.

It is therefore necessary to point out that the agropolitan approach is not intended to achieve a maximum level of self-sufficiency, or to expand the use-value economy to the virtual exclusion of values in exchange, or to oppose an urban-based industrialization at all costs. In emphasizing those elements which have been overlooked or neglected in traditional doctrine, we do not wish to suggest that they become the only elements.

Nor does an insistence on selective territorial closure mean an hermetic isolation from the world economy. The world economy exists, and if its further integration along functional lines is to become workable, the urban-based, corporate economy must be restricted to a non-competitive and, if possible, complementary realm. Corporate industry is non-competitive when it produces commodities that do not substantially duplicate the production of decentralized agropolitan industries. It is complementary where it develops backward and forward linkages with the thousands of small industries in agropolitan locations.

So long as corporate industry and business exist—and they will not only continue to exist but will probably expand—the movement of people from rural districts to the cities will also continue. The agropolitan approach is not meant to freeze the existing pattern of settlement. Its sole purpose is to make possible a development that is geared to the satisfaction of evolving human needs.

Over time, cities that are organized on agropolitan principles will grow, extending their reach over vast areas. But instead of destroying rural life, they will absorb it and, in absorbing it, transform it. And even though the exchange economy will expand relative to the economy of use values, at least for a time, the production of use values will continue to contribute importantly to national development. The agropolitan approach is a dynamic form of development. Except for a few basic principles, it does not follow any formulae but pursues the logic of its own evolution in specific settings.

Starting with an emphasis on basic needs—a sufficiency of livelihood—its ultimate purpose is to facilitate the satisfaction of emerging social and individualized needs. Only the initial conditions have been specified. Once begun, agropolitan development will pass through its own historical transformations.

23

The Self-Reliant City

DAVID MORRIS

The signs are there, harbingers of a new way of thinking. From the hills of Seattle to the arid flatlands of Davis, from the industrial city of Hartford to the university town of Madison, cities are beginning to redefine their role in our society. Long viewed as little more than real estate developers and social welfare dispensers, the municipal corporation is asserting the more important function of overall planning and development. Buffeted by natural resource crises beyond their control, cities are encouraging local sources of energy, food and raw materials. Burdened by deteriorating physical plants, cities are designing new, less expensive and more efficient life-support systems. Vulnerable to branch plant closings, cities are beginning to favor development that comes from within, that relies on hundreds of small businesses rather than one or two large factories.

The city is becoming an ecological nation which seeks to maximize the long term value of its finite piece of land by creating elegant, biologically-based systems. Local self-reliance is the goal. The term "local self-reliance" is defined in various ways by different disciplines. To the ecologist, local self-reliance means "closed loop systems" where the wastes of one process become the raw materials of another. To the economist, local self-reliance means capturing for the benefit of the local community the greatest amount of "value added" to the original raw material through processing and marketing. Local self-reliance, to biologist Russell Anderson is "a type of development which stimulates the ability to satisfy needs locally." It is "the capacity for self-sufficiency, but not self-sufficiency itself. Self-reliance represents a new balance, not a new absolute."

Consider the garbage we dispose of each day. Garbage is nothing more than mixed raw materials. The individual materials have a value. Once separated from the rest of the waste stream, the value of the material depends in large part on the degree to which it is processed into a useable final

Excerpted from David Morris, *The New City-States* (Washington, D.C.: Institute for Local Self-Reliance, 1982). Copyright © 1982 by the Institute for Local Self-Reliance. 2425 18th Street N.W., Washington D.C. 20009. 202-232-4108.

product. For example, a recycled aluminum can is worth about 17 cents a pound to community recycling centers (plus the indirect benefit of reducing garbage disposal costs). Compressing the cans into a smaller volume lowers the shipping cost to the central manufacturing plant, raising the value by 25 percent. Smelt the cans into ingots and the value rises again to more than 50 cents a pound. Convert the ingot into a consumer product like bicycle handlebars and the value of the aluminum doubles to more than a dollar a pound. The self-reliant city captures as much of this additional value as possible for the local economy.

The self-reliant city views itself as a nation. It analyzes the flow of capital within its borders and evaluates its "balance of payments." It recycles money much as it recycles goods. Every added cycle increases the community's wealth. Businesses are evaluated not only for the services or products they offer but for the way they affect the local economy. The results are often surprising. One MacDonald's restaurant in a Washington, D.C. neighborhood was found to be exporting out of the area more than $500,000 of its $750,000 monthly gross revenues. Of the $35 million the 30,000 residents, businesses and local governments of Carbondale, Illinois and Northampton, Massachusetts, paid for fuels and electricity in 1980, more than 85 cents on the dollar left the economy immediately. As the mayor of Auburn, New York, remarked, "It matters little to us whether a dollar goes to Saudi Arabia or Texas. The effect on the local economy is the same. We are losing control over a substantial part of our own resources." "Stop the Leakages" has become a rallying cry for those demanding local self-reliance. Whether the leakages are raw materials dumped into landfills, or branch stores that take the majority of their earnings out of the community, or retired people who can't find places to offer their time and skills the result is the same – the loss of valuable resources.

This new way of thinking about cities defies traditional political classifications. It is ideologically neither right nor left. To John McKnight of Northwestern University, the liberal sees everyone as a potential client; the conservative sees everyone as a potential consumer. The liberal thinks people want services; the conservative believes we want commodities. Each agrees that the individual citizen is not the actor but the acted upon. Those encouraging local self-reliance have a different philosophy. The individual is seen as a producer of wealth and an active participant in the political process of resource management. Production rather than consumption is the explicit priority for self-reliant cities.

Self-reliant cities minimize government but not necessarily governance. The very terms "citizen" and "cities" connote political authority. Practically, as communities take an active role in promoting local self-reliance, the traditional distinction between public and private sectors begins to blur. A good example is Oceanside, a rapidly growing, conservative Republican city in southern California. Its citizens believe the community should take an active role in promoting the general welfare. The city has a significant number of retired people. With rising energy prices cutting into fixed incomes, the city council investigated the potential for using solar energy to lower hot water bills. Because traditional financial institutions wouldn't provide adequate financing for people to pursue this option, the city council unanimously approved a program that creates an alternative method of financing this income- and energy-saving technology. Homeowners lease solar hot water systems directly from private firms. The city helps to market the systems, guarantees them, collects lease payments and reduces red tape associated with permits, building code applications and the like. To participate in the program, the private firm must post performance bonds, agree to a consumer complaint process and charge less than a maximum monthly amount. Within 60 days of the commencement of the program, more than $15 million had been committed by private firms for investment in this city of 80,000 people. Thus, the city is not only capturing the value of an indigenous resource—the sun—but it is assuming an aggressive and innovative role.

Local self-reliance is an inward-looking process. But its dynamic may have a major effect on our national economy. By viewing themselves as nations, cities emphasize special considerations that undermine one of the principal tenets of our Constitution—the continental free-trade zone. The unencumbered mobility of goods, capital and people across state and city boundaries was for many of the founding fathers the chief purpose of the Constitution. By the late nineteenth century, the Supreme Court was striking down almost any local restriction on commerce as unconstitutional. Yet, a century later, localities are being given considerable authority to influence the ease with which we transport people, goods and capital across political jurisdictions. Cities have been granted the right to limit population growth, in effect limiting people's right to move. Cities enact returnable bottle bills, in effect prohibiting corporations from selling products in certain kinds of containers within the city's political jurisdiction. Cities require public employees to live within city limits. Cities favor local businesses over those outside the city.

The courts have been ambivalent about spatially oriented policies. Some municipal bottle bills have been overturned as unfair burdens on interstate commerce. Zoning ordinances that favor small businesses have been overturned as unfair discrimination to large firms. Growth limitation ordinances have in some cases been overturned when the courts concluded that the severity of the action had not been justified by the local conditions.

In an age of scarce resources the issue of spatial bias will not disappear. As we become more aware of resource flows, the justification of "place" as the basis for decision-making increases. For example, most states require municipal corporations to purchase products at the lowest possible price. Cities may not pay more for a product simply because it is produced locally. These laws were enacted to simplify contracting procedures and to reduce the possibility of corruption. But what happens when the advantages of local production become significant? Take the case of Carbondale, Illinois. It owns 110 vehicles. The city now imports 100 percent of its fuel. The vehicles could, at minimal expense, be converted to operate totally on alcohol. The alcohol could be produced locally from local waste products. Even if the price of the local alcohol were slightly higher than that of imported gasoline, the benefits to the local economy and, as result, to the city through higher tax revenues would offset the price difference.

Energy, Integration and Recycling

The 2,000 percent increase in world crude oil prices between 1970 and 1980 adds to the burden of sore-pressed local economies. It also provides the motivation for a new conceptual model of the city. As gasoline, heating oil, natural gas and electricity prices soar, transportation becomes an important design consideration. The price of energy makes local self-reliance not only philosophically palatable but economically viable. Even as our school textbooks continue to extol the efficiencies of an integrated world economy, the rising cost of long distribution systems encourages us to think again. No longer is it economical to build a house with glue imported from one continent, wood from another, nails from another and fixtures from still another, to heat it with fuel that comes from still another part of the world, and to bring in water and electricity from several hundred miles away.

To illustrate the rising importance of distribution, today it costs twice as much to get food to our tables as it does to grow the food. Integration rather than separation will become the design criteria of the 80s. Rather than raise a tomato in California and eat it in Boston we will raise vegetables in Boston, in greenhouses warmed by waste heat from nearby factories or buildings. Small scale steel mills (the industry calls them minimills, or even neighborhood mills) already compete with conventional mills 10 times their size because they use locally available scrap metal. After an exhaustive study to ascertain how it could save energy, Portland, Oregon, concluded that a five percent savings could be accomplished simply by reviving neighborhood grocery stores. Once again integrating business and residence we can avoid the need to require a resident who wants a pack of cigarettes, a loaf of bread or a gallon of milk to drive a two-ton automobile to a regional shopping center.

Energy efficiency also encourages recycling. To make an aluminum can out of the original bauxite ore requires eight times the energy required to recycle an aluminum can. Similar savings come from recycling paper or other materials. In fact, the energy crisis may be considered a part of a larger materials crisis. Petroleum, natural gas and uranium are scarce, but so are many of our widely used construction and fabrication materials. As the shortages become more pronounced, the marketplace finds recycled materials more attractive.

A city of the size of San Francisco generates about 1,500 tons of solid waste per day. Broken down into component materials, San Francisco disposes of as much aluminum each year as is extracted from a medium-sized bauxite mine, as much copper as a small-sized copper mine and as much paper as is made from a good sized timber stand. The city itself is a mine. Its waste stream becomes the basis for new industries.

Manufacturing firms traditionally locate near their raw material supplies. Steel mills locate near iron ore deposits. Paper companies locate near forests. If our cities become mines for recycled material, we can expect industries to locate nearby. Since scrap manufacturing plants are smaller and less polluting, they can be located in populated areas and serve smaller market areas. An aluminum plant using recycled metal requires ten percent of the capital as one using virgin bauxite. Steel mills using scrap can be built with less than ten percent the capital, and can operate economically at less than five percent the output of conventional mills. The same holds true for paper mills using scrap material.

Rising energy prices also encourage decentralized energy generation. In an age of political uncertainty, long distribution lines have made our communities vulnerable. Social upheaval in Iran brings gas lines to Toledo. Grand Forks, North Dakota, waits to see whether Canada will cut off its natural gas supply.

Cities have begun to react to this dependence by moving toward energy self-reliance. Oceanside and Davis, California, mandate solar hot water systems for new homes. Springfield, Vermont, expects to complete the construction of a hydroelectric facility that will allow it to export power to the same central utility from which it had been purchasing power for almost 30 years. Clayton, New Mexico, gets 15 percent of its electricity from a wind turbine and Burlington, Vermont, gets about the same amount from wood.

Integration again becomes the key design element. Fort Collins uses the methane generated during the digestion of its sewage to fuel municipal vehicles and explores the potential for using the sludge as fertilizer for nearby cropland. Hercules, California, uses biological digestion processes to produce fertilizer, vegetables, meat and fuel from its sewage system.

Cities whose bureaucracies have been fragmented now realize that there is a synergy to municipal development. When individual parts reinforce one another, the whole becomes greater than the sum of the parts. The city is an integral system. Its public works structures are part of its life-support system. The way it uses the land area, the kinds of economic activities it encourages, and the way it uses natural resources combine to foster the general health of the city. Municipal planning for self-reliance must take into account many factors previously considered outside the province of the municipal corporation.

This new understanding comes as we enter the electronic age. New analytical technologies and low-cost computers give communities a much better understanding of their environment. The new resource maps are dynamic. They track the movement of capital — money — across city borders. They analyze the composition of the solid waste stream, check the quality of the air, water and soil, estimate the costs of new development, identify where buildings are losing heat and evaluate the skill levels of the unemployed. The inward orientation of local self-reliance is complemented by the outward orientation of new communications systems. New technologies allow communities to horizontally communicate with others, to share information outside the mass media networks.

Thus, the global village becomes a complementary metaphor to the globe of villages. Cities become enmeshed in a global network of information while they use modern science to convert sunlight, plant matter and abundant locally available materials into useful products. Long-distance trade in materials declines, while trade in information, culture and knowledge rises. Electronic trade replaces molecular trade.

Development: The Cost of Growth

During the post World War II era cities were addicted to growth. Yet they found that growth brings costs as well as benefits. Environmental legislation forced cities to estimate the impact of growth. Increasingly sophisticated computer models permitted cities to monitor the flow of resources through their borders.

What they found was profoundly disquieting. One suburb of San Francisco, Fairfield, found to its surprise and dismay that total tax revenues from a proposed new subdivision would pay only half of the required new police services and nothing for other services. A 1974 study of Madison, Wisconsin, estimated the cost of a new acre of development was $16,500 for installing sanitary sewers, storm drainage, water mains, and local streets. The figure did not include the acre's pro-rated share of the cost of new schools, fire stations, arterial streets, wells, landfills, etc.[1]

When Proposition 13 reduced the property tax revenues for California's cities many began to add public development costs to the private developers' bill. Santa Monica had one builder include 100 units of low-income housing, a day-care center, a public park and incentives for the use of mass transit. Another developer was required to include a grocery store on the first floor of a new office tower to meet the needs of the elderly.

As cities gained sophistication in the planning process they began to reevaluate the favored practice of courting big corporations to locate branch plants in their community. As Neil Pierce noted, this type of development often had a negative impact.

> When new industries are attracted from outside, they bring the well-advertised benefits of new jobs, orders for local suppliers, and a fresh infusion of money into a community. But there can be severe drawbacks. A firm with highly specialized labor requirements may bring its most highly paid workers with it. The jobs left for local residents may be few, menial or both. But local taxpayers will have to pay for new schools, roads, and other services for the newcomers. Capital investments to attract new firms have virtually bankrupted some communities—and even then they face the possibility that a big multinational firm may later decide there's even cheaper labor in Mexico or Taiwan and desert the area as rapidly as it came.[2]

The mating dance between cities and giant corporations had become too one-sided. One business magazine described the situation as a "rising spiral of government subsidies as companies play off city against city and state against state for the most advantageous terms."[3] Atlanta advertises its wares on Cleveland television programs and has opened an industry recruitment office in New York. In tiny Bossier City, Louisiana, the chamber of commerce encourages school children to write more than 900 letters to corporate executives telling them of the city's need for jobs, and its abundance of assets, such as clean air.[4]

When a city tries to negotiate with a giant corporation, it is a nerve-wracking experience, for it is a seller's market. The Detroit suburb of Trenton, population 24,000, gambled by refusing to give Chrysler Corporation the $36 million in tax breaks it had demanded in return for expanding its 4,400-employee engine plant. The City Council offered only $24 million because it felt the city needed the money for the school system. Edward M. Heffinger, mayor pro-tem of Trenton, nervously commented, "Our overriding concern was—what if we had guessed wrong here." Officials from Indiana, New York, and Ohio were waiting in the wings, wooing Chrysler. Finally, Governor Milliken of Michigan stepped into the fray, persuading the federal government to put up a long term, low-interest loan. In this instance, as with most, the final resolution turned more on one's political contacts with the federal government, than with anything the local government could do.

Their self-promotional activities constituted the benign side of the competition between cities for corporate investment. Cities often used their right to seize land to put together a site large enough to lure a corporation and then, at its own expense, to install the physical infrastructure necessary to service the industry, and finally, borrow money, while writing off local taxes for 10 or 20 years as a further enticement. When the stakes were high, a growing number of local officials were willing to exercise the full authority of the municipal corporation to attract large plants, even at the cost of destroying existing communities. One of the best examples occurred when General Motors announced it would build plants in cities in Kansas, Oklahoma, and Michigan only if the local governments met its demands. Cities that failed to accommodate GM, the third largest private corporation in the world, were informed they would not be considered. Several cities, including Detroit, agreed to all conditions. According to GM, its plant there would generate six thousand jobs; in return, GM wanted the city to clear a 465-acre site. Unfortunately, the 465-acre site was home to many people — Poletown, as it was called, was predominantly Polish and had strong social cohesion. When 90 percent of the neighborhood owners refused to sell, Detroit used a recently enacted Michigan statute called the "quick take" law that allowed a city to condemn private property for public purposes and take title within 90 days, whether or not the value of the property for compensation purposes had been agreed on. In March 1981 the Michigan Supreme Court ruled in favor of the city and its Economic Development Corporation. The court ruled that the city was exercising its powers of eminent domain for a public purpose, the creation of "programs to alleviate and prevent conditions of unemployment." However, in this instance, in order to create a maximum of six thousand jobs the city of Detroit razed 1,300 homes, 16 churches, and 143 businesses, destroying an entire cohesive community.

Ironically, attracting outside investment may well increase economic instability. Absentee-owned businesses tend not to be good neighbors. They cut back employment during down cycles and recessions more than locally based companies. They are less likely to purchase local services and products, such as legal assistance, financial consulting, capital borrowing and factor inputs.

The balance sheet of conglomerates is chillingly objective. Subsidiaries can be closed, not because they are losing money, but because they are not making enough. Said Joseph Danzansky, Chairman of Giant Foods, "But let's face it. Many stores are closed not because they operate at a loss, but because they are marginal and the capital can be more advantageously invested elsewhere." When Uniroyal closed its inner tube plant in Indianapolis, the *Wall Street Journal* noted, "Uniroyal could have kept the plant operating profitably if it wanted to, but under pressure from the securities markets, management decided to concentrate its energy on higher growth chemical lines. Many companies have grown too big to look at the small market."

Peter J. Bearse, economist in New Jersey, adds, "We know in New Jersey that the average size of economic units in most lines of activity has been increasing steadily. We know that the largest firms' units are likely to move longer distances when relocating."

Caught in a vicious cycle, cities end up competing for fewer and fewer large companies which have come to dominate certain major industries. Three companies sold 80 percent of the cold breakfast cereal in 1975. Three companies sold 80 percent of the home insulation in that year. Four sold 70 percent of the dairy products. One sold 90 percent of the canned soups.[5] Fewer than 30 giants owned over 20 percent of the cropland. Eight oil companies controlled 64 percent of proven oil reserves, 44 percent of uranium reserves, 40 percent of coal under private lease, and 40 percent of copper deposits.[6]

Yet it turns out that small businesses, not the giant corporations, are the backbone of local economies. In 1971, there were 12.4 million business enterprises of all sizes and kinds in America, including 3.3 million farms. Of that 12.4 million, over half (6.4 million) had gross sales of less than $10,000. Another 3.4 million failed to reach $50,000 in sales, and still another one million had $100,000 in yearly sales. Thus, nearly 11 million of the nation's 12.4 million firms, or 87.2 percent, had sales of less than $100,000 in that year.[7] Less than one percent of the service firms had multistore operations. Of the 275,000 manufacturing companies in the United States about 10 percent had more than 99 employees.[8]

A massive study of 5.6 million firms (representing 82 percent of the nation's private jobs) was conducted by David Birch. He tracked these firms over a seven-year period, from 1971 to 1978, and concluded that the country's biggest job producer was small firms. Two-thirds of all new jobs were created in companies employing fewer than 20 people. The top 1,000 firms on the *Fortune* list generated only 75,000 jobs, or just a little more than 1 percent of all new jobs created between 1970 and 1976.[9] Birch found that most jobs came from the start-up of the new firms, and the expansion of existing small businesses, destroying the myth that economic development is created by plant relocations and expansion by big corporations.

These figures gave an ironic twist to the frenzied competition among cities for giant plant locations. Cities, built on a foundation of thousands of small businesses, often found themselves in the position of forcing out small firms in order to make room for a branch of a larger corporation.

By the end of the 1970s, cities were beginning to understand the nature of their dilemma. They began to directly involve themselves in economic developments. In 1974 the Housing and Community Development Act provided Community Development Block Grants (CDBG), lump sum payments to cities which enabled them to coordinate community development and economic development planning. The 1977 amendments to this act expanded the economic development activities permitted under the CDBG program.

Increased funds and authority gave rise to dozens of local economic development corporations, with the power to acquire land, lease land, construct buildings and provide short and long term financing to businesses.

Cities are losing control over their capital as they lose control over their jobs and factories. In the late 1970s an older ethnic neighborhood in Chicago discovered that its residents had deposited $33 million in a local savings and loan association but had received back only $120,000 in loans. That discovery, made only after exhaustive and difficult research, led to the enactment of a federal law requiring financial institutions to invest a significant amount of their locally generated deposits in a local area. But no legislation could stop the hemorrhage of capital that accompanies the advent of electronic banking and money market funds. Not only neighborhoods within larger cities, but entire small- and medium-sized cities are now witnessing the largest outflow of local dollars in history.

With the advent of electronic banking and money market funds, the problem of capital outflow hit every small city in the country. Money market funds, centered in the nation's major cities, withdrew money from small communities and reinvested it in national corporations or federal securities. Money market funds grew from $11 billion in late 1978 to almost $800 billion in mid-1982. The American Bankers Association estimated that 50 to 70 percent of this growth was at the expense of financial institutions — and many in small towns. Many small city banks and savings and loan associations, to preserve their own profitability and liquidity, invested their own deposits in money market instruments rather than in their own communities. Elmor Romines, President of Progressive Federal of Houston, Missouri, says, "It's like a pipeline with a valve in every daggum community in this country." To individual residents and local financial institutions, the money market fund was an attractive investment. Each received security and a higher interest rate. But the price was a lack of funds lendable to local residents and businesses. The *Wall Street Journal*, commenting on the trend in mid-1982 concluded, "If the drain continues, less affluent, slower-growing areas of the country will have a tough time financing their local communities."

The City as Nation: Inventorying the Resource Base

The city has never been viewed as a producer of basic wealth. Mining and extraction are considered outside the capacity of urban areas. Even manufacturing is considered to need so much land area and to serve such large markets that it must locate outside cities. The urban community generally is seen as the site of finance, commerce and service industries. The self-reliant city changes this definition. The city becomes a producer of basic wealth and a processor of raw materials as well as a site of commerce and trade.

One of the most important problems will be to identify new sources of energy to heat our buildings, power our machines and fuel our vehicles. Fortunately, the dramatic price increases in fossil fuels during the 1970s spurred the creation of a vibrant industry to serve those interested in reducing energy imports and generating energy on-site. The $100 million energy conservation industry in 1973 had grown to $4 billion by 1979 and to $10 billion by 1982. That put it on a par with total Japanese imported car sales in the United States. *Business Week* predicts gross annual sales will reach $50 billion by 1990 equal to all car sales in the U.S. whether imported or domestically produced. It is an indication of how the times have changed that an industry which was only a bit player in the economy a decade ago has come to play such an essential role, while the automobile industry, a decade ago the centerpiece of our society, has become an economic albatross.

In moving toward an energy efficient community, cities can also rely on new technologies. Infrared cameras can locate building heat losses. Lights are now available that turn themselves off automatically when people leave the room and adjust their intensity levels to the amount of sunlight coming in the windows.

Existing buildings can save up to 80 percent of their energy with investments that repay themselves in fewer than ten years. Refrigerators are now commercially available that use 90 percent less electricity to provide the same cooling space as those in our homes today. Today's automobiles use 250 gallons a year compared to the 1,000 gallons a year used by those purchased a decade before.

Thus, the city seeking self-reliance can reduce its imported energy simply by making its physical stock more efficient. Moreover, new technologies now make it feasible for the city to become an energy producer.

Rising prices of natural gas make it desirable to tap into small deposits located under our cities. The Harbor School District in Erie, Pennsylvania, developed two wells between 1978 and 1980. To improve the payback, the school district converted its 34 vehicles, including 25 school buses, to compressed natural gas. The wells paid for themselves in 17 months, and the school district continues to find new cost benefits. The gas burns cleaner than gasoline and the carbon buildup on the engine has almost been eliminated. Tuneups have been extended to once every 24,000 miles rather than 12,000. Oil changes now occur every 6,000 rather than every 2,000 miles. Youngstown, Ohio, uses its natural gas resources in a different manner. It leases land at one of its municipal airports to a private company in return for a percentage of the gross revenue and a priority given to local businesses on gas sales from the land.

Sufficient sunlight falls on most of our city rooftops to heat our buildings. Unfortunately, the sunlight does not fall at precisely the time we need the heat. In some cities, 75 percent of the solar energy falls during the summer, yet 90 percent of the heating needs occur during the winter, when days are shorter and sunlight is less intense. These cities need to develop seasonal storage systems. Our household water tanks store 50 to 75 gallons of water. With only an inch or so of insulation, the water stays hot for 24 hours. Improving on the potential, Sweden and Canada have built immense underground storage tanks that are heavily insulated. Solar collectors convert the sunlight to heat during the summer. The heat is used during the winter months. Six or even nine months storage has proven economical in Sweden, whose latitude is more than 1,000 miles north of Boston, Massachusetts. Miamisburg, Ohio, has used a seasonal storage system called a solar pond to heat a part of one building since 1979.

Traditionally, more than 70 percent of the fuel burned in central stations is lost as waste heat. Less than a third is delivered as electricity. Today, more and more companies are building power plants that not only generate electricity but also can capture the waste heat for useful purposes. But since the cost of transporting heat long distances is very high, the best location for these cogeneration facilities is near the customer. Thus, the combination of smaller power plants and cogeneration moves electric generation back into our communities, reversing a century long trend. A 1978 study for the state of New Jersey concluded that almost 50 percent of the boilers in the state were over 25 years old and would soon require replacement. They could be replaced with devices that are up to 98 percent efficient, that is, that convert 98 percent of the energy value of the fuel source to electricity and heat.

By the early 1980s, rising electric prices had introduced a new term to the energy vocabulary—micro hydro. Run-of-the-river devices requiring no dams at all could generate power for fewer than 100 homes and still be competitive. Tens of thousands of backyard streams suddenly took on renewed economic importance. Cities that had been founded 200 years before on the shores of fast flowing rivers for a source of mechanical power began refurbishing their abandoned dam-sites. Some cities found new sources of water power. La Habra, California, installed a 100-kilowatt turbine in its water pipes.

The most exciting technology for on-site electric generation is a device developed for space use. The photovoltaic or solar cell converts direct sunlight into electricity. Until 1974, its only use was to power satellites. In 1974, one could outfit a residence for $2 million. By 1982, the price was $45,000 for household self-sufficiency, still too high for most households, but a 50-fold reduction in price in eight years. More than 500 homes already are equipped with solar cells. Many of these homes are located away from power lines. The cost of laying cable to the homes is greater than the cost of purchasing the solar devices and backup systems on battery storage systems. By 1985, industry and government experts agree these devices will be widespread in the residential and commercial sectors. Indeed, this technology is cost-effective at the household level first. Only as the price drops further does it become competitive for use in central locations. The reason for this apparent anomaly is that central facilities require large investments in land and arrays upon which to place the solar cells. Also, there is a ten percent loss of electricity in transmitting from a central facility.

General Electric, the company formed when Thomas Edison left the power plant business in the late 1880s, developed in prototype form a roof-top solar cell shingle in 1982. Not available yet commercially, these shingles will transform the roof into a power plant. GE eyes the two million homes that are re-roofed each year as its potential market.

Solar storage units, rooftop collectors, and another form of solar energy – food production – will require considerable space. One study done in the early 1970s found that among a sample of 86 cities with populations over 100,000, the average amount of vacant land available per capita was 2,279 square feet.[10] This ranged from a high of 6,279 square feet in the West South Central states, to 360 square feet in the Mid-Atlantic region. John Jeavons and Michael Shepard determined, on the basis of three years' growing experience, that a full, balanced diet may eventually be grown on as little as 2,500 square feet per person in a six-month growing season.[11]

To grow food, we need adequate water and fertilizers. The city is a giant nutrient machine, spewing out organic and human wastes. These can be used as fertilizers. In fact, municipal composting operations are increasingly commonplace around the country. One study of the Omaha–Council Bluffs area in Nebraska found that from sludge alone "more nutrients are available...than the average supplied by Nebraska farmers." It concludes, "By the year 2000, with increasing waste volume and rising fertilizer prices, benefits to the region's farmers in terms of supplying crop nutrients could exceed $1 million annually."[12] Another report concluded that the combined nitrogen disposed of by municipalities in America is greater than the total amount used in nitrogen fertilizers in the early 1970s.

Cities have the resource base to move toward local self-reliance. Not self-sufficiency, but independence – looking inward instead of outward, building on their scientific and technical knowledge to design systems that maximize the benefit to the city as a whole.

As cities look to retain as much economic value within their borders as possible, they will inevitably turn their attention toward manufacturing and processing. We are taught that large is best, that the model is the automobile assembly lines in Detroit, or the Gary, Indiana, steel mills. As we have had to reconceptualize our cities to see them as mines or power plants, so we must change our thinking about the scale required for efficient manufacturing. The self-reliant city can increasingly make it at home.

The City as Factory: Making It at Home

Harvard economist Joe Bain, in a classic study of economies of scale in manufacturing, concluded, "... after a century and a half of rapid industrial expansion, of extraordinary technical progress, and of generalized belief in the virtues of size, it still remains that the average factory in the United States or Great Britain employs only two or three score people..."[13]

Researchers have since come to a similar conclusion—most of the things we need could be manufactured within our larger urban areas. One study found that, if automobiles and petroleum products were excluded from the total, 58 percent of final goods consumption, by value, of a population of one million could be produced locally in small plants. Sixteen percent of the consumption needs could be produced by plants for a market population of 200,000.[14] Even very small factories raised production costs only slightly.[15] A shoe factory which produces for a city of 100,000 instead of a region of 500,000, may have production costs only five to ten percent higher. Since production costs only represent a small fraction of the selling price, such increases could be offset by eliminating middleman profits or reducing transportation expenses. Cities could, through their taxing or procurement policies, value locally produced items higher than those which are imported.

Most of these studies of plant sizes look at existing technologies. Economist John Blair described a more recent phenomenon, the rise of what he dubs "centrifugal technologies."[16]

> With plastics, fiberglass, and high performance composites providing high strength and easily processed materials suitable for an infinite variety of applications; with energy provided by such simple and efficient devices as high energy batteries, fuel cells, turbine engines, and rotary piston engines; with computers providing a means of instantaneously retrieving, sorting and aggregating vast bodies of information; and with other new electronic devices harnessing the flow of electrons for other uses, there appears to be aborning a second industrial revolution which, among its other features, contains within itself the seeds of destruction for concentrated industrial structures.

For example, in the late 1960s one plastics executive said: "A thermoforming mold made of epoxy costs approximately one to two percent of an equivalent steel stamping die, and we have yet to find out how many pieces can be run from a mold." Plastic-bodied cars can be produced at much less cost than steel-bodied vehicles. One observer notes, "The outside availability of power train components and the use of plastic bodies should reduce his capital costs markedly below what is currently required to enter the industry at any given level of output.[17] The close tolerances required of piston engines are not necessary for electric vehicles, reducing the need for both capital and labor. One British car manufacturer described the electric car as a "far less complex vehicle than the existing motor car and contains about one fifth of the parts that are in present-day cars." The tooling required to produce a plastic-bodied car in the late 1960s was about $1.5 million, compared to the $500 million then required to initiate production of conventional steel-bodied piston engine cars.

Internal combustion engine, steel-bodied car factories are economical only if they sell more than 150,000 vehicles a year. Conventional electric vehicle factories need sell only 7,000 medium-priced cars to financially survive. One enterprising Italian manufacturer has developed production techniques that can manufacture as few as 500 electric vehicles a year and still generate a profit.

In Nebraska, a problem—what to do with millions of car and truck tires—generated a new technology. The increased use of steel-belted radials makes it uneconomical to use conventional mechanical shredding processes for tires. But new techniques use liquid nitrogen to freeze the tire to hundreds of degrees below zero. The rubber is then pulverized. The steel and fiber is also captured. The powdered crumb rubber is then converted into a wide variety of products, from rubber soles to floorboard or road surfacing agents. Modern science again has taken a disposal problem and made it into a production process.

Hercules, California, a city of 7,000, wanted to grow, but the Environmental Protection Agency prohibited growth without a commitment to expensive new sewage treatment capacity. Bypassing federal strictures, the city chose to build a sewage plant called Aquacell with its own money. The system consists of an inflated polyethylene greenhouse cover built over three treatment lagoons. Duckweed and water hyacinths grow on the pond's surface, existing on nutrients in the waste water and screening out the sun to inhibit algae growth. The plants can be harvested or can be composted by themselves or along with the sludge to produce fertilizer. Harvested alone, the plants, high in protein, can become animal feed. Methane is generated during the digestion process, and can be used to fulfill some of the electrical requirements of the plant. The system can be built in modular form. Once again, modern science has created an elegant, integrated system that transforms a waste facility into a production plant.

The idea that there might be a variety of capital and labor tradeoffs in manufacturing was proven most dramatically by Ernst Schumacher and his London-based organization, the Intermediate Technology Development Group. In 1972 while visiting Zambia at the invitation of the president, he discovered a serious economic crisis; the farmers could not get their eggs to market because of a labor strike at the egg carton factory. Schumacher was surprised to learn that the factory was in the Netherlands. After returning to Europe he sought out the president of the company, and asked him whether it might be feasible to design a factory to meet only the needs of the small market of Zambia, which required but one million egg cartons a year. The president, speaking from 30-years' experience, answered that his factory was designed to be more efficient, and that if any factory were to produce egg cartons at less than the rate of one million a month it would have to produce them at a higher cost.

Undaunted, Schumacher set his team to work. Eighteen months later an egg carton manufacturing plant was operational in Zambia. It produced, not one million egg cartons a year, but only a third of a million, for there were three distinct egg market areas in the country, and three factories were needed. The plants produced egg cartons at the same unit costs, were more labor intensive, and used local materials. When industrial engineers were asked why they never designed a factory like that before, their answer was "Because no one asked us to."

In Chile, a colleague of Schumacher was asked if he could find a supplier of glass jam jars to replace those imported from Britain. The researcher recalled, "The mind boggles at the thought of a boatload of empty jam jars being transported there to be filled with jam, and then exported back again to the Western World. I thought that was basically crazy." He found that glass was made primarily from sand, limestone, soda ash, and a few trace elements like arsenic. Soda ash could be replaced with seaweed, but the glass would be slightly green. Arsenic could be eliminated, but there would be tiny bubbles in the glass. A furnace normally cost about 25,000 English pounds because it required highly sophisticated refractory materials. The reason why these materials were used was that the furnace was expected to last for 10 years. But if there were local refractory clay, and the people were prepared to reline every six months with refractory bricks, the proposed plant could produce one thousand jars an hour with local raw products for a modest investment.

This last example holds important lessons. Local self-reliance may require tradeoffs. A functionally equivalent product may be manufactured in a variety of ways, depending on how much the producer wants to substitute indigenous resources for imported resources.

We are cursed with giant central power plants, interlocking directorates between big corporations, big factories, and big government, production systems far removed from their markets, bloated bureaucracies which are on the whole unproductive, if not downright destructive, and hierarchical organizational structures which remove the top policymakers from the impact of their decisions. We are cursed but not condemned.

We are at a turning point in history. The opportunity exists to marry local political authority to the advantages of modern technology to make more independent, self-reliant communities. Only at the local level can we design humanly scaled production systems that meet our unique local requirements. We can seize the opportunity and potential that comes from a period of rapid social change and design a society in which we and our children would want to live. So far, to be sure, the positive signs are few. Yet they point the way to a new vision, a new context, and a new way of thinking.

Part Seven

Governance by the People
for the People

Empowerment of people is a central theme of people-centered development, and the development of people-responsive governance processes is one of its central concerns. The forms which such governance processes can take vary substantially. Some of the possibilities are examined by contributors to this section.

Alvin Toffler opens the section with an examination of what he sees as the current crisis of democratic governance. He argues that the demassification of society accompanying the passing of the industrial era is creating new demands for governance systems able to deal with substantially greater variety. His argument for increased experimentation with a variety of democratic forms of governance sets the stage for the contributions which follow.

Peter Berger and Richard Neuhaus argue the case for empowerment through pluralism based on a strengthened role for mediating structures — human-scale organizational units that stand between the individual and the impersonal megastructures of modern society. They suggest that an important source of alienation and of the deteriorating quality in the performance of social welfare functions can be traced to the bureaucratization of ever larger areas of the individual's lifespace. Instead of exacerbating these trends, they suggest that public policy should attempt to strengthen the role of the family, the voluntary association, the neighborhood, the small work group, and so forth.

A companion piece by Richard Nelson picks up on the theme of Berger and Neuhaus in relation to the problem of demands for quality day care. Nelson provides an exceptional organizational analysis, suggesting how difficult accountability problems can be resolved naturally and directly if services are organized in such a way as to make them truly accountable to informed users, even when publicly funded in part. He also demonstrates that many problems of social policy are not primarily allocational in nature; rather, they are organizational — requiring application of a type of analytical skill in short supply among policy analysts, whose skills are honed to address allocational analysis.

Grace Goodell returns the focus to the rural poor of the Third World. Her message is simple and direct. Development initiatives which assume that political development can be set aside to be addressed only after economic development is well underway reveal a fundamental ignorance of the true nature of the development process.

The final two chapters of this section address the role of voluntary associations in bringing fundamental changes to the social agenda in the United States and to the political processes through which that agenda is pursued. The chapter by the Exploratory Project for Economic Alternatives examines the growing role of intermediary organizations in solving local problems and in representing citizen interests. Finally, Jessica Lipnack and Jeffrey Stamps analyze as an organizational form the networking phenomenon which they maintain is reshaping America.

24

The Crisis of Democratic Governance

ALVIN TOFFLER

Democratic political institutions and processes, the mechanics of representative government, the entire apparatus of "democracy" as we know it — including voting, elections, parties, parliaments, and the like — are expressions not of some undying mystical human commitment to freedom but of the spread of industrial civilization that began in England 200 to 300 years ago.

This industrial civilization took the idea of representation (which like most ideas had rudimentary precedents in the ancient past) and merchandised it around the planet as the latest, most efficient, most humane form of government imaginable. As the industrial way of life spread, representative government, denatured or otherwise, spread with it. In fact, using shorthand, one might declare representative government — whether "capitalist" or "socialist" in form — to be the key political technology of the industrial era.

This era is now screeching to a halt. Industrial civilization is now in a state of terminal crisis, and a new, radically different civilization is emerging to take its place on the world stage. This does not mean that we are about to plunge ourselves voluntarily or simplistically back into some pretechnological way of life. Rather, it means that we are swiftly entering a new, more sophisticated stage of evolutionary development based on far more *advanced* yet more *appropriate* technologies than any known so far. This leap to a new phase of history is bringing with it new energy patterns, new geopolitical arrangements, new social institutions, new communications and information networks, new belief systems, symbols, and cultural assumptions.

Thus, it must also generate wholly new political structures and processes. I fail to see how it is possible for us to have a technological revolution,

243

a social revolution, an information revolution, moral, sexual, and episte-mological revolutions, and *not* a political revolution as well.

All this suggests that we need a fresh way to think about the political breakdown – the crisis of governmental competence – that we see all around us: the paralysis of parliaments, the ineptitudes of the giant governmental bureaucracies, the wild swings of political attention, focusing now here, now elsewhere, before any problem has been adequately understood, let alone solved. The erratic and ineffectual behavior of governments in the industrial world cannot be explained in conventional terms.

It is not because politicians and bureaucrats are stupid. It is not because of a conspiracy of the so-called right or left. It is not because greedy, rich people are corrupting and controlling our political institutions, though heaven knows they would like to. Nor does the crisis of ineffectuality arise because greedy, poor people are demanding too many "entitlements" from the system, as "neo-conservatives" would have us believe. Nor yet, for that matter, is it because we are witnessing the "general crisis of capitalism" that Marx predicted. Rather, it is because we are in the first stages of the "general crisis of industrialism" of which capitalism and socialism are both offshoots.

In this sense the breakdown of government as we have known it – which is to say representative government or parliamentary democracy or "indirect democracy" – is chiefly a consequence of obsolescence. Simply put, the political technology of the industrial age is no longer appropriate technology for the new civilization taking form around us. Our politics are obsolete.

To grasp why, let us for the moment lay aside all the other charac-teristics of political life (drama, ritual, struggle over power and resources, for example) and consider our present political system solely as a technology for the manufacture of collective decisions. This system – regardless of who runs it – is now, in my view, structurally incapable of making competent decisions about the world we inhabit.

A decision system suitable for one kind of environment may be totally ineffective or irrelevant in another – like a Seiko wrist-watch in the midst of a pre-historic band of nomads or an Exxon oil refinery in a world without fossil fuels.

The industrial age produced a specific decisional environment – one based on social homogeneity. The industrial revolution generated tremen-dous cultural, political, and technological pressures that converged to create uniformity in language, values, machines, work methods, architecture, political views, and life styles in general. If it did nothing else, the industrial revolution produced "mass society."

Yet the revolution gathering momentum today is carrying us precisely in the opposite direction. We are fast becoming far more socially, culturally, and politically diverse than ever before. We use more varied resources and tools, we fill more varied occupations and roles, we live more varied life styles than during the heyday of industrialism. Regional, sectoral, ethnic, and sub-cultural differences are looming into greater political importance as society, rapidly differentiating, moves away from homogeneity and toward heterogeneity. In short, we are shifting from a "mass society" to a "de-massified society"—and this has truly revolutionary (though largely misunderstood) implications for politics.

Thus it is becoming harder and harder to achieve consensus even locally, let alone nationally. Demands now pour in to the political decision-makers from a much wider range of special interests than before. Instead of having to deal with a few well-established mass constituencies, they now face political demands from a kaleidoscopic, continually changing set of temporary mini-constituencies. Instead of a few widely voiced, class-based slogans calling, say, for jobs or housing or social security, the political decision-maker today faces a clamor of competing, often contradictory demands from gay activists, ethnic sub-sub-minorities, regional power blocs, feminists, cultural and linguistic groups, gray panthers, Panama Canalers, anti-nuclear campaigners, single parents, solar freaks, and Sun Myung Moonies. In short, the decisional environment has been transformed.

Our political decision-making machinery, however, both legislative and executive, was never designed to cope with such high levels of diversity. It was designed, instead, to produce uniform, basically repetitive decisions for a much less differentiated environment, a simpler, more comprehensible and manageable environment. Designed to respond to mass movements, mass opinion, mass media, and large flows of relatively simple information, the system is now struggling against a tidal wave of de-massified mini-movements, de-massified opinion, increasingly de-massified communications media, and torrents of specialized data pouring in through fast-multiplying channels.

It should hardly surprise us if the result of this mismatch between our decisional technology and the decisional environment is a cacaphonous confusion, countless self-canceling decisions, noise, fury, and gross ineptitude.

If, moreover, our legislative and executive policy-makers are overloaded, what about those who implement their decisions in the civil service bureaucracy? Here the effects of our transformation from a mass to a de-massified society are even more explosive.

Take, for example, the "tax revolt" now raging in the United States. This revolt aims its attack at bureaucrats and government on the assumption that "government is doing too much," as though the entire problem were simply quantitative. But there is a far deeper reason for the tax revolt. For it we look at the huge government bureaucracies that were established during the industrial era, we discover that they, too, were designed to operate in a more homogeneous, repetitive, and predictable mass society. They were to the serivce economy what factories were to the goods economy: a tool for mass production.

As consumers have grown more diverse in the past twenty years or so, industry has responded through what executives term "product differentiation." Companies have competed to turn out different models, sizes, types, and styles for the increasingly segmented marketplace. Whether this product variation is good or bad, whether the differences are real or trivial are issues that can be explored elsewhere. Here it is only necessary to note that while goods producers responded quickly to growing social diversity, and service producers in the private sector did the same—witness the proliferation of different "package tours" in the travel industry—government bureaucracies have been far less adaptive. Constrained by anachronistic political boundaries, by well-intended but simplistic notions of "equality," by organizational ossification and rigidity, lacking even the spur of competition, the great government "service factories" are still, even now, pumping out essentially uniform services for an increasingly non-uniform population. Not surprisingly, the gap between what people need or want and what they get from government has grown to monstrous proportions.

The problem, therefore, is not simply that government does "too much"; the problem is that much of what it does is also simply wrong or too late. People who desperately need help don't get it. People in no need at all receive lush benefits. Programs designed in the nation's capital are not adequately tailored for local needs. Old programs that should have been slashed years ago continue to grind out whatever it is they grind out, while new ones proliferate beyond the ability of anyone to manage them. And instead of customized services for real individuals, the government service factories churn out their mass product for dehumanized "clients."

The crisis of government ineffectuality, in short, is qualitative as well as merely quantitative. Once again, in the bureaucracy as in the legislative and executive centers, we see a collision between descision structures designed for the old mass society and a civilization that is rapidly demassifying.

This by itself would be enough to account for many of our gravest difficulties. But this is by no means all that is meant by saying that our present political system is obsolete. For just as decision systems are designed to handle different levels of diversity, they are also designed to operate at quite different speeds. And if we add to the pressures generated by diversity those that arise from the acceleration of change, we drastically scale up the intensity of the decisional crisis.

Clearly, we no longer live in a world in which it might take a week for a congressional decision to get from Philadelphia to New York or Ohio. We now live in a communications net so tight that the slightest political sneeze in Zaire touches off instantaneous coughs, sniffles, or paroxysms in Peking, Paris, Brussels, or Washington, not to mention Moscow or Havana. Decisions that might have taken weeks to make in the past must now be made in hours. Experts are brought in. Computers are set to chattering. But the pressure for accelerated decision-making slams up hard against the increased complexity and unfamiliarity of the environment about which the decisions must be made. It is not as if the world were stable, routine, and predictable. It is surrealistic, with extremely complex events firing off at high speed. The result is that our political decision-makers swing wildly back and forth between doing nothing about a problem until it explodes into crisis and, alternatively, racing in with ill-conceived, poorly pre-assessed crash programs.

Any decision system is ultimately capable of handling only a given "decision load." The load gets heavier as needed decisions multiply, grow in complexity, or speed up. At some point the decision load is greater than the system can handle. At this point the fuses blow. And that, I think, is precisely what is happening to the political decision systems of all the high technology nations.

What we are witnessing is crushing decisional overload—in short, political future shock.

A political system is more than just a decision system, but if the decision system is malfunctioning, it becomes increasingly impossible to deal intelligently with the crucial issues of the day, from ecology and human rights to war, poverty, or relations with the nonindustrial world. Unless we can design an appropriate process for making collective decisions, one that fits the requirements of the new decisional environment, we face ultimate disaster.

A new decisional process, however, will not suddenly leap from the drawing board of social or political engineers. It will emerge, after repeated trial and error, from innovative experiments conducted by political activists. This, then, brings us back to the concept of anticipatory democracy.

There are essentially two contrasting ways to approach the crushing decisional overload at the center: one way is to attempt to further strengthen the center of government, adding more and yet more politicians, bureaucrats, experts, and computers in the desperate hope of outrunning the acceleration of complexity; the other is to begin reducing the decision load by sharing it with more people, allowing more decisions to be made "down below" or at the "periphery" instead of concentrating them at the already stressed and malfunctioning center.

One leads to ever-greater centralization, technocracy, and totalitarianism; the other toward a new, more advanced level of democracy, and there are quite hard-headed, nonaltruistic reasons for preferring the latter. For it is an obsolete myth that centralist or totalitarian decision-making is "efficient" while democracy only "muddles through." Looked at dispassionately, from the point of view of information or decision theory as distinct from political philosophy, democracy has marked virtues that the centralist or authoritarian decision system lacks.

Thus while czar or dictator may be able to act swiftly because he need not put up with opposing views, this proves to be an advantage only if his decision is intelligent or appropriate in the first place. Not only reward but risk is amplified in such a system, and risk in today's world can be shattering. Unchecked by democratic dissent and unrefreshed by new ideas from "below," the actions of any "czar" become increasingly error-prone, dangerous, self-amplifying—and often self-defeating.

By contrast, increasing channels for feedback, and especially negative feedback, between citizens and government decision-makers decreases the risk of error. It also means that errors, once made, can be more quickly and cheaply corrected. The less democratic feedback (and feedforward), the more decisions become divorced from reality, and the greater the danger that errors will go uncorrected until they escalate into crisis. Democracy, in this sense, is not just theoretically "nice"—it is highly "efficient."

This argument for participation, however, is not enough, since there is also a time factor at work. For citizen participation to be effective, it must concern itself increasingly not merely with "here and now" decisions but with those more basic decisions that influence the long-range future. In fact, participation without future consciousness is not democracy at all; it is a mockery of democracy. In leaving the long-range issues to others by default, citizens groups wind up participating—if at all—in the making of purely implementary decisions, squabbling over how to carry out the long-range designs of others.

This is why anticipatory democracy insists on fusing citizen feedback and future-consciousness. A perceptive observer of the movement will no doubt notice within it an uneasy tension between those who are essentially "participationist" (but not very future-oriented) and those who are "futurist" (but not very participationist). The essence of anticipatory democracy, however, is the recognition that one without the other is either foolish or futile, if not actively dangerous.

It should be clear by now that this emphasis on the future has nothing in common with those technocratic planners who think we need a "master plan" for the next quarter century or who hanker for consensus so we can all "get behind" a single vision. Both of these attitudes are holdovers from the mass society of the past. In fact, what counts most for those involved in A/D is not the formulation of some specific set of goals for city, state, or nation but the creation of a new decision process in which all goals, no matter whose, are continually reevaluated in the light of accelerating change. The essence of A/D is not the goal but the process by which we arrive at it.

Anticipatory democracy, therefore, does not promise that decisions made by ordinary citizens (even when these are aided by experts, as is often the case) will necessarily be "correct." It does not assert that citizens are capable of understanding technical matters without education or expert help. It does not necessarily seek to form, let alone compel, consensus. It does not lend itself easily to the rhetoric of either the so-called right or left. What it *does* do, however, is build a constituency for the future, and nothing could be more important.

It creates a large number of active citizens who—whatever other differences they may have—recognize that the time horizons of political life must be extended beyond the next election if we are all to survive.

This constituency for the future frees intelligent politicians and public administrators to do a better job even with the present inadequate decision tools. It frees them to speak openly and intelligently about long-range needs without sounding like kooks or cranks. It provides a base of support for far-sighted policies. It also promotes consideration of imaginative options and alternatives—including visionary pathways into the future—that normally are squeezed out of view by political polarization. In all these ways it improves the decision process.

If our present political technologies are failing, it is long past necessary to start imagining and experimenting with democratic alternatives, both representative and post-representative. Somebody must have fresh ideas ready when today's obsolete political structures collapse of their own weight, as I fully believe they must.

Those of us who prefer democracy to tyranny have a responsibility to do our homework before that time. If we do not prepare democratic alternatives, we can be sure that others will leap into the coming political vacuum. Unless we begin now to apply the principles of anticipatory democracy, we abdicate the future to those who would colonize it for totalitarian purposes.

25

To Empower People

PETER L. BERGER AND RICHARD JOHN NEUHAUS

Mediating Structures and the Dilemmas of the Welfare State

Two seemingly contradictory tendencies are evident in current thinking about public policy in America. First, there is a continuing desire for the services provided by the modern welfare state. Partisan rhetoric aside, few people seriously envisage dismantling the welfare state. The serious debate is over how and to what extent it should be expanded. The second tendency is one of strong animus against government, bureaucracy, and bigness as such. This animus is directed not only toward Washington but toward government at all levels. Although this essay is addressed to the American situation, it should be noted that a similar ambiguity about the modern welfare state exists in other democratic societies, notably in Western Europe.

Perhaps this is just another case of people wanting to eat their cake and have it too. It would hardly be the first time in history that the people wanted benefits without paying for requisite costs. Nor are politicians above exploiting ambiguities by promising increased services while reducing expenditures. The extravagant rhetoric of the modern state and the surrealistic vastness of its taxation system encourage magical expectations that make contradictory measures seem possible. As long as some of the people can be fooled some of the time, some politicians will continue to ride into office on such magic.

But this is not the whole story. The contradiction between wanting more government services and less government may be only apparent. More precisely, we suggest that the modern welfare state is here to stay, indeed that it ought to expand the benefits it provides — but that *alternative mechanisms are possible to provide welfare-state services.*

The current anti-government, anti-bigness mood is not irrational.

Excerpted from Peter L. Berger and Richard John Neuhaus, *To Empower People: The Role of Mediating Structures in Public Policy* (Washington, D.C.: American Enterprise Institute for Public Policy Research, 1977).

Complaints about impersonality, unresponsiveness, and excessive inter-ference, as well as the perception of rising costs and deteriorating service— these are based upon empirical and widespread experience. The crisis of New York City, which is rightly seen as more than a fiscal crisis, signals a national state of unease with the policies followed in recent decades. At the same time there is widespread public support for publicly addressing major problems of our society in relieving poverty, in education, health care, and housing, and in a host of other human needs. What first appears as contradiction, then, is the sum of equally justified aspirations. The public policy goal is to address human needs without exacerbating the reasons for animus against the welfare state.

Of course there are no panaceas. The alternatives proposed here, we believe, can solve *some* problems. Taken seriously, they could become the basis of far-reaching innovations in public policy, perhaps of a new paradigm for at least sectors of the modern welfare state.

The basic concept is that of what we are calling mediating structures. The concept in various forms has been around for a long time. What is new is the systematic effort to translate it into specific public policies. For purposes of this study, mediating structures are defined as *those institutions standing between the individual in his private life and the large institutions of public life.*

Modernization brings about an historically unprecedented dichotomy between public and private life. The most important large institution in the ordering of modern society is the modern state itself. In addition, there are the large economic conglomerates of capitalist enterprise, big labor, and the growing bureaucracies that administer wide sectors of the society, such as in education and the organized professions. All these institutions we call the *megastructures*.

Then there is that modern phenomenon called private life. It is a curious kind of preserve left over by the large institutions and in which individuals carry on a bewildering variety of activities with only fragile institutional support.

For the individual in modern society, life is an ongoing migration between these two spheres, public and private. The megastructures are typically alienating, that is, they are not helpful in providing meaning and identity for individual existence. Meaning, fulfillment, and personal identity are to be realized in the private sphere. While the two spheres interact in many ways, in private life the individual is left very much to his own devices, and thus is uncertain and anxious. Where modern society is "hard," as in the megastructures, it is personally unsatisfactory; where it is "soft," as in private life, it cannot be relied upon. Compare, for example, the social realities of employment with those of marriage.

The dichotomy poses a double crisis. It is a crisis for the individual

252 / GOVERNANCE BY THE PEOPLE FOR THE PEOPLE

who must carry on a balancing act between the demands of the two spheres. It is a political crisis because the megastructures (notably the state) come to be devoid of personal meaning and are therefore viewed as unreal or even malignant. Not everyone experiences this crisis in the same way. Many who handle it more successfully than most have access to institutions that *mediate* between the two spheres. Such institutions have a private face, giving private life a measure of stability, and they have a public face, transferring meaning and value to the megastructures. Thus, mediating structures alleviate each facet of the double crisis of modern society. Their strategic position derives from their reducing both the anomic precariousness of individual existence in isolation ·from society and the threat of alienation to the public order.

Our focus is on four such mediating structures – neighborhood, family, church, and voluntary association. This is by no means an exhaustive list, but these institutions were selected for two reasons: first, they figure prominently in the lives of most Americans and, second, they are most relevant to the problems of the welfare state with which we are concerned. The proposal is that, if these institutions could be more imaginatively recognized in public policy, individuals would be more "at home" in society, and the political order would be more "meaningful."

Without institutionally reliable processes of mediation, the political order becomes detached from the values and realities of individual life. Deprived of its moral foundation, the political order is "delegitimated." When that happens, the political order must be secured by coercion rather than by consent. And when that happens, democracy disappears.

The attractiveness of totalitarianism – whether instituted under left-wing or right-wing banners – is that it overcomes the dichotomy of private and public existence by imposing on life one comprehensive order of meaning. Although established totalitarian systems can be bitterly disappointing to their architects as well as their subjects, they are, on the historical record, nearly impossible to dismantle. The system continues quite effectively, even if viewed with cynicism by most of the population – including those who are in charge.

Democracy is "handicapped" by being more vulnerable to the erosion of meaning in its institutions. Cynicism threatens it; wholesale cynicism can destroy it. That is why mediation is so crucial to democracy. Such mediation cannot be sporadic and occasional; it must be institutionalized in *structures*. The structures we have chosen to study have demonstrated a great capacity for adapting and innovating under changing conditions. Most important, they exist where people are, and that is where sound public policy should always begin.

This understanding of mediating structures is sympathetic to Edmund Burke's well-known claim: "To be attached to the subdivision, to love the little platoon we belong to in society, is the first principle (the germ as it were) of public affections." And it is sympathetic to Alexis de Tocqueville's conclusion drawn from his observation of Americans: "In democratic countries the science of association is the mother of science; the progress of all the rest depends upon the progress it has made." Marx too was concerned about the destruction of community, and the glimpse he gives us of post-revolutionary society is strongly reminiscent of Burke's "little platoons." The emphasis is even sharper in the anarcho-syndicalist tradition of social thought.

In his classic study of suicide, Emile Durkheim describes the "tempest" of modernization sweeping away the "little aggregations" in which people formerly found community, leaving only the state on the one hand and a mass of individuals, "like so many liquid molecules," on the other. Although using different terminologies, others in the sociological tradition— Ferdinand Toennies, Max Weber, Georg Simmel, Charles Cooley, Thorstein Veblen—have analyzed aspects of the same dilemma. Today Robert Nisbet has most persuasively argued that the loss of community threatens the future of American democracy.

Also, on the practical political level, it might seem that mediating structures have universal endorsement. There is, for example, little political mileage in being anti-family or anti-church. But the reality is not so simple. Liberalism—which constitutes the broad center of American politics, whether or not it calls itself by that name—has tended to be blind to the political (as distinct from private) functions of mediating structures. The main feature of liberalism, as we intend the term, is a commitment to government action toward greater social justice within the existing system. (To revolutionaries, of course, this is "mere reformism," but the revolutionary option has not been especially relevant, to date, in the American context.)

Liberalism's blindness to mediating structures can be traced to its Enlightenment roots. Enlightenment thought is abstract, universalistic, addicted to what Burke called "geometry" in social policy. The concrete particularities of mediating structures find an inhospitable soil in the liberal garden. There the great concern is for the individual ("the rights of man") and for a just public order, but anything "in between" is viewed as irrelevant, or even an obstacle, to the rational ordering of society. What lies in between is dismissed, to the extent it can be, as superstition, bigotry, or (more recently) cultural lag.

American liberalism has been vigorous in the defense of the private rights of individuals, and has tended to dismiss the argument that private behavior can have public consequences. Private rights are frequently defended *against* mediating structures—children's rights against the family, the rights of sexual deviants against neighborhood or small-town sentiment, and so forth. Similarly, American liberals are virtually faultless in their commitment to the religious liberty of individuals. But the liberty to be defended is always that of privatized religion. Supported by a very narrow understanding of the separation of church and state, liberals are typically hostile to the claim that institutional religion might have public rights and public functions. As a consequence of this "geometrical" outlook, liberalism has a hard time coming to terms with the alienating effects of the abstract structures it has multiplied since the New Deal. This may be the Achilles heel of the liberal state today.

The left, understood as some version of the socialist vision, has been less blind to the problem of mediation. Indeed the term alienation derives from Marxism. The weakness of the left, however, is its exclusive or nearly exclusive focus on the capitalist economy as the source of this evil, when in fact the alienations of the socialist states, insofar as there are socialist states, are much more severe than those of the capitalist states. While some theorists of the New Left have addressed this problem by using elements from the anarcho-syndicalist tradition, most socialists see mediating structures as something that may be relevant to a post-revolutionary future, but that in the present only distracts attention from the struggle toward building socialism. Thus the left is not very helpful in the search for practical solutions to our problem.

On the right of the political broad center, we also find little that is helpful. To be sure, classical European conservatism had high regard for mediating structures, but, from the eighteenth century on, this tradition has been marred by a romantic urge to revoke modernity—a prospect that is, we think, neither likely nor desirable. On the other hand, what is now called conservatism in America is in fact old-style liberalism. It is the laissez-faire ideology of the period before the New Deal, which is roughly the time when liberalism shifted its faith from the market to government. *Both* the old faith in the market *and* the new faith in government share the abstract thought patterns of the Enlightenment. In addition, today's conservatism typically exhibits the weakness of the left in reverse: it is highly sensitive to the alienations of big government, but blind to the analogous effects of big business. Such one-sidedness, whether left or right, is not helpful.

As is now being widely recognized, we need new approaches free of the ideological baggage of the past. The mediating structures paradigm cuts across current ideological and political divides. This proposal has met with gratifying interest from most with whom we have shared it, and while it has been condemned as right-wing by some and as left-wing by others, this is in fact encouraging. Although the paradigm may play havoc with the conventional political labels, it is hoped that, after the initial confusion of what some social scientists call "cognitive shock," each implication of the proposal will be considered on its own merits.

The argument of this essay can be subsumed under three propositions.

The first proposition is analytical: *Mediating structures are essential for a vital democratic society.* The other two are broad programmatic recommendations: *Public policy should protect and foster mediating structures,* and *Wherever possible, public policy should utilize mediating structures for the realization of social purposes.* The research project will determine, it is hoped, whether these propositions stand up under rigorous examination and, if so, how they can be translated into specific recommendations.

The analytical proposition assumes that mediating structures are the value-generating and value-maintaining agencies in society. Without them, values become another function of the megastructures, notably of the state, and this is a hallmark of totalitarianism. In the totalitarian case, the individual becomes the object rather than the subject of the value-propagating processes of society.

The two programmatic propositions are, respectively, minimalist and maximalist. Minimally, public policy should cease and desist from damaging mediating structures. Much of the damage has been unintentional in the past. We should be more cautious than we have been. As we have learned to ask about the effects of government action upon racial minorities or upon the environment, so we should learn to ask about the effects of public policies on mediating structures.

The maximalist proposition ("utilize mediating structures") is much the riskier. We emphasize, "wherever possible." The mediating structures paradigm is not applicable to all areas of policy. Also, there is the real danger that such structures might be "co-opted" by the government in a too eager embrace that would destroy the very distinctiveness of their function. The prospect of government control of the family, for example, is clearly the exact opposite of our intention. The goal in utilizing mediating structures is to expand government services without producing government oppressiveness. Indeed it might be argued that the achievement of that goal is one of the acid tests of democracy.

It should be noted that these propositions differ from superficially similar proposals aimed at decentralizing governmental functions. Decentralization is limited to what can be done *within* governmental structures; we are concerned with the structures that stand *between* government and the individual. Nor, again, are we calling for a devolution of governmental responsibilities that would be tantamount to dismantling the welfare state. We aim rather at rethinking the institutional means by which government exercises its responsibilities. The idea is not to revoke the New Deal but to pursue its vision in ways more compatible with democratic governance.

Finally, there is a growing ideology based upon the proposition that "small is beautiful." We are sympathetic to that sentiment in some respects, but we do not share its programmatic antagonism to the basic features of modern society. Our point is not to attack the megastructures but to find better ways in which they can relate to the "little platoons" in our common life.

The theme is *empowerment*. One of the most debilitating results of modernization is a feeling of powerlessness in the face of institutions controlled by those whom we do not know and whose values we often do not share. Lest there by any doubt, our belief is that human beings, whoever they are, understand their own needs better than anyone else – in, say, 99 percent of all cases. The mediating structures under discussion here are the principal expressions of the real values and the real needs of people in our society. They are, for the most part, the people-sized institutions. Public policy should recognize, respect, and, where possible, empower these institutions.

A word about the poor is in order. Upper-income people already have ways to resist the encroachment of megastructures. It is not their children who are at the mercy of alleged child experts, not their health which is endangered by miscellaneous vested interests, not their neighborhoods which are made the playthings of utopian planners. Upper-income people may allow themselves to be victimized on all these scores, but they do have ways to resist if they choose to resist. Poor people have this power to a much lesser degree. The paradigm of mediating structures aims at empowering poor people to do the things that the more affluent can already do, aims at spreading the power around a bit more – and to do so where it matters, in people's control over their own lives. Some may call this populism. But that term has been marred by utopianism and by the politics of resentment. We choose to describe it as the empowerment of people.

Empowerment through Pluralism

By pluralism we mean much more than regional accents, St. Patrick's Day, and Black Pride Days, as important as all these are. Beyond providing the variety of color, costume, and custom, pluralism makes possible a tension within worlds and between worlds of meaning. Worlds of meaning put reality together in a distinctive way. Whether the participants in these worlds see themselves as mainline or subcultural, as establishment or revolutionary, they are each but part of the cultural whole. Yet the paradox is that wholeness is experienced through affirmation of the part in which one participates. This relates to the aforementioned insight of Burke regarding "the little platoon." In more contemporary psychological jargon it relates to the "identity crisis" which results from "identity diffusion" in mass society. Within one's group – whether it be racial, national, political, religious, or all of these – one discovers an answer to the elementary question, "Who am I?," and is supported in living out that answer. Psychologically and sociologically, we would propose the axiom that any identity is better than none. Politically, we would argue that it is not the business of public policy to make value judgments regarding the merits or demerits of various identity solutions, so long as all groups abide by the minimal rules that make a pluralistic society possible. It is the business of public policy not to undercut, and indeed to enhance, the identity choices available to the American people (our minimalist and maximalist propositions throughout).

This approach assumes that the process symbolized by "E Pluribus Unum" is not a zero-sum game. That is, the *unum* is not to be achieved at the expense of the *plures*. To put it positively, the national purpose indicated by the *unum* is precisely to sustain the *plures*. Of course there are tensions, and accommodations are necessary if the structures necessary to national existence are to be maintained. But in the art of pluralistic politics, such tensions are not to be eliminated but are to be welcomed as the catalysts of more imaginative accommodations. Public policy in the areas discussed in this essay has in recent decades, we believe, been too negative in its approach to the tensions of diversity and therefore too ready to impose uniform solutions on what are perceived as national social problems. In this approach, pluralism is viewed as an enemy of social policy planning rather than as a source of more diversified solutions to problems that are, after all, diversely caused and diversely defined.

Our proposal contains no animus toward those charged with designing and implementing social policy nor any indictment of their good intentions. The reasons for present pluralism-eroding policies are to be discovered in part in the very processes implicit in the metaphors of modernization, rationalization, and bureaucratization. The management mindset of the megastructure—whether of HEW, Sears Roebuck, or the AFL-CIO—is biased toward the unitary solution. The neat and comprehensive answer is impatient of "irrational" particularities and can only be forced to yield to greater nuance when it encounters resistance, whether from the economic market of consumer wants or from the political market of organized special interest groups. The challenge of public policy is to anticipate such resistance and, beyond that, to cast aside its adversary posture toward particularism and embrace as its goal the advancement of the multitude of particular interests that in fact constitute the common weal. Thus, far from denigrating social planning, our proposal challenges the policy maker with a much more complicated and exciting task than today's approach. Similarly, the self-esteem of the professional in all areas of social service is elevated when he or she defines the professional task in terms of being helpful and ancillary to people rather than in terms of creating a power monopoly whereby people become dependent clients.

Of course, some critics will decry our proposal as "balkanization," "retribalization," "parochialization," and such. The relevance of the Balkan areas aside, we want frankly to assert that tribe and parochial are not terms of derision. That they are commonly used in a derisive manner is the result of a worldview emerging from the late eighteenth century. That worldview held, in brief, that the laws of Nature are reflected in a political will of the people that can be determined and implemented by rational persons. Those naive notions of Nature, Will, and Reason have in the last hundred years been thoroughly discredited in almost every discipline, from psychology to sociology to physics. Yet the irony is that, although few people still believe in these myths, most social thought and planning continues to act as though they were true. The result is that the enemies of particularism ("tribalism") have become an elite tribe attempting to impose order on the seeming irrationalities of the real world and operating on premises that most Americans find both implausible and hostile to their values. Social thought has been crippled and policies have miscarried because we have not developed a paradigm of pluralism to replace the discredited assumptions of the eighteenth century. We hope this proposal is one step toward developing such a paradigm.

Throughout this essay we have frequently referred to democratic values and warned against their authoritarian and totalitarian alternatives. We are keenly aware of the limitations in any notion of "the people" actually exercising the *kratein*, the effective authority, in public policy. And we are keenly aware of how far the American polity is from demonstrating what is possible in the democratic idea. The result of political manipulation, media distortion, and the sheer weight of indifference is that the great majority of Americans have little or no political will, in the sense that term is used in democratic theory, on the great questions of domestic and international policy. Within the formal framework of democratic polity, these questions will perforce be answered by a more politicized elite. But it is precisely with respect to mediating structures that most people do have, in the most exact sense, a political will. On matters of family, church, neighborhood, hobbies, working place, and recreation, most people have a very clear idea of what is in their interest. If we are truly committed to the democratic process, it is *their* political will that public policy should be designed to empower. It may be lamentable that most Americans have no political will with respect to U.S. relations with Brazil, but that is hardly reason to undercut their very clear political will about how their children should be educated. Indeed policies that disable political will where it does exist preclude the development of political will where it does not now exist, thus further enfeebling the democratic process and opening the door to its alternatives.

As difficult as it may be for some to accept, all rational interests do not converge—or at least there is no universal agreement on what interests are rational. This means that public policy must come to terms with perduring contradictions. We need not resign ourselves to the often cynically invoked axiom that "politics is the art of the possible." In fact politics is the art of discovering *what* is possible. The possibility to be explored is not how far unitary policies can be extended before encountering the backlash of particularity. Rather, the possibility to be explored is how a common purpose can be achieved through the enhancement of myriad particular interests. This requires a new degree of modesty among those who think about social policy—not modesty in the sense of lowering our ideals in the search for meeting human needs and creating a more just society, but modesty about *our* definitions of need and justice. Every world within this society, whether it calls itself a subculture or a supraculture or simply the American culture, is in fact a subculture, is but a part of the whole. This fact needs to be systematically remembered among those who occupy the world of public policy planning and implementation.

The subculture that envisages its values as universal and its style as cosmopolitan is no less a subculture for all that. The tribal patterns evident at an Upper West Side cocktail party are no less tribal than those evident at a Polish dance in Greenpoint, Brooklyn. That the former is produced by the interaction of people trying to transcend many particularisms simply results in a new, and not necessarily more interesting, particularism. People at the cocktail party may think of themselves as liberated, and indeed they may have elected to leave behind certain particularisms into which they were born. They have, in effect, elected a new particularism. *Liberation is not escape from particularity but discovery of the particularity that fits.* Elected particularities may include life style, ideology, friendships, place of residence, and so forth. Inherited particularities may include race, economic circumstance, region, religion, and, in most cases, politics. Pluralism means the lively interaction among inherited particularities and, through election, the evolution of new particularities. The goal of public policy in a pluralistic society is to sustain as many particularities as possible, in the hope that most people will accept, discover, or devise one that fits.

It might be argued that the redirection of public policy proposed here is in fact naive and quixotic. A strong argument can be made that the dynamics of modernity, operating through the megastructures and especially through the modern state, are like a great leviathan or streamroller, inexorably destroying every obstacle that gets in the way of creating mass society. There is much and ominous evidence in support of that argument. While we cannot predict the outcome of this process, we must not buckle under to alleged inevitabilities. On the more hopeful side are indications that the political will of the American people is beginning to assert itself more strongly in resistance to "massification." In contradiction of social analysts who describe the irresistible and homogenizing force of the communications media, for example, there is strong evidence that the media message is not received uncritically but is refracted through myriad world views that confound the intentions of would-be manipulators of the masses. (Happily, there are also many often-contradictory media messages.) New "Edsels" still get rejected (though the Edsel itself is a collector's item). The antiwar bias of much news about the Vietnam War (a bias we shared) was, studies suggest, often refracted in a way that reinforced support of official policy. Promotion of diverse sexual and lifestyle liberations seems to be doing little empirically verifiable damage to devotion to the family ideal. Thirty years of network TV English (not to mention thirty years of radio before that) has hardly wiped out regional dialect. In short, and to the consternation of political, cultural, and commercial purveyors of new soaps, the American people demonstratè a robust skepticism toward the modern peddlers of new worlds and a remarkable inclination to trust their own judgments. We do not wish to exaggerate these signs of hope. Counter-indicators can be listed in abundance. We do suggest there is no reason to resign ourselves to the "massification" that is so often described as America today.

America today—those words are very important to our argument. While our proposal is, we hope, relevant to modern industrialized society in general, whether socialist or capitalist, its possibilities are peculiarly attuned to the United States. There are at least five characteristics of American society that make it the most likely laboratory for public policy designed to enhance mediating structures and the pluralism that mediating structures make possible. First is the immigrant nature of American society. The implications of that fact for pluralism need no elaboration. Second, ours is a relatively affluent society. We have the resources to experiment toward a more humane order—for example, to place a floor of economic decency under every American. Third, this is a relatively stable society. Confronted by the prospects of neither revolution nor certain and rapid decline, we do not face the crises that call for total or definitive answers to social problems. Fourth, American society is effectively pervaded by the democratic idea and by the sense of tolerance and fair play that make the democratic process possible. This makes our society ideologically hospitable to pluralism. And fifth, however weakened they may be, we still have relatively strong institutions—political, economic, religious, and cultural—that supply countervailing forces in the shaping of social policy. Aspirations toward monopoly can, at least in theory, be challenged. And our history demonstrates that the theory has, more often than not, been acted out in practice.

Finally, we know there are those who contend that, no matter how promising all this may be for America, America is very bad for the rest of the world. It is argued that the success of America's experiment in democratic pluralism is at the expense of others, especially at the expense of the poorer nations. It is a complicated argument to which justice cannot be done here. But it might be asked, in turn, whether America would in some sense be better for the world were we to eliminate any of the five characteristics mentioned above. Were the American people more homogeneous, were they as poor as the peasants of Guatemala, were their institutions less stable and their democratic impulses less ingrained—would any of these conditions contribute concretely to a more just global order? We think not.

Neither, on the other hand, are we as convinced as some others seem to be that America is the "advance society" of human history, or at least of the modern industrialized world. Perhaps it is—perhaps not. But of *this* we are convinced: America has a singular opportunity to contest the predictions of the inevitability of mass society with its anomic individuals, alienated and impotent, excluded from the ordering of a polity that is no longer theirs. And we are convinced that mediating structures might be the agencies for a new empowerment of people in America's renewed experiment in democratic pluralism.

26

Organizational Responses to Public Policy Issues: The Case of Day Care

Richard R. Nelson

While the public policy debate over day care has tended to define the problem as one of funding, that is as an "investment" problem, I propose that the problem essentially is organizational. The policy issue has arisen because of deep-seated changes in the structure of the American economy that are making increasingly problematic for many families the traditional mode for care of young children – the adult female of the family staying home with the child. While the pressures for the generation of organizational alternatives are obvious, the nature of a satisfactory alternative is far from clear.

Day care is an activity for which none of the standard organizational categories seems appropriate, and hence is requiring of sophisticated organizational design. But because the organizational aspects of the problem have not been recognized, there in fact has been very little serious organizational thinking. Many other problems are like day care in these respects, involving complex organizational issues that defy simple solutions, and a policy dialogue that fails to recognize this adequately.

The Prevalence of Child Care in the Home

Child care is a striking example of an activity whose prevalent mode of organization and governance has been different from the forms most studied by economists and political scientists. The resources involved are enormous.[1] Assume that child care was purchased by parents. In 1976 there were roughly 18 million American children under five years old. Existing federal day care standards require a minimum of one adult for every five children, or more than 3.5 million adults – double the number of teachers presently in our public schools. Even at a ratio of one adult for eight children (roughly the average in day-care centers), with a mean annual salary of

Excerpted from Richard R. Nelson, *The Moon and the Ghetto: An Essay on Public Policy Analysis* (New York: Norton, 1977), pp. 83–103. Copyright © 1977 Fels Center of Government, University of Pennsylvania. Reprinted by permission.

$6,000 per day-care worker (again about average) and total costs of about 1.3 times salary cost, the bill would amount to $18 billion a year.[2]

Of course, most child care is not transacted for by parents but is undertaken by the parents themselves. But the fact that no money changes hands in quid-pro-quo transactions means merely that the total does not show up in GNP accounts; the resources are no less real. The interesting issue is why most families have chosen to care for their own children rather than purchasing child care from others.

Obviously there are "preference" or "consumption" factors. Most families gain satisfaction out of caring for their own children—a not unmixed blessing, but still for many mothers a more attractive occupation than most available forms of employment for money. Social attitudes about what is best for the child, about the duties of mothers to their children, and about the proper economic role of women certainly have reinforced this factor. Nor are there compelling "efficiencies" from specialization and trade. While there are some economies of scale in child care, these are far less important than in many other activities, and specific training is not generally regarded as essential to good child care. Furthermore, as long as other activities are going on in the household—cleaning, cooking, or specialized economic activity for sale on the market, such as working on the family farm—the extra time cost of looking after children is less than it would be for an organization specializing in child care.

Finally, and of major importance when considering modes of extrafamily child care, there are questions of effective control of the way children are cared for. Parents may be wary of entrusting the care of their children to outsiders who may be fast-buck artists with no real concern for children's welfare, or may be incompetent, or may pursue goals in child rearing that run counter to those of the parents. The question of trust and confidence in judgment is a central issue in the care of one's children, and can best be resolved by doing it oneself.

These concerns notwithstanding, changing demographic patterns have resulted in decline in family size and in the percentage of her total years which a mother must devote to child care, thus making the pursuit of a career outside the home more attractive and realistic for many women. The result has been a substantial increase in the demand for extrafamily child care.

PUBLIC SUBSIDY OF DAY CARE

Almost all societies have expressed concern about the care and upbringing of young children and child care never has been purely a matter of family responsibility. There has been a long if erratic public involvement in the day care of preschool-age children. Under settlement house and similar auspices, day care has been provided for children of poor families where both or the only parent had to work. During the heavy wave of immigration, day-care nurseries were viewed by many Americans as a vehicle for acculturating the children of poor immigrants—in effect, a way of compensating for what was believed to be the poor upbringing such children got from their own parents. Day care traditionally has been a form of assistance advocated by social workers for the treatment of troubled families.[3]

Since 1960 there has been a significant increase in federal funding.[4] Public programs, by and large, have not operated directly on supply but have supplemented private demand by paying for day-care services provided under private (generally nonprofit) auspices. There have been two principal rationales behind the increase in public demand: one is the belief that mothers of families on welfare ought to go to work to gain family income; and the second is that children of poor and generally minority group families (blacks, chicanos) would benefit from the experience that can be provided in day-care centers compared to what they would receive within their families. Based on these arguments, federal funds for day care rose from less than $10 million in the early 1960s to $222 million in 1970. In 1970, approximately 250,000 children received at least some subsidy under federal programs.

THE ORGANIZATION OF EXTRAFAMILY DAY CARE

To a very considerable extent, the organization of nonsubsidized day care involves relatively informal arrangements—help through the extended family, or cottage industry. Of the children of full and part-time working mothers sampled in one study,[5] 80 percent were cared for by someone else in the family. For children of full-time working mothers, the figure was 53 percent. Similarly, a study of day care in the Washington, D.C. Model Neighborhood shows that 67 percent of the children of working mothers (full or part-time) were cared for by a family member of the child's home, 19 percent of them in the relative's home.[6] In 10 percent of the cases, the supplier was labeled a babysitter who either came to the child's house or cared for the child in their own home. This "sitter" category undoubtedly overlaps the "family day-care home" category of the Westinghouse Study, in which roughly 850,000 children were found to be cared for in outside homes in which one or more sitters looked after one to six children.

A portion of nonsubsidized day care, but virtually all of subsidized day care, is undertaken in more formal, and generally larger organizations, for which the term "day-care centers" customarily is reserved. Steiner reports that the number of day-care centers tripled between 1960 and 1969.[7] The Westinghouse Study, using somewhat different definitions, reports 17,500 centers in 1970 offering day care for seven or more children, looking after 575,000 children on a full-day basis and after additional children part-time. Sixty percent of the centers were proprietary; these accounted for about half of the children in day-care centers and received little subsidy. Most of the rest were nonproprietary; a small fraction were government operated. Many facilities were associated with community action agencies, and a few were run by public schools or state welfare departments. These nonproprietary and public centers were the principal beneficiaries of subsidies. Many provide quite elaborate day care, charging the parents less or at least no more than the proprietary centers.

While the circumstances have varied, depending on the nature of the legislation providing the subsidy (several agencies and programs were involved) and the policies of the local administrating agency, in many cases children eligible for day-care subsidy have no choice among centers. While "consumer sovereignty" is stressed in nongovernmental organizations, there seems to have been no intention of letting it play any role in monitoring the regime of subsidized day-care supply. This task has been left to the local government agencies providing the funds (welfare departments, community action or model cities organizations), to regulatory agencies (to monitor safety and space standards, etc.), and to chance.

It is widely agreed that this system has not worked very well. While most of the loud policy noise has been about the alleged need for more public funds, it is apparent that the existing supply of day care is often of shameful quality, that there is little control of cost, and that it is a very slow and cumbersome process to get day care expanded in areas of high excess demand.

ALTERNATIVE MODES OF ORGANIZATION AND CONTROL OF EXTRAFAMILY DAY CARE FOR YOUNG CHILDREN

Private demand for extrafamily day care will grow and will be augmented by public subsidy—perhaps for sound reasons, perhaps for poor ones. Particularly since public policy likely will be an active force behind the expansion, there is the deep obligation to consider carefully how extrafamily day care is to be controlled and organized.

Babysitting arrangements and family day-care homes will, and probably should, continue to provide a good portion of day-care supply. A major policy question is how to facilitate, support, and provide effective overview of noninstitutionalized day care. But the focus here will be on larger, more organized, day-care centers. What are the alternative ways in which demand can be organized? What forms of supply organization should be considered, and how do these link with demand organization? The following discussion will explore how demand and supply are organized under several different institutional regimes.

Evaluation of alternatives, of course, requires that there be some norm. The discussion will not involve explicit analysis of benefits and costs, but will be concerned with rather obvious failings of different regimes. Although gross, the schema seems capable of generating some insight into problems that might arise under different organizational alternatives.[8]

Day-care cooperatives. To many, the idea of providing day care through cooperation is attractive. As individual families become increasingly specialized and hence less able or less willing to provide care for their own children, communities might work out cooperative arrangements without formal organization. In effect, individual demanders of day care would get together and agree to share the "outside" work and the supply of babysitting, with, e.g., five families each agreeing to "sit" once a week.

There are two major difficulties with this kind of arrangement: one is the requirement for jobs with arrangeable hours, and the other is the instability and unreliability of informal arrangements. While there may be volunteers, mothers who "pay" for the care given their children by giving some of their own time to the center, and even a number of pure co-ops, experience with this approach suggests that it is viable for only small segments of society. To provide reliable day care for a large proportion of families, someone must be paid.

Distrust of private enterprise and the market. There appears to be near consensus among those discussing day care that private for-profit enterprise and the "market" represent an unsatisfactory way of organizing the activity. This belief seems to be held by many business leaders as well as by day-care officials.[9] This may appear strange in a country where private enterprise solutions tend to be exalted. What lies behind the apparent rejection?

Unregulated private enterprise – the market – performs the evaluation function by individual consumers deciding what and what not to buy. The supply adjustment is performed by firms seeking profit. An obvious problem with this regime, in its pure form, is that it does not take into account the public interest in quality child care. Many Americans believe that children of disadvantaged families ought to have better care than that which their parents will choose or can afford to purchase, and they are willing to back up their beliefs with money. It would be simple enough, however, to supplement private enterprise wth subsidies if externalities were the only complication.

However, there is a more basic objection to private enterprise. Although not spelled out explicitly, there apparently is a widespread feeling that private enterprise is not be be trusted, that the control exercised by consumer choice is not likely to be sharp-eyed or well informed about what is best for the children, and that the social responsibility in this matter requires better control.[10]

When considering services like child care, the costs of uninformed choice may be very serious. Furthermore, day care is normally provided when the parents are not present, and there is a severe problem of reliable display. The child cannot be considered qualified to evaluate the service.

The possibility of occasional sampling plus reports from the child gives some assurance that truly horrendous care is not the rule. But beyond this, how is the parent to judge? And if a parent cannot judge, how is the competitive market supposed to provide effective control?

Obviously the problem is more severe for some parents than for others. Some parents are quite expert in sizing up a place. In some communities there is considerable exchange of information. But for time-pressed inexperienced parents, in a community of like parents, consumer sovereignty is not likely to be an effective mode of public control.

The problem is compounded if public subsidy is to be provided. The public, like the individual parent, wants value for its money. But if a parent cannot judge quality, there is no assurance that public funds are accomplishing anything. In the absence of careful supervision, monies may go straight from the public fist into the pocket of the owner of the center without influencing the service provided. Clearly, worries of this sort are reflected in past policies that have been biased against providing subsidized day-care funds to proprietary centers.

One possibility is to supplement consumer sovereignty with various modes of quality and safety regulation, and this has been one approach taken in day care. However, it is recognized widely that the degree of overview that can be provided by regularly staffed agencies tends to be limited by resources, and that formal regulation is vulnerable to political pressures from the industry being regulated.

A LACK OF ENTHUSIASM FOR PUBLIC PROVISION

There is no inherent reason why public agencies should not provide goods and services to private individuals on a fee-for-service basis, supplemented by subsidy where appropriate. However, traditionally, public provision has been associated with severe restriction on consumer choice. If the public school system be the model, individual families would face a very limited choice among day-care centers. Their influence would have to be made felt, if at all, through "voice" rather than "exit," to use Hirschman's terms.[11] While a private-enterprise regime may place too much weight on the judgments of individual families, a regime of public provision tends to place too little weight on their judgments, and to restrict choice unduly, if experience with the public school system is a guide.

As has been proposed for public schools, providing families with a range of choice among institutions can lend more consumer weight to the evaluation machinery. However, as Downs has pointed out (in the case of school reform),[12] the traditional public sector supply adjustment machinery must be modified for increased consumer choice to be effective. In order for consumer "exit" to have influence, center directors must have some motivation to attract more children and the freedom to vary programs so as to make their centers more attractive. Resources must flow to them in accordance with their ability to attract customers; if they lose customers their resources must be cut back. The reward structure, decentralized mode of authority, and budget machinery that are required are quite foreign to the public sector as we now know it. No one has yet come up with an attractive proposal for making such a system work.

Public subsidy to private not-for-profit day-care centers. As indicated earlier, the general drift of public policy over the last decade or so has been, on the one hand, to augment private demand for day care by the provision of public subsidy for certain classes of children and, on the other, to support the evolution of private nonprofit organizations as the preferred delivery vehicle for subsidized day care. While this latter regime accounts for only a small fraction of today's extrafamily day care, in many discussions its rapid expansion is held forth as a target.

Such a regime is compatible with a wide range of mechanisms for organizing demand. Particularly if a considerable degree of consumer freedom of choice can be preserved, there are a number of attractions, at least on the surface, of the not-for-profit as the preferred mode of supply. The objectives of a not-for-profit organization can be defined in terms of the welfare of children and the provision of some particular kind of service, rather than in terms of profit. Within the constraints of financial viability, parents and other interested and expert parties can be given direct access to the processes that determine what is actually being done. Such a regime can, in principle, mitigate some of the more serious problems of lack of parental expertise or interest that make many people nervous about for-profit suppliers, and avoid the monopoly problem latent in a regime of total public provision.

However, unless there is effective overview, the not-for-profit label may be merely a tax dodge, and certainly does not afford much protection from gouging and poor care. While critics of a free-enterprise solution certainly are right in their suspicions of textbook economic arguments, surely many of these in arguing for not-for-profit centers are confusing a figleaf for a solution. Even were profiteering thereby avoided, there still would remain the problem of control of day-care management and of consumer choice. Perhaps the most important reason for the political success of the not-for-profits is that day-care professionals apparently prefer them, because they are a form that professionals are likely to be able to control. Despite its potential advantages as a way for blending professional overview and consumer sovereignty, as discussed above, the not-for-profit system has not allowed much influence to consumers; rather, children are often assigned to individual centers, the actual operation of which is pretty much under the control of day-care management.[13]

Still another difficulty with a regime of nonprofits is that it is neither fish nor fowl with respect to procedures for allocating and reallocating resources. In the absence of an overarching governmental hierarchy, there is no built-in administrative machinery for allocating resources among centers in order to accommodate changing patterns of demand, nor is there the automatic resource associated with for-profit organizations.

ELEMENTS OF A VIABLE SYSTEM

The organization problem for extrafamily day care is quite complex, and certainly will not be solved adequately by being shoved into one or another of our preconceived intellectual bottles. I shall sketch out here what seem to me the elements of a viable system.[14]

I already have committed myself to a system of mixed private and public financing and to some sort of mechanism of control on the demand side that involves a supplementation of consumer sovereignty. How might such a system be designed? One component of such a system certainly should be a mechanism to enable parental judgments to be relatively well informed about alternative day-care centers. This can be achieved in a variety of ways. One possibility would be to require the directors to write up the characteristics of their organization and services, and have these summaries available at a local day-care information and regulatory center, which would be responsible for verifying the claims. This procedure is integral to some of the proposed voucher schemes for elementary education. It is entirely possible to augment official inspection with more informal community inspection procedures.[15]

It is unlikely that such a simple patch-up will be sufficient. A more radical proposal is this. Parents and other interested parties should be able to observe centers in operation at times of their own choosing; each day-care center must operate, as it were, in a fish bowl. Such a requirement would not be viewed kindly by day-care management, whether that management be civil servants or private operators. However, licensing and subsidy regulations can make such operation mandatory. A key function of local regulation could be to check to see that these conditions of openness are being met; in effect, regulation would proceed in large part by seeing that parents and citizens are in a position to regulate.

Open operation can serve two ends. It can enable better-informed choices by parents among centers, thus supplementing the "information-posting" requirement discussed above. But, more important, it can enable parental and citizen overview of the operations of a center. It can facilitate the raising of a well-informed and relatively powerful consumer voice. For where quality is hard to judge, and where learning takes time and effort, control by means of exit or threat of exit is costly and likely to be ineffective. The various studies of day-care centers cited above, and the exposés of institutions delivering services with similar kinds of attributes, like nursing homes, suggest strongly that we must begin to think of nonconventional mechanisms for consumer and citizen overview. The "open institutions" proposal is put forth in that spirit.

Despite Hirschman's warning that a little exit can reduce the power of voice, it seems important to keep the possibility of consumer choice and exit as one of the instruments of control. Perhaps the most important reason for having a range of choices is that needs and tastes differ. Control through collective decisions by a group with diverse preferences involves the many difficulties inherent in the theory of public goods. If individual judgments are well informed, the ability of demanders to sort themselves out by picking their own suppliers contributes enormously to the effective operation of the system. There are important implications regarding the nature of day-care subsidy. If both choice and exit are to be given effective weight, children cannot be assigned to particular centers, nor can their access to subsidy be contingent upon their parents' choice over a very narrow range. Subsidy should in effect take the form of vouchers.[16]

It seems unwise to put too much weight on formal regulatory machinery, and the kinds of monitoring mechanisms discussed above reduce the requirements for formal regulation. Formal regulatory authorities cannot spend much time overseeing particular centers, and thus cannot substitute for continuous consumer or citizen overview. Formal authority generally is forced to use formal standards rather than personal judgments in regulating. Parents may judge that the center provides inferior services and may try to change policies. Or they may withdraw their children. The center may try to persuade them otherwise, but the parents' acts clearly are legitimate. It is something else when an arm of government withdraws a license. Here, due process requires more than the personal judgment of an inspector. Some specific code must be violated. Perhaps the most important role of regulation, under the proposed regime, is to protect and enforce "open" operation.

The requirements for information, openness, and a range of consumer choice, define much of what is needed in organizations that supply day care. So long as these conditions are met there seems no objection to public provision of at least a portion of day-care services, although traditional public provision does not seem to arise under these constraints. There are no innate objections to private, for-profit enterprise that operates according to these ground rules. However, private enterprise of this sort does not look like the textbook model.

Under circumstances where trust and openness, plus some freedom of consumer choice, are important, there is some evidence that private, not-for-profit organizations tend to spring up and take a large share of the market. Both Arrow and Klarman have noted this in the case of hospitals.[17]

Many private schools are not for profit. While I see no particular reason for public policy to encourage as a matter of principle the evolution of a nonprofit supply system, the kinds of requirements I have discussed will encourage such a development, and I see no reason for discouraging it.

While a system as described above would appear to be capable of monitoring day-care quality, there is a built-in weakness in the mechanisms that reallocate resources under a nonprofit regime. When demand for the services of a nonprofit center expands, what mechanisms induce its expansion? If it does not expand, what induces new entry at an appropriate location? While a regime of nonprofits with total revenue keyed to the number of children avoids much of the downward inflexibility associated with provision by a public bureaucracy, one would suspect sluggishness in expansion to meet new or expanded needs. Interviews with center directors and people responsible for overall day-care organization in Washington, D.C., reinforce these suspicions.[18] Center directors seem prone to meet excess demand by enlarging the waiting list rather than by enlarging the facility. Establishment of new centers in areas of excess demand appears to depend on the hard work of public-spirited citizens.

A regime of nonprofit institutions thus needs to be complemented by some kind of an overall planning body that is responsible for assessing day-care needs, and has some power to allocate day-care funds, particularly for the establishment of new centers. In what neighborhoods are there large unmet demands for day care? What hours do parents want day care? What components of day care do they consider most important and what are they willing to pay? Obtaining reasonable answers to these questions would be useful even were day care to be provided largely through unregulated private enterprise. Having some group responsible for getting answers to those questions, and with some significant influence on the allocation of funds, is essential in a regime of nonprofits.

The requirement for some kind of an overall planning body seems inherent in the other constraints placed on the solution, which preclude both public provision and private enterprise of the traditional sort. We currently are feeling the pains of not having faced, and certainly not having solved, this problem with respect to hospital investment. If we move toward something like a voucher system in the field of public education, we shall have to develop more effective planning machinery there.

CONCLUSION

This chapter has been concerned explicitly with extrafamily day care for young children, partly because it is of current policy importance and partly because most discussions of the issues either have ignored or have taken a highly oversimplified view of the economic organization questions involved. But along the way I have alluded to sectors that have characteristics quite similar to those of day care, at least in some of the following respects: there are both private and public interests in the good or service involved; and the good or service is divisible; effective evaluation of the alternatives requires that consumer sovereignty be assisted in various ways, both exit and voice are important control devices. Indeed, it is striking to note that a significant fraction of the articulated dissatisfaction with the micro-performance of the American economy involves sectors of this kind. The proposals for open operation and for an overall planning unit seem worthwhile exploring in a large number of these sectors.

27

Political Development and Social Welfare: A Conservative Perspective

GRACE GOODELL

The most common approach to building local capacity for economic development simply takes out to the poor the amenities we know they need, instructing them in how to use these improvements correctly: pumps, new seeds, clinics, electricity. On their part, the poor wake up one morning to find that their government has brought them one more thing not even of their asking—a vast irrigation system, or a tractor for every five villages—virtually free. We operate like surgeons on these etherized communities without so much as a nod of their consent.

Development practitioners justify the power that this approach gives the Third World elites and planners—and the concomitant sense of helplessness in the local people—by insisting that illiterates and poor people need others to make development decisions for them. Corrosive though this is for citizen responsibility and self-reliance as traditionally advocated by conservatives, and contrary though it is to American history, most World Bank projects and USAID programs set out to develop a nation in just this way. Such aid planners argue, when pressed, that the poor can and will direct their own development *after* their income has been raised for them. This, of course, denies the debilitating effects of paternalism on the grass-roots population during the "uplifting" process itself; it also glosses over centralization's irreversible entrenchment of power once control is firmly established at the national level.

The main purpose of involving the poor in their own development is to strengthen their initiative and critical abilities, and to help them build their own reliable channels for expression as well as for accountability. To achieve these goals, they and we must take their initiatives seriously. Except in desperate cases the material gains of "development" should serve mainly as a carrot to induce local people to acquire for themselves, *in the process*

Excerpted from Grace Goodell, "Conservatism and Foreign Aid," *Policy Review* (quarterly journal published by The Heritage Foundation), Winter 1982, pp. 111–32.

of achieving economic benefits, indispensable political skills and institutions which are far more difficult to establish (or to strengthen these when they already exist).

The trappings of economic development are transitory, but the fundamentals of political maturity will serve a society well, decade after decade, helping to prevent both anarchy and despotism. This *process* of responsible participation toward local and regional political maturity (or toward preserving those durable and effective political structures that already exist), should constitute a primary end of all development projects, and should determine what and how various economic goods come on the scene: *the complexity of a given economic benefit should never exceed the abilities and institutional capacities of local people to remain in control over it.* We might call such development "organic."

"Social" Development

Education is only part of the broader concept of "social development" which foreign aid has increasingly stressed, other aspects including programs in health, family planning, nutrition, slum clearance, urban drinking water, and better housing for the poor. This field of development has superseded the steel mills of the 1950s in its political appeal, and is becoming more and more popular among bilateral, international, and even private aid agencies — probably because Third World governments are asking for such programs.

Despite the fact that "social welfare" implies software, much of the assistance to these programs goes into buildings and equipment. This *quantifiable* hardware is then often taken as a measure of the actual services delivered. As Peter Bauer puts it, benefits are then equated with costs. Furthermore, *the planners* still decide from on high which national campaigns or Ministry-wide reforms are needed for village or slum society. The presence of the poor in the picture at last, as people — sick, ill-housed, or excessively numerous — in no way gives them any responsibility or power.

Worse still, the planners have deliberately distorted the meaning of "social" development by suggesting that it is furthered by improvements in health, education, housing, or a shift in the demographic pressure on resources. A malaria shot may keep me alive, thus contributing to my *physical* well being, but in doing so it has neither positive nor negative effects on my *social* well being.

Let us clarify the matter: *social* welfare is a question of relations between people and groups of people who make up a society. Inter-relationships are the stuff of society: the mortar between the bricks. Perhaps "economic" development is fostered in the short run by new cement plants or better bridges, but in no way do good drinking water and caloric charts constitute the "social" commonweal. They improve health. They are indeed badly needed, and we should help supply them. But we should do so in a way which is socially constructive, not claiming that hydrants or proteins are in themselves conducive to the relationships between individuals and groups in society. Social development might be much better served by legal reforms which enable people to relate to one another in a predictable manner, than by septic tanks for village homes. *Social* development must certainly not be confused with the provision of paternalistic government services.

By persuading us that health and education services equate with social welfare, planners and development elites have conveniently reduced an essentially relational matter to material hardware and bureaucratic services. This deflects our attention from the critical variable for development, the distribution of responsibility and power. In doing this, the planners, of course, retain control.

The *liabilities* of this policy, however, elude quantification. Since most planners are economists with little confidence in their ability to make qualitative judgments, the graver liabilities remain beyond their comprehension: local ennui, the solidification of centralized power, society's acceptance of corruption as a way of life (indeed, as a fair way to distribute resources!), and the uncontrollable enrichment of the rich. Most dangerous of all, our present approach legitimizes bureaucracy's claim to be its own competent watchdog.

Underlying Fallacies of Present Policies

The first assumption of western and Third World development planners which must be corrected is their assertion that local political expertise will somehow naturally evolve—or, more hopefully—*spring forth*, when people's standard of living or their literacy rate reaches a certain level.

It is simply not true that political stability will automatically follow upon economic prosperity. Almost two centuries ago, Edmund Burke showed the educated and very comfortable sectors of French society to be the most irresponsible politically. The staunchly middle-class and exceptionally literate support for Ayatollah Kohmeini's chaotic upheaval confirms Burke's observations. The solid force behind the Ayatollah is composed of university students and the bazaar merchants, shopkeepers, and traders, hardly the poor and ignorant. And surely the Red Guards' Cultural Revolution in China exemplified the same, as did the revolutions in Algeria, Cuba, Vietnam, and many parts of black Africa, driven as they were by middle-class intellectuals and bureaucrats rather than the unskilled masses.

In a fundamental sense the assumption that economic development comes first and political development will follow places the cart before the horse, since *indigenous* investment—the *sine qua non* of sustained economic development—waits for and is set in motion by indigenously rooted political stability. In the case of most Third World *elites*, it is true that once they have established a firm financial footing *outside* their own country, they are frequently willing to play roulette within the national economy at home, regardless of the political climate there. In their often reckless free-wheeling, they may impress economists with a mirage of rapid growth, particularly in one or several main cities. But by themselves these national and international elites cannot lay a solid foundation for sustained development. In the final analysis such apparent development must be complemented by the evolution of representative political institutions conducive to stability, and by investment and savings among a large part of the population as a whole, at the village and provincial levels. Ultimately, even in oil-exporting countries economic prosperity can only rise out of *broadly-based, local* saving, hard work, and initiative.

What then will prompt such long-term investment on the part of the population at large? Here, too, political development must precede the broadly based saving which sustained growth requires. Arbitrary political power, albeit benevolent and well fortified by statistical studies and obedient bureaucrats, simply cannot establish the essential underpinnings of pervasive social trust and predictability which *the majority* of people need for long-term risks. Not having bank accounts abroad, but rather being rooted in local conditions, most people will work just enough to get by, hoard their earnings, invest only in short-term prospects, or spend for "immediate gratification" if the political environment is unstable. *And,* without vigilant participation throughout the grass-roots levels, the arbitrariness of central power will remain, to discourage their thrift.

Thus, planners who hope that political maturity will *follow* that elusive attainment, "a higher standard of living," reveal their priority for externally-imposed rather than internally-generated development, and hence for flashy national monuments rather than enduring local foundations. The widespread predictability necessary for genuine development can never trickle down and out from a powerful and evermore consuming center. Local and regional political development must pave the way for broad-based initiative, saving, and investment which sustained economic growth requires.

The second mistaken assumption of development planners is their confidence that local political maturity can be *taught* through courses for bureaucrats in public administration or through farmers' classes in cooperative management, and so on. Similarly, planners consistently try to bring political maturity into existence through government-organized cooperatives, brigades, or village councils. But no single dimension of poverty more stonily resists formal correction from on high than political apathy and fragmentation in the slums and at the village and provincial level, where the vast majority of the Third World population resides. How can central power teach people to keep government excesses in check? Almost by definition, local political integrity can only be acquired through the tough lessons of continual practice, and even then may be jeopardized by brief periods of disuse.

A third error of development planners (which reveals their profound political naivete) is the assumption that the ability to sustain participation is innate in all people everywhere.

Few planners appreciate the fragility, complexity, and long evolution of the basic configurations which underpin any society's development. In fact many Third World peoples who once mastered a rich repertoire of local political skills have lost their expertise almost entirely; now they must re-learn the attitudes and re-create the organizations of local self-direction. As Edward Banfield indicated decades ago, poverty correlates very highly with political anomie. This is especially evident among the lowland and urban poor of the Third World, where people may never have enjoyed any community cohesion in the first place (coming together, as they may have, through recent migration, through the disruption of their settlements in plantation development, or through the coercion of landlords). More commonly, the social and political structures which once did flourish may have been destroyed by a particularly severe colonial regime, by the vast rural disruptions caused by World War II (especially in Asia), by centrally commanded and excessively rapid economic modernization, or by years of paternalistic government largesse. Possibly the most politically eroded rural areas in the Third World are the enormous lowland agricultural basins which have been the "beneficiaries" of gigantic World Bank transformation schemes over the past several decades.

In any event, it simply cannot be assumed that all peoples, particularly the poor, know how to form committees to implement or lobby for their interests, how to pool resources to embark on an enterprise together or to support one member in doing so, how to manage common funds by holding leaders accountable, or how to sustain a local organization for common interests or ends—nor can it be assumed that they will be able to start doing so when the need arises. It cannot be assumed that the ability to express disagreement with authorities is innate in everyone and will come forth in a crisis. Americans who have traditionally enjoyed such an active local political life take these political skills, indeed the fact of politics itself, for granted, when actually vigorous local participation varies considerably from culture to culture, and even from one group to the next within the same society.

A fourth myth that influences development planners is that political development can and will most easily wait until later. Planners who favor immediate transformations in the Third World may grant that the onslaught of development programs consolidates the power of a few national elites (though few see the significance of that for long-term development). Even those who do admit that large-scale and expensive development projects obliterate any social or political structures within the society at the grass-roots level, which might check the power of the elites (and *most* planners believe that the elites' legal or bureaucratic systems can check that power) — even those who admit to such social devastation then argue that a sturdy social fabric is not essential to development: once a given country is "developed," it can then solve the problem of centralization which we have created. The society will have gained "modernization" first, and then we can go back and make those little political repairs.

Putting Political Development First

Through carrying out projects which *they* define as important, people gradually learn punctuality, the ability to give and take criticism without personal offense, a lively insistence upon ledgers which everyone can inspect, and a responsibility towards enterprises beyond the family — all essential ingredients of economic growth. When *they* select leaders from among themselves for an undertaking that will command their own personal sacrifice, the poor frequently choose men and women with entrepreneurial skills and a firm sense of the bottom line. Of course, such indigenous entrepreneurs are rarely given scope when bureaucrats and landlords appoint leaders for the lower class.

Society-wide trust and predictability, and a stable political order, are essential for long-term economic growth. It appears that these essentials in turn can only evolve out of political participation, because no dictator and surely no Plan can provide the economic risk-taker with comparable assurances. Many Third World countries lack society-wide trust and predictability because efforts to spur the economy and to provide "infrastructure" — from the top — have raced ahead of concerns for these indispensable cultural and political foundations throughout the grass-roots.

Conservatives are correct who posit that the health of the commonwealth — its stability, and the creativity and civic commitment of its citizens — is dependent on decentralized political structures. Economic development and foreign aid policies should be founded on the process of building up local and provincial-level organizations, both public and private, to the principal end that political maturity will gradually take root throughout each new nation. This can only be done by beginning with small projects which do not overwhelm local organizational capacities, which strongly depend on local initiative, and which work towards local control. Projects, organizations and institutions must evolve *organically*, people themselves learning through trial and error rather than bureaucracies carrying out fiat from above or abroad.

Almost by definition most "modernization" efforts tend to erode traditional social groupings and associations. Urbanism, industrialization, a shift to the cash economy from subsistence agriculture, and "integration" into a nation state are forces which may threaten local and intermediate-level control which conservatives cherish. Since we may slow the speed of these forces but cannot reverse them, there is all the more reason why conservative economic development policy should "bend over backwards" to strengthen and if necessary to build strong participatory structures, fortifying the links between them.

Each actual step in the development process must fit the needs *as well as the growing capacities* of the local people, howsoever poor they may be.

28

Building Block for American Restructuring

EXPLORATORY PROJECT FOR ECONOMIC ALTERNATIVES

What are the building blocks of a more participatory society? A partial foundation is being laid in thousands of communities across the country. Based on the principles of "grass-roots" community organizing, local community groups are scoring significant victories in issues ranging from reforming utility rates to changing zoning laws, from building safer neighborhoods to preventing displacement of the urban poor.

Emerging Experience

An example is Baltimore, Maryland, a largely working class city on the Atlantic coast. A variety of neighborhood groups and block clubs have become a potent force in Baltimore city politics. In several parts of the city, important social services such as manpower training, youth and senior citizen activities, and health care are organized by these community organizations. Many have planning committees which work closely with city planners in order to influence, if not actually control, the direction of their community.

The function of Baltimore's community groups is not limited to the provision of services or to a mere advisory role. A number of organized efforts have won important political battles with city officials over neighborhood issues. For example, when the city government decided to route a highway through the heavily working class Southeast district, residents refused to accept it passively. A small number of activists organized a broad coalition of neighborhoods to protect their community. Not only did they succeed in halting the highway; they went on to form a permanent political alliance of community groups called the Southeast Community Organization (SECO). Determined to play a role in shaping decisions which affect its members' lives, SECO has defeated proposals to rezone the area for industrial use, solved the area's sanitation problem, sponsored an artisan's

Excerpted from Exploratory Project for Economic Alternatives, "Building Blocks for American Restructuring," in IFDA Dossier 16, International Foundation for Development Alternatives, Nyon, Switzerland, March–April 1980, pp. 39–48.

association (over half of its members are senior citizens), and formed a land bank to help residents purchase their own homes so as to protect the neighborhood against real estate speculation. SECO has inspired a number of other neighborhoods to organize community coalitions, and Baltimore has become a patchwork quilt of community-based political groups – the starting point for true decentralization of political power in the city.

State and local governments in many parts of the country are beginning to recognize the power of neighborhood groups. The National Association of Neighborhoods, based in Washington, disseminates policy information to its members, lobbies for neighborhood-centered legislation in the Congress, and generally works to increase the neighborhood movement's political efficacy. The general growth of neighborhood power has pushed many city governments into making provisions for substantial formal neighborhood and citizen participation in decision-making.

Sometimes, local government itself has been brought to encourage local citizen activism. The State of New Jersey has established a Public Advocate to represent individual citizens and the public interest in court cases against private corporations and government. Other states have followed suit with similar programs. These advocates have defended the rights of mental patients, opposed environmentally hazardous offshore oil drilling and the proposed construction of an offshore nuclear plant, and blocked or reduced many utility rate increases; in the process, they have chalked up a number of significant victories.

Moreover, elected officials are beginning to emerge from the neighborhood movement. In some cities, neighborhood activism is the easiest stepping stone to civic office. The platform of community control has also proven politically popular. Two years ago, Cleveland, Ohio voters elected a self-proclaimed "urban populist" mayor who served until 1980. Dennis Kucinich publicly announced his opposition to Cleveland's corporate and business elite. In a major battle to maintain public ownership of the city-owned electric utility, Kucinich allowed the public to decide by means of a referendum. A majority coalition of whites and blacks in Cleveland chose to increase the City income tax rather than sell the utility (a significant achievement in the national political atmosphere of tax revolt).

Other citizen coalitions have formed around the provision of basic social services. Innovations in health care and food marketing have cut costs and made services more responsive to consumer needs. For example, Health Maintenance Organizations (HMOs), decentralized pre-paid health care systems emphasizing preventive medicine, have been organized in many cities. They have pioneered imaginative consumer services such as follow-up calls to patients and community evaluation of physicians. HMOs often encourage patient participation in decision-making, making a traditionally elitist profession more responsive to the community's needs. The costs of these alternative health care systems, moreover, range from 15 to 50 per cent below standard health care costs. The Group Health Co-operative of the Puget Sound, in Seattle, Washington, provides health care at less than half the national average cost, while offering more services than normal third-party insurance coverage.

Food co-operatives also reduce prices while improving services. Often, they spur private sector competition to lower prices. When the Fort Greene Co-op opened in one of the poorest neighborhoods in Brooklyn, New York, two of its competitors immediately reduced their prices and cleaned up their stores. Food co-ops also discourage consumers from buying unhealthy or unnecessary products. Many take great pains to circulate information about the best bargains from the consumer's perspective, taking into account quality and nutritional value. The emphasis on consumer education not only helps consumers; it also encourages citizen participation in economic decision-making.

The same spirit of citizen participation and local self-reliance is beginning to manifest itself in the workplace as well – particularly in the growing experimentation with new forms of worker and community ownership. Throughout the northeastern and north central industrial region, cities faced with factory closings and economic dislocation are choosing to fight back rather than die. Workers are no longer simply packing up and relocating to more prosperous regions; instead, many are turning to alternative ownership plans.

One substantial success story is that of the South Bend Lathe Company in South Bend, Indiana. The company was on the verge of economic collapse after five consecutive unprofitable years. With some government help, five hundred employees bought the ailing firm. Today it is a thriving, profitable enterprise. According to surveys, the workers at South Bend Lathe have an unusually high level of morale, motivation, and commitment to the success of their company.

This is the common experience of employee-owned firms. Productivity usually increases dramatically, at times as much as 30 per cent. Workers adopt new attitudes toward their work, founded on greater self-confidence and a clearer understanding of their rights as workers. This, in turn, has influenced the way labor unions view worker participation experiments. In the past, the American labor movement has resisted such changes in the organization of the workplace on the grounds that the experiments were often mere cosmetic changes which allowed management to maintain control while feigning responsiveness to worker demands. Now, some unions are realizing that their involvement can assure that participation has a real content. For example, the United Auto Workers has initiated a joint union-management reorganization plan at a factory in Bolivar, Tennessee. Union and management agreed on four principles around which to reorganize the labor process; security, equity, democracy, and individuation. Through an on-going series of experiments—shorter work days, collective decision-making, classes on topics ranging from dye technology to ceramics, data processing to square dancing—workers and managers alike are developing structures to make work more satisfying.

In Youngstown, Ohio, a coalition of religious, community, and labor leaders struggled to preserve 5,000 jobs lost when a major steel mill—the biggest employer in this steel town—was closed over two years ago. Instead of allowing their city to decay like so many others in the northeast, the people of Youngstown banded together and proposed a solution: they would buy the steel mill and operate it as a community- and worker-owned co-operative.

The campaign was co-ordinated by Youngstown's religious leaders who formed the Ecumenical Coalition of the Mahoning Valley. Citizens and supporters raised $4 million in special "Save Our Valley" bank accounts as a sign of community support (the money was to have been exchanged for company stock once the new business, christened "Community Steel," was opened). Local politicians also joined the campaign. Not only did Youngstown's mayor and two Congressional representatives endorse the project; Ohio's two senators and the state's conservative Republican governor also were brought to support the effort. Traditional political divisions faded in the face of the overwhelming need for unity. The common cause was self-preservation.

Perhaps the most encouraging aspect of the Coalition's campaign was that it eventually earned the support of the powerful United Steel Workers union. Though suspicious of the community ownership plan for over a year, the union leadership finally changed its mind when it saw how strongly local union members supported the project. Through discussions with Youngstown steelworkers, the union developed a plan to cut unnecessary costs at the reopened Community Steel mill, assuring high productivity gains in the industry.

In spite of the united community effort, the attempt to reopen the Youngstown mill has so far failed. Although the federal government has supported many small-scale worker/community enterprises, it has so far refused to provide the substantial loan guarantees necessary to purchase the closed mill, modernize it, and launch Community Steel. (However, two new laws will aid worker-owned effort in the future.)

Despite the various local political and economic activities, there is a major weakness in the movement for local self-reliance and participatory democracy at the present stage of development. While organizing at the local level is diverse and often effective, it has yet to give birth to a serious national political movement to support local efforts. There has been some partially effective organizing on the national level, but it has been primarily around narrow issues. The success of some efforts, however, suggests the potential for national strategies to build a larger political movement on key issues.

The most visible and coherent national effort in the 1970s has been the environmental movement. Although environmental concerns are very old in the United States, the movement picked up considerable steam in the late 1960s and early 1970s, combining public education with intense legislative lobbying. Victories include enhanced public awareness of the environmental costs of economic actions, a variety of legislative acts (both state and federal) to tighten environmental regulations and protect certain unspoiled lands, and a general realization by most public policy-makers that "softer," less environmentally-destructive paths to economic growth must be explored.

A recent focus of many environmental (and other) groups has been the issue of nuclear power. Opposition to nuclear power has been strong among environmentalists for some time, but the recent Three Mile Island near-disaster spurred many others across the country into action. A major national rally was held in Washington, D.C. in mid-1980, drawing thousands of protestors. Similar rallies have also been held near nuclear power plants as people began to refuse to accept the risks of this form of energy. The number of people attending such protests has grown dramatically over the past year as economic and safety factors point increasingly to the sensibility of alternative energy forms. The anti-nuclear movement, however, has remained primarily just that: *anti*-nuclear. While many of its leaders advocate one or another alternative energy source (e.g., solar), the movement as a whole has not developed a full-scale alternate national energy plan. The focus on negative issues is limiting in terms of political efficacy, as it often leaves the movement on the defensive. Like the many and diverse community-based experiments mentioned above, single issue movements such as antinuclear organizing can lead to substantial social change only if they can be integrated into a comprehensive positive national political effort.

Another national effort which begins to point towards this goal is the Citizen/Labor Energy Coalition. C/LEC represents a wide variety of organizations and has fought corporate domination of energy resources. In the process the energy issue has become an important focus of progressive politics, combining local activism with national strategies targeting major centers of irresponsible corporate power. The Coalition has taken a sophisticated approach, combining the short-range goal of controlling energy prices with the longer-range aim of more public control over energy. A series of local and national protests have provided a forum of consumers to vent their frustrations; at the same time these have begun the process of cooperation and self-education necessary to develop new, alternative energy policies based on conservation and renewable energy resources. C/LEC is channeling significant public anger in a way that may provide a base for further political action.

Another effort is represented by Consumers Opposed to Inflation in the Necessities (COIN). COIN was formed in 1978 by approximately 70 consumer, labor, environmental, religious, senior citizen, minority and other groups to take the initiative in demanding anti-inflation policies founded on an equitable distribution of resources.

COIN has focused on inflation where it hurts people the most – in the necessities of life: food, energy, housing and health care. COIN has put forth both moral and economic arguments in articulating the goal of stabilized prices for life's necessities. COIN's activities have ranged from small, local teach-ins to a large national conference, from a mass literature-distribution effort to intensive task-force work to determine the most effective policies for each necessity sector.

Other broadly-based coalitions have also been working to build from individual citizen responses on political and economic questions to a larger national movement. The Progressive Alliance, initiated by United Auto Workers President Douglas Fraser, enjoys the support of a vast array of organizations and leaders from across the nation. This broad alliance is attempting to design a series of initiatives and positive proposals, particularly on industrial dislocations and health and safety issues.

In a similar vein the nascent Citizens Party was formed to put crucial issues of the 1980s into sharper political focus. A number of local and national activities have joined together to propose answers to a variety of questions of the new economic era, and to be sure that those questions are clearly put before the American people electorally. The Citizens Party has also been attempting to inject a more coherent progressive ideology into the political debate. It has begun to articulate an overall context in which people can view individual issues, thus commencing the process of individual and local cooperation in defining national goals and priorities.

Next Steps

Institutions which carry out and disseminate research are crucial to the creation of nationwide networks of participating communities with full awareness of the larger issues. The Conference on Alternative State and Local Public Policy, located in Washington, D.C., provides one forum for the exchange of ideas among progressive local leaders as well as a research center for policies facilitating local development. The National Center for Economic Alternatives provides another center, particularly on overall national economic issues. The Institute for Policy Studies has a broad mandate, with particular strengths in military and international issues. These groups are helping begin the integration process among community and national leaders and groups.

At the same time, a number of progressive religious leaders have started to put major political questions before their congregations, placing local and individual issues in their larger context. Many church leaders have begun to urge their followers to concern themselves with the major moral/political questions of the day, judging potential solutions in terms of the values of equity and democracy. Accordingly, the American church networks could well play an important role in bringing disparate movements into a broader focus. Their effectiveness was illustrated in the Youngstown, Ohio, case cited earlier. They gave legitimacy and leadership to the cause, and enabled community residents to see their struggle as part of a valuable moral and social effort – indeed, their slogan read "Save Youngstown, Save America." The recent involvement of a number of religious groups in such larger economic issues as inflation and unemployment is also likely to have significant impact.

During the 1980s, neighborhood groups in general could be playing a new and different role in the integration process. The multitude of grass-roots organizations have helped individuals cope with city living, and have made urban decision-making more responsive to citizen demand. By addressing central economic issues such as unemployment and inflation – *in the ways they affect local areas* – these groups could potentially provide models for national problem-solving and a structure for citizen participation in the planning process. But this requires a mechanism for expanding understanding of larger issues.

In this regard the COIN effort is instructive: COIN has launched a nationwide teach-in movement. Kicked off by a major national conference, COIN encouraged groups and individuals to sponsor public discussion of overall economic issues. The response has been encouraging. A wide range of groups have taken action to implement teach-ins, both on the state and local levels. Such public conferences have taken place in, or are planned for, approximately 40 localities across the country, sponsored by groups such as the California Tax Reform Association, the Catholic/Protestant Conference on Urban Ministry, a Michigan state legislator, consumers in Florham, New Jersey, the Maine Teachers Association, and part of W. Michigan University's Department of Economics. In these forums local citizens discuss and debate critical questions involved in developing an effective anti-inflation strategy. They share information and develop greater knowledge of the issues. Usually, the activities motivate the citizens to further action. Often, for instance, a local teach-in will result in the development of a community-wide coalition to study the local economy and take action on key local issues.

By initiating a process of cooperation on policy formation by a wide range of interest groups, such efforts could help provide focal points for a much broader progressive politics in the 1980s. The policies advocated would necessarily lead to a more democratic distribution of resources – and new tactics place local action within a national framework. The various national coalitions have stimulated citizen interest which thus could ultimately lead to a wider understanding and participation – *if* it is ultimately informed by a larger vision and an integrated strategy.

Conclusion

The historic problem of popular social movements in America has been the difficulty of establishing a politically effective national focus and organizational structure. This is the case with the movement for participatory democracy and local self-reliance. The challenge of the 1980s is to join the pieces of the democratic mosaic now beginning to emerge into a coherent design for a cooperative progressive national politics.

It is likely that the negative forces of traditional conservatism will remain dominant on the national level in the near future. The 1980s political campaigns may do little to clarify the basic issues. But the hegemony of outmoded ideas is beginning to crack. In urban neighborhoods, worker cooperatives, alternative energy projects, Americans are beginning to define new "paradigms" for social and economic change. And these are slowly being linked in the preliminary national strategies. Over the longer term, it is the emerging alternative paradigm that possesses the greater potential, if a coherent vision and fully developed strategy to implement it can be achieved. The immediate task is to link the "building blocks" of the new socio-economic model to broader issues of national politics – especially the control and redistribution of resources – and to positive proposals related to the international economic system.

29

Creating Another America:
The Power and the Joy of Networking

JESSICA LIPNACK AND JEFFREY STAMPS

Another America is not a place but a state of mind. Touching every area of our lives, there is Another America, not often seen on television or read about in newspapers. It is an Emerald City of ideas and visions and practical enterprises that people move in and out of depending on their moods and needs, a domain that is very new, and at the same time, very old.

In this special universe, health is perceived as the natural state of the body, cooperation is regarded as an effective way to meet basic needs, nature's ecological orchestra is revered as one unified instrument, inner development is valued as a correlate to social involvement, and the planet is understood to be an interconnected whole.

There is Another America and it is pulsating and expanding and unfolding through *networking*, an organic communications process that threads across interests, through problems, and around solutions. Networks are the meeting grounds for the inhabitants of this invisible domain. These flexible, vibrant organizations often exist without boundaries, bylaws, or officers. Networks are the lines of communication, the alternative express highways that people use to get things done. In crisis and in opportunity, the word spreads quickly through these people-power lines.

As short-lived, self-camouflaging, adisciplinary crosshatches of activity, networks are invisible, uncountable, and unpollable. Networks can be highly active one day, and totally defunct the next. Every time a network comes to life its form is a little different.

Networks are stages on which dissonance is not only tolerated but encouraged, yet consensus is a common goal. They are the experimental seedbeds in which people risk stretching their creativity. Networks are efficient and effective; feedback is as spontaneous as telephones, mailings, and meetings permit. Networks are often personal, friendly, supportive and affirming, critical and energizing. Networks can be intimate and immediate—at times they serve as our extended families, bonding people together as strongly as bloodlines.

There are spokespeople in Another America, but there are few exalted leaders, presidents, or boards of directors. There are people who serve as models, but there are few figureheads whose lives are to be cloned. There are entry points and connections—nodes and links—but there are few hierarchical structures along which individuals can advance. Another America exists everywhere, from the smallest towns to the largest cities, offering anyone who shares the vision the opportunity to participate.

There is nothing to be "won" in Another America: There are only problems to solve, using personal resourcefulness as the source of solutions. There are goods that are produced to be used but not consumed, and obsolescence refers to an antiquated value system that calls for winners and losers. Even the language people use is different: From a litany of overused clichés, people are finding novel ways to express themselves in optimistic, hope-filled phrases that help to create the reality toward which people are striving.

Outside the cement-block walls of the high-technology medical profession is a world in which people are learning to heal themselves and are reclaiming the two poles of the life cycle of bringing birth and death back into their homes.

In contrast to the high-speed competitive, militaristic America that we all know, there is Another America, which is measured, cooperative, and peaceful, yet alive with the promise of what life could be like if war were simply not a possibility.

Beyond the periphery of the fossil-fuel and nuclear-fission-intensive America, which threatens to expire within our lifetime and contaminate our offspring for generations to come, is a wellspring of ever-renewable energy resources that are heating people's homes and generating their electricity.

As the conventional politics and marketplaces of the machine age continue to break down, a value system is emerging in Another America that reflects deep concern with individual and collective human needs.

Sidestepping the stifling regimentation of rote learning that typifies much of education is a school without school in which people are learning from one another and teaching their children at home.

Meeting outside the temples and churches of organized religion is an ever-present chapel without walls in which people are growing from within, without paying obeisance to the patriarchal hierarchy or rigid dogma of established religions.

Alongside the official pronouncements that evolution happens over many, many lifetimes and is only a series of random mutations anyway is Another America, which knows in its heart that humanity is evolving very quickly, right now, and that we all are responsible for the outcome.

It is possible to live in both Americas at once and people are doing so all the time. Another America knows no national boundaries: It recognizes the interconnectedness of the entire planet. The impact of networks that offer a different eventuality for us all is slowly being felt around the globe, sidestepping the nation-state model that has dominated the earth for the past 400 years.

By looking within themselves—at their skills, their talents, and their local needs—people have found a gigantic reservoir of untapped resources that could be applied to remaking our civilization. By focusing in on hundreds of small issues, people discovered thousands of imaginative solutions. People use networking to solve small individual problems such as organizing play groups for babies as well as to tackle huge planetary problems such as nuclear proliferation. People network alone and they network together. When a few people get together to network, they usually form a group.

Networkers in various areas seem all to be saying the same thing: If you don't like what is, create something you do like. Regardless of whether they are designing programs for the elderly, initiating community alliances with prisons, exchanging information about home schooling, supporting options within holistic health, organizing against nuclear power, raising money to save an endangered species, creating a computerized community bulletin board, structuring a local skills-bank, forging a mountain commune, establishing a food co-op, starting a growth center, or building a windmill, all are verbalizing similar messages based on the same underlying values.

Another America exists as a pattern of connections and values, a complex lattice-work of hope and despair, anger and love, fantasy and reality, descriptions of problems, and examples of solutions. While some might say that optimism is unrealistic at this point in history, networkers counter with the belief that the future we create together is a matter of attitude and that while the doomsayers are important beacons, they spotlight only a portion of reality. Every day, every new situation, every new problem is a challenge and a potential for beneficial change.

Healing (health and life cycle) networks have formed because people want to be well.

Sharing (communities and cooperatives) networks have formed because people are happiest when they are actively working within their communities—whether geographic or conceptual.

Using (ecology and energy) networks have formed because people want to benefit from the earth's bounty without harming it.

Valuing (politics and economics) networks have formed because people want a sane politics and a fair economic system.

Learning (education and communications) networks have formed because people want to learn and they want to communicate—two interrelated human drives.

Growing (personal and spiritual growth) networks have formed because people quest for inner peace and for an understanding of the nature of the universe.

Evolving (global and futures) networks have formed because people have come to understand that nationalism, limitless growth, and political hegemony are antiquated ideas that ignore the reality that we are four and a half billion still-primitive people living on ten percent of the surface area of one small planet in one remote solar system of one of billions of galaxies dancing through space.

Of course, a clique that runs city hall from a booth at Joe's Diner is networking in the same way as an environmental coalition that plans strategy and trades information at a rotating potluck supper. An old-boy network that gathers at a country club is based on the same peer relationships and horizontal connections as a floating seminar of holistic health practitioners. It is not the network form or process which distinguishes a movement for social change from an elite breakfast club that runs an industry, nor is it bonds of values. The difference between *all* networks and the *particular* networks we selected to represent Another America lies in the values themselves.

Hine, Muller, and others have pointed out that networks are now most evident at the two extremes of power, but the ideologies in these sectors are utterly different. Since the life of a network lies in its values, then, says Hine:

> Perhaps one of the crucial tasks of the immediate future is to clarify and expose the underlying assumptions that provide the ideological "glue" for [networks] emerging at the various levels of the global social structure. The key to the future may very well be conceptual rather than organizational.

Our research on networks has led us to the discovery that a network, like the moon before the Apollo space flights, has a visible face and an invisible face. The visible face delineates an organizational structure whose features may include a title, a legal form, governing plans, personnel, offices, members, publications, and other attributes of an organized group of people doing some focused work together, or it may include none of these things. Regardless, a network also has an invisible face, which can be seen only by looking at the process of *networking*.

Eventually we realized that it was not useful to distinguish between networks and organizations. Rather, we came to regard the network as a type of organization, one that is significantly different from other types of organizations such as bureaucracies or hierarchies. We have identified ten aspects of networks that differentiate the free-form, adaptive nature of networks from the beadledom of bureaucracies and the rigidity of hierarchies.

The Structure of Networks: The Visible Face

Wholeparts. In contrast to bureaucracies, whose existence hinges on members who perform highly specialized tasks and who are totally dependent on one another, networks are composed of self-reliant and autonomous participants—people and organizations who simultaneously function as independent "wholes" and as interdependent "parts." Judy Norsigian, for example, is a unique person who participates in the Boston Women's Health Book Collective. The Collective, in turn, is a part of the National Women's Health Network, composed of groups and individuals. We have coined the word *wholeparts* to describe this fundamental feature of networks.

Levels. Unlike hierarchies, in which lower-level people (such as secretaries) have considerably less importance and power than those above them (such as managers), networks operate because of the integrated importance of all *levels* of structure and function. The person who types the newsletter performs as necessary a function as the person who writes it. Indeed, in a network, this is often the same person, a person who on another day may be licking stamps, answering the phone, or forming new goals.

While networks habitually dismiss the hierarchy model, they play freely with the concept of levels in their internal organization and external strategies. One example of the use of levels in networks is the antinuclear movement: Individuals belong to "affinity" groups that cooperate to form regional antinuclear organizations that, in turn, participate with other groups to plan, for example, a march on Washington. Each level—affinity group to national planning group—is seen as having integrity: "Smaller" levels are wholeparts included in "larger" levels that are also wholeparts. This abstraction translates into equal respect for all levels of human organization. We are attributing the pattern of "levels with respect for integrity" to networks without getting caught in the trap of authoritarian hierarchy.

Distributed. Contrasting with the bureaucratic tendency to centralize control and decision making, in networks power and responsibility are *distributed*. Whereas bureaucracies seek to bring people and power into the hands of a dominant authority, networks deliberately create a decentralized pattern of power with many people accountable for the work of a network. Similarly, while bureaucracies function along vertical lines, with information flowing up and orders flowing down, networks function along horizontal lines with information and ideas passing from person to person and group to group. Within the groups constituting a network, however, traditional authority lines may well be operative.

Mentally remove "command central" from an industrial-age institution. The likely result is either paralysis or disintegration, or both. Imagine a bureaucratic army with its headquarters blown away: a helpless, headless, fragmenting giant. Now remember how many times United States aircraft "destroyed" the guerrilla headquarters of the "Viet Cong." The jungle network endured, and won.

Fly-eyed. While bureaucracies tend to adopt single standards and policies, networks tolerate—and even encourage—many perspectives about goals and means. Although it may appear that the network "sees" only one point of view, on closer inspection the network has one apparent eye that embodies a plethora of others. Like its transparent, two-winged, flight-born relative, the network is *fly-eyed.*

At times, a network seems to "see" with one eye and "speak" with one voice, testifying to consensus around an idea or a strategy. Such moments of unanimity are important, because they often reveal the essential common values and bonds that explain the unity among the diversity of network viewpoints.

At other times, a network may appear to be a babble of disconnected concerns and interests, or an arena of internecine warfare. Hine calls this trait "the 'fission-fusion' characteristic that confuses observers and leads the bureaucratically-minded to see networks as 'lacking' in organization." Networks not only tend to put up with disagreement, in many ways they depend upon it. The forthright independence of the members keeps the network as a whole from being dominated by any single node.

Hydra-headed. While hierarchies are rigidly constructed with steps up a pyramid of ranks to a pinnacle that houses and exalts one revered leader or board of directors, networks have many leaders and few, if any, rungs of power. Like the Hydra, the nine-headed serpent which grew two heads each time one was cut off by Hercules, a network is *hydra-headed,* speaking with many equivalent but different voices at the same time.

The decade-long movement against the American war in Vietnam provides a dramatic example of mobile polycephalous leadership on a massive scale. Leadership sprouted everywhere, appearing and disappearing, incessantly moving, changing from moment to moment. Multiple leadership worked because there was a strong central core of values and assumptions that all members of the antiwar network shared either implicitly or explicitly.

In an active, dynamically growing network oriented to a change in the status quo, leadership may be even more than multiheaded and mobile. When a bureaucracy tries to suppress an unwelcome network, it may find itself confronting the second labor of Hercules. In multiple-leader networks, new leaders emerge in response to circumstance and need, and two heads will arise to fill a role left by the removal of any one head as needs demand.

The Process of Networking: The Invisible Face

To see the invisible face of a network requires a really different way of looking at organizations. Instead of focusing on offices, officers, and products, look at the purposes, roles, and connections. Instead of seeing the President in the Oval Office, look for the role of the presidency and consider the process of the executive function. It is through the perspective of process that the essence of networking really comes alive.

Relationships. While bureaucrats are obsessively concerned with concrete and quantifiable things – such as memos, products, or the number of pencils in the supply room – networkers are concerned with abstract and qualitative *relationships* between people. In a network, a person is always more highly valued than the paper s/he creates or files.

Networks seem invisible because so much of the meaning of networks is bound up in relationships: the links, connections, communications, friendships, trusts, and values that give the network its life. In a network, the spatial furniture can be quite minimal: a phone, index cards, file drawers, a room in the basement. For a contrast, imagine taking a snapshot of a bureaucracy. Our picture is filled with offices, equipment, and parking lots. Now try using time-lapse photography magically tuned to the vibrations of human relationships. A network is revealed as having a richly diverse ecology of intertwining patterns and flows, while a bureaucracy appears in stiff, frozen tracks of controlled, habitual movement.

Unlike a hierarchy, whose internal parts and external boundaries can be crisply mapped on a flow chart, a network has few clear inner divisions and has indistinct borderlines. A network makes a virtue out of its characteristic *fuzziness*, frustrating outside observers determined to figure out where a network begins and ends.

While some networks do indeed have limited, carefully defined memberships, and may even be closed to outside interactions, most networks are quite open and have a very loosely defined participantship. People drop into and out of networks: network offices open, move, and close frequently; and network patterns ebb and flow according to the needs of the participants and consequences of external events.

Nodes and links. Contrasting with bureaucrats, who scrupulously define their own specialized tasks and those of each underling, networkers play multiple roles, sometimes defying definition. In communicating, which is the main business of networks, a networker may in one moment serve as a *node*—an entry point or an end recipient—and in another moment serve as a *link*—a connector between nodes and conveyor of information.

If you sat as a fly on our wall one day, you might have observed an exchange something like this:

> Robin in Toronto calls us in Boston. He wants to demonstrate the virtues of computer conferencing at his college: do we have any suggestions? We do. Call Barry at the University of Toronto. By the way, does Robin know of any networks in computer-aided art? He does. Robin suggests that we call Jackie at MIT in Cambridge or Ron in Los Angeles.

When we suggest that Robin call Barry, we are functioning as a link while treating Robin and Barry as nodes. When Robin suggests that we call Jackie and Ron, Robin is doing the linking and we are being a node.

Me and We. Whereas hierarchies regard social organizations as more important then their human members, networks accord equal importance to the individual and the group. In the network, *me and we* reflects the balanced integrity of personal worth and collective purposes. Many networks express their vision as simultaneously encompassing the integrity and significance of the individual and concerned with the importance of cooperation and collective interests: they affirm both.

Values. While bureaucracies bind their members through mechanisms of reward and punishment (promotions and demotions), networks cohere through the shared *values* of their members. If a network could be drawn on paper, its lines of coherence would consist of the ideas that the participants agree upon, manifested in commitments to similar ideals.

Strangely, among the values of the industrial age is the unfortunate paradox that human value is itself devalued. To the old-style scientific observer, measuring stick and rat cage in hand, values seemed mired in subjectivity. Values are "intangible" and cannot be registered on instrument dials; consequently, scientists have said, values must be "unreal." In contrast, among the values of the networks of Another America is the value of *valuing* itself. Human values are considered "real" in Another America, and a concern with value is seen as essential for humane organization and purpose.

Peter and Trudy Johnson-Lenz, two very experienced and very thoughtful networkers, perceive four broad values "as the heart of the networking movement": (1) self-reliance; (2) interdependence; (3) self-interest; and (4) collective interest. Noting the obvious contrasts represented in their observations, they write:

> At first glance, these values may seem to be in conflict: self-

reliance with interdependence, and self-interest with collective interest. Yet from a broader perspective they can be seen as complementary opposites which when balanced together create a dynamic, workable whole.

In many respects, networks seem to involve a rediscovery of small-group interaction, a reaching back to more intimate forms of association before simple human relationships became obscured by hierarchy and bureaucracy. In other respects, networks reflect the leap forward, a form of organization with globe-encompassing capability that subsumes the enduring aspects of authority and bureaucracy.

Ultimately, networking is very personal. It begins with one person, threads through many others, and returns to one person. Networking is not a mass communications process. It is a person-to-person process with each connection made with gentle skill and great caring.

In the end, think of networking as Leif Smith does, as a journey, as a quest, as a never-ending process of seeking, integrating, and seeking once again.

You are an explorer traveling a universe that has no map.

Ask directions and follow them. Then allow yourself to get lost.

Take both paths—impossible to do in space, infinitely possible over time.

Go in circles. You may find they are spirals.

Enjoy long visits with people—in letters, on the phone, and, best of all, in person.

Allow youself to love the people you network with, and soon you will be networking with many.

Stay in touch—with others and with yourself.

Remember that you are the gateway to the networking universe.

Part Eight

Emerging Frameworks

30

People-Centered Development: Toward a Framework

DAVID C. KORTEN

The dominant logic of the industrial era was a production logic and its dominant goals were production-centered. Its values, systems, and methods were geared to the exploitation and manipulation of natural resources to produce an ever-increasing flow of standardized goods and services and to the creation of a massified consumer society to absorb them. It created great bureaucracies that organized society into efficient production units — centrally controlled and functionally defined — and a trading and financial system that linked all the nations of the globe. Its management systems were designed to maximize rates of increase in system throughput and the health of its societies was judged largely by indicators of such increase on the premise that they translated automatically into corresponding improvements in human well-being.

The persistence of this paradigm, even in the face of accumulating evidence of its limitations, is a reflection of the extent to which it has become embedded not only in individual value systems and institutional structures, but also in the available theoretical frameworks and methodologies that dominate problem identification and solution processes at both individual and institutional levels. Absorbed in crisis management attempts to forestall the collapse of outmoded and overstressed systems of the global political economy, most of society's leaders continue to rely on the only ideas and instruments at their command — those of what appears to be a past and dying era. This may help explain why their best efforts seem so often only to exacerbate the problems they seek to resolve.

An Alternative Development Paradigm

The postindustrial era faces conditions quite different from those of the industrial era and presents important new potentials to enhance human growth and well-being, equity, and sustainability — the central concerns of people-centered development. But to realize these potentials the develop-

ment actions that shape the postindustrial era must be guided by a new paradigm based on alternative ideas, values, social technique, and technology.

There is reason to believe that such a paradigm is currently emerging
from a global process of collective social invention. The dominant logic
of this paradigm is that of a balanced human ecology, its dominant resources
are the inexhaustible resources of information and creative initiative, and
its dominant goal is human growth defined in terms of greater realization
of human potentials. As articulated by Guy Gran, it assigns to the individual
the role not of subject, but of actor "who defines the goals, controls the
resources, and directs the processes affecting his or her life."[1] People-
centered development places substantial value on local initiative and
diversity. It thus favors self-organizing systems developed around human-
scale organizational units and self-reliant communities.

Production is critically important to the goals of human well-being and
self-realization which are the very heart of the concept of people-centered
development. The sense of self-worth derived from participation in productive activity is as important to achieving a high quality of life as is
participation in consuming its products. The performance of a production
system must therefore be assessed not only in terms of the value of its
products, but also in terms of the range of society it includes as participants
and the quality of the worklife it provides for them. One critical distinction
between production-centered and people-centered development is that the
former routinely subordinates the needs of people to those of the production
system, while the latter seeks consistently to subordinate the needs of the
production system to those of people.

An understanding of the distinction between people-centered and
production-centered development is essential to choosing social technique
appropriate to the aims of the former, since planning methodologies and
organizational forms are not neutral with respect to purposes or values.
Social techniques of production-centered development, for example, includes
command-system forms of organization, many of the presumably "value
free" methods of decision analysis, social research methodologies based on
the principles of the classical physical sciences, functionally defined production systems, and analytical tools that externalize people and environment.

The social techniques of people-centered development stand in marked
contrast. They feature forms of self-organization that highlight the role of
the individual in the decision process and call for the application of human
values in decision-making. Its knowledge-building processes are based on
social learning concepts and methods. The territorial rather than the
functional perspective dominates the planning and management of its
production-consumption systems. And its use of frameworks of human
ecology in analysis of production choices and performance not only intern-

alizes people and environment but makes them the very foundation of the analytical process.

Action Themes for People-Centered Development: Beyond Decentralization

Achieving the purposes of people-centered development implies a substantial decentralization of decision-making processes, but a good deal more is involved than the simple delegation of formal authority. Basic styles and methodologies of decision-making must also change. For example, if expert-dominated, nonconsultative modes of central decision-making are simply replicated at lower levels, local decisions may be no more responsive to human needs than those made centrally. Decision-making must truly be returned to the people, who have both the capacity and the right to inject into the process the richness – including the subjectivity – of their values and needs. Decision processes should be fully informed by whatever analysis available experts can provide, but only as one of several data inputs available to the many participants.

A variety of structural changes is implied. Relaxing the accountability of local leaders to the center does not in itself ensure their accountability to local people. If central controls over resources and essential services are relaxed, they must be replaced by new and appropriate mechanisms that place control in the hands of those whose lives they affect, rather than in the hands of officials who bear little of the consequences of their actions. The necessary mechanisms are built and institutionalized in local structures and values only with time.

The organizational technologies of production-centered development are oriented primarily to the needs of command systems. They emphasize legal charters, formal authority, control structures, and budgetary processes. The self-organizing learning systems of people-centered development complement such formal structures with a variety of organizational technologies which are less formal and more rapidly adaptive. Important among them are informal networks built around people, values, and information flows in response to particular interests and needs as circumstances dictate; and more permanent social groupings, such as family, neighborhood, church, and voluntary associations, which provide social support and stability at a more personal level.

Achieving a society which is both oriented to people-centered purposes and at the same time consistent with existing technical, social, environmental, and political realities is likely to involve structural and normative changes, as well as development of new social and technical capabilities throughout the society. Three themes are basic: (1) focusing public policy thought and action on the creation of enabling settings which encourage and support people's efforts to meet their own needs and to solve their own problems at individual, family, and community levels; (2) developing organizational structures and processes that function according to the principles of self-organizing systems; and (3) developing territorially organized production-consumption systems based on principles of local ownership and control.

The changes implied cannot be mandated and will not occur abruptly. They must emerge through evolutionary processes, as an outgrowth of the efforts of countless individuals. These can be greatly facilitated by the appropriate choice of social technique.

The Creation of Enabling Settings

The potentials for solving social problems through local self-help action have barely been tapped.[2] Even so, current settings are generally hostile to such action.[3] Modernization has been accompanied by a trend toward professionalizing, centralizing, and publicly funding an ever-growing number of activities that once were the province of the individual, the family, and the community—from health care, home building, and neighborhood renewal to day care and care of the elderly. Self-interested professional and bureaucratic monopolies have come to control nearly every sector of human activity and have successfully fashioned a complex web of governmental regulations that sustain their interests, from building codes to professional licensing requirements. But the financial and managerial burdens of professional bureaucratized approaches to meeting basic human needs are proving too much for even the wealthiest of nations, to say nothing of the depersonalization, inefficiency, and general ineffectiveness of many such programs.

There is an important distinction between government acting *to meet a need for people* and government acting *to create an enabling setting within which people can be more effective in meeting those needs for themselves*—as demonstrated by Nelson (chapter 25) and Bailey (chapter 9). Most tragic of all are government actions taken in the name of development that actually undermine existing local self-help capacities. For example, many large-scale irrigation schemes displace small local associations through which people have mobilized to meet their own irrigation needs, substituting centrally funded and managed systems accountable only to a central bureaucracy.[4] Some governments, such as the Philippines,[5] are building national agency capacities to enable rather than displace existing local self-help capacity in irrigation. There is growing realization that in nearly every area of resource and social services management—from forestry to public health—there are opportunities for achieving similar changes in orientation.[6]

Such fundamental reorientation in public policy perspectives is not achieved easily. The creation of enabling settings calls for much more varied and sophisticated analysis than does dealing with more conventional allocative planning decisions, which commonly involve little more than budgeting resources between existing bureaucracies and programs. The creation of enabling settings may require changes in the law, the restructuring of incentives, and the development of new local capacities.[7] It almost inevitably requires fundamental reorientation in the purposes, structures, and operations of government bureaucracies—away from direct service delivery or resource management to local capacity building and support.[8]

Development of Self-Organizing Structures and Processes

Research in the United States has found that small firms produce as much as twenty-four times the number of innovations per research and development dollar produced by large firms and that the largest firms seldom produce the major advances in their industries. A study of the most successful large corporations of America and Japan concluded that they circumvented the sluggishness of more typical large firms by organizing around small units that operated almost as independent businesses. They fostered small maverick research groups that worked separately from their parent organization on problems of their choice. The firms found that their smaller production facilities were consistently their most efficient. Theoretical economies of scale often fail to materialize in real-world settings. Small is not only beautiful—it is often more efficient, even in big business.[9]

Psychologists have long recognized the important contribution of group membership to basic human well-being. Membership in a group provides a source of emotional support and identity, a security in one's being, based on love and affection—quite apart from one's value in an economic sense. Such a group serves as what Berger and Neuhaus (chapter 24) call a mediating structure, insulating the individual from the shocks of the larger society within which he or she is only one among faceless millions.

Networks that connect both individuals and primary groups are another important human-scale organizational technology with tremendous potential. One of the major social phenomena of the past decade has been the growing prominence of informal networking structures, which have proven to be major factors in creating a global consciousness of the environmental crisis, human rights, the tragedy of human poverty, and the population crisis.[10] Networks are both the mechanism and the manifestation of an upsurge in local initiatives dealing with a seemingly limitless array of human concerns, from peace to personal growth and from health care to energy conservation. They work through local action to shape local realities, while at the same time influencing national and even global political commitments (chapter 28).

It is important to bear in mind that the formal structures of hierarchy and the informal processes of networking are not substitutes for one another, but rather complements. Neither is viable without the other. The challenge therefore is not to seek to replace hierarchies with informal structures, but rather to strengthen primary social groups and networks as supplements to these hierarchies – in particular as sources of social support, innovation, and social action.

It would be appropriate to our times to consciously invest in building networking skills as an essential part of the educational process. A recent Harvard Business School study finds that building, maintaining, and using networks is one of the most important and time-consuming activities of effective general managers. It concludes that not only is this crucial function largely ignored in conventional management education, but also that many of the techniques commonly taught in formal management courses are actually counterproductive in that they interfere with this essential process.[11]

Production-centered industrial society was all too prone to suppress such natural human forms of organization in the name of productive efficiency. Its organizational ideal, the modern bureaucracy, was based on an organizational theory that called for total depersonalization – treating people of a given rank and specialty as interchangeable units and expecting all relationships to be impersonal and rule-bound. Rather than rejoice that people do tend to establish human relationships within even the most stifling of formalistic bureaucracies, it commonly looked upon such behavior as a subversion of efficiency and technocratic norms. Even more suspect by the traditional standards was any tendency on the part of members of such a bureaucracy to establish a personal relationship with a client – treating him or her as an individual and responding to particularistic needs rather than applying detached universalistic criteria in rendering service or exercising regulatory power.

Substantial effort has been made to transplant these production-centered bureaucratic value systems into Third World development agencies. Such efforts have been well-intentioned, seeking to address a very real need – the reversal of long-standing traditions that held public office to be private property bestowed by a grateful ruler as a gift to be exploited for maximum personal economic advantage. Such individualistic personalism is both dehumanizing – in the sense that it treats others only as objects for exploitation – and a serious barrier to development. But the substitution of one form of dehumanization for another is not the only alternative; another is to build a system based on recognition of the essential humanity of both one-self and others. It is not a simple alternative, but is no more difficult than attempting to inject total depersonalization – and it has a substantially greater human appeal.

The past decade has seen a resurgence of interest in development approaches that seek to emphasize human values over production values. But only quite recently has it been recognized that there is a basic contradiction between such values and a primary reliance on depersonalized and depersonalizing development bureaucracies as the major instruments of development action.

There is nothing either immutable or sacred about bureaucratic structures. They can and do change in response to effective leadership and strong member commitment to a new vision. And there are numerous alternative forms of organization which are at the same time more human *and* more effective and efficient by conventional economic criteria.

One of the important challenges of people-centered development is to reorient the major development bureaucracies of government to become organizations that appreciate and enhance the humanity of both their members and the citizens they are intended to serve. Such organizations are generally built around innumerable primary groups that function as teams in setting and meeting local objectives and are joined not only by relatively stable formal hierarchies, but also by continually evolving networks of informal relationships. They have many important and appropriate roles in relation to self-reliant communities, but these must be carefully examined and defined. To define them as long-term conduits of external resources to mobilized villagers is to deny the basic principle of self-reliance and to reduce the villagers to clients rather than contribute to their development as creative citizens. Guy Gran suggests the following as appropriate—indeed essential—roles of the reoriented development bureaucracy.

> Defenders against assaults by elites; idea brokers and catalysts on matters of social mobilization; trainers of local group organizers; and advisors on the social implications of technology choice, market information, legal and political empowerment, and credit mechanisms.[12]

As formidable as the achievement of the proposed reorientation may appear at first to be, encouragement is found in the successful experience of a few such agencies that have already undertaken pioneering efforts to redefine their roles from management of resources for the people to strengthening of the people's capacity to manage their own resources. Such changes are difficult to achieve and involve comprehensive shifts in structures, norms, and operating procedures, brought about only through long and often difficult processes of social learning. As in the case of the large corporations that have learned to work as small businesses, one model for the large development agency seeking to achieve such change is to approximate the processes by which smaller development organizations have developed successful programs.[13] This involves creating a successful community-level prototype that allows the organization to learn what is required to be effective at that level and then gradually refining the methods and building the organizational capability required to expand their application (see chapter 18). Networks and coalitions have proven particularly helpful in these efforts in breaking down the structural resistance of such organizations to fundamental change, by serving as the essential organizational mechanisms through which institutional learning is accelerated and sustained.[14]

LOCAL RESOURCE CONTROL: A TERRITORIAL PERSPECTIVE

Productivity, equity, and sustainability in a crowded and ecologically stressed world depend on the establishment of direct linkages between people's uses of the environment and the personal consequences of those uses. This implies a strong attachment of people to place. The freelance logger whose income is a simple function of the number of trees he cuts is likely to have a somewhat different perspective on resource management that that of the tree farmer who sees his and his children's livelihoods as dependent on the continuous regenerative yield of a given piece of land.

The corporate form of ownership which has become such a prominent feature of industrial society has tended to separate ownership from management and to leave both ownership *and* management largely divorced from attachment to place, with ownership broadly diffused and management largely itinerant. Thus the prevailing pattern for a great many localities has been for control over much of their productive asset base gradually to pass to outside interests with little stake in the particular community and its future. Often national and community officals have been unwitting accomplices in this process of transferring ownership outside the community in the name of economic development. While commonly recognized as a problem of the developing countries, it is also true in the developed countries, as demonstrated by the study of American cities reported by Morris (chapter 23).

Application of the conventional economic logics of scale, specialization, capital investment, and comparative advantage has been carried to such lengths that these valid concepts, in some cases, have become disfunctional. Governments, both local and national, searching for investment capital and foreign exchange earnings, compete with one another for the privilege of turning over control of their local economies to outside interests by giving them special economic advantages not offered to their own citizens and taxpayers. The result is to concentrate economic power in organizations that have no attachment to place and no accountability to people or in many instances even to governments. This lessens the control that even national governments have over their own economies and weakens their ability to exercise their most basic responsibilities to protect and promote the well-being of their citizens.[15]

The economic logic of open borders, free movement of goods and capital, and comparative advantage has been thoroughly demonstrated by the remarkable economic and technological accomplishments of the industrial era. But it is a logic that works its miracles only within limits and with certain costs. It has combined with the logic of scale and the mechanisms of corporate ownership to separate control over productive resources from the human and environmental consequences of their use. And it has created a global system so interdependent that it may have become dangerously unstable and nonadaptive.[16] Future well-being depends on tempering that logic with the logic of local self-reliance.

The logic of local self-reliance is the logic of place, people, and resources bound into locally, self-sustaining human ecological systems. This territorial perspective internalizes social and environmental costs and benefits (see chapter 21). It is a logic of local control and diversification, and of overall system redundancy. Application of this logic helps to cushion the overall system from localized shocks and to facilitate local adaptation to changing conditions. The result is a system less vulnerable to disruption from international political blackmail, acts of terrorist sabotage, and military attack.

Local self-reliance as a development strategy involves giving first priority to the creation of conditions that enable the people of an area better to meet their own needs using local resources under local control. Where local needs cannot realistically be met locally, they are met through external markets, to which the area's surplus production is sold as well. The more basic the needs, such as food, shelter, and energy, the greater the priority placed on local production. Under this strategy, appropriate measures of system performance assess both the degree to which local needs are met with a minimum of *material* exchange between local economies, and the degree to which the system supports a high level of *information* exchange between and within these local elements to achieve rapid growth and dissemination of knowledge and technology. Thus self-reliance is not to be confused with self-sufficiency, isolation, or the closing of local borders. Nor does it involve a denial of modern technology. Indeed it calls for application of highly advanced technologies, especially those that are information intensive.[18]

The role of territorial units such as local governments clearly becomes central in the coordination of local development policy. Larger functionally defined organizations that span the borders of these self-reliant communities are engaged primarily in the development and distribution of information, particularly in the form of technology suited to self-reliant local development— less in the actual production and transportation of goods. The performance of both territorial and functional organizational units is judged by the extent to which they contribute to the creation of enabling settings for self-reliant local development, the maintenance of communication links between local units, and the development and exchange of technical knowledge for local adaptation and application.

The introduction of a territorial perspective, combined with policies that provide strong support for local resource control, is particularly important to the situation of Third World countries. There the results of applying the conventional tools of production-centered development planning have been especially tragic. The logic of these tools has created a substantial bias toward capital- and energy-intensive investments that characteristically expand the output of the modern sector without providing any prospect of meeting the employment needs of rapidly growing populations. Indeed, these investments often compete with the traditional sector on which the vast majority of the population depends for its livelihood. From the perspective of people-centered development there is a special irony in this bias toward displacement of the traditional sector. For in contrast to the modern sector, it is highly labor-intensive – providing livelihoods for all that the modern sector fails to absorb – and it makes extensive use of recycling as a primary source of raw materials (see chapter 13).

In recognition of this reality, rural development efforts in Third World countries are giving growing priority to programs that emphasize local community control and management of local resources. This includes efforts to place irrigation facilities under the control of water user associations, and forest lands under small producer management. These and related efforts seek to restructure control and ownership so that those who are in the best position (by virtue of residence) to maximize sustainable productivity of the natural resource base have the means and the incentive to do so.

POWER BUILDING

It is evident that powerful political interests are well served by the institutions of production-centered development. The question is thus raised, From what sources will come the power to challenge these interests? It is necessary to address the question from the perspective of the long-term processes of re-creation by which human society has evolved – by which old ideas, social technique, and technology have continuously given way to the new. Sometimes armed conflict has proved necessary to clear away the old and to provide the setting for the new. But it is important to bear in mind that conflict and confrontation themselves do not *create* the new. Indeed, in their more extreme forms, such as armed revolution, they can be highly destructive of many of the very values, skills, and leaders needed to create the new society they claim to seek. In a choice between destruction of the old and creation of the new as a social change strategy, preference should normally go to the latter.

Death and regeneration are both basic to evolutionary process. But one of the most basic principles of this process is that regeneration must *precede* death, or else that line of evolutionary development terminates. Dead parents produce no offspring to occupy the space they have left. If people-centered development is to emerge, it will be as an offspring of the production-centered industrial era. It will be conceived in the knowledge, possibilities, and necessities created by that era. It is, however, still in its gestation period. Achieving its independent viability depends for the moment on the continued survival of its parent.

The objective of building power for people-centered development is best served through action to hasten creation of the new, rather than through political confrontation to hasten the passing of the old. The gestation process is already well along—an outgrowth of a collective act of human creation that has no visible organizational structure, no headquarters, and no budget; knows no national boundaries; and transcends traditional ideological and political affiliations. Its participants act not as formal office holders, but as individual human beings seeking the creation of a more human society. They come from among the marginalized and the powerful, the poor and the wealthy, the illiterate and the well-educated.[18] The majority are found outside the halls of power and the pages of the leading news magazines. With less stake in maintaining the past they can sometimes see more clearly the nature of present realities. Less in the limelight and thus less pressured to provide immediate solutions, they have more freedom to experiment in the creation of the alternative ideas, social techniques, and technologies that are the basic elements of the power-building process. Indeed, these three creative tasks define an important part of the power-building agenda of people-centered development.

The industrial era has been a period of remarkable human accomplishment, creating potentials for advancement to a new evolutionary stage in which all people may have the opportunity to become and grow as full human beings. The ideas, values, and social techniques of production-centered development were instrumental in the creation of this potential and contributed in important and powerful ways to the achievement of human purposes appropriate to their time. There is reason to believe, however, that realization of the same potential that was a product of the old paradigm will come only through reliance on the alternative ideas, values, social techniques, and technologies of people-centered development. The creation of such alternatives presents an important and immediate human challenge.

Notes

CHAPTER I

1. The "long-term multifold trend" of Western society was delineated by Herman Kahn and Anthony Wiener in *The Year 2000* (New York: MacMillan, 1967). It includes as components increasingly sensate values (empirical, this-worldly, humanistic, pragmatic, manipulative); bureaucratic and meritocratic elites; centralization; accumulation of scientific and technical knowledge; institutionalization of technological change; modernization and industrialization; increasing affluence; population growth; urbanization; increasing importance of services and information-related activities; increasing literacy and education; innovative and manipulative social engineering; increasing tempo of change.

2. More recent survey data, especially that reported by SRI International's "Values and Lifestyles" program and by Daniel Yankelovich in his 1982 book *New Rules*, indicates that the fraction of the United States adult population emphasizing "inner-directed" values grew even more rapidly after the mid-1970s, and in the early 1980s amounts to something over a fifth. It seems to be rather evenly distributed over age, income, and similar demographic variables.

3. Aldous Huxley wrote of this new-yet-old core belief system in *The Perennial Philosophy* (New York: Harper and Brothers, 1945); others have used the term "the perennial wisdom." Essentially, in all the durable spiritual and religious traditions, despite the apparent diversity of their exoteric or public forms, there seems to be an esoteric, inner-circle understanding which is more or less the same around the world and through the centuries. This core "perennial wisdom" asserts an intuitive "supraconscious" awareness that may occur spontaneously or be fostered by any of various spiritually focused disciplines. This awareness is recognized by the individual as his/her own "higher will," and also as in some sense not separate from the corresponding higher minds of his fellow human beings.

This "perennial wisdom" has had a profound effect on all civilizations. In Western civilization it has been an intermittently visible stream throughout the history of Christianity. In its Hermetic, Cabalistic, Sufistic, Rosicrucian, and Freemasonry forms it greatly influenced the history of the Middle East, Europe, and North America. In its Eastern forms, particularly Zen Buddhism and Vedanta, it has had a marked influence over the past twenty years or so, especially in the English-speaking world. By the 1980s it had become quite clear that the "perennial wisdom" is not, as once thought, irrevocably incompatible with Western science. Rather, they seem to have in some sense a complementary relation to one another. As research into human consciousness has advanced in recent years, it seems to point increasingly toward reaffirmation of the "perennial wisdom."

4. Based on N. B. McEachron, "Forces of Societal Transformation in the United States," EPRC Research Memorandum no. 13. SRI International, Menlo Park, Ca., September 1971.

CHAPTER 3

1. I am using the words "man," "men," and "mankind" out of linguistic convenience rather than sexist bias. Unfortunately there is no equivalent in English of "der Mensch."

2. In this discussion I am drawing heavily on Paul Colinvaux, *The Fates of Nations: A Biological Theory of History* (New York: Simon and Schuster, 1980) for terminology and general concepts. I have serious reservations, however, about the historical theory that he derives from them.

3. Cf. Olwen H. Hufton, *The Poor of Eighteenth-Century France, 1750–1789* (Oxford: Clarendon Press, 1975), passim, on this and equally harrowing topics.

4. Another of Napoleon's characteristic contributions to French *civilisation* was police licensing of prostitues.

5. Cf. Marvin Harris, *Cannibals and Kings: The Origins of Cultures* (New York: Random House, 1977), chap. 2. I have relied on this brilliant book for much of the information on historical anthropology.

6. Paul Colinvaux, *Why Big Fierce Animals Are Rare* (Princeton, N.J.: Princeton University Press, 1978).

7. A modern-day illustration of this came up by coincidence in an oral honors examination in the history department only a few days after I had given this talk. In Rumania as the human population grew rapidly after World War I, the animal population shrank dramatically and meat virtually disappeared from the peasants' diet. Indeed, they even had to give up eating the more expensive cereal crops and fell back on maize, previously thought good only for hog feeder. I owe this freebie to William Segal.

8. This pattern of intensification and depletion is the overall thesis of Harris, *Cannibals and Kings*. His book is a study of the chronological stages that this cyclical process has passed through as new technologies have been invented.

9. Cited by Geoffrey Barraclough in "Culture and Civilization," *New Republic*, 22 December 1979, p. 28.

10. Charles Krauthammer, "Rich Nations, Poor Nations," *New Republic*, 11 April 1981, pp. 20–23.

CHAPTER 4

1. Charles Darwin, *Origin of Species* (New York: Macmillan, 1962).

2. C. H. Waddington, *The Listener* (London), 13 February 1952.

3. Ludwig von Bertalanffy, "General System Theory and Psychology," in J. R. Royce, ed., *Toward Unification of Psychology* (Toronto: Toronto University Press, 1970).

4. Primates are the only animals with stereoscopic color vision.

5. T. C. Cheng, *Symbiosis (Organisms Living Together)*: New York: Pegasus, 1970), p. 11.

6. G. G. Simpson, *The Major Features of Evolution* (New York: Columbia University Press, 1953).

7. J. S. Haldane, *The Philosophy of a Biologist* (Oxford: Clarendon Press, 1935).

8. The experimentor is usually not considered to be part of the experiment, and thus, the energy "lost" in the experiment is not observed as being translated

into new *information*. Looked at as a more holistic system, the experimentor must be treated as a part of the experiment. Brillouin postulated this with his concept of "negentropy" although he believed that the information obtained was always less than the energy lost and in this way, held fast the idea of entropy. If we look at the relationship of the physical system to the experimentor's mental system we derive a very different picture from that of Brillouin's negentropy; we see instead a demonstration of syntropy—higher not lower order.

9. M. Calvin, *Chemical Evolution* (New York and Oxford: Oxford University Press, 1969).

10. M. Rubner, *Das Problem der Lebensdauer und Seihe Beziehunger zu Wachstum und Ernahrung* (Munich and Berlin, 1908).

11. A. Arshavsky, "Musculoskeletal Activity and Rate of Entropy in Mammals," in Grant Newton and Austin H. Riesen, eds., *Advances in Psychobiology*, (New York: Wiley-Interscience, 1972). Human life-span and intensive work may be as directly related as the life-span of cattle and horses; that is, while horses will expend far more active energy than cattle they live twice as long or longer. As Arshavsky notes, active approaches to stimuli prove to be a positive factor and avoidance (or self-sparing for comfort) is negative. The Soviet Institute of Gerontology states that "Man could live longer if he were allowed to work longer," a fact which is frequently and tragically verified by the deterioration that so often accompanies idle retirement.

CHAPTER 6

1. Ludwig von Bertalanffy, *Problems of Life* (New York: John Wiley and Sons, 1952).

2. Richard L. Meier, *Science and Economic Development* (New York: John Wiley and Sons, 1956).

3. Kenneth E. Boulding, "The Consumption Concept in Economic Theory," *American Economic Review* 35 (May 1945): 1–14; and "Income or Welfare?," *Review of Economic Studies* 17 (1949–50): 77–86.

4. Fred L. Polak, *The Image of the Future*, vols. 1 and 2, trans. Elise Boulding (New York: Sythoff, Leyden and Oceana, 1961).

CHAPTER 7

1. Dorothy Pitkin, "One Woman's Death—A Victory and a Triumph," ed. R. C. Townsend, in Elisabeth Kuebler-Ross, *Death: The Final Stage of Growth* (Englewood Cliffs, N.J.: Prentice-Hall, Spectrum Books, 1975), pp. 107, 116, 116.

2. Ian L. McHarg, *Design with Nature* (Garden City, N.Y.: Doubleday/Natural History Press, 1971), p. 11.

3. Ibid., p. 15.

4. Ibid., p. 9.

5. Ibid., p. 29.

6. Beatrice Willard, et al., "The Ethics of Biospheral Viability," in Nicholas Polunin, ed., *Growth without Biospheral Disasters?* (London: Macmillan, 1980).

7. Barry Commoner, *The Closing Circle: Nature, Man and Technology* (New York: Knopf, 1971), pp. 81–111.

8. Howard T. Odum, *Environment, Power and Society* (New York: Wiley-Interscience, 1971), pp. 274–303.

9. For an introduction to the New Alchemy Institute and its founder, John Todd, see *What Do We Use for Lifeboats When the Ship Goes Down?: Conversations with Robert Reines, John Todd, Ian McHarg, Paolo Soleri, and Richard Saul Wurman*, by "my" (New York: Harper and Row, Colophon. 1976), pp. 67–97.

10. Ibid., pp. 77–79.

11. Ibid., pp. 95–97.

12. Erik Eckholm and Lester R. Brown, *Spreading Deserts: The Hand of Man* (Washington, D.C.: World Watch Institute, 1977), pp. 29–30.

13. Matthias Johannessen, *Sculptor Asmundur Sveinsson: An Edda in Shapes and Symbols* (Reykajavik: Iceland Review Books, 1974), p. 63.

14. Eugene C. Bianchi and Rosemary Radford Ruether, *From Machismo to Mutuality: Essays on Sexism and Woman-Man Liberation* (New York: Paulist Press, 1976), p. 61.

15. Jean Hersey, *The Shape of a Year* (New York: Charles Scribner's Sons, 1967), pp. 137, 96, 104, 102.

16. May Sarton, *Plant Dreaming Deep* (New York: Norton, 1968), p. 138.

CHAPTER 8

1. Jerome B. Wiesner and Herbert F. York, "National Security and the Nuclear Test Ban," *Scientific American* 211, no. 4 (1964): 27.

2. Garrett Hardin, "Interstellar Migration and the Population Problem," *Journal of Heredity* 50 (1959): 68; Sebastian von Hoernor, "General Limits of Space Travel," *Science* 137 (7 December 1962): 18–23.

3. Jon von Neumann and Oscar Morgenstern, *Theory of Games and Economic Behavior* (Princeton: Princeton University Press, 1947), p. 11.

4. John Heaver Fremlin, "How Many People Can the World Support?," *New Scientist* no. 415 (29 October 1964): 285.

5. Adam Smith, *The Wealth of Nations* (New York: Modern Library, 1937), p. 423.

6. William Forster Lloyd, *Two Lectures on the Checks to Population* (Oxford: Oxford University Press, 1833), reprinted (in part) in Garrett Hardin, ed., *Population, Evolution, and Birth Control*, 2d ed. (San Francisco: W. H. Freeman, 1969), p. 28.

7. Alfred North Whitehead, *Science and the Modern World* (New York: Menton, 1948), p. 17.

8. Hardin, ed., *Population, Evolution, and Birth Control*, p. 46.

9. Scott McVay, "The Last of the Great Whales," *Scientific American* 216, no. 8 (August 1966): 13.

10. Joseph Francis Fletcher, *Situation Ethics* (Philadelphia: Westminster, 1966).

11. David Lack, *The Natural Regulation of Animal Numbers* (Oxford: Clarendon Press, 1954).

12. Harry Girvetz, *From Wealth to Welfare* (Stanford, Calif.: Stanford University Press, 1950).

13. Garrett Hardin, "A Second Sermon on the Mount," *Perspectives in Biology*

and Medicine 6, no. 366 (Spring 1963): 366.

14. U. Thant, "Thirty Governments Review Human Rights Appeal," *International Planned Parenthood News*, no. 168 (February 1968): 3.

15. Kingsley Davis, "Population Policy: Will Current Programs Succeed?," *Science* 158 (10 November 1967): 730–39.

16. Sol Tax, ed., *Evolution after Darwin*, vol. 2 (Chicago: University of Chicago Press, 1960), p. 469.

17. Gregory Bateson, Donald D. Jackson, Jay Haley, and John Weakland, "Toward a Theory of Schizophrenia," *Behavioral Science* 1 (1956): 251–64.

18. P. Goodman, *New York Review of Books* 10, no. 8 (23 May 1968): 22.

19. Alexander Comfort, *The Anxiety Makers* (London: Nelson, 1967).

20. Charles Frankel, *The Case for Modern Man* (New York: Harper, 1955), p. 203.

21. John D. Roslansky, *Genetics and the Future of Man* (New York: Appleton-Century Crofts, 1966), p. 177.

CHAPTER 9

1. Ian R. Smith, *A Research Framework for Traditional Fisheries*, ICLARM Studies and Reviews 2 (Manila: ICLARM, 1979).

2. W. L. Collier, Harjadi Hadikoesworo, and Suwardi Saropie, *Income, Employment, and Food Systems in Javanese Coastal Villages*, Southeast Asia series no. 4 (Athens, Ohio: Ohio University, Center for International Studies, 1977).

3. D. S. Gibbons, *Public Policy towards Fisheries Development in Peninsular Malaysia: A Critical Review Emphasizing Penang and Kedah* (Proceedings of the Seminar on the Development of the Fisheries Sector in Malaysia), in *Kajian Ekonomi Malaysia* 13 (June–December 1976): 89–124; Shuichi Nagata, "Some Problems of Crew Labour in the Trawl Fishing of Northwest Malaysia," in G. T. Means, ed., *The Past in South East Asia's Present: Selections from the 1977 Proceedings of the Canadian Council for South East Asian Studies* (Hamilton, Ontario: Canadian Council for South East Asian Studies, 1978), pp. 128–40.

4. D. Pauly, "History and Present Status of the San Miguel Bay Fisheries," in D. Pauly and A. N. Mines, eds., *Small-Scale Fisheries of San Miguel Bay, Philippines: Biology and Stock Assessment*, ICLARM Technical Reports 7 (Manila: ICLARM; Institute for Fisheries Development and Research, University of the Philippines in the Visayas; and the United Nations University, Tokyo, 1982); N. A. Navaluna and E. Tulay, "Costs and Returns of Small and Medium Trawlers," in I. R. Smith and A. N. Mines, eds., *Small-Scale Fisheries of San Miguel Bay, Philippines: Economics of Production and Marketing*, ICLARM Technical Reports 8. (Manila: ICLARM; Institute for Fisheries Development and Research, University of the Philippines in the Visayas; and the United Nations University, Tokyo, 1982); and M. Vakily, "Catch and Effort in the Trawl Fishery," in Pauly and Mines, eds., *Small-Scale Fisheries of San Miguel Bay, Philippines: Biology and Stock Assessment*, pp. 65–94.

5. This project was a cooperative effort between the Institute of Fisheries Development and Research, University of the Philippines in the Visayas, and ICLARM. The project was funded in part by grants from the United Nations University and the Philippine Council for Agriculture and Resources Research.

6. A. N. Mines, D. Pauly, N. A. Navaluna, and M. Vakily, "The Physical Environment," in Pauly and Mines, eds., *Small-Scale Fisheries of San Miguel Bay, Philippines: Biology and Stock Assessment.*

7. Pauly, "History and Present Status of the San Miguel Bay Fisheries."

8. Conner Bailey, *Small-Scale Fisheries of San Miguel Bay, Philippines: Occupational and Geographic Mobility*, ICLARM Technical Reports 10 (Manila: ICLARM; Institute for Fisheries Development and Research, University of the Philippines in the Visayas; and the United Nations University, Tokyo, 1982).

9. L. R. Yater, "Problems in the Fishery as Received by the Fishermen," in C. Bailey, ed., *Small-Scale Fisheries of San Miguel Bay, Philippines: Social Aspects of Production and Marketing*, ICLARM Technical Reports 9 (Manila: Center for Living Aquatic Resources Management, Institute for Fisheries Development and Research, University of the Philippines in the Visayas; and the United Nations University, Tokyo, in press.

10. Bailey, *Small-Scale Fisheries of San Miguel Bay, Philippines: Occupational and Geographic Mobility.*

11. E. B. Villafuerte and Conner Bailey, "Systems of Sharing and Patterns of Ownership," in C. Bailey, ed., *Small-Scale Fisheries of San Miguel Bay, Philippines: Social Aspects of Production and Marketing.*

12. Since this paper was written, all trawlers greater than three gross tons have been banned from fishing within San Miguel Bay.

13. In 1981 U.S. $1.00 equaled approximately 8 Philippine pesos.

14. Pauly, "History and Present Status of the San Miguel Bay Fisheries."

15. I. R. Smith and A. N. Mines, "Implications for Equity and Management," in I. R. Smith and A. N. Mines, eds., *Small-Scale Fisheries of San Miguel Bay, Philippines: Economics of Production and Marketing.*

16. Navaluna and Tulay, "Costs and Returns of Small and Medium Trawlers."

17. Pauly, "History and Present Status of the San Miguel Bay Fisheries."

18. Rural banks in the Philippines are privately owned. Loans to fishermen are unsecured but 80 percent of the loan is guaranteed by the government. Nonetheless, past experience with low repayment rates on similar government programs (Smith, *A Research Framework for Traditional Fisheries*) has made local bankers reluctant to issue further loans to fishermen without additional guarantees of the kind willingly provided by wealthy trawler operators.

CHAPTER 10

1. P. A. Yotopoulos and J. B. Nugent, *Economics of Development: Empirical Investigations* (New York: Harper and Row, 1976); M. P. Todaro, *Economic Development in the Third World* (London: Longman, 1977).

2. For a detailed sketch of the neoclassical paradigm of development, see G. M. Meier and R. E. Baldwin, *Economic Development: Theory, History, Policy* (New York: Wiley, 1957), chapter 3.

3. It was quickly and perhaps quite rightly pointed out, e.g., by V. K. R. V. Rao, that the assumptions of Keynesian analysis, in particular the underutilization of all factors of production simultaneously, and Keynes' emphasis on the short run were not applicable to LDCs and their long-run growth problems. Therefore, even Keynesian unemployment has been dismissed in the orthodox literature of devel-

opment economics. See Rao, "Investment, Income and the Multiplier in an Under-developed Economy," *Indian Economic Review* (February 1952); reprinted in A. N. Agarwala and S. Singh, eds., *The Economics of Underdevelopment* (London: Oxford University Press, 1958), pp. 205–18.

4. A Leijonhufvud, *On Keynesian Economics and the Economics of Keynes* (New York: Oxford University Press, 1968); R. W. Clower, "The Keynesian Counter-Revolution: A Theoretical Appraisal," in F. H. Hahn and F. Breckling, eds., *The Theory of Interest Rates* (London: Macmillan, 1965), pp. 103–25; H. P. Minsky, *John Maynard Keynes* (New York: Columbia University Press, 1975); and R. Barro and H. Grossman, *Money, Employment and Inflation* (Cambridge: Cambridge University Press, 1976).

5. W. A. Lewis, "Economic Development with Unlimited Supplies of Labour," *Manchester School of Economics and Social Studies* 22 (May 1954): 139–97; and J. C. H. Fei and G. Ranis, *Development of the Labor Surplus Economy: Theory and Policy* (Homewood, Ill.: Irwin, 1964).

6. D. W. Jorgensen, "The Development of a Dual Economy," *Economic Journal* 71 (June 1961): 309–34.

7. The facts of high and generally growing urban unemployment rates and the persistence of urban-rural wage and income differentials have, of course, at long last, been recognized, but unfortunately the result has been to stimulate still further variations on the old theme. For example, Harris and Todaro attempted to treat unemployment as an endogenous variable which equalizes rural marginal productivity and the expected urban wage rate, i.e., the urban wage rate weighted by the probability of securing employment. See J. R. Harris and M. P. Todaro, "Migration, Unemployment and Development: A Two-Sector Analysis," *American Economic Review* 70 (March 1970): 126–42.

8. L. C. Thurow and R. E. Lucas, "The American Distribution of Income: A Structural Problem" (U.S. Congress, Joint Economic Committee, 1972).

9. P. A. Yotopoulos, "The Population Problem and the Development Solution: Interactions, Especially in Agriculture," *Food Research Institute Studies* special issue (1977), chapter 5.

10. According to the neoclassical price adjustment mechanisms, the labour-displacing bias of technological change would prompt changes in relative factor prices, allowing full employment equilibrium to be maintained. Detailed empirical investigations of the relevant technological changes by Day and Singh and Day, however, suggest that the magnitude of the labour-displacing bias of technological change is so great that it is totally unrealistic to expect that factor prices and hence factor proportions would ever adjust to such an extent as to offset the influence of technological change. See R. H. Day, "The Economics of Technological Change and the Demise of the Sharecropper," *American Economic Review* 57 (1976): 427–49; and I. Singh and R. H. Day, "A Microeconomic Chronicle of the Green Revolution," *Economic Development and Cultural Change* 23 (July 1975): 661–86.

11. T. Y. Shen, "Economies of Scale, Expansion Path, and Growth of Plants," *Review of Economics and Statistics* 47 (1965): 420–526; and P. A. David, *Technical Choice, Innovation and Economic Growth* (Cambridge: Cambridge University Press, 1975).

12. R. R. Nelson, "A Diffusion Model of International Productivity Differences

in Manufacturing Industry," *American Economic Review* 58 (December 1968): 1219–48.

13. R. B. Sutcliffe, *Industry and Underdevelopment* (Reading, Mass.: Addison-Wesley, 1971).

14. Ibid., p. 324.

15. S. A. Resnick, "The Decline of Rural Industry under Export Expansion: A Comparison among Burma, Philippines and Thailand, 1870–1938," *Journal of Economic History* 30 (March 1970): 51–73.

16. W. F. Stolper and P. A. Samuelson, "Protection and Real Wages," *Review of Economic Studies* 9 (1941): 58–73; and P. A. Samuelson, "International Factor-Price Equalization Once Again," *Economic Journal* 59 (June 1949): 181–97.

17. This can be shown to be true only if there are at least as many products with common technology as there are factors primary to both countries. See P. A. Samuelson, "Prices of Factors and Goods in General Equilibrium," *Review of Economic Studies* 21 (1953-54): 1–20.

18. W. P. Travis, "Conditional Protection and Industrial Employment," in W. Van Rijckeghem, ed., *Employment Problems and Policies in Developing Countries* (Rotterdam: Rotterdam University Press, 1976), pp. 87–102.

19. A. Emmanuel, *Unequal Exchange: A Study of the Imperialism of Trade* (New York: Monthly Review Press, 1972).

20. Ibid.; L. Mainwaring, "A Neo-Ricardian Analysis of International Trade," *Kyklos* 27, no. 3 (1974): 537–53.

21. A. O. Hirschman, "How to Divest in Latin America and Why," in A. O. Hirschman, ed., *A Bias for Hope* (New Haven: Yale University Press, 1971), chapter 2, p. 228.

22. J. M. Keynes, *The General Theory of Employment, Interest and Money* (London: Macmillan, 1936); D. Patinkin, *Money, Interest and Prices* (Evanston, Ill.: Row Peterson, 1956).

23. Financial economies of this sort are often used to justify cooperative or collective buying and selling operations. In practice, however, such schemes all too often serve only to place additional bureaucratic layers between producers and consumers and to offer a few well-placed, well-heeled individuals new possibilities for skimming off the cream and leaving the sediment to settle.

24. The same point of the existence of *financial* economies of scale is made by Raup for US agriculture – only that he considers this bias as a corollary of policy actions rather than as a logical consequence of the operations of the market mechanism.

We have credit policies that cheapen the cost of credit for large borrowers. We have tax policies that encourage vertical integration, agglomeration and farm size enlargement. We tax unearned income in the form of capital gains more leniently than we tax earned income. We use investment tax credits and accelerated depreciation to hasten the substitution of machines for labour, with the result that these policies are of greatest advantage to those sectors of the economy that are relatively most highly mechanized. We adopt farm commodity price support programs that are flat-rate supplements to price, and thus yield benefits that are a linear function of output. If there are any economies of size available through farm size enlargement, this system gives a differentially larger reward to the larger firms. These policies are not scale-neutral. Taken together, they create incentives for farm land buyers to shift attention from efficiency and productivity criteria to a search for rewards in the form of farm expansion, agglomeration and land value appreciation.

25. R. F. Harrod, "An Essay in Dynamic Theory," *Economic Journal* 49 (1939): 14–33; *Towards a Dynamic Economics* (London: Macmillan, 1956); and *Economic Dynamics* (London: Macmillan, 1973); and H. Nikaido, "Harrodian Pathology of Neoclassical Growth: The Irrelevance of Smooth Factor Substitution" (Los Angeles: University of Southern California, Working Paper 7709, 1977).

26. M. Friedman, *A Theory of the Consumption Function* (Princeton, N.J.: Princeton University Press, 1957).

27. See, for example, W. A. Lewis, *The Theory of Economic Growth* (London: Allan and Unwin, 1955).

CHAPTER II

1. In 1979 the exchange rate was approximately US $1.00 = 15 Taka or 1 Taka = US 06.6 cents.

2. One seer equals 0.93 kilograms.

CHAPTER 12

1. This scenario draws on a number of papers presented at a conference on seasonal dimensions of poverty held at the Institute for Development Studies at Sussex in 1978. In addition we acknowledge a special debt to the work of Susan Schofield, in particular her article, "Seasonal Factors Affecting Nutrition in Different Age Groups and Especially Preschool Children," *Journal of Development Studies* 11 (October 1974): 22–40.

CHAPTER 13

1. This definition is borrowed from the Philippine Council for Agriculture and Resources Research (PCARR)–sponsored Workshop on Landless Rural Workers (WLRW), Los Banos, 8–9 December 1978.

2. Staff of the Technical Board of Agricultural Credit (TBAC), "Socio-Economic Survey on Landless Rural Workers in Three Selected Barangays," preliminary report (Manila: Government of the Philippines, 1978).

3. Rafael S. Espiritu, "Access and Participation of Landless Rural Workers in Government Programs"; and Antonio Ledesma, "Socio-Economic Aspects of Filipino Sugar Farm Workers: Three Views from the Cane Fields" (Papers presented at WLRW, Los Banos, 8–9 December 1978).

4. Staff of the Technical Board of Agricultural Credit (TBAC), "Socio-Economic Survey."

5. See Espiritu, "Access and Participation," and Yujiro Hayami, *Anatomy of a Peasant Economy: A Rice Village in the Philippines*, (Los Banos: International Rice Research Institute, 1978).

6. Espiritu, "Access and Participation."

7. E. Tejada, "Socio-Economic Study of Landless Rural Workers In A Sugarcane

Plantation in Negros Occidental" (Paper presented at WLRW, Los Banos, 8–9 December 1978).

8. Erik D. Eckholm cites similar trends around the world in *The Dispossessed of the Earth: Land Reform and Sustainable Development,* World Watch paper no. 30, (Washington: World Watch, June 1979).

9. A. Ledesma, "Rice Farmers and Landless Rural Workers: Perspectives from the Household Level," International Rice Research Institute Saturday Seminar Paper, 28 October 1978, mimeographed.

10. Gelia Castillo, *Beyond Manila: Philippine Rural Problems in Perspective* (Los Banos: University of the Philippines, 1977).

11. Ledesma, "Rice Farmers."

12. G. E. Dozina, Jr. and R. W. Herdt, "Upland Rice Farming in the Philippines," 1973, mimeographed.

13. D. J. Ganapin, "Factors of Underdevelopment in Kaingin Communities," unpublished paper.

14. Bureau of Forestry Development Census, (Manila: Government of the Philippines, 1972).

15. Ganapin, "Factors of Underdevelopment."

16. PCARR, "Indicators for Philippine Agriculture, Forestry, Fishery and Mine Resources," (Los Banos: Philippine Council for Agricultural Resources and Research [PCARR], 1977).

17. Anacleto Duldulao, *An Integrated Project for Kaingin Control in the Philippines: A New Approach to Forest Conservation, Phase I Socio-Economic Profile Survey of Kainginero-Cooperators – October 1976–December 1977* (Los Banos: University of the Philippines).

18. An average of 5 tons per hectare for root crops and an average of 0.4 metric tons per hectare of upland rice is produced, according to the United Nations Development Program/Food and Agriculture Organization (UNDP/FAO), *The Philippines, Shifting Cultivation, Demonstration and Training in Forest Range and Watershed Management* (Manila: UNDP/FAO, 1978).

19. Castillo, *Beyond Manila.*

20. UNDP/FAO, *The Philippines.*

21. Ibid.

22. Felipe Abraham, "The Nasipit Experience" (Paper reporting rate of natural forest regeneration on protected logged-over areas for USAID-sponsored conference, Improved Utilization of Tropical Rainforests, Washington, D.C., May 1978).

23. Virginia Holazo, "Philippine Municipal Fisheries: A Review of Resources, Technology and Socio-Economics," *Fisheries Today* 2 (May 1979).

24. Ian Smith, Miguel Puzon, and Carmen Vidal, *Philippine Municipal Fisheries: A Review of Resources, Technology and Socio-Economics.* (Joint unpublished report by the Fishery Industry Development Council [FIDC] and the International Center for Living Aquatic Resources Management [ICLARM]).

25. This figure is derived from a mean of 4,500 pesos based on results from sixteen small socio-economic barrio studies completed in 1976–77. Using food indices, the 4,500 pesos equates to a household income of 3,900 pesos in mid-1975. We have adjusted the figure to facilitate comparison among the poor groups.

26. Smith et al., *Philippine Municipal Fisheries.*

27. Ibid.

28. "How the Fuel Price Increases Will Affect the Fishing Industry," *Farming Today* 5, no. 9 (September 1979).

29. National Environmental Protection Council, *The Philippine Environment* (Manila: National Environmental Protection Council, 1978).

30. W. P. David, "Watershed Protection" (Seminar paper, Department of Agricultural Engineering, University of the Philippines, Los Banos, 1975). David reports on five years of research and shows that slash-and-burn farming for rice and corn results in soil losses through erosion of from 60 to 85 metric tons of topsoil per hectare, per year.

31. Landsat Photos, 1976 (National Environmental Protection Council, UNEP/ESCAP Regional Seminar on Environment and Development, Bangkok, August 1979).

32. A. V. Revilla, South East Asian Regional Center for Graduate Study and Research in Agriculture (SEARCA) professorial lecture, published in *Conservation Circulation* (Los Banos: Department of Forestry Extension, University of the Philippines College of Forestry, 1977).

33. National Economic and Development Authority (NEDA), *Five-Year Philippine Development Plan, 1978–1982.* (Manila: Government of the Philippines).

CHAPTER 14

1. The description of the municipal system is based on original research undertaken by the author in 1974–76, the results of which were first presented in an unpublished project report; see Haiti, *Plan de développement de Port-au-Prince et de sa Région Métropolitaine*, phase 3, vol. 3, *Infrastructure* (Nations Uniées/CONADEP/TPTC, February 1976).

2. Government officials sometimes suggested that because the standpipes were not equipped with shut-off mechanisms or with basins, they were a principal cause of the system losses. There was, to be sure, some degree of wastage involved. However, at the best of times, when all the spigots were flowing freely, the combined outflow of all standpipes was between 20 and 25 l/s, or about 2.5 percent of source inflows. The standpipes were clearly not responsible for much of the loss in the system.

3. Haiti, *Infrastructure.*

4. It was hopeless to attempt to fight fires with water from hoses attached to fire hydrants. There were few of them to begin with, about one for each 20-hectare area of urban land, and fewer still that could operate at all. Among the operational ones, the irregularity of flows made it difficult to predict whether a particular hydrant would have water pressure behind it or not. This was particularly the case in the dry season, when water flows were severely restricted and fire hazards particularly acute. The more typical method of dealing with fire was to bulldoze a clear area around it to prevent spread, and then to let it burn out. When major fires did occur, the area damaged generally tended to be extensive.

5. Haiti, *Infrastructure.*

6. The description of the private market is based in part on the original research identified in note 1, above, and in part on additional research undertaken in 1976–77. The latter was partially financed by a grant from the Office of Urban Development,

USAID, and the results were presented in abridged form in another unpublished report; see S. Fass, *The Economics of Survival: A Study of Poverty and Planning in Haiti* (unpublished report prepared for the Office of Urban Development, USAID, October 1980).

7. In addition to the approximately 1,200 homes that had regular contracts for delivery by tanker truck, variation in piped water service to homes with connections could raise the number over a short period by as many as another 3,000. The gross revenue figure of $980,000 per year is therefore something of an underestimate.

8. Haiti, *Infrastructure.*

9. Ibid.

10. Haiti, *Plan de développement de Port-au-Prince et de sa région métropolitaine,* phase 3, vol. 5, *Habitat,* Nations Uniées/CONADEP/TPTC, February 1976).

11. The surveys referred to are those which were used to prepare the reports identified in notes 1 and 6, above.

12. Average daily per person nutritional components in Port-au-Prince were 1,580 calories, 40 grams of protein, and 44 grams of carbohydrate. In more tangible terms this means that 20 percent of children grow normally, 46 percent suffer from first-degree malnutrition, and 30 percent from second-degree malnutrition; see K. W. King, "Nutrition Research in Haiti," in V. Rubin and R. P. Schaedel, eds., *The Haitian Potential: Research and Resources of Haiti* (New York: Teachers College Press, 1975).

CHAPTER 15

1. M. Ahluwalia, "The Dimensions of the Problem," in H. Chenery et al., *Redistribution with Growth* (Oxford, 1974).

2. See K. Rafferty, *Financial Times,* 10 April 1974, p. 35, col. 5; M. Lipton, "Urban Bias and Rural Planning," in P. Streeten and M. Lipton, eds., *The Crisis of Indian Planning* (Oxford, 1968), p. 85.

3. F. Muir and D. Norden, "Common Entrance," in P. Sellers, *Songs for Swinging Sellers,* Parlophone PMC 1111, 1958.

4. Nobody who, like myself, has worked in Bangladesh could miss the combination, not rare in Asia or East Africa, of (1) extreme poverty, especially in villages; (2) a responsive peasantry "raring to go" with improved techniques; (3) a system that steers 70 to 80 per cent of scarce savings, skills and political energy into a tiny, inefficient but influential urban sector. Even a total cure for urban bias – given the momentum of outgoing projects – could not efficiently slash this proportion *at once* to, say, 40 to 55 per cent. But clearly movement towards a cure is the first requirement.

CHAPTER 19

1. The term paradigm-shift refers to a radical break with the reigning conventional wisdom that informs the accepted practice of science. See Thomas S. Kuhn, *The Structure of Scientific Revolutions,* 2d ed. (Chicago: Chicago University Press; and the discussion in Imre Lakatos and Alan Musgrave, eds., *Criticism and the Growth of Knowledge* (London: Cambridge University Press, 1970).

2. The most complete American formulation of the blueprint model of planning is found in Rexford Tugwell's writings; see Salvador M. Padilla, ed., *Tugwell's Thoughts on Planning* (Puerto Rico: University of Puerto Rico Press, 1975).

3. National planning conforms to this model only in the instance of socialist economies where central planning has replaced markets – and in countries of mixed economy, chiefly in the Third World, where national investment planning has been instituted. For trenchant critiques of central economic planning, see Rudolph Bahro, *The Alternative in Eastern Europe* (London: NLB, 1979); and Charles Lindblom, *Politics and Markets: The World's Political-Economic Systems* (New York: Basic Books, 1977).

4. See Allen Heskin, "Crisis and Response: An Historical Perspective on Advocacy Planning," *Journal of the American Planning Association* 46 (January 1980): 50–63.

5. Daniel P. Moynihan, *Maximum Feasible Misunderstanding: Community Action in the War on Poverty* (New York: Free Press, 1969).

6. Janice Perlman, "The Neighborhood Movement in the 1970s: Grassroots Empowerment and Government Response," *Social Policy*, September–October 1979; and Harry C. Boyte, *The Backyard Revolution: Understanding the New Citizen Movement* (Philadelphia: Temple University Press, 1980).

7. E. F. Schumacher, *Small Is Beautiful: Economics As If People Mattered* (New York: Harper and Row, 1973).

8. Ivan Illich, *Tools for Conviviality* (London: Fontana/Collins, 1975).

9. John Dewey, *The Public and Its Problems* (New York: H. Holt, 1927); *Liberalism and Social Action* (New York: G. P. Putnam's Sons, 1935); and *Experience and Education* (New York: Collier, 1938).

10. Lewis Mumford, *The Culture of Cities* (New York: Harcourt, Brace, 1938).

11. Edgar H. Schein, *Process Consultation* (Reading, Mass.: Addison-Wesley, 1969).

12. Charles Hampden-Turner, *Radical Man: The Process of Psycho-Social Development* (Garden City, N.Y.: Anchor, 1971).

13. Edgar S. Dunn, *Economic and Social Development: A Process of Social Learning* (Baltimore: Johns Hopkins University Press, 1971). See chapter 17 in this anthology.

14. Donald Schon, *Beyond the Stable State* (New York: Random House, 1971); Donald Michael, *On Learning to Plan and Planning to Learn* (San Francisco: Jossey-Bass, 1973); John Friedmann and Barclay Hudson, "Knowledge and Action: A Guide to Planning Theory," *Journal of the American Institute of Planners* 40 (January 1974): 2–16; and Chris Argyris and Donald Schon, *Theory in Practice* (San Francisco: Jossey-Bass, 1975) and *Organization Learning* (Reading, Mass.: Addison-Wesley, 1978). See chapter 18 in this anthology.

15. The best account of planning as a cybernetic process adapted to "turbulent" environments is Magoroh Maruyama, "Heterogenistics and Morphogenetics: Towards a New Concept of the Scientific," *Theory and Society* 5 (January 1978): 75–96. See also Paul R. Lawrence and Jay W. Lorsch, *Organization and Environment: Managing Differentiation and Integration* (Boston: Harvard University Graduate School of Management, 1967).

16. See John Friedmann and George Abonyi, "Social Learning: A New Model

for Policy Research," *Environmental Planning A* 8 (December 1976): 927–40; and John Friedmann, "Innovation, Flexible Response, and Social Learning: A Problem in the Theory of Meta-Planning," in R. W. Burchell and G. Sternlieb, eds., *Planning Theory in the 1980's: A Search for Future Directions* (Brunswick, N.J.: Transaction Books, 1978), pp. 163–78, "The Epistemology of Social Practice: A Critique of Objective Knowledge," *Theory and Society* 6 (July 1978): 75–92; and *The Good Society* (Cambridge, Mass.: MIT Press, 1979).

17. Few planners are familiar with Mao Tse-tung's theoretical writing in which special prominence is given to the relation of theory to practice in the transformation of society. See his essay "On Practice" in Mao Tse-Tung, *Four Essays in Philosophy* (Peking: Foreign Language Press, 1968).

18. David C. Korten, "Community Organization and Rural Development: A Learning Process Approach," *Public Administration Review* 40 (September–October 1980): 499.

19. See Michael Polanyi, *The Tacit Dimension* (Garden City, N.Y.: Anchor, 1967).

20. See Friedmann, *The Good Society.*

21. Ibid., pp. 112–19.

22. Paul K. Feyerabend, *Against Method: Outline of an Anarchistic Theory of Knowledge* (London: NLB, 1975).

23. The social function of claims to rationality is to ignore the broader value implications of planning. It places planning, and specifically allocative planning, at the service of dominant business interests, a value commitment that remains invisible behind the screen of scientific objectivity. See Henrika Kuklick, "Chicago Sociology and Urban Planning Policy," *Theory and Society* 9 (November 1980): 821–46.

CHAPTER 20

1. Z. Bauman, F. G. Burke, L. K. Caldwell, M. Crozier, J. Friedmann, B. M. Gross, R. Shafer, and P. J. D. Wiles, Executive Committee, International Group for Studies in National Planning (INTERPLAN), "Attitudes and Beliefs on National Planning," in B. M. Gross, ed., *Action under Planning: The Guidance of Economic Development* (New York: McGraw-Hill, 1967), pp. 281–99.

2. Hasan, Ozbekhan, *Les fonctions internationaux de Paris: Roles et vocations,* publication no. 39 (Paris: La Documentation Francaise, 1973).

3. R. Ackoff, *Redesigning the Future* (New York: John Wiley and Sons, 1974).

CHAPTER 21

1. Bruce F. Johnston and William C. Clark, *On Designing Strategies for Rural Development: A Policy Analysis Perspective* (Baltimore: Johns Hopkins Press, 1982); Dennis Rondinelli, "The Dilemma of Development Administration: Coping with Complexity and Uncertainty in Control Oriented Bureaucracies," *World Politics* 24 (October 1982); Frances F. Korten, "Stimulating Community Participation: Obstacles and Options at Agency, Community and Societal Levels," *Rural Development Participation Review* 2 (Spring 1981); J. K. Satia, "Developmental Tasks and Middle Management Roles in Rural Development," in David C. Korten and Felipe B. Alfonso, eds., *Bureaucracy and the Poor: Closing the Gap* (West Hartford, Conn.:

Kumarian Press, 1982), pp. 76–85; Jon R. Moris, *Managing Induced Rural Development* (Bloomington, Indiana: International Development Institute, Indiana University, 1981); Marcus D. Ingle, "Reaching the Poor through Development Assistance: An Overview of Strategies and Techniques," Development Project Management Center, Technical Assistance Division, Office of International Cooperation and Development, U.S. Department of Agriculture, Washington, D.C.; and Anil K. Gupta, "Monitoring of Rural Projects Through People's Participation," *EKISTICS: The Problems and Science of Human Settlements* 48 (November–December 1981): 434–42.

2. David C. Korten and Norman T. Uphoff, "Bureaucratic Reorientation for Participatory Rural Development," National Association of Schools of Public Affairs and Administration Working Paper no. 1 (Washington, D.C.: NASPAA, 1981). John C. Ickis, "Structural Reponses to New Rural Development Strategies," in Korten and Alfonso, eds., *Bureaucracy and the Poor*, pp. 4–32; David F. Pyle, "From Project to Program: The Study of the Scaling-Up/Implementation Process of a Community-Level Integrated Health, Nutrition, Population Intervention in Maharashtra (India)" (Ph.D. diss., Massachusetts Institute of Technology, Cambridge, Mass., 1981); George H. Honadle, "Fishing for Sustainability: The Role of Capacity Building in Development Administration," Integrated Rural Development Working Paper no. 8 (Washington, D.C.: Development Alternatives, Inc., 1981); Jerry VanSant, "Local Action for Development" (Paper prepared for the World Conference of the Society of International Development, Baltimore, Maryland, 20 July 1982); Coralie Bryant and Louise G. White, *Managing Rural Development: Peasant Participation in Rural Development* (West Hartford, Conn.: Kumarian Press, 1980); Norman T. Uphoff, John M. Cohen, and Arthur A. Goldsmith, *Feasibility and Application of Rural Development Participation: A State-of-the-Art Paper*, monograph series no. 3 (Ithaca, N.Y.: Rural Development Committee, Cornell University, January 1979); and Milton J. Esman and John D. Montgomery, "The Administration of Human Development," in Peter Knight, ed., *Implementing Programs of Human Development*, World Bank Staff Working Paper no. 403 (Washington: World Bank, 1980), pp. 183–234.

3. This case is abstracted from George Carner and David C. Korten, "People Centered Planning: The USAID/Philippines Experience," working paper no. 2 (Washington, D.C.: NASPAA, 1982). The case is also reported in David C. Korten and George Carner, "Reorienting Bureaucracies to Serve People: Two Experiences from the Philippines," *Canadian Journal of Development Studies* (forthcoming). For other cases of people-centered planning applications see David C. Korten, "Social Development: Putting People First," in Korten and Alfonso, eds., *Bureaucracy and the Poor*, pp. 201–21.

4. For key reviews of the need for donor reorientation see Judith Tendler, *Inside Foreign Aid* (Baltimore, Maryland: Johns Hopkins University Press, 1975); Harry W. Strachan, "Side Effects of Planning in the Aid Control System," *World Development* 6 (April, 1978): 467–78; Robert Chambers, "Project Selection for Poverty-Focused Rural Development: Simple is Optimal," *World Development* 6 (February 1978): 209–19; E. Philip Morgan, "Managing Development Assistance: Some Effects with Special Reference to Southern Africa," *SADEX* 1 (January–February 1980), African Bibliographic Center, Washington, D.C.; Coralie Bryant, "Organizational Impediments to Making Participation a Reality: 'Swimming Upstream' in AID," *Rural Development Participation Review* 1 (Spring 1980): 8–10; and David C. Korten,

"Community Organization and Rural Development: A Learning Process Approach," *Public Administration Review* 40 (September–October 1980): 488–511.

5. For a complete description of the guidance provided by AID/Washington see *Guidance for the Country Development Strategy Statement (CDSS)*, AIDTO CIRC A–384, 16 September 1978.

6. Milton H. Esman, *Landlessness and Near-Landlessness in Developed Countries* (Ithaca, N.Y.: Cornell University Center for International Studies, 1978). The method of analysis was also influenced by studies done by the Indian Institute of Management at Ahmedabad in Dharampur Taluka of Gujarat State. See Ranjit Gupta, "The Poverty Trap: Lessons from Dharampur," in Korten and Alfonso, eds., *Bureaucracy and the Poor*, pp. 114–35.

7. See also George Carner, "Survival, Interdependence, and Competition Among the Philippine Rural Poor," *Asian Survey* 22 (March 1982). See chapter 13 in this anthology.

8. See Jasper Ingersoll, Mark Sullivan, and Barbara Lenkerd, "Social Analysis of AID Projects: A Review of the Experience," report written under AID contract no. OTR-147-80-79 for the Agency for International Development, Washington, D.C., June 1981; and Marcus D. Ingle, "Reaching the Poor through Development Assistance."

9. Based on Kenneth Boulding, "The Economics of the Coming Spaceship Earth," in *Environmental Quality in a Growing Economy*, published for Resources for the Future, Inc. (Baltimore, Md.: Johns Hopkins University Press, 1966). See chapter 6 in this anthology.

10. John Friedmann and Clyde Weaver, *Territory and Function: The Evolution of Regional Planning* (Berkeley and Los Angeles: University of California Press, 1979). The following section is based on this work; our concept of people-centered development was substantially influenced by their concept of "agropolitan" development. See chapter 22 by Friedmann in this anthology. See also John Friedmann, "The Active Community: Toward a Political-Territorial Framework for Rural Development in Asia," *Economic Development and Cultural Change* 29 (January 1981): 235–61.

CHAPTER 22

1. The "broad consensus" emerging from the 1976 World Employment Conference is ambiguous about the meaning to be attributed to basic needs. It appears that the use of basic needs as a strategy for *welfare planning* carried the day. As an alternative approach to *territorial development*, the use of basic needs was mainly championed by the poorer countries of the Third World and certain socialist countries. International Labour Office, *Meeting Basic Needs: Strategies for Eradicating Mass Poverty and Unemployment* (Geneva: ILO, 1977).

2. This obviously excludes the very young, the very old, the infirm, and others who are precluded by their physical condition of engaging in useful work.

3. It is important to point out that basic needs do not refer to physiological minima. All needs are culturally mediated and will consequently vary among societies and according to the level achieved in the development of their productive forces.

4. In formal terms, this is an expression of the principle of commutative justice.

5. A. Helman, "The Distribution and Allocation of Consumer Goods in the Kibbutz" (Ph.D. diss., London School of Economics and Political Science, 1974).

6. A. Heller, *The Theory of Needs in Marx* (London: Allison and Busby, 1976).

7. An earlier version of the agropolitan concept was presented in J. Friedmann and M. Douglass, "Agropolitan Development: Towards a New Strategy for Regional Development in Asia," in United Nations Centre for Regional Development, *Growth Pole Strategy and Regional Development Planning in Asia* (Nagoya, Japan: UNCRD, 1975).

8. For details of China's development experience, especially with a view to its territorial base, see H. Schenk, "Concepts behind Urban and Regional Planning in China," *Tijdschrift voor Economische Sociale Geografie* 65 (1974): 381–88; J. G. Gurley, "Rural Development in China 1949–72, and the Lessons to Be Learned from It," *World Development* 3 (1975): 455–71; Joint Economic Committee, Congress of the United States, *China: A Reassessment of the Economy* (Washington, D.C.: GPO, 1975); C. Salter, "Chinese Experiments in Urban Space: The Quest for an Agropolitan China," *Habitat* 1 (1976): 19–36; and S. Paine, "Balanced Development: Maoist Conception and Chinese Practice," *World Development* 4 (1976): 277–304. One of the best overall formulations of Mao Tse-Tung's thoughts on China's development is found in his 1956 speech, "On the Ten Great Relationships," which also forms the basis of Paine's analysis; see S. Schram, ed., *Mao Tse-Tung Unrehearsed: Talks and Letters, 1956–1971* (London: Penguin Books, 1974).

9. K. Griffin, *The Political Economy of Agrarian Change: An Essay on the Green Revolution* (London: Macmillan, 1974); D. Lehman, ed., *Agrarian Reform and Agrarian Reformism: Studies of Peru, Chile, China, and India* (London: Faber and Faber, 1974).

10. Formal equality of *results* is a Procrustean bed. Only the most iron social discipline would be able to enforce it, right down the line, for every member of a social group. See W. Harich, *Kommunismus ohne Wachstum? Babeuf und der "Club of Rome"* (Hamburg: Rowohlt, 1975).

11. Under agropolitan conditions, the primary spatial system arises from the intersection of cultural, economic, and political attribute spaces. A secondary system of nodal structure is superimposed upon this pattern, reflecting functionally integrated activities that co-exist but are subordinate to territorial interests.

12. According to common practice in the United States, an area is considered *urbanized* when it lies adjacent to a city of at least 50,000 people and has a minimum settlement density of 100 housing units per square mile. Using the 1970 average size of household of 3.17, this translates into a population density of 120 persons per square kilometre. At the older ratio of 4.0 persons per household, the density would be 152 per square kilometre.

A proposed agropolitan density of 200 per square kilometre of cultivated land is thus an arbitrary standard which does, however, suggest an "urban" density pattern. Variations of these dimensions can obviously be used. It might be noted, however, that with the proposed size-density function, the entire agropolitan area would be accessible by bicycle within, at most, one hour.

13. Urban agropolitan districts would be self-governing areas which would be designed for a reasonable mix of industrial, agricultural, and residentiary functions. Their densities would tend to be higher than rural districts, requiring more careful land use and environmental planning. One important objective of urban planning for agropolitan development would be the reduction of average travel time within

the city, especially the journey to work.

14. Self-reliant development was the subject of the 24th Pugwash Symposium which was held at Dar-es-Salaam, Tanzania, 2–6 June 1975; see Pugwash Symposium, "The Role of Self-Reliance in Alternative Strategies of Development," *World Development* 5 (1977): 257–66.

15. M. Goldberg, "On the Inefficiency of Being Efficient," *Environment and Planning A* 7 (1975): 921–39.

16. Recent studies have explored the variety of energy sources that can be tapped for rural development. See V. Somil, "Intermediate Energy Technology for China," *World Development* 4 (1976): 929–37; and National Academy of Sciences, *Energy for Rural Development*, report of a panel of the Advisory Committee on Technology Innovation (Washington, D.C.: NAS, 1976).

17. The case of China's rural industrialization has been the most thoroughly documented of any experience outside the industrial West. See J. Sigurdson, "Rural Industrialization in China," in Joint Economic Committee, Congress of the United States, *China: A Reassessment of the Economy*, pp. 411–35.

18. H. Gilbert, "The Argument for Very Large Cities Reconsidered," *Urban Studies* 13 (1976): 27–34.

19. According to H. Dandekar and S. Brahme ("Role of Rural Industries in Rural Development" [Paper prepared for the Binational Interdisciplinary Seminar on Rural Development, Gokhale Institute of Politics and Economics, Poona, India, 1977], pp. 23–24), who base their conclusions on a series of carefully executed village surveys in Maharashtra State (India):

> It is unrealistic to conceive of building up rural industries that utilize local products to meet local demand. Just as the urbanite's preferences lead him to buy imported goods wherever possible, so also the villager's preferences lead him to buy the product of the city wherever possible. From our case studies, it is apparent that with the growing integration of the rural-urban economy, the traditional industries are on the decline. . . . To succeed, a rural industry has to latch into the urban economy and make a profit from urban money. There is either not enough surplus in the village to allow the industry to thrive or what surplus there is, is already largely flowing to the city. One must therefore accept that a successful rural industry may not develop many forward or backward linkages in the villages around it and come to terms with the limited role that rural industries can play in rural development.

This gloomy conclusion is not, however, justified. The "industries" described by the authors include not only the traditional village but also the raising of livestock (chickens, pigs, milch cows). To accept the statement that rural "industries" have only a "limited role" to play in rural development is, therefore, tantamount to saying that the livestock has no future in the region studied by the authors, unless it is organized by corporate (urban) interests. By the same perverted logic, one could say that a *national* industry has to latch into the *international* economy and make a profit from *international money*.

Conclusions such as these are not convincing. If traditional rural industries do not succeed in India, it is because very little effort has been made to diversify the rural economy, building up the rural infrastructure in ways that will permit diversification to occur. A solution where half the males are earning money in distant cities, leaving their villages to women, children, and old men is not a satisfactory solution from a territorial (basic-needs) point of view. It is, of course, entirely acceptable to corporations.

20. The introduction of use values into the development calculus would automatically put an end to the vicious practice of "pricing" work performed outside the market economy according to the current subsistence rate for labour. If the myth can be disestablished that wage rates accord with productivity "at the margin," then also the concept of an "industrial reserve army" would disappear, as the production of use values in the community could simply not be *reduced* to an exchange-relation, whatever the artifice. See B. Stuckey, "The Spatial Distribution of the Industrial Reserve Army (Manuscript; Starnberg: Max Planck Institute, 1977).

21. M. Gaviria, *Ecologismo y ordenación del territorio en España* (Madrid: Cuadernos para el Diálogo, 1976).

22. D. S. Paauw and C. H. Fei, *The Transition in Open Dualistic Economies: Theory and Southeast Asian Experience* (New Haven: Yale University Press, 1973).

23. Because they are important to alternative development approaches, a good deal has been written about small-scale entrepreneurs. Among the more important studies are R. B. Buchele, *The Development of Small Industrial Entrepreneurs as a Tool of Economic Growth*, Working Paper no. 31 (Honolulu, Hawaii: East-West Technology and Development Institute, 1972); B. Dinwiddy, *Promoting African Enterprise* (London: Overseas Development Institute, 1974); K. Hart, "Small-Scale Entrepreneurs in Ghana and Development Planning," *Journal of Development* 6 (1969-70): 104-20; P. F. Kaplan and C. H. Huang, "The Industrial Modernity of Filipino Small-Scale Industrial Workers," *Economic Development and Cultural Change* 24 (1976): 799-814; P. Kilby, *African Enterprise: The Nigerian Bread Industry* (Stanford: Stanford University Press, 1965); P. Marris and A. Somerset, *The African Entrepreneur: A Study of Entrepreneurship and Development in Kenya* (New York: African Publishing Co., 1972); and E. W. Nafzinger, *South-Indian Industrialists: A Profile of Entrepreneurs in Coastal Andhra*, Working Paper no. 34 (Honolulu, Hawaii: East-West Technology and Development Institute, 1972). The broader question of the viability of small-scale enterprise is discussed by, among others, M. Bienefeld, "The Informal Sector and Peripheral Capitalism: The Case of Tanzania," in J. Oxenham, ed., *Human Resources Research*, special issue of *Bulletin* 6, Institute of Development Studies, Sussex University, 1975; and T. G. McGee, *Hawkers in Selected Southeast Asian Cities* (Report presented at a conference on the "Role of Marginal Distribution Systems in a Development," Kuala Lumpur, Malaysia, 23-26 September 1979.

24. This does not mean that modern (i.e. western) technology should be forbidden. It does mean that its use should be carefully planned so as to *protect* the wage-goods sector of the agropolitan economy against unreasonable competition from the corporate (national and transnational) sector. One way to do this would be through social pricing of imported machinery and raw materials and through the elimination of subsidies in the corporate sector.

25. A. T. Mosher, *Thinking about Rural Development* (New York: Agricultural Development Council, 1976), pp. 46-50.

26. J. F. C. Turner, *Housing by People: Toward Autonomy in Building Environ-*

ments (New York: Pantheon, 1977).

27. G. E. Johnson and W. E. Whitelaw, "Urban-Rural Income Transfers in Kenya: An Estimated Remittances Function," *Economic Development and Cultural Change* 22 (1974): 473–79.

28. In India and Pakistan, for instance, rural savings rates of 4–13 percent are reported, and this is without counting the enormous income unjustly transferred to landlords and the corporate urban sector; K. Griffin and A. R. Khan, eds., *Growth and Inequality in Pakistan* (London: Macmillan, 1972), p. 203.

29. B. Galjart, "Peasant Cooperation, Consciousness, and Solidarity," *Development and Change* 6 (1975): 75–84.

30. Essays on economic planning in China are extremely instructive on this point. See A. Donnithorne, *The Budget and the Plan in China: Central-Local Economic Relations*, Contemporary China Papers no. 3 (Canberra: Australian University Press, 1972); "Centralization and Decentralization in China's Fiscal Management," *The China Quarterly* no. 66 (1976): 328–39; and N. Lardy, "Economic Planning in the People's Republic of China: Central-Provincial Fiscal Relations," in Joint Economic Committee, Congress of the United States, *China: A Reassessment of the Economy*.

31. J. Friedmann and G. Abonyi, "Social Learning: A Model for Policy Research," *Environment and Planning A* 8 (1976): 927–40; and J. Friedmann, "The Epistemology of Social Learning: A Critique of Objective Knowledge," *Theory and Society* 6 (1978): 75–92.

CHAPTER 23

1. Elizabeth Bardwell, *Less Is More* (Madison, Wis.: Capital Community Citizens, 1974).

2. Neil Pierce, "Smokestack Chasers Who Miss the Point," *Washington Post*, 30 May 1977.

3. *Business Week*, 21 June 1976.

4. *Wall Street Journal*, 22 March 1978.

5. Representative Morris Udall, *National Journal*, 30 July 1977.

6. Jeremy Rifkin and Ted Howard, *Who Shall Play God?* (New York: Dell, 1977), p. 105.

7. Charles Mueller, testifying in hearings on "The Future of Small Business in America," Report to the Committee on Antitrust, Consumers, and Employment of the Committee on Small Business, U.S. House of Representatives, 95th Congress, 1978.

8. Barry Stein and Mark Hodex, *Competitive Scale in Manufacturing: The Case of Consumer Goods*, (Cambridge: Center for Community Economic Development, 1977).

9. David Birch, *The Job Generation Process* (Cambridge: MIT Press, 1979).

10. Ray M. Northern, *Vacant Urban Land in the American City* (Corvalis: Oregon State University, 1971).

11. John Jeavons, 1972–1975 Research Report Summary on the Biodynamic French Intensive Method (Palo Alto: Ecology Action, 1976).

— 12. Roger Blobaum, *The Use of Sewage and Solid Wastes in Metropolitan Omaha* (Washington, D.C.: Roger Blobaum and Associates, 1979).

13. Joe S. Bain, *Barriers to New Competition* (Cambridge: Harvard University

Press, 1956).

14. Stein and Hodax, *Competitive Scale in Manufacturing*.

15. See, for example, F. M. Scherer, "Economies of Scale and Industrial Concentration," in Harvey J. Goldschmid, H. Michael Mann, and J. Fred Weston, eds., *Industrial Concentration: The New Learning* (Boston: Little, Brown, 1974).

16. John Blair, *Economic Concentration* (New York: Harcourt Brace Jovanovich, 1972), p. 151.

17. Data taken from hearings on Economic Concentration, part 5, Subcommittee on Antitrust and Monopoly, 1967.

CHAPTER 26

1. Despite the general parochialism, several studies deal with these topics, and to these this study is indebted—e.g., K. J. Arrow, in his "Uncertainty and the Economics of Medical Care," *American Economic Review*, December 1963, developed a provocative discussion of nonprofit organizations. Several economists have considered the family, e.g., J. Mincer, "Labor Force Participation of Married Women: A Study of Labor Supply," in National Bureau of Economic Research, *Aspects of Labor Economics* (Princeton: Princeton University Press, 1967), and G. Becker, "A Theory of the Allocation of Time," *Economic Journal*, September 1965.

2. Basic data are from *Day Care Survey of 1970* (Washington, D.C.: Westinghouse Learning Corporation for the Office of Economic Opportunity, 1972). Henceforth, this study will be referred to as the Westinghouse Study. The Office of Child Development recommends a day-care program that costs roughly three times this figure. For a discussion of day costs per child, see D. Young and R. R. Nelson, *Public Policy for Day Care of Young Children* (Lexington, Mass.: Lexington Books, 1973).

3. For an excellent discussion of the history of day care, see G. Fein and A. Clarke-Stewart, *Day Care in Context* (New York: John Wiley and Sons, 1973).

4. For a more detailed account, see Steiner, *The State of Welfare*, and Young and Nelson, *Public Policy for Day Care*.

5. F. Low and T. Spindler, *Child Care Arrangement of Working Mothers in the United States* (U.S. Department of Health, Education, and Welfare, Children's Bureau publication no. 461, 1968).

6. R. Zamoff and L. Vogt, *Assessment of Day Care Services and Needs at the Community Level* (Washington, D.C.: Urban Institute, 1971).

7. Steiner, *The State of Welfare* (Washington, D.C.: Brookings Institution, 1971).

8. In effect, the framework is a generalization of the "anatomy of market failure" approach.

9. See F. Rudderman, *Child Care and Working Mothers* (Washington, D.C.: Child Welfare League of America, 1958). In particular, see table 12, p. 78.

10. The flavor comes through strongly in Rudderman, *Child Care and Working Mothers*.

11. O. Hirschman, *Exit, Voice, and Loyalty* (Cambridge: Harvard University Press, 1970).

12. A. Downs, "Competition and Community Schools," in *Urban Problems and Prospects* (Chicago: Markham Press, 1970).

13. See particularly the chapter by Emma Jackson in Young and Nelson, *Public Policy for Day Care*.

14. See Young and Nelson, *Public Policy for Day Care.*

15. Ibid.

16. If one insisted upon racial integration, or certain other kinds of groupings of children, as a goal or constraint, then the issue becomes more complicated.

17. Arrow, "Uncertainty and the Economics of Medical Care," and H. Klarman, *The Economics of Health* (New York: Columbia University Press, 1964), particularly chapter 5.

18. See the chapter by Jackson in Young and Nelson, *Public Policy for Day Care.*

CHAPTER 30

1. Guy Gran, *Development by People: Citizen Construction of a Just World* (New York: Praeger, 1983), p. 146.

2. Bruce Stokes, "Local Responses to Global Problems: A Key to Meeting Basic Human Needs," *World Watch Paper 17*, (Washington, D.C.: Worldwatch Institute, February 1978).

3. Whyte argues that significant social inventions can occur even within quite hostile settings, demonstrating the power of the creative resources of human beings. William Foote Whyte, "Social Inventions for Solving Human Problems," *American Sociological Review* 47 (February 1982): 1–13. The potentials for such invention within *enabling* as contrasted to basically *hostile* settings has hardly been tested.

4. In one nearly tragic case, a foreign donor designed and funded an irrigation project budgeted to cost more than U.S. $55 million for a Southeast Asian country. The area which the system was to "irrigate" was already being served by nearly 200 strong local irrigator associations. The project proposal barely made reference to these existing systems, which the project would have largely displaced. Fortunately tragedy was forestalled when a group of social scientists spoke truth to power, bringing the situation to the attention of the head of the national agency responsible for implementing the project. He immediately halted the work and ordered the preparation of a completely new design in collaboration with the existing associations, one intended to strengthen rather than to displace them. Whether this very expensive project will in the end result in improvement in the irrigation services already available in the area is not at all certain, but at least it is now less likely the project will do serious harm. Unfortunately such decisive action by agencies intent on obtaining foreign donor funds is all too rare, while the waste of funds incurred in such ill-conceived efforts is common.

5. Frances F. Korten, *Building National Capacity to Develop Water Users' Associations*, World Bank Staff Working Paper no. 528, Washington, D.C., July 1982.

6. See Bruce Stokes, *Helping Ourselves: Local Solutions to Global Problems* (New York: Norton, 1981).

7. See Frances F. Korten, "Community Participation: A Management Perspective on Obstacles and Options," in David C. Korten and Felipe B. Alfonso, eds., *Bureaucracy and the Poor: Closing the Gap* West Hartford, Ct.: Kumarian Press, 1983. pp. 181–200.

8. See John C. Ickis, "Structural Responses to New Rural Development Strategies," in Korten and Alfonso, *Bureaucracy and the Poor*, pp. 4–32; and David C. Korten and Norman T. Uphoff, "Bureaucratic Reorientation for Participatory Rural

Development," NASPAA Working Paper no. 1 (Washington, D.C.: NASPAA, November 1981).

9. Thomas J. Peters and Robert H. Waterman, Jr., *In Search of Excellence: Lessons from America's Best Run Companies* (New York: Harper and Row, 1982).

10. Hazel Henderson, *Creating Alternative Futures: The End of Economics* (New York: Berkeley Publishing, 1978); and John Naesbitt, *Megatrends: Ten New Directions Transforming Our Lives* (New York: Warner Books, 1982).

11. John P. Kotter, "What Effective General Managers Really Do," *Harvard Business Review* 60 (November–December 1982): 156–62.

12. Guy Gran, *Development by People: Citizen Construction of a Just World* (New York: Praeger, 1983), p. 146. See also David C. Korten and Norman T. Uphoff, "Bureaucratic Reorientation for Participatory Rural Development."

13. David C. Korten, "Community Organization and Rural Development: A Learning Process Approach," *Public Administration Review* 40 (September–October 1980): 480–510. One of the more fully documented cases from current experience is the Philippine National Irrigation Administration. See F. Korten, "Building National Capacity"; David C. Korten, "The Working Group as a Mechanism for Managing Bureaucratic Reorientation: Experience from the Philippines," NASPAA Working Paper no. 4, (Washington, D.C.: NASPAA, May 1982).

14. The use of networking processes to achieve the reorientation of a major development bureaucracy is described by D. Korten, "The Working Group Mechanism."

15. "A 'Check-Is-in-the-Mail' Tactic," *Business Week*, 1 November 1982, p. 89.

16. "Worry at the World Banks," *Business Week*, 6 September 1982, pp. 80–83; and "The IMF and Latin America," *The Economist*, 11–17 December 1982, pp. 19–25.

17. Naesbitt, *Megatrends: Ten New Directions Transforming Our Lives.*

18. Alvin Toffler, *The Third Wave* (New York: William Morrow, 1980).

19. Guy Gran suggests that

> to the extent that such a democratic vision more accurately crystallizes and works toward the breath of real human concerns, it will attract adherents from the sterile materialism of capitalism, the unrealistic utopianism of state socialism, and the oppressive bureaucracies of both. (*Development by People*, p. 146).

ABOUT THE EDITORS

David C. Korten, Ph.D. (Stanford, 1968), MBA (Stanford, 1961) is Asia Regional Advisor on development management to USAID under contract with the National Association of Schools of Public Affairs and Administration on a project funded by the Agency for International Development. He is also Visiting Professor of Social Development Management at the Asian Institute of Management in Manila, Philippines. A former member of the faculties of the Harvard University graduate schools of Business and Public Health, he has extensive experience as a development management consultant, researcher, and teacher throughout Asia, Latin America, and Africa. He has served as Academic Director at the Instituto Centroamericano de Administracion de Empresas (INCAE) in Nicaragua, and Assistant Dean of the College of Business Administration at Haile Selassie I University in Ethiopia. Recent articles include: "Community Organization and Rural Development: A Learning Process Approach" (1980), "New Issues, New Options: A Management Perspective on Population and Family Planning" (1979), and "Management for Social Development" (1977). Previous books are: *Bureaucracy and the Poor* (1983), *Population and Social Development Management* (1979), *Casebook on Family Planning Management* (1977), *Planned Change in a Traditional Society* (1972).

Rudi Klauss, Ph.D. (University of Rochester, 1977) is Director of a development management improvement project at the National Association of Schools of Public Affairs and Administration which is funded by the Agency for International Development. A former member of the faculty of The Maxwell School, Syracuse University, he has conducted research, consulting and teaching in the field of management in the U.S. as well as in Asia, Africa and the Middle East. Other work experience has included six years in program and administrative positions with the Peace Corps and two years at the U.S. Office of Personnel Management. He has written numerous articles on management and has published two previous books, *International Development Administration* (1979), and *Interpersonal Communication in Organization* (1982).

OTHER TITLES FROM **KUMARIAN PRESS**

Bureaucracy and the Poor edited by David C. Korten and Felipe B. Alfonso
"An exceedingly important book for practitioners and social theorists." William Foote Whyte, Cornell University and former President, American Sociological Association.
Paper ISBN: 0-931816-52-1 $9.95

Managing Rural Development with Small Farmer Participation by Coralie Bryant and Louise B. White
A practical manual that develops extensive strategies for managing and co-ordinating the participatory development process.
Paper ISBN: 0-931816-52-1 $6.95

Dharma and Development by Joanna Macy
Illustrates how a proper synthesis of religious traditions, pragmatism and innovation can engender personal well-being and successful community development.
Cloth ISBN: 0-931816-74-2 $15.75 Paper ISBN 0-931816-74-2 $8.75

Catalysts of Development by Terry Alliband
An analysis of the role of voluntary agencies in rural development.
Paper ISBN: 0-931816-03-3 $12.50

Microcomputers in Development by Marcus Ingle, Noel Berge and Marcia Hamilton
"The primary source of information about computers that managers should have." Norman Weatherby, Ph.D., Center for Population and Family Health, Columbia University.
Paper ISBN 0-931816-03-3 $12.75

Training for Development by Rolf P. Lynton and Udai Pareek
"A very comprehensive textbook on the theory and practice of training." *Training and Development Journal*
Paper ISBN: 0-931816-25-4 $8.95

Managing Development: The Political Dimension by Marc Lindenberg and Benjamin Crosby
"Provides new insight into methods of analyzing an important managerial contingency." *Public Administration and Development*
Paper ISBN: 0-931816-12-2 $9.95

For more information, a copy of our catalog, or to place an order, write or call:

Kumarian Press, Inc.
630 Oakwood Ave, Suite 119
West Hartford, Ct. 06110

(203) 524–0214

Orders from individuals must be prepaid. Include $1.50 shipping and handling for first book and 25 cents for each additional book.